A HISTORY OF THE

FROM 30 B.C. T

A HISTORY OF
THE ROMAN WORLD
FROM 30 B.C. TO A.D. 138

BY

EDWARD T. SALMON

London and New York

First published 30 November 1944
Second edition 1950
Third edition 1957
Reprinted 1959
Fourth edition 1963
Fifth edition 1966
Sixth edition published 1968 by Methuen & Co. Ltd

First published as a University Paperback 1968
Reprinted seven times
Reprinted 1987

Reprinted 1989, 1991, 1995
by Routledge
11 New Fetter Lane, London EC4P 4EE
29 West 35th Street, New York, NY 10001

Printed in Great Britain by
J. W. Arrowsmith Ltd, Bristol

ISBN 0–415–04504–5

PREFACE TO THE THIRD EDITION

TO discover that yet another reprinting of his work has become necessary is indeed a flattering experience for an author even when, as in the present instance, he knows full well that it is due to the fascination of the subject matter and not to any particular merits of his own. Besides affording gratification, however, it also imposes the obligation to introduce improvements wherever possible; and in the case of a reprinting as distinct from an entirely new edition this was bound to present some difficulties. For reasons of economy it was decided to reprint the present edition from plates cast from the text of the previous one, and this inevitably meant that any textual changes had to be contained within the pagination and indeed the lineation of the earlier edition. This, of course, imposed a limitation on the amount of alteration possible and necessarily involved rigorous compression and careful manipulation of language. I can only hope that in the process lucidity has not suffered, that an unjustified and certainly unintended dogmatism has not emerged and that the modifications of the text do not seem too awkward or too grotesque. For modifications there are, and the publishers have uncomplainingly and generously allowed them to be quite numerous. The attempt has been made not only to correct earlier mistakes and slips but also to bring the volume up to date with post-war work on the period with which it deals. The chapters on Augustus' reorganization of the State, in particular, have been extensively revised; Appendix IV has been completely rewritten, and so has the Bibliography. I hope that, as a result, the work will be found more useful, although I do not expect to escape the reproach that my account of the various aspects of life in the first century and a half of the Roman Empire is rather thin. This is a single, not very large volume on a very large subject; and the constitutional and political, the social and economic, the military and the art historian will all no doubt find the treatment summary. I myself, for instance, greatly regret that the scale of the work does not permit a fuller account of the responsibility of the great families for the shaping and continuity of imperial policies. But in a book of modest size, which does not pretend to be anything more than an introduction to the history of the

Early Empire, the temptation to go exhaustively into one topic at the expense of others had to be resisted as far as possible.

In general, the ancient names have been used except in cases where the modern name has become so familiar that to use any other would convey an impression of pedantry or might even confuse the reader. Thus, for Roman Britain the nomenclature adopted is the one most familiar to speakers of English.

Documentation has been reduced to a minimum in order to save space. It should not be taken to imply any reluctance on the author's part to acknowledge his obligations to his fellow-workers in the field. This book, in fact, makes no claim to originality : it merely seeks to provide a reasonably up-to-date synthesis of the history of the Early Empire. The bibliography will appear similarly sketchy : for it consists almost exclusively of books which have appeared recently, are likely to be available in most libraries, and are themselves well documented. From them the student desirous of consulting earlier works, and especially works in foreign languages, will be able to obtain all the information he requires.

Nowadays it is often fashionable to decry historical works in which individual personalities seem to be given undue attention ; and some readers may regret that the framework of the present volume is the traditional one of the lives of the various Emperors. The following pages, however, will make it clear that the author's choice of this method is not due to any lack of interest in the life of the Roman world as a whole. The study of the Roman Empire has always exercised a marked fascination for citizens of its modern British analogue. This is particularly true in the case of one who received his early instruction in the subject at the great Australian University of Sydney, continued his studies at Cambridge, and is now a member of a Canadian University.

E. T. SALMON,
Summer 1956   HAMILTON, ONTARIO

PREFACE TO SIXTH EDITION

Recent work on the Roman Empire has dictated that a number of changes be made for this latest reprinting, which can accordingly be regarded as a new edition. The list of bibliographical items that has been added does not pretend to be complete. It does, however, direct attention to books where the interested student will find mention of most recent work of consequence.

June 1968   E. T. SALMON

CONTENTS

PART I

THE FOUNDING OF THE PRINCIPATE

CHAPTER I

AUGUSTUS PRINCEPS

CHAPTER II

ITALY

CHAPTER III

THE PROVINCES

CHAPTER IV

THE FRONTIERS AND BEYOND

CHAPTER V

THE LITERATURE OF THE AUGUSTAN AGE

PART II

THE JULIO-CLAUDIAN EMPERORS

CHAPTER I

TIBERIUS

CHAPTER II
GAIUS

CHAPTER III
CLAUDIUS

CHAPTER IV
NERO

PART III
THE ITALIAN EMPERORS

CHAPTER I
ANARCHY

CHAPTER II
VESPASIAN

CHAPTER III
TITUS

CHAPTER IV
DOMITIAN

CHAPTER V

FLAVIAN FRONTIERS

CHAPTER VI

THE ECONOMIC LIFE OF THE EMPIRE

CHAPTER VII

LITERATURE BETWEEN A.D. 50 AND 100

PART IV

THE NON-ITALIAN EMPERORS

CHAPTER I

NERVA

Chapter II
TRAJAN

Chapter III
HADRIAN

Chapter IV
THE RISE OF CHRISTIANITY

CHAPTER V

LITERATURE AND ART IN THE EARLY SECOND CENTURY

APPENDICES

MAPS

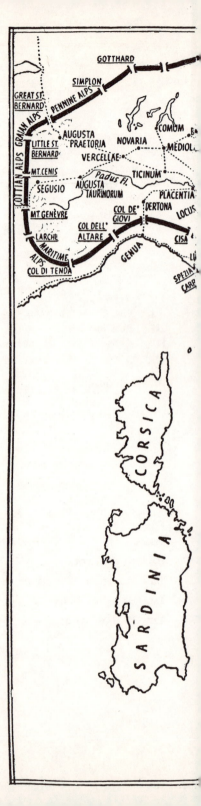

ITALY

Names of
Modern Towns
underlined

Scales

0 20 40 60 80
Roman Miles

0 20 40 60 80
English Miles

Roman Roads ·········

BRENNER
MONTE CROCE
CARNIC ALPS
TARVISIO
PREDIL
PIEDICOLLE
JULIAN ALPS
TRIDENTUM
Via Claudia Augusta
AQUILEIA
BIRNBAUM
MUM
Athesis Fl.
VICETIA
VERONA
ALTINUM
PATAVIUM
ENONA
MANTUA
Via Postumia
HOSTILIA
TORIUM
DRIACUM
BRIXELLUM
Padus Fl.
RAVENNA
PARMA
MUTINA
BONONIA
Via Aemilia
Rubicon Fl.
ARIMINUM
PUAN ALPS
LUCA
Arnus Fl.
APENNINES
PISAURUM
FANUM FORTUNAE
AE
VOLATERRAE
ARRETIUM
Via Flaminia
ANCONA
ASISIUM
FULGINIUM
MEVANIA
CASTRUM TRUENTINUM
Via Cassia
SATURNIA
SPOLETIUM
INTERAMNA
Via Salaria
ASCULUM
Via Aurelia
Via Clodia
OCRICULUM
NARNIA
HADRIA
ATERNUM
CENTUMCELLAE
Tiber?
REATE
Via Claudia
Fucine Lake
Via Valeria
CORFINIUM
SULMO
CAERE
FIDENAE
TIBUR
Arno Fl.
ARPINUM
ROMA
OSTIA
TUSCULUM
PRAENESTE
ANAGNIA
ATINA
AQUINUM
AESERNIA
Alban Hills
Via Latina
Via Appia
SETIA
VENAFRUM
AEQUUM TUTICUM
LUCERIA
AECAE
ANTIUM
CALES
Via Traiana
CANUSIUM
RUBI
BARIUM
TARRACINA
SINUESSA
Mt. Tifata
CAPUA
Aufidus Fl.
VENUSIA
VENAFRUM
Volturnus Fl.
CUMAE
NOLA
Mt. Vesuvius
Pandateria
MISENUM
PUTEOLI
NEAPOLIS
POMPEII
Mt. Vultur
Via Appia
HERCULANEUM
Capreae
SALERNUM
BRUNDISIUM
TARENTUM
Via Popilia
MARE ADRIATICUM
MARE
TYRRHENUM
Sila Mountains
RHEGIUM
SICILIA

PART I

THE FOUNDING OF THE PRINCIPATE

CHAPTER I

AUGUSTUS PRINCEPS

§ 1. THE RESTORATION OF PEACE

THE previous volume has described how the Roman Republic failed. A period of confusion, unrest, civil strife and violence of all kinds had finally culminated in the emergence of one man as the supreme arbiter of the destinies of the Roman world. Octavian [1] was now in a position to impose his will as he saw fit. The day of the Republic is done ; the rule of the Caesars begins.

This failure of the Roman Republic was caused very largely by the reluctance of the Romans to change their methods of government and their political institutions generally. Conservatism and tenacity are no doubt valuable traits in a nation's character ; but conservatism may degenerate into mere obstinacy, and frequently obstinacy can be cured only by bloodshed.

The malady of the Roman Republic was caused by its attempt to govern a large Mediterranean empire with the political and administrative machinery of a city state. By means of various makeshifts and legal fictions the city on the banks of the Tiber did for a long time manage to administer the Empire with this inadequate political machinery. But ultimately the system broke down, and in the resulting anarchy Octavian fought his way to pre-eminence. His problem now was to settle the affairs of the Roman world and to place the Roman state once again on a stable basis.

One thing was, or should have been, clear ; a genuine restoration of the Republic, a return to the *status quo ante*, was out of the question. The advice, which the third-century historian Cassius Dio makes Maecenas give to Octavian, is a neat and correct appraisal of the problem with which the young man was faced : " The cause of our troubles is the multitude of our population and the magnitude of the business of our

[1] To use the name commonly given him before 27 B.C. ; he, however, called himself Caesar, not Octavian.

1

government ; for the population embraces men of every kind, in respect both of race and endowment, and both their tempers and their desires are manifold ; and the business of the State has become so vast that it can be administered only with the greatest difficulty." [1]

A reversion to the previous state of affairs being out of the question, Octavian had to seek for some other and better solution.

Antony and Cleopatra died in August of 30 B.C. in the city of Alexandria whither Octavian had followed them. After their death he did not return to Italy immediately. He was content to let his deputy, Maecenas, govern in the west, while he busied himself with the task of restoring order in the east. It was not until August of 29 that he reached Rome to celebrate a magnificent triple " triumph " for his victories in Illyricum, Actium and Egypt, without any allusion being made, however, to the fact that his victories had been gained, in part at least, at the expense of Roman citizens. Octavian throughout his life showed that he well understood the value and uses of propaganda. So now in 29 Antony was officially ignored and Octavian was represented, not as the party leader (*dux*) who had managed to snatch victory for his own clique, but as the man who had saved the civilization of the west. His court poets were soon assiduously spreading the tale that Cleopatra's victory would have infallibly meant the orientalization of Europe.

The long list of extravagant honours which had been accorded the youthful conqueror by Senate and People before he reached the city need not be given here ; as Dio says,[2] it would be quite superfluous to mention the prayers, the images, the front-seat privilege and similar distinctions. Such flattering attentions did not turn his head or divert him from his object ; and by August of 29 this far-sighted and prudent man surely realized that his object ought to be to regularize his own position in the State, if possible. At that moment he occupied a position that was quite extraordinary and had all the marks of a makeshift. His task was to terminate the temporary aspect of his extraordinary position, while at the same time ensuring that matters did not relapse once again into anarchy. The return from an abnormal to an ordered government is never easy.

But, although the problem was pressing, he could not address himself to it immediately. Before he could give much thought

---

[1] Cassius Dio, LII, 15.   [2] *Ibid.*, LI, 19, 3.

or attention to his own future position in the State, he had to restore a semblance of order and an atmosphere of confidence throughout the shattered Roman world. This task engrossed him for two years, and he discharged it brilliantly.

Lavish games and doles of grain were a traditional method for diverting public attention from public uncertainties. By a liberal dose of *panis et circenses* Octavian kept the public from brooding on recent calamities. A vast programme of spectacular public works—temples, basilicas, roads—also helped to create the impression that stability had returned. By paying his own debts, by overlooking the debts of others to the State and by rehabilitating impoverished senators, he restored financial confidence; interest dropped to one-third of the usual rate. Simultaneously he removed the prevailing military atmosphere. The temple of Janus was ceremoniously closed. It was his desire to convince men that normal, civilian life had returned: this was going to be no period of proscriptions. Antony's former supporters with relief heard him declare that all incriminating correspondence had been burnt. Obtaining land for his veterans either by purchase or by mulcting communities which had supported Antony, Octavian began a large-scale demobilization. In the year 30 he found himself at the head of a huge army numbering some sixty legions. Within a few years these had been reduced to twenty-eight. Over 100,000 of his veterans were paid their gratuities in full and then disbanded. For the most part they were sent to old and new colonies either in Italy or in the provinces.[1] In Italy alone Octavian founded twenty-eight colonies, while in the provinces we find his veterans in such places as Acci Gemella (Spain), Carthage (Africa), Parium (Mysia) and Berytus (Syria). As a result of these various measures confidence gradually returned. The world began to breathe more easily. No doubt it was only lavish spending that enabled Octavian to carry out these measures. The spoils of war, above all the treasure of Egypt, defrayed the bill. But he must at least be given full credit for taking the time and the trouble to do the job thoroughly.

He was now free to give serious study to the question of his own personal position in the State. By temperament he was circumspect and prudent; and the fate of Julius had strengthened his natural tendency to caution. Therefore he was unlikely at this stage to impose upon the Roman world the final form which his constitution was to assume, even if indeed he already

---

[1] His new foundations were almost exclusively in the west.

had a full mental image of the changes he proposed to make. Throughout his life Octavian was content to make haste very slowly. He preferred the tentative method of moving with the inevitability of gradualness from one precedent to another. Ultimately a new constitution did emerge. But it was the result of a long process of trial and error. Octavian felt his way very cautiously, preferring to let arrangements grow out of experience.

As early as 36 B.C. he had been careful to be formally granted the personal inviolability of a plebeian tribune. He had diligently noted all the political lessons of the preceding three-quarters of a century, and on more than one occasion during that period military leaders with political ambitions had found it most expedient to have a tribune closely associated with themselves. Sulla's reforms had demonstrated that in any proposed constitutional changes the tribunes could not be overlooked. Octavian, however, was technically debarred from becoming a plebeian tribune, since he was officially patrician. No doubt he could, like Clodius, have had himself adopted into a plebeian family, but he preferred not to follow this example. His action in 30 B.C. in getting a Lex Saenia passed to empower him to create new patrician families shows that for him the patrician stock had a definite value. The Roman instinct was towards an hierarchical system of society, and Octavian's natural inclination was always either to share in, or to adapt his behaviour to, Roman prejudices and preferences. At one time he apparently flirted with the idea of becoming tribune, but by 30 B.C. he hardly wanted the actual office with its limited tenure : the tribune's prerogatives, without the actual office, would suit him better. These were offered him now (30), but his tribunician sacrosanctity apparently sufficed for the time being.[1] The view that other powers of the tribunes now came his way cannot be proved, and as official documents from his " reign " regard 23 B.C. as the first year of his Tribunician Power, that would appear to be the time when he obtained a tribune's powers without a tribune's limitations. Nevertheless in the next year (29) we find him preventing a tribune-elect from proceeding to office.

From early in his career Octavian was called Imperator.

[1] At this time he also seems to have received the right of hearing appeals from certain judicial decisions.

Under the Republic this was a title, a *cognomen* borne by a pro-magistrate who had been hailed *imperator* by his troops after a victory but had not yet re-entered Rome. Under the Empire *imperator* continued to be thus used as a *cognomen* (see below, p. 33); but it was used also as a *praenomen* and ultimately developed into the title Emperor. The change began with Octavian. In 38 he replaced his *praenomen* Gaius with Imperator, indicating that he was *imperator* supreme, defender of Rome against all threats: after 30, when his military position was unassailable, he de-emphasized but did not discard this *praenomen*.[1] Indeed, during military campaigns outside Italy, he wore the purple robe—which was more red than purple—of an *imperator*; and soon the Emperor became the only person entitled to wear such a garment.

Here clearly there was a standing reminder to all men of his pre-eminence. Pre-eminent he certainly was; as he himself put it later, the State was in his hand. But the Ides of March warned him that he must not be autocratic as well as pre-eminent. Roman republican sentiments had to be respected. He probably desired to respect them; almost certainly he shared his countrymen's conservatism. At any rate he was particularly careful to interest himself in activities where conservative forces normally have most scope. The various priesthoods excited his lively attention.

Technically Lepidus, the ex-triumvir, and not Octavian, was Chief Pontiff and therefore head of the state religion; and Octavian scrupulously refrained from depriving Lepidus of the office, contenting himself with the office of augur. But *de facto* he became head of the various priestly colleges. When the Senate empowered him to fill the numerous gaps which proscriptions and civil wars had made in them, Octavian was granted the right to add as many members to them as he chose. He addressed himself to the task seriously and by thus establishing the religious rites and ceremonies upon which public well-being depended he obtained a reputation for constitutional correctness. In the process he also gained some extraordinary distinctions. The Salii henceforth included his name in their litany; the Senate enacted that libations should be poured to him at all banquets and that priests and People should offer prayers for

---

[1] But with him the *Praenomen Imperatoris* was not an official title. Octavian's three immediate successors (Tiberius, Gaius and Claudius) did not adopt it officially. It became a regular part of the imperial titulary after A.D. 69.

the saviour of the State ; [1] the consul for 29, Valerius Potitus, actually offered public sacrifices and vows on his behalf.

Although such distinctions inevitably contributed to his personal prestige (*auctoritas*), thereby sharply differentiating him from other men, they contained nothing in them to excite republican qualms.   On the contrary, Octavian carefully avoided shocking the old republican traditions.   When he became consul for the sixth time in 28, with the tried and trusted Agrippa as his colleague, men noted that normalcy appeared to have returned : the *comitia* were restored, the consuls were ceremoniously placed on terms of strict equality with one another, and at last after twenty years consuls passed their full twelve months in Rome.   There they proceeded to conduct a census of the People and to revise the list of senators.

For these actions they might expect to win approval.   For the last previous census of the whole people had been taken as long ago as 70 B.C., and the Senate was popularly believed to stand in need of purging.   Ever since Julius had appointed a flock of senators, the suspicion was nursed, whether justifiably or not, that the Senate's numbers were swollen by unworthy members ; Julius' senators were a subject for popular jokes. Octavian's action in striking some two hundred names from the senatorial list probably did not evoke resentment.   Even after his action the Senate still had some eight hundred members, enough for it to discharge its duties properly and efficiently, provided that senators took those duties seriously ; and since a senatorial decree of 29 virtually enforced attendance at Senate meetings by forbidding members to leave Italy without Octavian's permission, the senators obviously were expected to take their duties seriously.   Octavian himself was appointed Princeps Senatus in this year (28 B.C.).

To carry out this census Octavian and Agrippa did not take the office of censor.   The duties of the censor in the early days of the Republic had been discharged by the chief executives of the State ; it was not until 443 B.C. that the censorship became a separate office from the consulship.[2]   In 28 the two friends revived the ancient practice and wielded their *censoria potestas* as consuls.   This must not be imputed to mere antiquarianism on their part.   Octavian was positively eager to

[1] In 29 Senate and People dedicated a monument to him in the Forum, *re publica conservata*.
[2] Livy IV, 8.

avoid the office of censor, since through the centuries the censors
had come to be regarded as holding a whip-hand over the
Senate.   It was they who kept the list of senators, and it was
in their power to eject quite arbitrarily any members of whom
they disapproved.   Octavian now, as later, was anxious to
avoid the appearance of constraining people, especially senators,
against their will.[1]   As censor he would have exposed himself
to the charge of dragooning the Senate ; as consul wielding
censorial powers he might hope to convey the impression that
the Senate readily collaborated in the proceedings.

By thus somewhat ostentatiously avoiding the show of
power while retaining the reality, Octavian hoped so to increase
his prestige (*auctoritas*) that men would acquiesce willingly in
his proposed constitutional changes.   Actually his prestige was
so high that his desires were not likely to be openly disputed.
All of his actions so far had been officially confirmed by a
senatorial decree of January 1, 29 ; and to render his future
actions acceptable he now passed a kind of amnesty act.   It
is described by Dio : " Since Octavian had given many illegal
and unjust orders during the strife of the Civil Wars, and
especially during the triumvirate with Antony and Lepidus,
he annulled all these in one edict, fixing his sixth consulship
(28 B.C.) as the limit of their validity." [2]   This may not have
been a complete act of amnesty, but it is safe to assume that it
put an end to injustices such as the disabilities under which the
children of the proscribed still laboured.   The act met with
general approbation.   The legend *libertatis populi Romani vindex* on coins of 28 refers, however, not to this act of amnesty,
but to the abolition of abnormal consulships.

Octavian's popularity was also heightened by the undeniable
fact that the Roman world was passing weary of recurring
disorders.   Civil wars and proscriptions, in addition to removing
many elements of opposition, had had the effect of making
most men long for the return of an era of stability and peace.
Anyone who gave promise of ushering in such a period was sure
of a following ; and Octavian's propagandists had been assuring
the Roman world ever since 40 B.C. that the Golden Age was
soon to return.[3]   Now was the time for Octavian not only
to fulfil his promise and restore constitutional government, but

---

[1] Cassius Dio (LIV, 13, 1) makes it clear that this was Octavian's
motive in always declining the office of censor.

[2] *Ibid.*, LIII, 2, 5.   [3] See Vergil, *Eclogue* iv.

also to create the best constitution. Accordingly when he entered on his seventh consulship in 27 B.C., with Agrippa once again as his colleague, he proceeded to the attempt to define his future position in the state.

§ 2.   THE " RESTORATION OF THE REPUBLIC," 27 B.C.

On January 13, 27 B.C., Octavian announced to the Senate that he planned to lay down his supreme power. His own particular partisans, who had presumably been warned beforehand, greeted the announcement with cries of protest. The result was that the subsequent settlement altogether lacked an appearance of coercion.

Bowing to the cries of protest Octavian consented to accept the commission from the Senate to administer in a proconsular capacity a certain, definite group of those provinces which his lieutenants were then governing and all of which he had placed at the free disposal of the Senate and People. It is uncertain whether the People provided his exceptional position with a legal basis by meeting in an Assembly and ratifying the Senate's action. Thus Octavian received the special commission of a promagistrate. There was nothing unprecedented about this. Pompey's position under the Gabinian Law is an obvious analogy. Nor was it a novel idea for this vast proconsular power to be conferred upon him for a period of years (ten actually). After the Conference of Luca in 56 Pompey, Crassus and Caesar had each of them received similar extended commands, and Pompey had exercised his through his own personal lieutenants. The fact that Octavian obtained this proconsular power while also holding the consulship at Rome, was, it is true, rather more unusual.[1] But for this one could conveniently cite the position of Pompey in 52 as a precedent.

Octavian's Imperium Proconsulare,[2] as we shall henceforth call it, concentrated great power in his hands, since the provinces which he was " invited " to administer were precisely those that contained large standing armies. A corollary to this was that he had to have the power of making war or peace, and hence the right to make treaties with whomsoever he chose. In effect Octavian obtained the command of so much of the armed

---

[1] Some scholars indeed deny that this cumulation of *imperia* could ever have occurred. See Appendix IV.

[2] The term is not used of the settlement of 27 ; but the fact, in the present writer's view, is indisputable. See Appendix IV.

strength of the Empire that the military destinies of the State were in his hand. The justification for this was that the Senate during the preceding century had repeatedly shown itself incapable of controlling the soldiers, so that it was necessary to place them under the firm hand of a member of the Julian family, which had already demonstrated its ability to manage them.   But though the arrangement might be a safeguard against the renewed outbreak of civil war, it was also a permanent obstacle to any genuine independence of decision or judgment by Senate or People.   In the last analysis the wishes of the man who controls the soldiery must always be respected ; and if Octavian later became occasionally impatient at the Senate's unwillingness to take a strong line of its own on questions of policy, then his huge *provincia* with its vast armed establishment was really responsible.

Normally the *imperium* of a promagistrate did labour under one disadvantage : it could not be exercised inside Rome itself, for only the *imperium* of the urban magistrates was valid within the *pomerium*.   But in the case of Octavian even this restriction did not apply, for so long as he held a consulship he actually was one of the urban magistrates.

Although his Imperium Proconsulare thus made him really the supreme arbiter of the State, it was technically a special commission deriving from the Senate and Roman People. Moreover consular elections had been normalized. Hence he claimed to have restored the Republic from his own authority to the free disposal of the Senate and Roman People.

This claim superficially seemed not unjust. For the settlement of January 13, 27 contained nothing for which republican precedents could not be adduced : as Octavian himself later expressed it, he assumed no office inconsistent with ancestral custom. Nor did the extraordinary honours, which were gratefully voted him by the Senate three days later on the motion of the ex-consul L. Munatius Plancus, contain anything specifically unrepublican.   The posts and lintel of his door were respectively decked with laurel and oak-leaves, and a golden shield lauding his virtues was set up in the Senate-house.   But such honorific compliments had been paid to successful commanders at least as early as the third century B.C.

The name " Augustus " was one of the honours bestowed on him on this occasion, and as a further mark of respect, it was also given to the month Sextilis. The name immediately won

wide currency : indeed from that time on he has always been
known as Augustus. But we must not think that, simply
because the name has become so celebrated, its assumption by
Octavian was a startling innovation. The word was actually
an adjective, and for Octavian to be called Augustus might seem
to be no more extraordinary than for Sulla to be labelled Felix
or for Pompey to be styled Magnus. The name " Augustus "
did indeed contain mystical and religious connotations ; inevitably it would remind Romans of that other augur, Romulus,
who had founded the city *augusto augurio*. But simply because
the epithet was carefully and astutely selected it was not therefore a radical departure from former practice. It was after
all only a name, not an official title.

In 27 B.C. Augustus prudently avoided any title that might
imply that he held some exceptional office. He was content
to rely on his personal prestige rather than on any official
position : [1] indeed he himself cites the alleged fact that his
magisterial colleagues had equal executive authority with
himself as proof that he had in very truth restored the
Republic.

There have been historians, modern as well as ancient, who
regard his statement as the simple truth ; but it is difficult to
agree with them. To the average Roman, restoration of the
Republic would mean only one thing : the surrender of the
reins of government and the direction of affairs to the senatorial
group. Under Augustus' constitutional arrangements, the
Senate did undoubtedly obtain very great honours and prerogatives. But Augustus was careful to retain the military,
that is the ultimate, power in his own hand. As Machiavelli
points out, a prince is liable to deceive himself in the estimate
of his strength unless he has an armed force of his own ; subjects will continue to show loyalty and goodwill, and will
continue to remain faithful, only to princes capable of defending
them. Octavian was determined not to be without an army
devoted to himself. Under such circumstances, if there were
any eventual clash of wills, that of Augustus would inevitably
prevail. In other words, the Senate was not a sovereign
body ; even its power of discussion was circumscribed after 27,
when Augustus instituted a kind of Privy Council, which
acted as a standing committee for the Senate and decided what
business should be brought before it. This Senate Committee
consisted of the consuls, one member from each of the other

[1] See M. Grant, *From " Imperium " to " Auctoritas "* (1946), *passim* :
Grant exaggerates the constitutional aspects of Augustus' prestige
(*auctoritas*).

boards of magistrates, and fifteen senators chosen by lot; it served for six months.[1]

Presumably the consuls of 27–23, 5 and 2 B.C. were the magisterial colleagues who were supposedly on equal terms with him, since the consulship was the only actual magistracy he ever held henceforth. But it was not the consulship that made him powerful. Nor can other holders of *imperium*, the governors of senatorial provinces for example, be regarded as his real equals after 27 B.C.: for his *imperium*, even though probably not specifically defined as superior (*maius*) to theirs in 27, undoubtedly transcended theirs in actual practice.

Augustus' claim to have restored the Republic must therefore be regarded as a piece of propaganda, whose object was to convince men that he was no more than what he represented himself as being, viz., the first citizen of a free community. To describe his position he assumed no special title; he was shrewd enough to call himself merely *princeps*, the leading man, a term which in the plural had been familiar to Roman ears for centuries and in the singular to Roman ears for the closing years of the Republic. They had heard it applied to Pompey and to Caesar;[2] its adoption by Augustus would not come as a surprise or shock. The appellation was strictly unofficial; it was not a shortened form of the title *princeps senatus* (which position, however, Augustus undoubtedly held). It carried with it the suggestion of personal pre-eminence in civil affairs, just as the name Augustus contained a mystical connotation of religious awe.

It was his anxiety to avoid the hated titles of Rex or Dictator that led Augustus to adopt this term. As a result the system of government which he organized is called the Principate. At exactly what year it is legitimate to refer to it as an Empire (that is, as something ruled by an Emperor) is a matter of some dispute. Actually from 27 B.C. onwards the title Empire is justified; although it was not until four years later that Augustus candidly admitted that his position in the State was quite apart and virtually possessed the formal continuity of a legitimate monarchy.

The Princeps at once proceeded to demonstrate that his great powers would be employed to assure the well-being of Italy by repairing the great arterial highways. He himself took care of the Via Flaminia while various henchmen looked after the other roads.

---

[1] The *semenstria consilia* of Suet., *Aug.* 35; cf. Cass. Dio, LIII, 21, 4.

[2] Cic., *De Domo Sua* 66; Suet., *Iul.* 29.

Shortly thereafter, however, he imitated Solon of Athens and left the city. He felt that his presence was needed in the western provinces, and he seems to have taken with him his nephew Marcellus and his stepson Tiberius, both of them striplings of about fifteen years of age. During the latter half of 27 he was in Gaul. He passed 26 and 25 in Spain and did not arrive back in Rome until the spring of 24.

§ 3.   THE SETTLEMENT OF 23 B.C.

On his return he found that the settlement of 27 had not been successful in winning over the constitutionalists. The sage Augustus knew that, if stability was ever to return, national unity must be achieved. So far as the army, the moneyed equestrian class and the proletariat were concerned, he could unite them in support of himself ; the difficulty was to conciliate the senatorial oligarchy. .Yet it was sound common sense to prevent what had formerly been the governing class from becoming permanently disgruntled, for they were the guardians of the Roman tradition which Augustus valued so highly, and besides this he could make good use of their abilities. A world-wide empire cannot be ruled indefinitely by martial law ; Augustus needed men to help him in the work of administration, and the only men with the necessary experience belonged to the senatorial families. But his alleged restoration of the Republic had at the most elicited only a very grudging co-operation from them. They were unconvinced that there had been any return to truly constitutional government.

As early as 26 they showed themselves unresponsive. In that year M. Valerius Messalla Corvinus was appointed Prefect of the City (*praefectus urbi*). The title, but not the actual office, was ancient. In the days of the monarchy an official with this title used to be appointed to preside in the courts and deal with emergencies whenever the king himself was absent. After 367 B.C. the Urban Praetor took over these functions, so that the need for an official like the City Prefect disappeared.[1] In appointing Messalla, Augustus was seeking to honour a known republican, but the intended rôle of this new City Prefect, to maintain public order, not to conduct the Latin Festival, made his action unpopular. The senatorial nobles regarded the appointment as unrepublican, and Messalla resigned after a few days.

Certain distinctions accorded August between 27 and 23 were also distinctly unrepublican. In 26 when Cornelius Gallus,

---

[1] Except when all the magistrates were absent for the *Feriae Latinae*.

the first Prefect of Egypt, committed suicide, his estate was awarded him and thanksgiving sacrifices were made ; in 25 he was actually exempted from certain specific enactments.[1] These honours were actually voted by the Senate itself, either because it felt constrained to pay them to the master of the armed services or perhaps because it maliciously sought to make his ascendancy conspicuous.

Senatorial resentment certainly existed. Augustus suspected conspiracy as well and c. 23 the republican Fannius Caepio and Varro Murena (consul, according to some) were executed. Their guilt cannot be proved. Nevertheless here was a clear warning that some changes would have to be made. What especially rankled was his perpetual consulship. Under the Empire the consulship was to decline in importance ; but its ultimate fate should not blind us to its importance in the twenties B.C. and even much later. In Augustus' day, the consulship represented the goal of men's ambitions. It was the office to which the senatorial class especially aspired, and to them its permanent monopolization by Augustus was an affront. Augustus presumably did not retain the consulship from 31 to 23 merely for reasons of vanity. Perhaps he was feeling his way : he may have been seeking a method for exercising the consul's authority without holding the consul's office. Or possibly he was attempting to create an enduring tradition of his own personal preeminence. Once assured that he could wield a consul's powers without actually being consul, he resigned the office, and arranged for notorious republicans to be consuls for what remained of 23. Herein he was hardly following the advice of Maecenas, since the latter was no longer participating in public life.[2] Henceforth Augustus regularly avoided the consulship (see below, p. 124).

Thereby he did more than just remove a source of senatorial chagrin. He also made available an extra post to qualify men for administrative appointments ; and the desire to obtain trained and experienced administrators surely influenced Augustus to relinquish the consulship.

Augustus may also have had another reason for revising the settlement of 27. It seems certain that he desired not only to retain his power himself but also to perpetuate it. For this he

---

[1] Cassius Dio, LIII, 28, 2 wrongly says that he was placed above the law in general.

[2] By now Augustus and Maecenas had become estranged. The conspiratorial Murena was Maecenas' brother-in-law, according to Dio (LIV, 3).

would need a successor of Julian blood : the various armies were unlikely to be reconciled to anyone else. If he himself died soon, the experienced Agrippa would necessarily have to take charge;[1] but the eventual succession of the Julian stock must be unmistakable. Now his young nephew Marcellus, although technically a Claudian, did have Julian blood : he accordingly in 23 was marked out for the succession. The steps which under the Republic were normally taken to assure a man's political future had already been taken for Marcellus. In 25 he had been married to the fourteen-year-old Julia, Augustus' only child, and in 24 by special dispensation of the Senate he was granted the right to hold magistracies at an earlier age than normal. Now he became aedile without having first held the quaestorship, and he was permitted to stand for the consulship ten years before the usual age.

These measures ensured Marcellus' rapid political preferment, but they did not render his succession inevitable. Augustus himself technically only held a special commission : how could this be bequeathed to someone else ? Augustus was already facing the recurring problem of the Principate, that of the succession. In 23 this was brought home to him very vividly. He had already had a serious illness in 25 ; in early 23 he fell desperately sick. As he expected to die, he doubtless wanted to establish the succession firmly ; yet he could not do so without making a mockery of his claim to have restored the Republic. To have associated the youthful Marcellus with him in the Imperium Proconsulare, that is, to have instituted a " secondary proconsular *imperium* "[2] of the type that later was not uncommon, would have directed attention to the arbitrary powers which he in fact possessed ; and Augustus was not anxious to remind men that his position enabled him to exercise such wide and sweeping unconstitutional powers. Accordingly, the most he could do in 23 was to reflect that Marcellus was at any rate his son-in-law.

When Augustus recovered from his illness he proceeded to modify the settlement of 27. He resigned the consulship on July 1 and was replaced by a well-known republican, L. Sestius Quirinalis. The other consul, Piso, was also a republican : both men had fought against the triumvirs at Philippi. It cost Augustus little to make this gesture of conciliation to the republican elements ; it involved no real diminution of his

---

[1] As in 30 he handed his signet ring to Agrippa, thereby authorizing the latter to act in his name.

[2] The expression is Mommsen's. (*Röm. Staatsr.* II, p. 1145 f.)

military power, since he still retained his Imperium Proconsulare ; indeed it was now officially recognized as superior (*maius*).[1] He did not even lose such consular powers as he wanted ; for these were soon granted to him by special decree.   The consulship, unlike the proconsulship, carried with it the right to exercise the *imperium* inside Rome ; accordingly when Augustus resigned the consulship, it was enacted that his Imperium Proconsulare should not lapse when he entered the city.   The consul also had the right to call the Senate together and to place the first item of business before it (*ius primae relationis*).   Both rights were conferred upon Augustus, although not simultaneously. It was not until 22 that he obtained the right to convene the Senate : to have re-acquired many consular powers at once would have stultified his gesture in resigning the consul's office. Augustus was even slower in obtaining some of the consul's outward privileges : it was not until 19 that he obtained the right to sit between the consuls in the Senate and to be attended by twelve lictors.

If Augustus occupied what republican elements would regard as an unconstitutional position, it was actually because of his unfettered Imperium Proconsulare :[2] it had a time limit but virtually no other restriction.   By virtue of it he could constrain anyone to obey his slightest wish.   He was not, however, eager to parade this fact : his plan was not to dragoon, but to win willing co-operation ; consequently the more this power was disguised the better.   Accordingly he now set out to convince men that his exceptional position, which was obvious to all, was to be attributed not to his Imperium Proconsulare but to something else, and could be given a legal, constitutional appearance.

Since 36 he had enjoyed some of a plebeian tribune's privileges.   He now in 23 obtained the Tribunician Power (*tribunicia potestas*), which comprised all a tribune's ordinary, and some quite extraordinary, prerogatives.   Conferred upon him for life, it both revealed and legalized his position as unique.[3]   In 27, he could speciously argue, his position was republican ; in 23 it was not.   His new office, lacking both time-limit and colleague (unless he co-opted one), differed immensely from the consulship.   Yet this revolutionary innovation might not provoke

[1] On *imperium maius* see H. Last in *Journ. Rom. Stud.*, XXXVII (1947), pp. 157–64.

[2] See R. Syme in *Journ. Rom. Stud.*, XXXVI (1946), p. 149.   Dio (LIII, 32, 5) styles Augustus' *imperium* perpetual : by which he means that henceforth Augustus held it until his death.

[3] This legal admission that one individual was now in an extraordinary position meant that the Republic had now formally become an Empire.   Actually, of course, it had become such years earlier.

bitter opposition ; for, since tribunes traditionally safeguarded citizens against the caprice of *imperium*-holding magistrates, Augustus could represent his new, unrepublican position as deriving from powers that were popularly associated with the protection, not the repression, of citizens. Moreover the Tribunician Power enabled him to transact business with Senate or People, since a tribune possessed *ius agendi cum populo et cum senatu* : hence, his power to legislate. To emphasize the way it made his position exceptional,[1] he commenced a new epoch with it. The day he obtained it (26 June apparently) officially began his " reign " : henceforth public documents are dated by the years of the Tribunician Power. (Later Emperors made the day they assumed Imperium Proconsulare their *dies imperii* : below, p. 206. After 98 *tribunicia potestas* was apparently renewed annually on December 10, the plebeian tribunes' " New Year," not on the anniversary of its original conferment.)

These stratagems achieved Augustus' purpose. The Tribunician Power did come to be regarded as the basis of the Princeps' power. Henceforth the length of an Emperor's reign is determined by the number of years he holds the Tribunician Power. Velleius gives the official view : according to him the *imperium*, even a *maius imperium*, was inferior to the Tribunician Power.[2]

Besides serving to disguise the military basis of his position, Augustus' Tribunician Power might also render the nomination of a successor more feasible. The problem of the succession arose from the fact that the Principate originated as a special commission which theoretically could scarcely outlive the one appointed to discharge it. Conferment of the Tribunician Power upon an individual would designate him as the successor much more definitely than certain marriage arrangements or premature magisterial appointments would do. Actually Augustus did not take such a colleague in the Tribunician Power until 18 B.C. ; but once he did so, the colleague would be regarded as the Emperor's equal : for him to succeed to the Emperor would not only be easy, it would seem perfectly natural, if not indeed *de rigueur*.

To make the Tribunician Power thoroughly respectable

---

[1] Tacitus (*Ann.*, III, 56, 1) makes it clear that Augustus sponsored the view that the Tribunician Power, " the phrase for the supreme dignity " (*summi fastigii vocabulum*), was pre-eminent over the *imperium*.

[2] Velleius Paterculus, II, 99, 1.

Augustus apparently caused the Senate to confer it and the People to ratify it in a special Assembly (*comitia tribuniciae potestatis*). Consequently, although it may be very obvious to us that the real basis of Augustus' power was military, to contemporaries it was ostensibly legal.

Later on we find that the various powers and prerogatives of the Emperor were consolidated and conferred by a single comprehensive piece of legislation, the so-called *Lex de Imperio*.[1] The earliest known specimen of such an enactment belongs to A.D. 69 ; Dio however implies that a similar act of legislation, no doubt very much less comprehensive, was also passed on behalf of Augustus in 23.[2]

§ 4. CONSOLIDATION

Augustus hoped that the ship of state would henceforth be sailing in less stormy seas. In this hope he was not disappointed, although certain of his more personal expectations did prove vain. Late in the year 23 Marcellus died, and Augustus had to renew the search for a successor. A person of Julian ancestry still seemed to be indicated, but none was available. Augustus therefore was obliged to select a regent who, in case of necessity, should hold the reins of power until some Julian appeared. Needless to say the regent chosen was the trusted Agrippa. In 23 Augustus had sent Agrippa to the provinces beyond the Ionian Sea (the so-called *transmarinae provinciae*), a move which was later alleged to be a device to eliminate any possibility of friction between him and Marcellus. Actually Agrippa was in the east as the Emperor's deputy invested with *imperium* : possibly he was engaged on some secret diplomatic mission to the Parthians ; or more probably Augustus wanted him there because trouble seemed imminent.[3] When Agrippa returned to Rome in 21, he was straightway married to Marcellus' widow, Julia. Augustus' hope presumably was that the union would produce a male offspring who would be his grandson and inherit Julian blood ; Agrippa would act as regent until the boy grew up. Agrippa's intended rôle was indicated clearly in this year 21, when, Augustus being absent from Rome, Agrippa was in charge there. Apparently Agrippa held no official position on

[1] Dessau, *Inscriptiones Latinae Selectae*, 244.

[2] LIII, 32, 5.

[3] Josephus, *Antiquitates Judaicae*, XV, 10, 2 (§ 250) : XVI, 3, 3 (§ 86).

this occasion : yet his authority was not questioned, since he was the Princeps' mouthpiece. Incidentally this demonstrates how effective was Augustus' control of the machinery of government.

Nevertheless Augustus was discreet enough not to advertise his supremacy. On various occasions during the remaining years of his principate he obtained additional powers, privileges and prerogatives. As a matter of fact there was nothing to stop him from simply taking them, yet he always preferred to have them conferred upon him with formal correctness. Indeed he sometimes refused the proffered additional powers—he could never be induced to hold the dictatorship, the censorship, or " an annual and perpetual consulship "—while he accepted others only with considerable reluctance. In this he was not always necessarily insincere. There were undoubtedly many things which he could quite safely leave to the competence of others. In fact he was prepared and indeed eager to have the Senate bear its full burden of administrative duties ; and the Senate was probably flattered at the prospect. Certainly at first the senatorial nobility displayed political enthusiasm : the riots at consular elections in the late twenties B.C., while deplorable, are indicative of genuine political exuberance.

But in the last analysis the Senate could not make any decision independently of Augustus. The senators must have been always conscious that the Emperor's ratification was needed for everything. Moreover the Senate had to rely almost exclusively on persuasion in order to get its policies carried out ; if more than persuasion were needed, then the Emperor had to be called in, for only he had an adequate backing of armed force, and the policy thus carried into effect ceased to be senatorial. The Senate might possess great moral influence ; it did not possess final authority, and this being so, its administration was bound to suffer. A body that is not sovereign will have the greatest difficulty in obtaining efficiency : lacking the power to be really efficient, it will soon lack the incentive. This was especially true of the Senate, which for administrative purposes depended on the urban magistrates, men who were changed annually (if indeed not more frequently), and were usually very inexperienced.

Consequently it is not surprising that popular demand in Rome asked Augustus to assume control of certain services where efficiency was urgently required. If these were services that touched his own position closely he never hesitated; his usual practice was to appoint *curatores* to supervise the services concerned. Thus in 22 B.C., at the request of the people, he assumed responsibility for maintaining the grain supply (*cura annonae*), the immediate cause being a serious grain shortage. As usual there was a republican precedent: Pompey had been put in charge of the grain supply in 57. Henceforth the maintenance of an adequate supply devolved upon the Princeps, who c. A.D. 8 instituted an equestrian prefecture for this service. (But ex-praetors supervised the actual grain doles: see p. 56, n. 4.) Similarly before his reign ended Augustus assumed the *cura* of roads and of the water supply.

Nor did Augustus always wait to be invited to take charge; he might take the initiative himself. In 21, when the aedile M. Egnatius Rufus gained great popularity by organizing his slaves into a fire-brigade, Augustus moved swiftly to suppress what might easily develop into a private army. He had Rufus executed in 19 and formed a public fire brigade (*vigiles*), consisting initially of six hundred public slaves. This corps was placed under his direct administration. It is characteristic of Augustus, however, that in this matter too he felt his way gradually. The organization of the fire-brigade was not regularized until twenty-five years later (A.D. 6), when seven cohorts of Vigiles, each one thousand men strong, replaced the previous inadequate corps of six hundred. Each cohort looked after the safety of two of the fourteen " regions " into which the city had been divided in 7 B.C. Incidentally the formation of this semi-military body provided some outlet for the military energies of freedmen, who were admitted to it but rigorously excluded from the army. The corps was commanded by an equestrian Prefect.

Thus even matters that concerned only the city of Rome came more and more to be supervised by the Princeps. Perhaps that is why Augustus, despite his previous rebuff by Messalla, definitely instituted the office of City Prefect, whose duty was to safeguard public order during his own absence from the capital.

§ 5.   THE LEGISLATION OF 18 B.C.

In the year 18 B.C. Augustus for the first time specifically named a successor by making Agrippa his colleague in the Tribunician Power. The Imperium Proconsulare probably explains why Augustus waited until this year to make the gesture.

Always anxious to appear constitutionally correct and never desirous of attracting attention to his possession of this supreme *imperium*, Augustus had never hitherto shared it with a colleague, for it would have been constitutionally dubious procedure for him to delegate to an individual the sovereign power which was supposed to be conferred only by the People. Moreover if he nevertheless did so, he would openly advertise that though he paraded the Tribunician Power, what he really valued was the Imperium Proconsulare. Yet his successor, if he was called to the office suddenly, would urgently need the *imperium* ; the Tribunician Power by itself, without its backing of armed force, was not enough. Augustus therefore waited until his own tenure of the Imperium Proconsulare expired in 18. It was conferred afresh, of course, in the same year (as he knew that it inevitably would be) ; but this time it was almost certainly conferred upon Agrippa as well for a period of five years. This measure was put through quietly and inconspicuously, so inconspicuously indeed that the ancient sources do not explicitly mention it : [1] the ostentation was reserved for Agrippa's assumption of the Tribunician Power. Fundamentally, however, Agrippa's Imperium Proconsulare was the more important, and it was primarily to get him invested with it that Augustus had any constitutional arrangements at all made in the year 18.

Augustus had characteristically felt his way forward to this step. Agrippa's *imperium* in 23, while not a secondary Imperium Proconsulare, nevertheless had probably made him the superior of the governors of imperial provinces (and possibly certain senatorial ones), and had thus prepared him for the higher *imperium*.

Thus in 18 B.C. Agrippa became a co-regent with Augustus. If the latter were suddenly to die, Agrippa would automatically become Princeps. But the Principate did not now become a dual one with two equal rulers. Of the co-regents Augustus clearly enjoyed priority, for although Agrippa's Tribunician Power, like Augustus', was annually numbered, it had a five-year limit : Augustus' was annual and perpetual.

Concurrently with these succession arrangements in 18 B.C.

---

[1] Dio (LIV, 12, 4) merely says that Augustus conferred upon Agrippa " other privileges almost equal to his own, including the Tribunician Power." But in 17 B.C. Agrippa was exercising powers over both imperial and senatorial provinces : in other words he possessed *imperium maius*. (For a contrary view, see M. Grant, *From " Imperium " to " Auctoritas,"* p. 428.)

Augustus seized the occasion for a general reorganization of the State. He conducted another revision of the Senate, with the intention of reducing its membership to three hundred. In republican times this would have been a task for the censors. But Augustus was no more eager now than earlier to assume this office ; on the contrary he seems to have tried to discredit it ; at any rate, the office had been temporarily revived in 23 and entrusted to a pair of worthless nonentities. Augustus himself did at various times perform the functions normally discharged by the censors,—the general supervision of public morals, the solemn purification of the State, the revision of the lists of senators, knights and citizens generally, and the letting of public contracts. He actually discharged some of these duties at five-year intervals, the traditional period between censorships, although the more prominent of the censor's duties were reserved for the years in which his Imperium Proconsulare came up for renewal.

In 18 B.C., to avoid the appearance of bringing constraint to bear on the Senate, he proposed an ingenious scheme to revise its list of members : he would select thirty senators who in their turn would proceed by various stages of co-optation to select the others. This scheme actually proved unworkable, and ultimately Augustus was obliged to make that personal selection which he feared would appear autocratic. Perhaps to render it more palatable, he named six hundred senators instead of the three hundred originally intended.[1]

Augustus also discharged other censorial functions in 18 B.C. He refused to become *curator morum*, but he did exercise a general supervision of public morals and conduct, and promulgated the Julian Laws. In effect these laws constituted a new code, for they made provision for criminal law and legal procedure as well as for moral reform.

When the constitution of a state is altered, a revision of its legal code becomes inevitable. At the very least the law of treason will require reshaping. The crime of treason (*maiestas*) was not easy to define. According to Cicero treason was committed when one detracted in any way from the dignity, great-

---

[1] On the occasion of a later revision of the Senate in A.D. 4 Augustus tried a different scheme. He nominated ten men from whom three were chosen by lot as the commissioners to revise the senatorial roll (*tresviri legendi senatus*). This scheme also proved unsatisfactory and was never repeated.

ness or power of the People or of those to whom the People had
given power.   Under the Empire treason came to be interpreted
as any offence or insult offered to the Princeps in deed, writing
or speech.   This interpretation was for the most part established
by precedents in the reign of Augustus' successor, but the legal
authority for the interpretation seems to derive from the Julian
Laws of 18.   The law on what the Romans called *vis*, that is
arbitrary conduct either by a public official or by a private
individual, likewise came to be related closely to the person of
the Emperor.

The Emperor in fact became a High Court.   This development was natural since, in theory at least, any Roman magistrate could take judicial cognizance of an alleged crime, although
from very early times the citizen's right of appeal to the People
had limited his power to inflict punishment.   This clumsy procedure had been modified beginning in the second century B.C.,
when the People commissioned magistrates (praetors usually)
to try more important cases in permanently established jury-
courts.[1]   Their verdicts were inappellable ;   under the late Republic appeal, properly speaking, had not existed.   As Augustus
possessed the highest *imperium* of all—by his proconsular *imperium* he exercised, even in Rome, a jurisdiction similar to
that of a governor in his province—a High Court was naturally
entrusted to his competence.   And he could hear appeals in it.
Possibly in 30 B.C. he had obtained some form of appellate jurisdiction.   The appeal procedure was regularized *c*. 18 B.C.   As
Augustus possessed the ultimate authority in certain provinces,
the actual governors of which were technically only his deputies,
he logically had to allow appeals to himself from their judgments.
Ultimately Roman citizens everywhere obtained the right to
appeal to Caesar.

His High Court steadily encroached on the public jury-courts.
To help him in legal decisions the Princeps imitated the republican magistrates and called in as assessors a group of experts who
constituted his *consilium*.[2]   This *consilium*, however, was quite
unofficial until Hadrian organized it formally in the second
century.

---

[1] Sulla (see Volume V, p. 132) established a number of such permanent jury-courts (*quaestiones perpetuae*), where charges of maladministration, treason, bribery and corruption, and the like were investigated.

[2] This judicial *consilium* must be sharply distinguished from the
semenstre consilium, or Senate Committee (for which see above, p. 10).

Under the Empire the Senate also sat as a High Court. This too was probably a development from the fact that a magistrate could take judicial cognizance of a crime. The investigating magistrate would gather round him for assistance and advice a *consilium*—a group of assessors virtually equivalent to our jury. The High Court of the Senate in origin would seem to have been the court of the consuls who had used the Senate as their *consilium*. At the time of the Catilinarian conspiracy, for instance, it seems to have functioned in this way. When the Senate was first formally constituted as a High Court is not quite certain. It first became prominent in this way during Tiberius' reign, but it may have sát as a court in 40 B.C. and from 4 B.C. senatorial commissions tried cases of provincial extortion.

The *iudicia publica*, the normal type of jury-court under the Late Republic, did not disappear under the Empire : their jurors were henceforth drawn from the Equestrian Order only. To preside over them and thus to make the civil law function smoothly was in fact one of the praetor's principal duties. However, the *iudicia publica* did not try the more notorious cases. *Causes célèbres* invariably were heard in the court of the Emperor or of the Senate. Accordingly the activities of the *iudicia publica* under the Principate have been rather neglected, despite the Younger Pliny's descriptions of what happened in them.

The Julian Laws of 18 were concerned with public morality as well as with the criminal code and jurisdiction ; and it was a much more difficult thing to restore public morale than to prescribe rules and regulations governing legal procedure. There was something rotten in the State, and Augustus proposed to set it right.

The inevitable aftermath of the prolonged period of civil wars had been a relaxation of morals and a growth of cynicism. Anarchy and lack of responsibility in public life usually find their counterparts in private life : traditional standards of conduct tend to lose their value and meaning, they are despised and consequently disappear. If they are not quickly replaced by fresh rules for the behaviour of society, there ensues a period of emotional and spiritual confusion, marked by a general lack of principles and by an uncertainty as to what constitutes right and truth. Sallust, Vergil, Horace, Livy and other writers make it abundantly clear that in the second half of the last century B.C. Rome was living in a moral vacuum. One cer-

tainly should not make a sweeping generalization and assert
that every section of the population throughout all Italy was
similarly affected.   The masses throughout the peninsula were
basically sound and were still living as they had lived for
centuries, by observance of their traditional rules of life.   But
the governing class at Rome had lost its spiritual bearings, and
this class, though small, was very important ; ultimately it set
the tone of life in Rome, and the habits and customs, that came
to prevail in the capital, were as a rule finally adopted in the
municipalities of Italy.   Therefore the spiritual dry-rot of the
governing class in Rome could be expected gradually to spread
throughout the peninsula ; and the pace would accelerate when
the younger generation, a generation that had grown up in the
moral vacuum and had not inherited a sound political experience,
reached the years when it would have to take its part in state
affairs.   Augustus realized that his great power entailed corre-
spondingly great responsibility.   Unlike the famous French
monarch, he was not prepared to let the deluge follow him ;
he felt it his duty to promote some kind of moral and spiritual
regeneration.

He had already made some attempt to re-establish the spiritual
basis of the State, for ever since 28 B.C. he had been trying to
rehabilitate the traditional cults of Italy.   He himself relates
how he dedicated new temples, or rebuilt old ones, or in other
ways fostered a religious revival.   He even contemplated the
restoration of the Etruscan sacred league.   There is no reliable
evidence, however, that he introduced moral legislation in
28 :   that was reserved for 18.

The re-establishment of family life seemed to him the best
way to rescue the coming generations.   The decay of family life,
especially among the small governing class, was no doubt caused
by a number of factors.   The rather haphazard methods for
entering on the conjugal state were not in themselves very
conducive to respect for the marriage tie ; nor should the
effects of the influx of wealth be forgotten.   As a result of the
Punic Wars money had poured into a Rome that had not even
used it until a few years previously.[1]   It accumulated in the
hands of the governing classes ; and before they had learnt to
invest and apply it sensibly the period of civil disorder and
confusion had begun.   The consequent economic insecurity
produced a frantic search for excessive liquidity and a tendency

---

[1] Salmon, *Samnium and the Samnites*, p. 277.

to spend money on material comforts. When men find their possession of their property uncertain in the extreme, they are not likely to take a very long or responsible view of their investment obligations. A generation intent on material comforts will not find conjugal, much less parental, fetters very attractive : it will scramble for more money in order to indulge itself the better.

It was not only the male sex that was affected. By the last century B.C. many women were wealthy in their own right, and by then custom no longer sanctioned any very rigorous marital control over them ; so that they too sought self-indulgence. Men who in any event preferred personal pleasures to wedlock found in the behaviour of women like the notorious Clodia yet one more excuse for avoiding matrimony ; and it was easy enough to avoid, since in Rome the dividing line between marriage and mere cohabitation was always fairly slim.

The growing disinclination to marry led inevitably to a fall in the birth-rate, especially in the small governing class. This brought another evil in its train : legacy-hunting. Wealthy but childless people naturally attracted the seeker after easy money. The legacy-hunters lavished all kinds of flattering attentions upon their prospective benefactors ; and such attentions might be agreeable enough to induce men not to run the risk of losing them by marrying. It was a vicious circle : the prevailing aversion to wedlock resulted in legacy-hunting, and legacy-hunting encouraged celibacy.

To remedy the situation Augustus passed laws on the relations between the sexes. The Julian Laws of 18 B.C., however, were not an unqualified success. They needed supplementary legislation and obtained it, in A.D. 9, when the Lex Papia Poppaea was passed. As it is not easy to separate the two sets of enactments, it will be convenient to describe all of Augustus' moral legislation at this point.

The *Lex Iulia de Maritandis Ordinibus* aimed at promoting marriage. It specifically recognized the right of Roman men, except Senators, to contract legal marriages with freedwomen. It also forbade parents to restrain their children from wedlock and testators to stipulate that their beneficiaries should be single. The act placed disabilities upon unmarried citizens : Roman spinsters were obliged to pay a special tax, while unmarried women over fifty and unmarried men over sixty were debarred from certain types of legacy.   Family men on the other hand, especially family men of the governing class, were distinctly favoured.   The Right of Three Children (*ius trium liberorum*) was evolved, so that men of senatorial rank who had served the State by producing offspring could advance on their official career at an age below the legal minimum.   In the event of a tie at the consular elections the candidate with the more children was declared elected, and after the election the consul with the greater number of children was reckoned senior.   Parenthood also increased one's chances of a provincial appointment.   In the lower strata of society a freedman, by becoming the father of three or more children, was released from the hold which his *patronus* normally held over a portion of his estate.

The *Lex Iulia de Adulteriis Coercendis* sought to discourage divorce.   Hitherto the marriage tie had had few legal regulations to protect it : public opinion, in the form of the censor's stigma, frowned on but hardly prevented divorce.   Augustus now established a public court where people taken in adultery and those who aided them were put on trial and, if found guilty, severely punished.   Banishment to islands, together with the forfeiture of at least a third of one's property, was the penalty laid down.   An action brought against an erring partner automatically involved an action for divorce.   Thus divorce and, with it, marriage were regularized and some of the casualness disappeared from marital relations.

Augustus' illusion that men can be legislated into continent behaviour caused him also to pass laws limiting the size of houses and even of meals.   Such sumptuary legislation presumably was no more successful than similar efforts in the same field both before and after his day.

§ 6.   THE SECULAR GAMES ;   CAESAR-WORSHIP

Augustus could now claim that the wounds of the State, moral as well as political, had been healed.   A new era of general prosperity and well-being could be anticipated.   Therefore he had no hesitation in announcing that the Golden Age, which Vergil had so confidently predicted in 40 when the youthful Octavian was first emerging into power, had at last arrived. Nothing short of a magnificent celebration was worthy of the occasion, and such a celebration was duly solemnized in 17 B.C. at the Secular Games (*ludi saeculares*).

The idea of a cycle of epochs (*saecula*) was familiar to many ancient peoples; it may have reached the Romans by way of the Etruscans. Antiquarians had calculated that each epoch had lasted for 100 years and that the Tenth and Golden Age of Rome should have begun in 49 B.C.; yet that was actually a year of civil war. Augustus now induced the Fifteen Men who supervised the Sibylline Books (*XV viri sacris faciundis*), one of whom was M. Cocceius Nerva (great-grandfather of the future Emperor), to make pronouncements which could be interpreted as meaning that the Tenth Age really began in 17 B.C. Accordingly in June of that year the New Age was magnificently ushered in with a ceremonious festival. A fitting culmination to it was provided by a choir of boys and maidens, singing the hymn expressive of the spirit of the New Age, which Horace had been commissioned to write. The selection of Horace as the laureate on this occasion is significant. It was due partly to the fact that he was now the foremost poet of Rome (Vergil having died in 19), but partly to the fact that he was a comparatively recent convert to the régime. While Vergil had been welcoming the prospect of a Golden Age, Horace, recently escaped from the republican defeat at Philippi, had been giving expression to very different sentiments.[1] For him now to emerge as the official eulogist of the New Age meant that in his own person he offered living proof of the manner in which old wounds had been healed.

But it was not only the poet who symbolized the spirit of the New Age. The festival itself chiefly honoured, not the Capitoline Jupiter, traditionally the supreme god of the Roman world, but Apollo: Horace's hymn was sung on the Palatine as well as on the Capitol. Augustus in fact was deliberately setting up the Palatine as a kind of religious rival to the Capitol; the Palatine Triad of Mars Ultor, Apollo and Venus received far more official support than the ancient Capitoline Triad of Jupiter, Juno and Minerva. The fact that the Julian house traced its origin back to Venus no doubt helped to dictate the choice of divinities; but family pride was not the main motive for this shift of religious emphasis.

Augustus was very conscious of the multiplicity of nations in the Roman Empire. There was no common language, no common culture, no common way of life, no common conception of national destiny. Yet if the Empire was ever to be united,

[1] See Vergil, *Eclogue* IV and Horace, *Epode* XVI.

it could only be as the result of some common loyalty, some common idea which all its component members shared. Augustus tried to find that common idea in the field of religion. For this the old Capitoline Triad, essentially a local Italic cult, obviously could not serve. Hence he instituted a new Palatine Triad. But the Palatine was becoming increasingly identified with the imperial family that lived there. Hence the Palatine Triad was only ancillary to the real core of the new cult, which we can call by its traditional name of Caesar-worship.

This undoubtedly was inspired to a very large extent by the well-known practice of ruler-worship in the Eastern Mediterranean. The Caesar-worship of the Roman Empire, however, differed in some important particulars. When the Augustan principate was established, the Hellenized inhabitants of the east quickly realized that they were once again subject to the personal rule of a monarch, and they were quite ready to establish the formal practice of personal worship of him. In such worship the language was often extravagant, although the word " god " was probably not meant to indicate anything more than extreme exaltation of rank. Such deification of himself, however, did not appeal greatly to Augustus, even though he could scarcely take the extreme step of rigorously suppressing such proof of devotion. There is evidence to prove that he was personally worshipped in the eastern provinces, e.g. in Egypt, where he received the adulation customarily lavished on a conqueror.

But the career of Antony had taught him that eagerness for such extravagant honours was politically dangerous. He also realized that if he were to seek some idea that the whole Empire could share in common, he was not likely to find it in what was essentially an eastern practice, for the west would not accept it. Consequently he hit upon an ingenious compromise that was acceptable to east and west alike. He combined the eastern tendency to worship the ruler with the western tendency to revere dead ancestors, the most national and sacred of Rome's religions. He did not, officially, countenance personal worship of himself either at Rome or in the provinces : the poetic licence of his court poets and his inability to restrain his eastern subjects from voting him extravagant honours should not blind us to the conservative features in his religious innovation. What he did was to encourage the worship of the imperial house in conjunction with the worship of the goddess Roma.

He thus suggested that the imperial house and the State were virtually one, or at the very least that their fortunes were inextricably bound together.

The cult took different forms in various parts of the Empire. In the provinces the provincials paid worship to " Rome and Augustus," Roman citizens to " Rome and the Deified Julius " (since Romans, while prepared to honour dead ancestors, would feel the impropriety of addressing prayers to a man who was still alive). In Italy Augustus did not go this far, for he did not introduce direct worship of the imperial house into any of the state cults ; but he shrewdly sanctioned its introduction into the family cult of the Lares, the cult about which all Romans felt deeply. Under these forms Italians worshipped the *genius Augusti* or the *numen Augusti*, so that when they prayed for the welfare of their own families, they also prayed for the welfare of the imperial family. (See further below, pp. 66–7.)

A great and rapid extension of the new Caesar-worship took place after 12 B.C., when Augustus succeeded Lepidus as Pontifex Maximus. But even before then it had been gradually growing ; the Secular Games festival must have contributed not a little to the new spiritual basis that the State found under the Empire.

§ 7.   THE AUGUSTAN BUILDING PROGRAMME

The revival of religion contributed markedly to Augustus' vast building programme. He did not indeed confine himself to religious architecture, but he executed many works of public utility, such as docks, granaries, shopping centres, aqueducts and the like.[1] On the whole it was public monuments that chiefly engaged Augustus' attention. So far as we know, there was no systematic housing programme under government supervision, nor even any careful town-planning at Rome, though there was such in other Italian towns such as Augusta Praetoria (*Aosta*).[2] In the capital such planning as was attempted, was in connexion with temples, shrines and similar public buildings. According to the *Res Gestae* Augustus restored eighty-two temples ; and he built many new ones. In these enterprises, which were spread over his whole reign, Augustus had many

---

[1] Agrippa's Aqua Virgo is an outstanding example.

[2] There was also much building activity in the provinces : the famous Pont du Gard near Nîmes belongs to the Augustan era.

helpers. Agrippa and, after his death in 12 B.C., Tiberius deserve almost as much credit as Augustus himself. Less exalted personages also bore their share of the burden, notably Asinius Pollio and Gaius Maecenas, who transformed the Esquiline rubbish heaps into parks.

To make a list of all the Augustan buildings and to give a detailed description of them in this volume is obviously impossible. We can barely allude to the embellishment of the Campus Martius where Augustus and his coadjutors either built or restored such famous monuments as the Ara Pacis Augustae with its beautiful bas-reliefs; the Augustan Mausoleum; numerous porticoes; the Saepta Julia; Agrippa's Baths; the Theatres of Pompey and Marcellus; the Pantheon, and several other temples. On the Palatine there rose the splendid Temple of Apollo, while in the Forum Romanum beneath it Augustus completed Julius Caesar's re-orientation, built new edifices and restored old ones. Few are the buildings flanking the Roman Forum that do not owe something to the Augustan building programme. In addition Augustus constructed his own Forum slightly to the north-west and enclosed therein an imposing Temple to Mars Ultor. On the Capitoline Hill overlooking this he erected temples to Jupiter Feretrius and Jupiter Tonans.

In these enterprises use was made of the building materials commonly employed under the Republic: the various kinds of volcanic tufa, the marble-like travertine, the excellent Roman bricks, and the concrete of which the red pozzolana is the base. But in addition to these white marble from the Carrara quarries near Spezia now began to be extensively used. Augustus also copiously imported the various coloured marbles that are found in the countries fringing the Mediterranean: hence his famous boast that he had found a city of brick but left one of marble.[1]

§ 8. IMPERIAL POWERS AND TITLES

The Secular Games, by ushering in the New Age, intimated that Augustus now regarded his reforms, political, moral and spiritual, as firmly established. In this he was not mistaken: from now until the end of his life in A.D. 14 he was called upon to make few major changes in the system which he had fashioned. He did alter electoral procedures [2] and regularize

[1] Suetonius, *Augustus*, 28, 3.   [2] See below, pp. 39, 57, 126.

the periodic accretions to the Princeps' prerogatives and powers : none of these, however, fundamentally altered the constitution as the reforms of 27, 23 and 18 B.C. had left it. Some of them were little more than honorific ritual, such as the New Year's ceremonies at which senators individually renewed the oath to him and citizens brought small gifts of money with which he dedicated statues in the various *vici* (or wards) of the city. The title *pater patriae*, conferred in 2 B.C., suggests that the State was in his power like a *familia* in a father's : but it added nothing specific to his powers.

Other honours were of greater importance. For example, he obtained the sole right of coining in the precious metals. Under the Republic the Senate controlled the coinage ; and under Augustus it continued to coin the bronze token money, minting it at Rome. But even in republican times generals in the field had been allowed to strike coins ; and Augustus as *de facto* commander of the armed forces established his own mints outside of Italy. After 15 B.C. the gold coins for the whole Empire and the silver coins for the west were minted at Lugdunum. The silver coins for the east were struck at Antioch.

But Augustus not only issued the coins, he also controlled the state finances. Under the Principate the finances were under the charge of three departments.[1] One of these, the public treasury (*aerarium Saturni*), was nominally supervised from 23 B.C. onward by the Senate, acting through two annual praetors. However, as it was unable to carry on without subventions from the Emperor, and as the services which made the heaviest demands on it (the grain and water supplies and the highways) were administered by the Emperor's *curatores*, it must have been effectively controlled by him.

The second financial department was the military one (*aerarium militare*), instituted by Augustus in A.D. 6 and supported by the proceeds of the 1 per cent sales tax and the 5 per cent inheritance tax. It paid out military pensions, and the Emperor administered it directly through three ex-praetors.

But the most important financial institution consisted of the Emperor's own accounts, the various *fisci*, which ultimately (probably under Claudius) were united into one single centralized *fiscus*. Augustus employed freedmen to manage these accounts, which were founded on spoils of war, and the Emperor's private income, derived from his privately owned and

[1] See A. Garzetti in *Athenaeum*, XXXI (1953), pp. 298–327 and F. Millar in *Journ. Rom. Stud.*, LIII (1963), pp. 29–42.

inherited estates (*patrimonium Caesaris*).   In practice, says
Dio, it was extremely difficult to keep his official and private
accounts separate.

The Emperor also became virtually the only source of new
law.[1]   This was a development from the republican practice of
allowing any official possessing *imperium* to interpret the law.[2]
Like the magistrates and promagistrates of the Republic, the
Princeps could issue a summary of the principles of the law as
he understood them ; and from this to the actual promulgation
of new laws was but a small step.   By *c.* A.D. 135 an Emperor's
edicta (fiats), *decreta* (judicial decisions), and *rescripta* (written
replies on legal points) were known collectively as his *constitutiones* and had recognized legal validity.   Augustus' measures
were more informal than this (they were colloquially styled *dicta
principis*), but were legislative in practice.   Sometimes, too, the
Emperor became a source of new law indirectly through the
pronouncements of eminent jurists, to whom he had delegated
the power of giving binding opinions on points of law : under
the Republic the *responsa* of leading jurists, while greatly
respected, had not possessed such legal validity.

In his official titles Augustus was careful not to advertise
his exceptional powers.   Epigraphic evidence reveals that he
used only five titles.   The inscriptions do indeed contain, in
addition to the titles, the designations Imperator Caesar Augustus.
These, however, were not titles but names, Imperator being a
praenomen, Caesar in effect the *nomen*, and Augustus a *cognomen*.[3]

The five titles used by Augustus on official documents were :
pontifex maximus, consul, imperator, tribunicia potestas, pater
patriae.[4]   These were all republican titles with the exception

[1] For the Senate as an ostensible source of new law see below,
p. 39 and n.

[2] The analogy of British judge-made law, although obvious, is far
from exact.

[3] Later these names virtually did become titles, since the successors
of Augustus assumed them and they became a regular feature of the
imperial nomenclature.   Tiberius adopted Augustus ;   Claudius in
effect made Caesar a title (it came especially to denote the heir apparent) ;
Nero apparently regularized the title of Imperator (under Vespasian it
displaced Princeps as the popular designation of the Emperor).

[4] Later Emperors sometimes omitted the title *pater patriae*, and
sometimes added *censor* (after Claudius) and *proconsul* (after Trajan).
The order finally adopted for the imperial titles usually was : pontifex
maximus, tribunicia potestas (II, III, etc.), imperator (II, III, etc.),
consul (II, III, etc.), censor, proconsul.

of the Tribunician Power, and its implications were not alarming to constitutionalists. It is noteworthy that Augustus' formidable Imperium Proconsulare was not explicitly recognized in the official titulary : it was only obliquely indicated by the title *imperator* (which must not be confused with the *praenomen imperatoris*). Technically this title meant that the troops had hailed Augustus as *imperator* (the so-called imperial salutation). Only the Emperor could be so saluted since the generals who did the real work and earned the salutation were serving under his superior *imperium* : technically they were only his subordinates, so that any salutations they received belonged to him. In other words the title *imperator* could be given only to one who possessed the Imperium Proconsulare.[1] Trajan was the first Emperor who openly included *proconsul* in his list of titles ; and even in his case it was officially used only when he was away from Italy.

§ 9.   ENSURING THE SUCCESSION

Augustus' policy was to achieve national unity and avoid any recurrence of civil war. The succession of a non-Julian would almost certainly provoke pretenders to put forward their claims : armed conflict would result.[2] Augustus accordingly sought a successor of Julian ancestry. After Marcellus' death in 23 he looked to his daughter Julia and Agrippa to provide one. Their union proved fruitful, for Julia bore a son, Gaius, in 20, and another, Lucius, in 17 B.C. Henceforth Augustus' hopes for the succession centred on his grandsons, and he revealed his purpose unmistakably in 17 by adopting both boys, who became the young ' Caesares.'

As his grandsons were still too young to be employed in administrative duties, Augustus was obliged to fall back on the services of their father Agrippa and of the Claudian stepsons whom Livia had brought him, Tiberius and Drusus. Of the

[1] A short-lived exception to this was the commander in Africa who, down to the reign of Gaius, was directly responsible to the Senate and not to the Princeps.

[2] Augustus' judgment in this respect was vindicated in the ensuing half-century. Of his Julio-Claudian successors, the two Claudians (Tiberius and Claudius), although suitable candidates for the purple, were greeted with revolts on their accession ; the two Julians (Gaius and Nero), although obviously unfitted for imperial responsibilities, succeeded without incident. See *Journ. Rom. Stud.*, XXXIII (1943), 2.

loyalty of Agrippa there could be no doubt.   The behaviour of
the stepsons was also loyal enough, whatever their views on
Augustus' attempt to perpetuate the supremacy of the Julian
family over the heads of the old Roman aristocracy.   It is said
that the younger, Drusus, was opposed to the Principate and
favoured a genuine restoration of the Republic ;   the elder,
Tiberius, was also republican in sentiment, to judge from his
subsequent actions.

In 16 B.C., when Agrippa had returned to the East, Tiberius
was praetor and Drusus was quaestor, although each was under
age for his office.   Sigambri and others now defeated the legate
Lollius along the Rhine.   So Augustus left T. Statilius Taurus
as City Prefect and took Tiberius thither.   Augustus soon moved
on to Spain ;   while his stepsons, Drusus as well as Tiberius,
remained in the north.   Both served there with distinction
during the next four years.

In 13 B.C. Augustus and Agrippa both returned to Rome.
Drusus became governor of the Three Gauls, and Tiberius held
the consulship.   Augustus' Imperium Proconsulare was renewed
for another five years, as was also the Tribunician Power of
Agrippa.   On this occasion, as distinct from 18 B.C., Agrippa's
imperium maius was specifically mentioned ; and he immediately
left Rome to exercise it in Pannonia.[1]

In the spring of 12 B.C. Agrippa returned to Italy, but died
soon after.   His death robbed Augustus not only of a loyal
friend and supporter, but also of one who could serve as Emperor-
regent in the event of the sudden demise of the Princeps.
Augustus' grandsons, Agrippa's children by Julia, were still
unavailable as successors because of their tender years : the
third of them, indeed, was not born until after his father's
death (hence he was usually called Agrippa Postumus).
Augustus accordingly made provision for a sudden emergency
by forcing his elder stepson Tiberius to divorce the wife of whom
he was genuinely fond, Vipsania (Agrippa's daughter by an
earlier marriage), and marry Julia, who was now a widow for
the second time (11 B.C.).   This dubious favour, however, was
the only immediate sign that Tiberius stood next in line for
the succession ; apparently his intended function was to be that
of guardian to the young Caesars.

Soon Tiberius became the sole adult support of the Princeps,
for his younger brother Drusus, after some brilliant military

[1] Cassius Dio, LIV, 28, 1.

campaigns in the north which finally took him as far as the River Elbe, was killed by a fall from a horse (9 B.C.). Augustus, conscious no doubt of his own increasing years, now made Tiberius' intended rôle of Emperor-regent clear. When the Princeps' Imperium Proconsulare came up for renewal in 8 B.C. it was prolonged for a ten-year period, and Tiberius was apparently named to share it with him.[1] In 6 B.C. Tiberius obtained the Tribunician Power for a period of five years.

But in the same year Augustus made it unmistakably clear that the succession was really intended for his Julian grandsons, and that Tiberius the Claudian was merely intended to be a stop-gap regent. Augustus now set propaganda in motion to prepare the Roman world for the premature election of the fourteen-year-old Gaius to the consulship. Nevertheless, the boy was not actually appointed consul in this year. In the next year Gaius assumed the *toga virilis* and was formally introduced to public life by no less a person than Augustus himself, who actually became consul for the occasion. It was now that Gaius was designated consul, with the proviso, however, that he would not actually hold the office until five years had elapsed. He was also given the right to attend Senate meetings ; and as a further indication of his ultimate position in the state he was saluted as Princeps Iuventutis, chief of the youthful members of the Equestrian Order.[2] The same ceremonies were repeated exactly three years later for Gaius' younger brother Lucius.

Meanwhile, however, Augustus had lost the services of Tiberius. The latter, in the very year in which he had obtained the Tribunician Power (6 B.C.), had forsaken public life and retired to the island of Rhodes. His motive has long been a subject for speculation. Presumably it was not just disappointment because his great services seemed to be rather slighted. He surely understood why Augustus refused to recognize the title of *imperator* with which his troops had saluted him in 12 and 11 B.C., and why the Emperor did not allow him to celebrate the triumphs which the Senate had voted him on those occasions : Tiberius must have realized that only the holder of

---

[1] This is not expressly stated in the ancient sources : but they invariably reflect Augustus' practice of keeping a close-drawn veil over his Imperium. From 8 B.C. on Tiberius has the title of *imperator* on inscriptions, and only a holder of Imperium Proconsulare would be so described. (Dessau, *Inscr. Lat. Sel.*, 95.)

[2] See below, p. 55. The title usually, and after A.D. 70 invariably, designated the heir apparent to the reigning Princeps.

Imperium Proconsulare was entitled to such honours.[1] He
equally well understood Augustus' insistence on a Julian successor : his intended rôle of Emperor-regent must have been
plain to him.   But these measures could not be palatable, and
they were coupled with other grievances.   Relations between
him and his stepson, the youthful Gaius, were strained.   Above
all, he was forced to live in wedlock with the immoral Julia,
whose profligacies increased with age.   Tiberius, while loyally
prepared to do his public duties even though they were not gratifying to himself, could see no reason why in addition he should be
obliged to endure private infamy at the hands of Julia.   He was
not eager to become Emperor in any case ; and he simply did not
want the position at all if he had to take as his Empress a
woman who obviously intended to make him a mere cuckold.
The story that Tiberius himself, on his arrival in Rhodes,
imitated Julia's lubricity is untrustworthy, although such conduct on his part would not be altogether incomprehensible.
Actually he devoted himself on the island to literary and scientific
pursuits, and in particular to the study of astrology.   He may
have cited Agrippa's journey to the east in 23 as an analogy for
his own retirement thither in 6, but this it certainly was not.
Agrippa had gone to the east in the public service ; Tiberius'
motive was the private one of terminating his relations with
Julia.

Finally Augustus himself was obliged to recognize that
Tiberius' low opinion of Julia was justified.   In 2 B.C. her
flagrant adulteries led the Princeps to banish her to the island
of Pandateria.   Tiberius thereupon requested permission to
return to Rome.   But Augustus, coldly furious at what he
regarded as his stepson's defection in 6 B.C., refused to grant
it.   It is hardly necessary to add that in the next year (1 B.C.),
when Tiberius' Tribunician Power expired, Augustus refused to
renew it, and Tiberius became a private citizen.

Meanwhile the Princeps' grandsons, the young Caesars, were
growing up and were beginning to fill their destined rôles.   In
4 B.C. Gaius was among Augustus' advisers on an affair of state,
and in 2 B.C. both he and his brother assisted at the dedication

[1] See above, p. 33.   Augustus on each occasion did the next best
thing : in 12 Tiberius was awarded the *triumphalia ornamenta* (the right
to retain permanently the insignia worn at a triumph (on this see A. A.
Boyce in *Class. Phil.*, XXXVII (1942), pp. 130–41)) ; and in 11 he celebrated an *ovatio*.

of the Temple of Mars Ultor in Augustus' new Forum. In 1 B.C. Gaius was given a commission in the eastern provinces, being invested with a special proconsular *imperium* for the purpose ; and three years later his younger brother, Lucius, was given a similar appointment in the west. Augustus now, probably at Livia's urging and with the haughty consent of Gaius, relaxed his anger to some extent ; in A.D. 2 Tiberius was permitted to return to Rome, but only to private life. In A.D. 3, when Augustus' Imperium Proconsulare was again renewed for ten years, Tiberius was not named as his colleague. Neither was anyone else for that matter.

Fate, however, again intervened and obliged the Princeps to use the services of Tiberius, for the young Caesars died, Lucius in A.D. 2 and Gaius in A.D. 4. Augustus now had little choice. Tiberius was the only member of his household who had experience enough either to help the Princeps now or to carry on in the event of his sudden demise. Accordingly in A.D. 4 he adopted Tiberius as his son and granted him the Tribunician Power again, this time for a ten-year term. Furthermore, since Tiberius henceforth appears with the title of *imperator* on inscriptions, he presumably again became colleague in the Imperium Proconsulare : he certainly was exercising a special *imperium* immediately afterwards on the Rhine frontier.

But Augustus was careful not to adopt Tiberius alone. He still wished to ensure the ultimate succession of a Julian. Therefore he made his surviving grandson, the youthful Agrippa Postumus, legally his son at the same time as Tiberius. Still further to demonstrate that the succession was intended for the Julians and not the Claudians, Tiberius was obliged to adopt his brother's son, his nephew Germanicus, and so to relegate his own son, Drusus, to the position of second choice, and to grant privileges of seniority to Germanicus. The latter, it is true, was technically Claudian ; but he had Julian blood, and his Julian connexions were strengthened at this time by marriage, his bride being Augustus' granddaughter Agrippina. Such marital unions were the traditional method for ensuring a man's political future. Augustus' object was that Germanicus and Augustus' direct descendants, Germanicus' children, should succeed instead of Drusus or Drusus' descendants.[1] As before, Tiberius' obvious rôle was that of Emperor-regent.

---

[1] Germanicus was soon given needed military experience by serving with Tiberius in Pannonia ; and he was made consul in A.D. 12.

Tiberius could not have been particularly enamoured of these arrangements, since he could not have had a very high opinion of either Agrippa Postumus or Germanicus. The former was a brutal lout, whom in A.D. 7 Augustus had to banish ; the latter, to judge from his subsequent career, was headstrong and opinionated. Both youths, however, had Julian ancestors and were blood relatives of the Princeps : Agrippa Postumus was the grandson of Augustus himself and Germanicus was the grandson of his sister Octavia ;[1] and Tiberius loyally agreed with Augustus' decision that the Principate must belong to the Julians. In succeeding reigns, however, rivalry between the Julian and Claudian branches of the imperial house was to play an important rôle.

This time death did not play havoc with Augustus' arrangements, and during the remaining ten years of his reign Tiberius gradually came to be more and more closely associated with his adoptive father. The old Emperor had to rely heavily on Tiberius' military capacity. In A.D. 13, when the Imperium Proconsulare of both and the Tribunician Power of Tiberius came up for renewal, the stepson was explicitly recognized as sharer in both. Tiberius was co-regent, just as Agrippa had been in 18 B.C.

But on this occasion the senior partner in the co-regency did not outlive his associate. Augustus passed away at Nola in August of A.D. 14. In the *laudatio funebris*, which Tiberius delivered, the old Emperor was compared not unfavourably with Hercules ;[2] and in September he was voted divine honours. Henceforth he was known as *Divus Augustus*, the Deified Augustus. To his successor he bequeathed a Roman world that enjoyed external security and internal peace. Externally the boundaries of the Empire had been firmly indicated. Internally a new constitution had been patiently devised which paradoxically men found acceptable because Augustus had carefully used and adapted the old republican institutions. The new feature was the way in which the old republican institutions were combined.

[1] Scandal even said that Germanicus was the grandson of Augustus : Suet., *Claudius*, 1, 1.
[2] Bayet, *Origines de l'Hercule romain, passim.*

CHAPTER II

ITALY

§ 1. THE SENATE AND ITS POWERS

THE *real* basis of the Principate was the Emperor's military power. The *legal* basis, however, was his special commission from the Senate and People. But the People's ratification of the Senate's choice was a mere formality ; hence one can say that, in legal theory, the Senate actually appointed the Emperor. Thus the Senate ostensibly had very great power. The official version was that it was fulfilling its "ancient functions." It administered numerous provinces, and theoretically Italy as well, since it controlled the consuls, who still possessed the nominal authority over Italy ; and it could claim to exercise supervision over the treasury, the grain and water supply of Rome and the highways.

Under the Empire the Senate numbered somewhat under six hundred. *C.* 4 B.C. it became one of the two High Courts from whose verdict there was no appeal. It also possessed legislative functions. Nominally it was one of the two sources of new law ; and in our period the Emperors usually preferred to issue their legislation in the form of *senatus consulta*.[1] In addition to these powers the Senate shortly obtained elective functions. After A.D. 14 it elected the magistrates and even before then it and the judiciary knights " designated " consuls and praetors. The Senate even retained some of its pristine powers in external affairs, since we hear occasionally of foreign envoys coming to it ; and there is at least one instance of the Senate, rather than the Princeps, pronouncing a client king to be " a friend of the Roman people."

These extensive powers, privileges and prerogatives of the Senate have led some scholars to conclude that the Principate was intended to be a dyarchy, a joint rule of Emperor and

---

[1] Under Augustus apparently *senatus consulta* were not, strictly speaking, laws. They were resolutions taken by the Senate and tendered as advice to the magistrates. These latter, however, never failed to act on them, so that they were laws *de facto*. Consequently legal hair-splitting was soon forgotten and the Senate acquired the right to make laws directly.

Senate : the Roman world was, as it were, divided between them. Actually the spheres of Princeps and Senate cannot be thus neatly separated : *senatus consulta*, for instance, and after 23 B.C. the Princeps' *imperium* were valid everywhere. Augustus never intended a dyarchy conception of the Principate to prevail. He was willing to have the Principate popularly regarded as the rule of the Senate with the Princeps as its guide, philosopher and friend. But the so-called dyarchy was no more of a reality than the restoration of the Republic. Theoretically the Senate might appoint the Princeps, actually it was the other way round ; the Emperor gave very close attention to the composition of the Senate.

Under the Empire Roman society was strictly hierarchical, the classes in descending order of rank being the Senatorial Order, the Equestrian Order, the common people (*plebs*), the freedmen and the slaves. The Senatorial Order, which had the right to wear the laticlave (a tunic with a broad purple stripe), was the class from which the Senate was recruited, and the Princeps controlled its membership.

In exercising this control Augustus adhered to certain traditions which the republican censors had observed in appointing senators. By Sulla's day the office of quaestor automatically conferred membership in the Senate. Augustus adhered to this practice, with modifications. Under his arrangements some men began their careers before the quaestorship. He intended to use senators in high posts involving military as well as administrative duties and consequently insisted that any who planned to enter his service should do some serious soldiering before entering the Senate. Such *viri militares* might serve long periods as *tribuni laticlavii* ; they were the real governing minority of the Empire. Senatorials aiming at purely civilian careers sometimes served as legionary tribunes for a year but could reach the quaestorship without doing so.

§ 2. THE SENATORIAL CAREER

Membership in the Senatorial Order was obtained either through birth or imperial grant. Senators' sons entered it easily, if not automatically. Men not so favoured could be " adlected " into it by the Princeps, for he had the right to bestow the laticlave upon those whom he thought worthy of it ; normally the men so adlected were taken from the Equestrian

Order. But a capital qualification was also necessary. This qualification from 13 B.C. onwards, if not before, was 1,000,000 sesterces. The source of this wealth was normally landed property, since senatorials were forbidden to participate, openly at any rate, in trade, and they no longer had opportunities of making fortunes out of politics, war booty, or at the expense of provincials.[1] The estates from which the senatorial families obtained their income were largely situated in Italy : even later, when non-Italians began to become senators, they were obliged to invest at least a third of their capital in Italian land. Occasionally the Emperor gave a money grant to an impoverished but worthy family to enable it to retain its senatorial status.

Senators might carve glittering careers in the Emperor's service. The administrative capacities of all aspirants to it were first tested in minor offices before they were even allowed to become candidates for the quaestorship, the first step in the *cursus honorum* proper. They were obliged to serve, for at least a year, in one or more of the so-called lesser magistracies that comprised the vigintivirate.[2] They performed their above-mentioned military service usually as *tribuni militum* (that is, officers in a legion), but sometimes as *praefecti alae* (that is, officers in the auxiliary cavalry). After these necessary preliminaries, and on attaining twenty-five years of age, a man could become a candidate for the quaestorship.

The quaestors held office for a year (December 5 to December 4) and under the Empire numbered twenty. A quaestor's duties were varied and, unlike those of some other city magistrates, not unimportant. They might take him outside of Italy : the quaestor, in fact, was the only urban magistrate who left Rome during his term of office. It was in the quaestorship particularly that a man demonstrated his administrative ability. He might serve as a financial official in the senatorial provinces (*quaestor pro praetore*) ;[3] or, after Claudius, he might serve as an official at the public treasury (*quaestor urbanus*) ; or he might serve as a liaison officer between the Emperor,

[1] Some senatorial families, however, did make money from usurious practices in the provinces.

[2] The " twenty men " consisted of three moneyers (*tresviri monetales*), three police commissioners (*tresviri capitales*), four city engineers (*quattuorviri viis in urbe purgandis*), and ten police court magistrates (*decemviri slitibus iudicandis*).

[3] Normally ten were so employed.

the Senate and the consuls (*quaestor principis*, *quaestor consulum*).[1] The quaestor automatically became a member of the Senate, Augustus in this particular preserving Sulla's arrangement.

The quaestorship, however, was only the first step. The consulship was still regarded as the crown of the senatorial career, and there was keen competition for it. This might seem surprising, for under the Empire the city magistracies, and not least the consulship, steadily lost their importance. The explanation is that most of the really important posts in the Roman world, such as the City Prefecture, the bigger provincial governorships and the higher military positions, were open only to ex-consuls. After the quaestorship, a man's next step was to serve for a year as one of the ten plebeian tribunes or as one of the aediles. Patricians, who obviously could not serve in plebeian offices, were not unnaturally exempted from this step by law.[2] Under the Republic neither office had been an obligatory step in the *cursus honorum*. Augustus insisted on either one or the other, since otherwise the unpopular offices would have had difficulty in attracting candidates.[3]

The third step was the praetorship, an office reserved for men of thirty or over and tenable for twelve months (January 1 to December 31). In Augustus' last years the praetors numbered twelve, and their principal and by no means unimportant duty was to preside in the various law-courts (*iudicia publica*). Until A.D. 44 praetors were also in charge of the public treasury. Actually the office was not burdensome, since usually there were more than enough praetors to discharge the duties required of them.

Two years after the praetorship, when a man would be at least thirty-three years of age, he could present himself as a candidate for the consulship. In practice, however, a *novus homo* rarely did so. Only the descendant of a consul could hope for the consulship until at least ten years after his praetorship. During the period of waiting he need not live a quiescent life. He might be appointed, either by the Emperor or by the Senate,

---

[1] There were regularly two *quaestores principis*, both patrician.

[2] This enabled the Emperor to show his favour. The number of genuine patricians now being small, he sometimes pronounced a man " patrician " and thereby relieved him or his children of one of the more tiresome stages in the official senatorial career.

[3] Cassius Dio, LV, 24, 9.

to some important praetorian post, usually in the provinces. A man was normally forty-two and well trained in public administration by the time he became consul; but this was a matter of more importance for subsequent posts than for the consulship itself, for this was more or less of a sinecure with duties of a largely ceremonial kind.

The Emperor's control over a man's senatorial career did not consist merely in starting men of obscure origin on their way by adlecting them into the Senatorial Order; it could be exercised at every step of the way both for those who were senatorials by birth and for those who were such by adlection. Since no one could even expect ultimate high preferment without first serving as an officer in the army, and since it was the Emperor who issued commissions, he decided who should and who should not begin a senatorial career. Thereafter he had the power to make or break every aspirant. This imperial control was the outcome of the Emperor's desire to keep potential conspirators out of influential positions and to obtain administrative efficiency. Under the Republic magistrates, as often as not, had been elected for purely political reasons: it was not their fitness to discharge their eventual duties which procured their election, but rather some totally extraneous consideration, such as the number of clients' votes controlled by their families. The imperial system, for all its nepotism, did aim at obtaining really qualified men for the important posts. Therefore to avoid the uncertainties of electoral caprice, the Emperor discreetly supervised the preselection of candidates.

The republican consul had had the right of announcing candidates' names (*nominatio*). When presiding at elections he accepted or refused nominations at his own discretion and literally drew up the list of candidates. Until 23 B.C. Augustus possessed this right by virtue of being consul. After 23 he continued to exercise it, but indirectly: candidates asked him to submit their names in the justifiable belief that no presiding magistrate would dare exclude the Princeps' nominees. Later emperors sometimes " nominated " the same number of candidates as there were vacancies and made their election a mere formality. Augustus himself rarely resorted to this stratagem, but apparently did so for the consulships of A.D. 8.

Another republican tradition was that of ex-consuls electioneering in person for their candidates. This was known as *suffragatio.* Augustus undoubtedly practised it, canvassing the tribes himself on behalf of those he favoured.

Even more persuasive was his written support (*commendatio*). After A.D. 8, being too frail to canvass in person, Augustus merely published a list of those he " commended ", and " Caesar's candidates " were forthwith elected. The two *quaestores principis* were normally appointed thus. The consulship, however, was keenly contested, and there is no epigraphic evidence of anyone becoming consul as *candidatus Caesaris* under Augustus. On the contrary, since bribery occurred at consular elections, they could hardly have been foregone conclusions. Evidently for the higher magistracies Augustus and his immediate successors used indirect methods to block or promote candidates, employing *commendatio* only for minor offices.[1] Later emperors had fewer scruples and used it widely. The *Lex de Imperio Vespasiani* of 69 nakedly parades the imperial right to " commend ".

Thus did the Princeps ensure the election of those he approved, whether *nobiles* or *novi homines*.

§ 3. THE CONSULSHIP UNDER THE PRINCIPATE

Once the imperial system began to function smoothly, the number of posts open to ex-consuls showed a tendency to multiply, because of the growing need of the administrative machine for experienced officials. Even in republican times the annual magistrates had not been able to carry out unaided all the duties required of them in Rome alone. Accordingly *curatores* (commissioners) had been appointed, as and when necessary, to perform specific tasks, e.g. the repair of roads. Augustus regularized such curatorships by organizing them as permanent commissions of senators under the presidency of an ex-consul. His motive, says Suetonius, was " to increase the number of those taking part in the administration of the Republic." [2] Amongst other things these boards supervised the Grain Supply (until A.D. 8), the Water Supply, the Highways, the regulation of the Tiber, Public Works.

Augustus also used ex-consuls extensively for various other

---

[1] But not all of them : *candidati Caesaris* for the unpopular offices of aedile or tribune were very rare. For Tiberius' practice, see Tacitus, *Annals*, I, 14, 6 ; 81, 1–3.

[2] Suetonius, *Augustus*, 37, 1.

specialized tasks. When the infirmities of age began to limit his physical activity, he " entrusted to three ex-consuls the embassies sent to Rome by peoples and kings ; these sat separately and gave audience to the envoys and replied to their requests, except in cases where it was necessary for the final decision to be taken by the Emperor and the Senate." [1]   It was likewise ex-consuls who heard appeals from the provinces and who in A.D. 6 formed the commission for effecting economies in public expenditures.   They quite certainly were to be found in the Senate Committee. Augustus also regularly sought the advice of ex-consuls on all matters of public importance, if we may judge by the practice of Tiberius, who did so in the conviction that he was thereby following his predecessor.

In the early part of his reign Augustus apparently relied almost exclusively on ex-consuls from his own household or immediate entourage. But his increasing need of ex-consuls and the ravages of death among his own household soon rendered a wider choice both necessary and inevitable. Increasingly after 5 B.C. he used the device of a shortened consulship to supply the need, and from A.D. 2 onwards the abbreviated consulship became a permanent feature of the constitution. Six months was the regular duration of the office under the Julio-Claudian emperors. After A.D. 69, however, it became normal for three, and sometimes more, pairs of consuls to hold office in the same year. The pair that assumed office on January 1 were called *consules ordinarii* : they gave their names to the year, unofficially if not on official documents. The later pairs of consuls were called *consules suffecti* : often they were appointed early in the year. It was rare, especially before A.D. 69, for a man to hold the consulship twice, while a third consulship was the highest honour that a private individual could obtain under the Empire. Hence there was a regular, constant supply of ex-consuls available. [2]

The shortened consulship not only ensured an adequate supply of these necessary officials but also distributed the consulship more widely. This tended to remove a prime cause of dissatisfaction with Augustus' régime : it helped to allay the suspicion that he was anxious to secure the ascendancy of himself only and of his own faction. Once his personal position

[1] Cassius Dio, LV, 33, 5.
[2] See F. B. Marsh, *The Founding of the Roman Empire* (2nd ed.), p. 250 f.

was firmly established, Augustus' horizon had widened to include a vision of a genuinely national unity. The comparative failure of the settlement of 27 B.C. and the tactful but insistent exhortations of men like Horace presumably contributed to Augustus' conversion from the rôle of party politician. After 23 B.C., if not before, his primary aim was to prevent the recurrence of old schisms. His insistence that his deal with Parthia paid off old scores with that power indicates his anxiety to unify the nation : he knew that all Romans, whatever their political affiliations, were passionately eager to see the defeat at Carrhae avenged. But he needed to do more than settle accounts with Parthia to unite the whole of Italy behind him. National unity could never be achieved so long as the proud, old senatorial families remained unreconciled ; and unreconciled they would assuredly remain so long as they were excluded from the consulship, for the holding of the consulship had become traditional with them : houses like those of the Metelli, Aemilii, Servilii and Lentuli regarded the exalted office as almost their birthright. So long as the consulship remained an annual office, it would have been impossible to satisfy the aspirations of both the members of his own faction and of all the old republican families : there simply were not enough consulships to go round. But by shortening the term of office the number of consulships was automatically increased, and thereby it became possible to satisfy the political aspirations or the vanity of all.

As a result Augustus succeeded in winning over the republican elements in the state. Seneca's assertion that " Augustus enrolled the whole regiment of his intimates from the enemy's camp," although sweeping, is not without a basis of fact.[1] The first pair of consuls to take office after Augustus relinquished his continuous consulship in 23 B.C., the Emperor's laureate at the Secular Games in 17 B.C., and the ex-consul who proposed in 2 B.C. that the title " Father of the Fatherland " (*pater patriae*) be officially conferred upon Augustus, had all fought on the republican side at Philippi.

But others besides the old republican clique obtained a share in the sudden plethora of consulships. Consulships were now also available for " new men," and Augustus' policy in this respect is noteworthy. He is customarily criticized for a lack

[1] Seneca, *De Clementia*, 1, 10, 1.

of liberality. Julius Caesar, so the argument runs, had shown by his readiness to grant either the Roman citizenship or the inferior Latin Right to foreigners that he realized how such methods of assimilation had made Rome's expansion sure and lasting ; whereas Augustus was always reluctant to extend the citizenship.[1] Augustus' niggardliness with the citizenship has been exaggerated, even though his vision was certainly narrower than that of Julius. The latter saw nothing incongruous about a whole province possessing Roman citizenship and thereby enjoying roughly equal status with Italy ; Augustus' conception was different. In general he allowed only particularly favoured individuals in the provinces to acquire Roman citizenship. On the other hand the whole of Italy enjoyed it in his reign. His success in unifying the whole country south of the Alps was of even greater importance than his success in reconciling the various political factions at Rome. It had the effect of placing Italy in a class apart from the provinces, and set it up, as it were, as the mistress of the Empire.[2] But it was Italy, and not just Rome, that occupied this privileged position.

On the other hand if Augustus' outlook was more circumscribed than that of Julius, it was by no means so narrow as that of the oligarchical clique who had been in fact the government during the last century B.C. This is clearly shown by what happened to the consulship. Under the Republic this office had been virtually monopolized by a handful of senatorial families ; and if any outsider made his way into this zariba of noble exclusiveness he was almost certainly someone who had been actually born in Rome. All *novi homines* were exceptions ; those who did not come from Rome itself were positive curiosities. Even men who came from a long-enfranchised Italian municipal town found it almost impossible to win the consulship. Marius and Cicero, the men from Arpinum, were but the exceptions that proved the rule : in both cases it was a fortuitous combination of circumstances that led to their election, and neither of them lived down his non-Roman origin

[1] Suetonius describes how on one occasion the Princeps was perfectly willing for a non-citizen to be granted exemption from taxation but not to obtain citizenship. (*Augustus*, 40, 3.)

[2] He divided the whole country into eleven districts (*regiones*) for administrative purposes. On this, see R. Thomsen, *The Italic Regions* (Copenhagen, 1947).

entirely. All of this was in line with the tradition of selfishness which had been steadily growing since the Hannibalic War. The Romans had only been induced under duress to grant the citizenship to Italians in 90–89 B.C., and even then they had tried to make the grant nugatory. It is hardly surprising, therefore, that they should regard the highest office in the State as reserved not merely for Roman citizens but for Roman citizens from Rome.

Augustus changed this. His consuls came not only from families that no one had ever heard of (witness Agrippa), but also from all parts of Italy. As a consequence the Senate became representative of the aristocracy of all Italy and not merely of the aristocracy of Rome.[1] It was indeed left to a later emperor to go even further and throw the consulship open to Roman citizens from the provinces. But in Augustus' day neither Roman public opinion nor probably the Princeps himself was ready for such a step. That fact, however, does not lessen the importance of his action in enlarging the group from which consuls could be selected. After 5 B.C. *consules suffecti* became common : many were *novi homines*. Thus, between 18 B.C. and A.D. 3, of fifty-two consuls only fourteen came from " new " families ; whereas between A.D. 4 and 11 no fewer than eleven out of twenty-nine were such, practically all of them *suffecti*.[2]

§ 4.   IMPERIAL CONTROL OF THE SENATE

Besides controlling the composition of the Senate, Augustus regulated its procedure. In 11 B.C. he reduced the size of the quorum needed to pass a valid *senatus consultum*, and in 9 B.C. he made the quorum variable according to the business under discussion. In addition he rigidly supervised attendance ; as early as 29 B.C. he forbade senators to leave Italy without permission, and the fine for absence from meetings was increased (in 17 and again in 9 B.C.). On the other hand the publication of the Senate's transactions was discontinued.

The Emperor's right of *suffragatio* and *commendatio* restricted the elective functions which the Senate acquired after A.D. 14. Its deliberative, legislative, executive and judicial functions, for all their appearance of independence, were similarly hampered.

---

[1] Dessau, *Inscr. Lat. Sel.*, 212, col. II, 1. 4.

[2] The " old " families that supplied the *ordinarii* were supporters of the Principate : Syme, *Rom. Revolution*, p. 372.

In theory the Senate might appoint the Emperor, in actual
practice it merely ratified the Emperor's, or failing him the
army's, choice of a successor.[1]

The Senate, in fact, could hardly discuss anything without
the Emperor's prior permission. For his Senate Committee
prepared business for submission to the Senate and was not
likely to submit anything of which he disapproved. Moreover
in A.D. 13 this Senate Committee had its term of office prolonged
(from six months to a year) and became more non-senatorial in
complexion : henceforth it might include such " others as the
Princeps might at any time call upon for advice." (Under
Augustus' successor these " others " included friends of the
Princeps, who were not even of senatorial status and who
served not one year only but as long as he saw fit).[2] Likewise in A.D. 13 the Senate Committee ceased to play a purely
probouleutic rôle : henceforth it could also legislate itself
directly, for it could pass resolutions which did not need the
Senate's ratification but had themselves the force of *senatus
consulta*. Thus although the Senate possessed power to legislate, it could nevertheless only pass those laws to which
the Princeps was not opposed, while at the same time it
was powerless to prevent him from enacting whatever he
wished. Is it surprising that before the Principate was very
old the Senate became very unwilling to discuss anything
until it had ascertained the Emperor's attitude ? The
Emperor sometimes revealed his attitude by displaying his
proposed measures in the senate-house before bringing them
forward, in order that senators might suggest amendments
if they so desired. It is improbable that any of them so
desired.

Augustus was eager for the Senate to exercise its right to
discuss problems freely ; he was content to remain unobtrusively
in the background. But his reluctance to set in motion the
machinery that constrained the Senate does not mean that the
machinery did not exist. A less tactful or more tyrannical
Princeps could reduce the Senate to a rubber stamp.

This was particularly true in the sphere of international
relations. Even in republican times it had been a disadvantage
to have foreign policy in the hands of the Senate. Since this

[1] But legally the Imperium Proconsulare could not be granted by
the army.

[2] This, of course, meant the end of it as a *Senate* Committee.

assembly could neither leave Rome nor delegate its powers very easily, the representatives of other powers had to come to Rome, a matter that might not suit either the convenience or the dignity of the power concerned. Moreover, foreign nations naturally prefer to deal with the element in the state that has the real power : with the element whose power is only nominal, their relations can hardly extend beyond the interchange of formal courtesies, and that, in fact, was as far as the Senate of the Empire could go in the field of foreign policy. Foreign envoys did occasionally come to it ; but the power to make peace or war, to conclude treaties with foreign states, to conduct negotiations with client kings rested with the Princeps. Thus the conduct of foreign policy was effectively in his hands.

Even in that part of the Roman world for whose administration the Senate was directly responsible, namely Italy and the senatorial provinces, the Senate did not possess the ultimate authority. In Italy the Emperor participated more and more directly : his *curatores* supervised the highways and the grain supply, and he was really responsible for public order, since the police and fire brigade were both under his charge. Furthermore, his personal force, the Praetorian Guard, formed the garrison of Italy. In the senatorial provinces likewise the Senate's sway was by no means unrestricted. Inscriptions from Cyrene reveal that from the earliest days of the Principate the Emperor could exert his authority in the senatorial provinces if he so desired. Moreover, he could transform them into Caesarian provinces or transfer their small garrisons elsewhere.

In the judicial sphere, perhaps, the Senate wielded more genuine power. In particular it took cognizance of offences committed by senators, equites or provincials. As early as 40 B.C. it was exercising judicial functions,[1] although it was not until Tiberius' reign that it became really important as a high Court. Nevertheless Tacitus implies that the Princeps could and did influence its legal decisions. The Senate accordingly tried to make its judgments conform invariably to the wishes of the Princeps. An accused person, of whom the Emperor was believed to disapprove, was certain to be condemned no matter what the merits of his case. Augustus complained that " he was the only man in Rome to whom it was not permitted to set limits to his displeasure with his friends."

Augustus really tried to contribute to the prestige and

[1] It apparently condemned Salvidienus Rufus in 40, just as it did Gallus in 26 B.C.

authority of the Senate ; and his successor, at any rate in his first years, punctiliously consulted the Senate on all matters of policy. But it is clear enough that the Senate enjoyed no real power or independence. How could it, when the senatorial nobles depended on the Emperor not only for their early advancement but also for their later appointments ? Under the circumstances the attitude of hopeful and ambitious senators towards the Princeps was bound to become one of increasing deference, if not of servility. The restoration of the Republic was pure fiction, a sham and a show, the aim of which was to win the active co-operation of the republican elements in the state. In this Augustus succeeded admirably : many of his former bitter opponents accepted posts of responsibility and discharged their duties faithfully and well. But, as Tacitus says, " Augustus gradually absorbed into himself the functions of Senate, magistrate and laws." [1] It is possible, of course, that he did not consciously intend all power to become thus concentrated in one man's hands. But it is far more probable that Augustus, a far-seeing political realist if there ever was one, was not blind to the implications of his various measures. Impressed by the fate of Julius, he was content to make haste slowly and to take each forward step cautiously. But that hardly alters the fact that from the beginning he probably intended to be supreme in the State, with helpers indeed but no rivals. The Senate might give the impression that it was directing affairs; Augustus himself knew better. In his view a state or an empire could not be properly and efficiently governed by divided authority ; accordingly he saw to it that the authority was not divided ; in the last analysis it rested with him and with him alone. He was prepared to divide executive function but not actual power.

This was to have momentous consequences. It meant inevitably that really serious business could not be entrusted to the Senate. More and more the Senate's time came to be taken up with discussing matters of trivial importance. And Satan always finds something for idle hands to do. Many members of the Senatorial Order, avoiding the Emperor's service and appointments abroad, devoted themselves to a frivolous pursuit of pleasure and to a luxurious competition in social ostentation: the deterioration in the Roman character in imperial times, which many writers have observed, was due in part to the sense of

[1] *Annals*, I, 2, 1.

frustration which the noble families came to feel. Others of them, instead of treading the path of refined and sensuous luxury, devoted themselves in a sterile kind of way to the study of philosophy, a study that was really barren of spiritual comfort.[1] Yet others had recourse to far more dangerous pursuits. It is not far-fetched to suggest that one of the reasons for the numerous anti-imperial conspiracies, which members of the Senate were so prone to plot in the Early Empire, was their impatience with their rôle of dignified nonentities and their desire to make the Principate truly senatorial instead of imperial. A class that had been accustomed to command was not content just to provide imperial officials. The curious thing is that the Senate preserved this attitude for so long despite its changing personnel. Under the Early Empire the old republican nobility was gradually replaced by new senatorial families, yet these new families seem automatically to have adopted the outlook of the republican oligarchs. The conservatism of the Senate of the Early Empire and its conviction of its peculiar historical rôle may be a phenomenon, but it is a fact.

§ 5. THE EQUESTRIAN ORDER

The knights (*equites*) were in a different category. They were, indeed, an organized order, but lacked a deliberative council of their own. They were the other great property-owning class, and were usually very loyal to the Princeps.

Ever since the days of Gaius Gracchus the Equestrian Order had possessed a very real *esprit de corps*, to which it usually gave expression by quarrelling with the Senate. Augustus found for the knights a place in the State where their interests and those of the Senate would not clash.

The supply of qualified men produced by the senatorial *cursus honorum* was limited, since the number of magistracies was fixed ; the shortened consulship added but few, since before A.D. 69 it was often held for six months. On the other hand the number of posts for which incumbents had to be found showed a tendency to increase. The emergence of a new element in the State, such as the Princeps, inevitably meant a wholesale creation of new posts. The new posts, not being republican survivals, could not be regarded as magistracies ; indeed it was

[1] So at least one would infer from the *Meditations*, which Marcus Aurelius wrote over a century and a half later.

prudent to keep them entirely separate from the old republican machinery. Augustus did not wish to get openly out of harmony with republican traditions or to risk offending the pride of the great republican houses by virtually asking them to become his personal servants. They regarded themselves as his social equals and he was wise enough not to discourage their delusion.

Instead he turned to the Equestrian Order. With the administrative experience they had gained in their tax-farming and other financial operations under the Republic, the knights were quite competent to fill posts in the growing if still rudimentary civil service. In fact it was in the imperial civil service that the Equestrian Order found the great outlet for its talents. Incidentally this brought about a lasting *concordia ordinum* : the knights now had a better use for their energies than to waste them in squabbles with the Senate ; they could enter upon a career which might culminate in one of several new big prefectures.

It is obvious that the magistrates and ex-magistrates could not discharge all their administrative duties alone and unaided. Minor officials, clerks and the like were necessary. Under the Republic, however, these less important instruments of government had not been supplied by a regularly organized civil service. The State no doubt did supply some clerical help ; but the magistrates and ex-magistrates, lacking a real executive machinery or staff, usually had to invoke the services either of their friends or of the slaves, freedmen and clients of their own households. It was thus that provincial governors obtained their staffs ; Sulla obtained many of his small officials by similar means ; and the services rendered by Oppius or Balbus to Julius Caesar are well known. In imperial times the Princeps did not by any means dispense with the services of his own household, but since he was directly administering more than half the Empire, a very large and salaried imperial civil service was bound to become a necessity. Augustus accordingly organized a new executive. In later centuries this body grew into a huge bureaucracy, and fastened a ruthless iron grip on the whole State and finally strangled the Empire. In Augustus' reign, however, the civil service was still quite rudimentary : as usual, he had to make haste slowly. Men of birth were reluctant to be the servants of just another aristocrat ; consequently when the Emperor went beyond his own household, he did not always obtain the services of the Equestrian Order. In fact the civil service was by no means filled exclusively by knights : freedmen were frequently used as procurators and (in the first century) even as prefects.   In the lower branches of the civil service even slaves were used.

It was not until it was obvious that the Principate was permanent and the Princeps was the executive chief, whose agents wielded a formidable power, that men of birth became eager to join his civil service.   It was not until Hadrian's reign that the knights literally became the civil service.   Nevertheless they were commonly used from the earliest days of the Principate, especially as financial officials, for which their experience obviously qualified them.

To regularize the employment of knights, Augustus used his *de facto* censorial powers to reorganize the Equestrian Order. It had originally been a body of aristocratic cavalry.   Each knight was provided with a horse by the State and had his name entered on a roll kept by the censors.   Under the Republic the censors had gradually enlarged the Order, by enlisting not only cavalrymen of the upper classes who were of military age, but also men who might never have sat on a horse in their lives yet could afford membership in the organization.   From 67 B.C. or earlier the property qualification for membership was 400,000 sesterces : indeed men who possessed this equestrian census would often pose as knights even though not formally enrolled as such.[1]   The equestrian privileges were substantial : knights served in the jury-courts,[2] had preferred seats in the theatre and wore distinctive insignia, a gold ring and the angusticlave (a tunic with a narrow purple stripe).

The wealth of the knights was usually derived from business and commerce, for they were financiers and bankers by tradition.   This presumably explains why under the Empire freedmen, whose skill in commerce was notorious, frequently made their way into the Order : the genuinely Roman knight had a flair not so much for legitimate business as for speculation at the provincials' expense, and under the Principate such speculation was not as easy as it had been earlier.

Since Augustus' aim was to have the Equestrian Order composed of able and not merely of wealthy men, he was very careful in his reorganization of it.   Henceforth membership was

---

[1] In the last century B.C. the censors' lists were not very accurately kept.

[2] Under the Empire the jurors in the *iudicia publica* were men of equestrian census.

obtained either by birth or by appointment. Senators' sons, who had not yet held a magistracy,[1] belonged to it automatically but usually only temporarily. It was, however, chiefly recruited from the Emperor's appointees, for inclusion in the equestrian roll depended on the Princeps' approval. Veteran centurions from the army, wealthy residents of country towns and sometimes freedmen obtained equestrian status. There was no difficulty in keeping up the numbers of the Order, since the prosperity which the Pax Romana brought made it increasingly easier for men to acquire the equestrian census.

As the knights were now likely to serve in administrative posts involving the command of troops, Augustus restored the ancient connexion between the Equestrian Order and military service. All knights under thirty-five years of age were organized in six *turmae* and required to parade before the Princeps on horseback every July 15 ; presumably a similar ceremony was staged in Italian and provincial towns for the benefit of knights who did not reside in Rome. The cadets participating in this *travectio equitum* obviously represented Roman upper-class youth. They were, in fact, the youth (*iuventus*) par excellence, and they usually selected a member of the imperial house, the one most likely to succeed the Emperor, as their *princeps*.[2]

Under the Empire the title prefect, not unknown for *equites* serving the State in republican times, was the highest equestrian honour. Mere participation in the *travectio* did not win it. Ambitious *equites* had to do real military service. As in the case of other imperial institutions, the scheme developed gradually ; but by Claudius' reign regular *militiae equestres*, as they were called, had been organized. The career knights were appointed by the Emperor to various officer posts in the army, which were reserved for members of their Order. The *eques* normally began his military career as *praefectus cohortis* (that is, commander of an auxiliary cohort) ; he then became *tribunus militum*[3] (that is, staff officer in a legion) ; after that he

[1] The tenure of a magistracy would commit them to the senatorial career. Prior to this they may have been known as *equites illustres*.
[2] In Flavian times the title *princeps iuventutis* regularly designated the heir apparent.
[3] Normally a legion had five such equestrian (or angusticlave) tribunes ; the sixth tribune was senatorial (or laticlave) and was usually second in command of the legion and destined for high military rank.

obtained the post of *praefectus alae* (that is, commander of an auxiliary cavalry squadron). It was an exceptional privilege for a knight to be excused part of this military service ; the so-called six months tribunate (*tribunatus semestris*) was rarely bestowed, and the knight usually served in the *militiae equestres* for ten years or so. Even after that he might continue to serve in a military capacity : for example, he might become a cohort commander in the fire brigade, police force or Praetorian Guard.[1] Often, too, before his army service, he had held office in his home town. Now he was ready for administrative appointments in the form of various procuratorships.

In republican times the term *procurator* never designated a servant of the State but rather the agent of a wealthy individual or corporation. Therefore it was appropriate that, under the Principate, the title should be given to men who were essentially the personal agents of the Emperor.[2] By the second century it had become usual for the procuratorships to be held in a more or less regular order, but in the first century, and least of all in the reign of Augustus, there was no such regular equestrian *cursus*.

The procurators served the Princeps in various ways : for example, as fiscal agents in the provinces or as governors of relatively small, and scantily garrisoned, but not necessarily unimportant provinces. The gradually extending sphere of their operations meant that these men, who theoretically were only agents, acquired wide powers : under Claudius, for example, they obtained jurisdiction within their own financial departments. They thus became public officials.

By faithful and efficient service in various procuratorships knights qualified for the various prefectures. The prefectures reserved for knights were, in ascending order of importance : Prefect of Traffic, of the Fleet,[3] of the Fire Brigade, of the Grain Supply,[4] of Egypt, of the Praetorian Guard, this latter obviously

---

[1] *Tribunus cohortis vigilum, urbanae, praetoriae.* For good measure an *eques* sometimes had obtained additional military experience by serving as *praefectus fabrum* (a semi-military officer), or *praepositus vexillationibus* (commander of detachments from a legion), or even sometimes *praefectus castrorum* (a kind of glorified quartermaster in a legionary camp, who, however, was usually an experienced ex-centurion).

[2] Freedmen, as well as knights, often bore the title.

[3] Down to A.D. 69 the Prefect of the Fleet was regularly a freedman.

[4] After A.D. 8. This Prefect must not be confused with a senatorial Prefect of the Grain Dole (*praefectus frumenti dandi*).

being a very powerful individual.[1]   These equestrian posts were
so attractive that many individuals who were eligible for the
senatorial career deliberately selected the equestrian instead.
This automatically debarred them from the more important
provincial governorships which were assigned only to senators,
but the equestrian posts were not greatly inferior.

§ 6.   THE PLEBS

The Senatorial and Equestrian Orders did not really share
in the political power but merely in the executive functions of
the Emperor.   Even this much was denied to the vast mass of
free-born Roman citizens (*plebs*), who did not belong to either
Order.   Their rôle in the government of the Empire, legally at
any rate, came to be pretty completely passive.   This, however, like other features of the Principate, was a very gradual
development.

Until A.D. 14 the People retained the right of electing the
urban magistrates, although from A.D. 5, if not earlier, ten
special centuries of senators and judiciary knights " designated "
the men who were to be elected as consuls and praetors.   Until
then in the first years of the Principate the urban elections
excited genuine interest.   After A.D. 14 they were transferred
to the Senate.

The legislative power of the Assembly also did not disappear
immediately.   Indeed it was apparently never formally abolished, but merely faded away : even as late as *c.* A.D. 97 Nerva
issued a piece of legislation in the form of a law of the
People instead of as a decree of the Senate.[2]   This, of course,
did not alter the fact that the Emperor was *de facto* the only
source of new law.

The Roman *plebs* also retained, in form, another political
right.   On the accession of a new emperor they met in a
special Assembly and passed a law which ratified the Senate's
choice and formally conferred upon the new Princeps the
Tribunician Power.   The so-called Lex de Imperio dating from
A.D. 69 survives in part.   This obviously was a mere formality,
not a sign of genuine political initiative.

So far as participation in public life was concerned, the
inhabitants of the Italian and even of the provincial munici-

[1] A prefect's office which had existed in republican times, e.g. the
prefecture of the city, was reserved for senators.

[2] Augustus occasionally legislated by means of *plebiscita* of the
Concilium Plebis.

palities were better off than the *plebs* of Rome. In the towns of Italy there was real political life in our period. The cities usually managed their local affairs through their own magistrates, the chief of whom were called either *duoviri* or *quattuorviri*.[1] These enjoyed the right of jurisdiction, in civil cases mostly, and, after their term of office, normally became members (*decuriones*) of the local senate (*curia*). This latter was the governing body of the municipality, and membership in it was a high but expensive honour. Elections for the local magistracies at Pompeii and presumably elsewhere were keenly contested, and the local senates really governed, thus providing a healthy political outlet. It was, however, a comparatively minor one, for the sphere of competence of these officials was purely local. They were, in fact, only the instruments through which the central government indirectly ruled the Empire, and gradually the rule of the central government became more and more immediate. Its direct interference in the local affairs of the Italian municipalities commenced about A.D. 100 and ultimately (long after our period) became universal and complete.

The Roman *plebs* does not seem to have bitterly resented its exclusion from political activity. From Augustus' time onward, all organizations or clubs (*collegia*) of a potentially political nature were suppressed. Yet the *cives Romani* acquiesced. For this there were several explanations.

Even in republican times the participation of the lower orders in politics had been more nominal than real. The great noble houses had really controlled the popular Assemblies through their dependents (*clientes*). The substitution of a Princeps for an oligarchical clique did not make a great deal of difference as far as the *plebs* was concerned. The urban mob could not have been conscious of any great loss of political power,[2] especially when the Princeps paraded his sensitivity to its moods and caprices, and showed concern to keep it fed and amused.

The needs of the Roman *plebs* were to a certain extent cared for by something analogous to the social legislation of our own day. Nor were such measures confined to Rome : muni-

---

[1] A town with the status of *colonia* usually had *duoviri*, a town with the status of *municipium* had *quattuorviri*.

[2] This would be even truer of Italians in general : for, although Roman citizens, they had only on rare occasions come to Rome to vote in the Assembly.

cipal residents also obtained free games, and at the end of the first century a system of public maintenance for poor children was instituted in the towns of Italy and later spread to the provinces.

Regarded as social legislation, the grain doles and free games went either too far or not far enough. In that they pampered a large proportion of the Roman population and bred in it irresponsible expectations, they went much too far. A system which encourages many members of a community to demand something for nothing and which makes public duty the responsibility of a comparatively small section is vicious ; at Rome it bred a spirit of dependence to which the paternalism of the Later Empire was obliged fatally to cater.

Though Augustus reduced the number of recipients of the monthly grain-dole at Rome, there were between 150,000 and 200,000 of them in the Early Empire. What proportion they formed of the city's total population we cannot say ; but as a measure of social legislation the *frumentationes* were inadequate. The grain-dole alone could not keep these people alive : man does not live by bread alone, he also needs housing and clothing. Therefore the pauperized mob had to implement its grain-dole from other sources. The cash distributions by the Emperors (*congiaria*) no doubt came in handy ; but they were only occasional windfalls. In general it was the noble and wealthy houses that came to the rescue. By means of food distributions or actual money doles,[1] they contributed to the support of swarms of dependents.

In the first century A.D. the idea of patronage, which was inherited from the Republic, was still deeply rooted. It permeated all spheres of Roman life. Client kings were the dependents of the Princeps ; poets were the dependents of belletristic millionaires ; slaves were the dependents of their masters ; freedmen were the dependents of their ex-masters. It was perhaps natural, therefore, for the poorer plebeians to be the dependents of the opulent nobles. In return for gifts of food and money doles, the plebeian clients rendered their noble patrons various services : for instance, they would pay an early morning courtesy call at the patron's mansion, and escort him to and from the heart of the city as he went about his day's business.

[1] Some of the Emperors, notably Domitian, legislated against such cash disbursements, but apparently with no permanent success.

Such services (*officia*) gratified the patron's vanity and encouraged the client's habits of frivolous idleness. In addition there was one type of " service " that was an unmitigated evil. The clients might fawn on their patrons, flatter them and even shower them with gifts in the hope of receiving a legacy. The professional satirists undoubtedly paint an exaggerated picture of society : the Roman world did not consist of two groups of people, those with legacies to bequeath and those who schemed to inherit them. Nevertheless legacy-hunting was very common and was fostered by the trend towards celibacy and childlessness.

Neither did the central government provide fully for the people's spiritual needs : gladiatorial shows, mock naval battles, horse races and the like provided excitement but only ephemeral satisfaction. Men's minds seek something to believe in, and the empty formalism of Caesar-worship did not provide it. The growth of numerous foreign mystery-cults is indicative of the need.

At the outset of Augustus' reign the citizens of Rome were perhaps stirred by the unification of Italy and the panorama of Empire. The restoration of order and discipline, and Augustus' religious revival, also helped to end the physical and mental chaos that had characterized the last years of the Republic. With a firm system of government and some sense of values re-established the citizens of Rome in Augustus' day were no longer living in a moral vacuum. Life, however, does not stand still. The Principate was bound to grow and develop. But in its growth and development the urban population had little share ; they were little more than spectators. This inevitably had its effect, for their attitude to the Empire in many ways came to be one of curious detachment. It is significant that the urban mob did not find its way into the army in any quantity ; it was content to accept passively whatever benefits the Empire had to bestow rather than actively defend them.

The upper classes rather than the masses became the repository of the Roman spirit. The exclusion of the *plebs* from any share in the responsibility for the government of the Empire would have led to this in any case, but popular apathy became more marked as the Italian element in the population was diluted more and more. The *plebs* was largely recruited from ex-slaves, and these, although often superficially romanized with a veneer of Roman culture, were certainly not representative of the Roman spirit, for they had little sense of continuity with Rome's past.

Gradually even the upper classes became indifferent, since they were usually recruited from below. This was, indeed, a slow process ; for adlection into the higher Orders was generally reserved for men who showed themselves worthy of the honour. In our period numerous inscriptions ostentatiously testify to the public spirit of the upper classes. But even in them the Roman spirit was largely passive ; it tended to express itself in nostalgic glorification of the past, and the archaizing tendency of the Emperor Claudius was symptomatic of this attitude. The upper classes were not actively bringing any positive contribution of their own and, as the Roman strain in them gradually disappeared, their sense of imperial destiny became less marked and the fires of patriotism burned lower.

This development might have been prevented by a universal system of fairly extensive education. But the State evinced little concern in this. It was not until c. A.D. 75 that the Emperors took any active interest in public education, and even then they were chiefly concerned to give some formal training to the classes from whom they obtained their officials ; school education was never free or compulsory.

Clearly Rome must have contained many idle people, whose physical and mental needs were only inadequately cared for. However, by no means all of the *plebs* were unemployed. The very satirists who convey that impression also describe men's vocations in Rome. Even though a certain number tried to subsist exclusively on public and private charity, the majority, even including many of the recipients of free grain, surely followed some trade or livelihood. Certain it is that we hear of jurists, doctors and teachers ; of shop-keepers, hawkers and auctioneers ; of builders, artisans and labourers ; of musicians, dancers and jockeys. Estimates vary as to the population of Rome in the Early Empire, but assuredly it was so large that the satisfaction of its needs must have given employment to many free people, even if we make allowance for the fact that slaves performed a good deal of the work.

The existence of skilled workmen and of many and varied callings is also attested by the numerous guilds of Rome. These bodies (*collegia*) were social and burial clubs, and as such were not subject to the general ban on organized associations. Membership in them was apparently not restricted : freedmen and even slaves are found in them, the tendency being for men of the same calling to form their own guild.

In the towns of Italy the percentage of idlers must have been lower than at Rome. It is significant that Rome seems to have been the only Italian city heavily dependent upon imports of overseas grain : in other words, many Italians got their living by land-work. Nor were the Italian municipalities peopled solely by agriculturists and pastoralists : the city par excellence of the guilds is Ostia, not Rome.

The standard of living of the workers could not have been high. Rash generalizations should not be formed from the existence at Pompeii of luxurious houses like those of the Vettii. The literary sources indicate that, at Rome at any rate, the working classes were housed in overcrowded quarters which were so poorly constructed that there was serious danger of their collapsing. The fire hazard was also an ever present peril ; while the filthy condition of the streets must have made these slums very malodorous places. Conditions in the smaller Italian towns were probably better, but still left much to be desired. The great bathing establishments and other public conveniences, which the Emperors and even private philanthropists provided, no doubt made up for some of the inadequacies in housing. The mass of the *plebs* nevertheless must have lived a very dingy life. Nor did Trade Unions exist for social betterment. The guilds were not really analogous to these, for they were more concerned with improved conditions for the next life than for this : they were essentially funerary colleges whose main purpose was to provide deceased members with decent burials.

If the standard of living was low and inadequate provision was made for the physical, mental and spiritual needs of the *plebs*, whether unemployed or not, one might ask why the lower orders acquiesced so readily in the Principate. The answer is probably to be sought in the security with which the Principate provided them. They were protected against external military attack, and they lived under the rule of law. Nor was it martial law : even though the Princeps did maintain his position by means of his control of the armed forces, the Principate was not a mere military autocracy. The civil law functioned, and to the inhabitants of Italy this has always been a matter of prime concern. They have always shown a

disposition to believe not so much in any abstract theory of
government as in a system that works : and the Augustan
system did work. The relation of citizen with citizen was
regulated by law, and the average man could go about his
daily business with the comforting assurance that he was not
exposed to the arbitrary caprice of his neighbour. His life and
property were protected ; no longer was he liable to find himself
summarily ejected from house and home by the passage of
some confiscatory agrarian law. It has often been remarked
that the reigns of terror, which Emperors like Gaius, Nero and
Domitian instituted, did not affect the masses : the sufferers
were a handful of nobles. For that matter, even in their cases,
due forms of law were generally observed : convictions were
usually procured by means of perjured evidence and similar
corrupt practices.

No doubt law enforcement left much to be desired. The
evidence suggests that the streets of Rome were permanently
blacked out and anything but safe after nightfall. The police
arrangements, though an improvement over those of the
Republic, were still inadequate. Footpads and roisterers were
not curbed as rigorously as they ought to have been. Even so,
the ordinary Roman citizen lived and worked, bought and sold,
married and brought up his family in an ordered society.

The civil law, once it was set in motion, must have been well
administered. In general we hear little of the *iudicia publica*
under the Principate, largely no doubt because Tacitus and
Suetonius were more interested in treason trials before the
High Courts of Princeps or Senate. Presumably the public
courts, over which the praetors presided in Rome and the local
magistrates in the municipalities, functioned smoothly. The
wheels of justice were in continuous operation, and the humblest
Roman citizen had access to the law : his patron saw to that.
It was one of the merits of the patronage system that it safeguarded the legal rights of the ordinary citizen.

In this respect the Italians were better off than the
provincials. The provincials did, indeed, also live under the
majesty of the law : their own local magistrates presided over
civil cases and the provincial governors over criminal. But for
them the benefits were fewer. They were not only at a disadvantage as compared with Roman citizens in such things as
appointments to the better governmental posts and probably
trade and industry as well : but they also did not benefit from

the civil law in quite so full a measure as Italians. They inhabited " provincial soil," and this fact alone prevented them from establishing legal title to landed property.   Moreover, they might be harshly treated by imperial officials and, unless they had acquired Roman citizenship, they had no redress in the form of an " appeal to Caesar."   Italians, moreover, were less heavily taxed ; they only paid indirect and occasional taxes : a 5 per cent inheritance tax, a 1 per cent sales tax,[1] a 5 per cent manumission tax, and the harbour dues, thus escaping the direct taxes which provincials were obliged to pay.[2]

The *plebs*, despite their exclusion from political life, were not disgruntled.   But the hierarchical system of the Principate did leave the majority of citizens more or less passive members of the State.   The *plebs* could display little initiative, originality or enterprise even in material things.   They made little contribution to the civilization in which they were living ; they were scarcely a part of the living organism of the Empire.   Under the circumstances it is not strange if they were not imbued with any high conception of service to the State.   The upper classes in the Early Empire were willing to spend their money on public projects : the *plebs* lacked the means to make such a display. They were not even enthusiastic about defending the Empire : from the earliest days of the Principate, the Princeps had to seek soldiers outside of Italy.   It is worth adding, however, that these seeds of decay did not produce a truly rank crop of unspirituality until after the period with which this volume deals.

§ 7.   THE FREEDMEN

Besides the ordinary Roman citizens who were free-born (*ingenui*), there were the freedmen (*libertini*).[3]   Under Roman law an ex-slave acquired the citizenship of the man who manumitted him ; hence in Rome and Italy freed slaves became Roman citizens.   This generous provision was offset somewhat by official discouragement of manumission.   Even in republican times there was a manumission tax, and Augustus tried to keep

---

[1] 4 per cent in the case of sales of slaves.

[2] However, the provincials also escaped the inheritance tax for which the Italians, as Roman citizens, were liable.

[3] A freedman was a *libertinus* to the free-born population in general ; he was a *libertus* to his own patron (i.e. his ex-master).   The old view that *libertus* is an emancipated slave and *libertinus* his offspring is untenable for our period.

manumissions within bounds by passing discriminatory legislation against freedmen who (largely no doubt to evade the
manumission tax) had been irregularly liberated or were under
thirty, so that they could not obtain the Roman citizenship
automatically.[1] Despite official discouragement, however,
manumission was frequent and *libertini* were numerous. But
they were not fully privileged citizens, for a freedman owed
definite obligations to his former master—a liability which had
been generally recognized under the Republic and was enforced
by law under the Principate. The Lex Aelia Sentia of A.D. 4
compelled freedmen to respect their patrons, to pay them various
small duties, and to refrain from bringing legal actions against
them. In particular, the freedman had to discharge any services
which the patron had stipulated at the time of manumission
should continue to be given him. The patron was also entitled
to a share in the freedman's estate. In return the patron
safeguarded his freedman's legal interests and generally acted
in loco parentis.

The freedman was also under certain disabilities compared
with the mass of free-born citizens. Politically he had fewer
rights than they. Not only could he be tortured if haled into
court ; he also could not hold any magistracy, either in Rome or
the municipalities, or serve as priest to any of the old Roman
gods or as a soldier in the Praetorian Guards, Legions or
Urban Cohorts. Socially he was under a stigma from which he
could not escape by hiding his status, for his name advertised
his servile origin.[2] He could indeed wear the citizen's *toga*,
but with it he was obliged to wear a special freedman's cap
(*pilleus*). Not only was he debarred from the Senatorial and
Equestrian Orders, but he was forbidden to intermarry with
the Senatorial.[3] Indeed, even the free-born son of a freedman
could not normally become a member of the Senatorial Order :
only the grandsons could hope for that distinction. In private
life, too, the freedman's inferior social status was made no less
plain, for the haughty free-born Roman was inclined to regard
the freedman with contempt. In the first century A.D. freedmen

---

[1] They were the so-called Junian Latins. They could obtain the
citizenship by marrying and producing offspring.

[2] The freedman took his patron's *praenomen* and *nomen* and kept his
own slave name as a *cognomen*.

[3] This did not prevent senatorials, and even emperors, from having
freedwomen concubines.

were often served inferior viands at dinner parties; and they must have been subjected to many similar irritations.

Nevertheless the freedman possessed certain advantages. He was after all a Roman citizen; and Roman citizens in Italy, whether *ingenui* or *libertini*, were better off than provincials. They were living on Italian soil, the privileged part of the Empire, and consequently escaped the land-tax and the poll-tax. Probably, too, the lower orders at Rome did not feel the same prejudice against the freedmen that a Tacitus or a Juvenal did. After all many, indeed most, members of the urban *plebs* themselves had some servile blood in their veins. The freedmen, and for that matter even slaves, were freely admitted to the guilds; they actually dominated and monopolized some of them. Intermarriage between *ingenui* and *libertini* was common; in particular, patrons often married their freedwomen. Moreover the freedmen had certain rights to compensate for their disabilities. They might not serve in the Guard, Legions or Urban Cohorts; but service in the Vigiles was open to them and at first was actually reserved to them.[1] Their exclusion from Roman priesthoods was partly offset by their virtual monopoly of the priesthoods for the non-Roman deities and even more by their prominent rôle in the official Caesar-worship. The freedman would naturally become associated with the cult as it was formally practised in his community. From Rome he acquired the Latin language that enabled him to enter into the world of Mediterranean thought. The Roman peace gave him personal security and the opportunity to obtain material comforts. To some freedmen this must have been a far cry from the barbarian lives of their immediate forbears. The freedman was inevitably conscious of his debt to Rome and the Emperor from whom these blessings flowed; *Roma et Augustus* consequently commanded his allegiance,[2] and he played a prominent rôle in the new cult. At Rome after 7 B.C. the worship of the Lares Compitales (between which stood the Genius Augusti) was supervised by Ward-masters (*magistri vicorum*) of freedman status; by *c.* A.D. 50 there were 265 such *magistri*. In the municipalities[3] it was usually freedmen who were elected as

---

[1] It was not popular with them, however, since it involved both discipline and danger. In any event freedmen were normally too old at the time of their liberation to be of much use in a military capacity.

[2] This is also true of provincials who obtained the Roman citizenship.

[3] In the western part of the Empire at any rate: in the east only *coloniae* show Augustales.

Seviri Augustales to promote Caesar-worship. These Augustales were not magistrates, but they were granted the insignia of such, and their office did carry social distinction with it, ranking second only to that of decurion in public esteem. It was, in fact, a very expensive office to keep up: the Augustales normally had to pay a large fee on election and they were expected to provide games and shows.[1] Almost certainly the prejudice against freedmen was much less marked in the municipalities than at Rome.

Freedmen could obtain the status of *ingenui*, for the Emperor might bestow upon a *libertinus* the Right of the Gold Ring (*ius anuli aurei*), which automatically put him on a level with the free-born and even made him eligible for equestrian status. The proportion of freedmen who obtained this symbolic gold ring was presumably small, although their absolute numbers must have been high. In the second century many knights were not only of freedman extraction but actually freedmen themselves. A *libertinus* who obtained the Gold Ring did not, however, cease to be *libertus*: he still owed his obligations to his own personal patron.

The literature of the Early Empire stresses the ubiquity of the freedmen. Many of them remained in the households of their former masters, serving as secretaries and the like, but many went out into the world to seek their fortunes. The majority of these undoubtedly did not rise above the lowly and even the menial occupations. They would make their living as artisans or workmen, as attendants or messengers for the urban magistrates and pontiffs, as clerks and shopkeepers. But not a few of them rose higher. Freedmen were notably successful in commerce and industry: they often possessed greater business ability than the native-born Roman and some of them amassed large fortunes. Very many of them came from the Hellenized portions of the Empire: Juvenal sneers about the Syrian Orontes flowing into the Tiber. But their origin from countries with an old civilization stood them in good stead: as often as not, they were better educated than their patrons and were men of some intellectual attainments, an advantage which enabled them to succeed in what we would call the liberal professions. Such success naturally did not endear them to the native-born

[1] The Augustales were apparently elected by the decurions. On the vexed question of *Augustales* and *VI viri* see G. E. F. Chilver, *Cisalpine Gaul* (1941), pp. 198–207.

Romans; indeed a good deal of the prejudice against freedmen can be safely attributed to mere jealousy.

But it was the astounding eminence to which a comparative handful of freedmen attained that, more than anything else, evoked the ire of native-born Romans. These were the Emperor's personal freedmen (*liberti Caesaris*). Augustus, like Cicero and other republican nobles, used freedmen as his personal agents to manage his private affairs. Free-born Romans were not willing to act as a man's personal agents (i.e. as his servants) for his private affairs : Roman sentiment was opposed to the employment of *ingenui* in such posts. But it was very difficult to distinguish between the Princeps' private and public affairs (as Augustus himself implies in his *Res Gestae*). For instance, it was scarcely possible to separate his private property (*patrimonium Caesaris*) from the public monies with whose supervision he was entrusted, and this remained true even after the organization of the central imperial treasury (*fiscus*). Inevitably therefore the freedmen secretaries, who were originally intended to supervise his private property, came to supervise his public accounts as well ; and what was true of the Emperor's finances was true of his other activities. Thus in effect the *liberti Caesaris* became highly-placed civil servants. They did not, indeed, as a rule hold important administrative posts, although down to A.D. 69 the Prefect of the Fleet was regularly a freedman and in Tiberius' reign there was a freedman Prefect of Egypt.[1] But they did come to occupy positions of power and influence in the imperial court : they were the vested interests that spring up behind any political system. The *liberti Caesaris* attained to greater eminence under Augustus' successors, and especially under Claudius, whose institution of a centralized bureaucracy made the imperial secretaryships posts of importance. The three chief secretaries were those who supervised respectively the imperial correspondence in general, the imperial accounts, and petitions to the Emperor (*liberti ab epistulis, a rationibus, a libellis* : the Emperor's legal secretary, *a cognitionibus*, and literary adviser, *a studiis*, were of lesser importance). These three secretaries, standing as they did between the Princeps and the rest of the world, wielded very considerable power. All classes of the population, not excepting even the Senate, had to cultivate their good graces : many

---

[1] Under Augustus the unscrupulous Licinus was financial superintendent of Gaul.

anecdotes survive to illustrate the servility of senators before them. The story that the Emperor Claudius was mere putty in their hands is apocryphal, for he, and not they, initiated the policies of his reign ; but it reflects the resentment of free-born Romans that the posts which they had at first scorned to fill should have developed into positions of all-pervading influence and be monopolized by low-born upstarts, who did not hesitate to parade their insolent arrogance. Succeeding Emperors took note of this resentment ; and from the time of Vitellius they sought to conciliate the upper classes by gradually transferring these positions to knights. Henceforth individual imperial freedmen could still be the personal favourites of the Emperor, but the power of the *liberti Caesaris* in general declined. Domitian increased the rôle of the knights in the imperial civil service ; Trajan controlled his *liberti* closely ; Hadrian eliminated them almost entirely from the higher posts in the civil service.[1]

It was the spectacle of freedmen in the great secretaryships that chiefly excited the wrath and jealousy of the upper classes. They were still content to let freedmen fill the less influential and humbler positions in the Emperor's service. From the beginning of the Principate the numerous procurators needed by the Princeps were frequently freedmen, and freedmen procurators are still encountered throughout the second century A.D.

The *liberti Caesaris*, of course, formed only a fraction of the total number of freedmen. The vast majority had to make their way without the advantage of being the Emperor's personal agents. There was, however, one privilege which all freedmen held in common, and it was one which they valued highly : any children born to them after their manumission were *ingenui*. Such children could not, indeed, enter the Senatorial Order, but that disability did not distress them unduly, for being free-born they could hope to escape the stigma that attached to their fathers. The latter, to help them avoid it, usually gave their children good old Roman names. In this way the *plebs* was constantly being recruited from the libertine class and became heavily infected with servile blood in consequence. One estimate reckons that in the Early Empire not more than 10 per cent of Rome's population was of purely

[1] However, the legal secretary continued to be a freedman down to the beginning of the third century.

free-born extraction.[1] In the municipalities the freedmen were probably less numerous. But even there they were far from few : Petronius' *Satiricon* clearly implies that.

§ 8.   THE SLAVES

Below the freedmen and constituting the lowest stratum of all in the population were the slaves. Legally they were only chattels without personal rights, whom their master could treat virtually as he pleased. Some masters no doubt availed themselves of their legal right to act with great brutality towards their slaves : nineteenth-century America cannot claim any monopoly of Simon Legrees. Instances occur of slaves attacking their masters, despite the prescribed penalties ; [2] and there was a saying that a man had as many enemies as he had slaves. This is evidence of the brutalizing process involved in Roman slavery.

Nevertheless under the Empire the general tendency was in the other direction. One reason for this was the increase in the number of home-born slaves (*vernae*). The Pax Romana caused a drop in the number of slaves acquired by conquest, and incidentally it probably saved modern Italy from a colour problem.[3] Home-breeding, therefore, kept up the supply, and slaves born in the household were traditionally better treated than the purchased variety. But apart altogether from this, there was a growth of humanitarianism. Roman Stoicism, with its doctrine of the brotherhood of man, encouraged this attitude : Seneca, for instance, urged the duty of kindness to slaves. But it was probably the slaves' manifold usefulness that impressed the practical Romans most favourably. Slaves had long ceased to be exclusively farm labourers housed in horrible *ergastula*, nor were they just unskilled workers. Some of them, of course, discharged very menial duties, but in our period they might perform any conceivable task. Intellectually many slaves, especially those from the eastern regions, were

[1] On the subject of race mixture at Rome, see T. Frank, *Amer. Hist. Rev.*, XXI (1925–6), pp. 689 ff.

[2] If a master was murdered, the law prescribed death for *all* his slaves.

[3] The Nubians, who were in such demand as litter-bearers and porters generally, cannot have been exceptionally numerous. On the humaner aspects of Roman slavery, see W. L. Westermann, *Journ. Econ. Hist.*, II (1942), pp. 149–63.

superior to their masters. Hence (to adopt modern terms) we find white-collar, as well as black-collar, slaves. They might serve as business managers, overseers, secretaries, clerks, accountants, or school teachers; and great numbers of them were highly skilled artisans. Schools were actually established to give slaves very specialized training. The argument that slave labour, being less efficient, is not much more economical than free labour, is only valid if the free labour has a standard of living almost as low as the slave labour. This apparently was the case in the Roman Empire; but it was the extensive use of slave labour that kept the living standards of the free workers depressed. Facilities were not provided for the training of highly skilled and competent free technicians; consequently the skilled craftsmen in the numerous, if not large, industrial establishments were often slaves: for example, the artists who produced the widely diffused Arretine pottery were mostly slaves. This employment of slaves may account for the lack of industrial inventiveness in the Empire; it certainly accounts for the amelioration in the slaves' condition. To use highly skilled workmen despitefully, to abuse and brutalize them was no more sensible than to maltreat the delicate machinery of a modern factory. The slaves, in short, had acquired a definite value; and it is human nature to treat with care the things we value.

Thus the humanitarian teachings of the Roman Stoics were the result, rather than the cause, of a kindlier attitude to slaves. Indeed, others besides the Stoics regarded the slaves as fellow-humans and not mere chattels. The free workers, who were in daily association with the slaves labouring alongside them and freely mingling with them, must have been impressed with their essential humanity; and the Roman public could not have been unimpressed by the useful work which public slaves performed in keeping the water supply flowing and in putting out conflagrations for twenty-five years during Augustus' reign.[1]

Thus there was a growing tendency for masters not to treat their slaves harshly; indeed, there are many instances of mutual attachment between slaves and their owners. The slaves were almost always encouraged to build up a personal fund of their own (*peculium*) by saving their earnings and

[1] Until A.D. 6, when the Vigiles were regularly organized, the city firemen were slaves.

perquisites. They could also have a home life of their own; for although a union between slaves was technically only *contubernium* and not legal wedlock, servile family relationships were respected.

The law, as often, lagged behind public opinion, and it was a long time before the humaner attitude towards slaves was reflected in the written statutes. But Roman jurisprudents enunciated the doctrine that all men are free according to the law of Nature, and emperors introduced remedial legislation. Claudius *c*. A.D. 50 enacted that sick slaves, who were deserted by their masters, should be free if they recovered. Under Vespasian *c*. 75 a female slave could, under certain circumstances, obtain her freedom if prostituted by her master.[1] Domitian *c*. 90 forbade the mutilation of slaves. Hadrian early in the second century refused to countenance the sale of slaves for immoral or gladiatorial purposes and may have forbidden the execution of slaves by their masters.[2]

Manumission of slaves was frequent. Many slaves bought their freedom out of their accumulated savings; others had it conferred upon them for their faithful services; to others it was granted in their masters' wills.

Roman society thus was strictly hierarchical; the lines of demarcation between the various classes were sharply defined. But the lines were not inviolable; they could be and very frequently were crossed. Each class in the population was regularly recruited from below as well as from births inside its own ranks. At the bottom were the slaves. From their ranks came the freedmen, the outward symbol of whose status was the close-fitting cap. They, in their turn, could be recruited into the free-born *plebs*, who were entitled to wear the plain toga. Plebeians, however, could obtain admission into the Equestrian Order and thereby acquire the right to the angusti-clave. It was from the Equestrian Order that new members were usually adlected into the Senatorial Order; the external indication of their status was the laticlave. Above the Senatorial Order, but recruited from it, was the Princeps, who might be arrayed in purple. And it was possible to trans-cend even this dizzy height: the Princeps could look forward to deification.

---

[1] It was not, however, until *c*. 200 that a blanket prohibition of the prostitution of slaves was enacted.

[2] This latter law, however, was perhaps passed by Hadrian's successor.

§ 9. THE GARRISON OF ITALY

By reason of its privileged position Italy stood apart from
the rest of the Roman world. This is seen even in its military
establishment. Whereas the normal garrison of a province
consisted of legions and auxiliary troops, that of Italy was the
Praetorian Guard. This famous corps got its name from the
body of picked soldiers who in republican times had normally
attended a holder of the *imperium*. It did not, however, so
much resemble a unit of this type as the private armies which
Greek " tyrants " or Roman demagogues regularly raised.
Theoretically it was the Princeps' bodyguard ; actually his
picked, personal guard was a select body of German troops, the
Praetorian Guard proper being stationed, under Augustus at
least, in various Italian towns.[1] In the Early Empire it normally consisted of nine infantry cohorts, each of one thousand
men recruited almost exclusively from Italy and commanded
by a tribune.[2] A cavalry squadron was attached to each cohort.
Some emperors increased the number of cohorts.

The Praetorians did not go into battle unless the Princeps
or some member of his family took the field. They were, in
fact, a very pampered corps, who served for sixteen years, were
paid thirty-two *asses* a day, and received a bonus of 5,000
denarii on their discharge. Such conditions of service were much
less onerous than those of the legionaries ; and legionaries were
not eligible for service in the Guard. The Command of the
Guard as a whole was entrusted to prefects who, despite their
equestrian rank, were sometimes of obscure origin. Usually,
for safety's sake, they were two in number, although instances
of a sole commander can be adduced.[3]

Besides the Praetorian Guard Italy contained in Augustus'
last years the city police of Rome, i.e. the three (later four)
Urban Cohorts, commanded by the City Prefect. Service in
these was for twenty years. As the Vigiles can be reckoned
as part of the garrison of Italy, it is clear that the military
establishment of the peninsula was not inconsiderable.[4]

[1] Augustus normally kept three cohorts in Rome and six in other
parts of Italy. He apparently first organized the Guard in 28 B.C.
[2] Usually an ex-centurion from a legion.
[3] Notably Sejanus in Tiberius' reign and Burrus in Nero's.
[4] For the Imperial Navy, which had its headquarters in Italy, see
below, pp. 100–1.

CHAPTER III

THE PROVINCES

§ 1. THE DIVISION OF THE PROVINCES

IN January of 27 B.C. when Augustus, or Octavian as he then was, " consented " to administer a large area of the Empire, he was granted a special ten-year commission. The sphere of his authority (his *provincia*) was large and formidable : the provinces of Spain, Gaul and Syria. It did not indeed embrace all the provinces where troops were either actually, or likely to be, stationed ; but it did include most of them. This fact enabled Augustus to encroach gradually on the provinces nominally left to the control of the Senate, for since he alone possessed military power that was really adequate, it was inevitable that, if warlike operations ever should become necessary in a province, either through internal uprising or external attack, his services would be required.

Gradually but ineluctably it came to be clearly recognized that there were two types of provinces : the " armed," which needed the presence of soldiers, and the " unarmed," which after a long period under Roman rule were orderly and peaceful.[1] It is true that even when Augustus' sphere of competence had expanded beyond his three original areas of Spain, Gaul and Syria, it did not include Macedonia, Illyricum and Africa : and these, between them, at first contained a quarter of the Empire's armed strength (seven legions and possibly more). Strabo therefore is anticipating later developments when he asserts that the Emperor obtained all the armed provinces. But Macedonia soon became an unarmed province ; Illyricum was transferred to Augustus *c.* 11 B.C. ; and the garrison of Africa passed to the Princeps' control in the reign of Gaius. Thus by A.D. 40 Strabo's statement had come true : by then the Emperor did control all the provincial armies.

No doubt the official justification for this allocation of the Empire's armed forces was the Senate's repeated failure to

[1] These latter, of course, must have contained some small military units to maintain public order. When they needed larger military forces, their governors were entitled to ask for detachments (*vexillationes*) from the legions of neighbouring " armed " provinces.

control ambitious men who possessed both the *imperium* and an army : the Princeps could be expected to keep such men in their place.   But the real reason for the arrangement was Augustus' realization that if he once relinquished his military power he would be reduced to the same impotence as Pompey in 61 B.C.   The Princeps accordingly saw to it that the preponderance of military power remained in his hands.   As usual, precedents could be adduced.   Sulla, Pompey, Crassus, Caesar had all of them received essentially similar commands, and Augustus could claim, with legal if specious justification, that he was not a military autocrat but merely a Roman promagistrate invested with very wide powers for a period of years.   There were, after all, other provinces which remained as heretofore the care of the Senate.

The provinces therefore henceforth fell into two groups : the imperial or Caesarian provinces, which were administered by the Princeps, and the senatorial or public provinces, for whose government the Senate was responsible.   But the Princeps' *auctoritas*, unchallengeable because backed by *imperium*, enabled him to interfere in the senatorial provinces if for any reason he so desired.   It was by interfering in this way that Augustus stealthily enlarged his original sphere of competence ; and even after the definite division of the provinces between Princeps and Senate his interference did not entirely cease.

In seeking to introduce more order and regularity into all matters pertaining to the provinces Augustus followed republican usages where possible ; but, as usual, he proceeded cautiously, so that only after his day (*c.* A.D. 80 actually) can the system of provincial administration, which became normal under the Principate, be clearly discerned.

When Rome first acquired transmarine possessions, they were governed by the regular *imperium*-holding magistrates. But gradually the practice had arisen of assigning the provinces to ex-magistrates, who as proconsuls or propraetors administered them in the name of the Senate and Roman People.   In the absence of any central Department of State for the Provinces senatorial supervision tended to be rather lax : in fact the Senate found it very difficult to control recalcitrant governors, to whose tender mercies the provincials were only too frequently exposed.

Under the Principate some of the features of this Republican system were retained, but many new ones were introduced.

Augustus himself was largely responsible for the reorganization, his successors merely modifying some of the details of his arrangements. The republican connexion between the city magistracies and provincial governorships was retained : provinces continued to be assigned to ex-consuls and ex-praetors. Actually the old magistracies might not have attracted candidates, had they not led to these coveted provincial appointments. Augustus, like Sulla, was aware that the threat to the constitution came from ambitious governors who could use the military forces of their provinces to stage a *coup d'état* : this danger had been inevitable whenever the same man remained in the same province for any length of time. But, like Pompey, he also realized that only men who did retain their office for a length of time were likely to obtain the experience necessary for capable and efficient administration. His problem was to get experienced men without endangering the state. He did so partly by rigorously enforcing the regulations of the *cursus honorum*, and partly by keeping the armed provinces under his own control. Most men who passed through the *cursus honorum* stood a reasonably good chance of becoming governors in the senatorial provinces, although usually care was taken that the lot did not fall on them until a number of years after they had held their magistracy. This latter precaution may have been suggested to Augustus by Pompey's enactment of 52 B.C., which stipulated that an interval of at least five years must elapse between the tenure of a city magistracy and a provincial governorship. Whatever Pompey's motive for this piece of legislation, Augustus rightly saw how it would promote administrative efficiency.

§ 2.   THE SENATORIAL PROVINCES

The senatorial provinces were assigned by lot, the governors serving for a year, but frequently longer. The use of the lot would scarcely promote efficiency ; but in the years before the ex-magistrate was appointed, he presumably would have acquired useful experience to qualify him for his post. In any case the senatorial provinces did not make particularly heavy demands on the administrative capacities of their governors. If a situation arose where they were likely to do so (for example, a threatened foreign invasion), the lot was abruptly jettisoned and the Emperor could invoke his power of intervention so as to procure the appointment of the right man and for the length of time that might prove necessary. As early as the reign of Augustus we find the Princeps appointing a governor to a senatorial province ; and in the next reign the Princeps kept governors of senatorial provinces in office for as long as six years.

Governors of senatorial provinces, like all provincial governors since Sulla, were styled proconsuls. Actually only Africa and Asia regularly obtained ex-consuls,[1] the usual rule being for a ten-year interval to elapse before the former consul obtained his governorship. The governors of the other senatorial provinces were actually ex-praetors and normally received their appointment five years after holding their magistracy.

At Augustus' death the following were the senatorial provinces : Achaea [2]; Africa; Asia; Baetica [3]; Bithynia [4]; Crete-Cyrene ; Cyprus [3]; Gallia Narbonensis [3]; Macedonia [2]; Sicily.

§ 3.   THE IMPERIAL PROVINCES

The governors of the imperial provinces were never styled proconsuls ; the proconsular authority in their provinces and of course the supreme command of their military forces belonged to the Princeps himself by virtue of his Imperium Proconsulare. Though the governors of the more important imperial provinces were ex-consuls or ex-praetors, both alike were called *legati pro praetore*. They were naturally appointed by the Princeps and for as long as he liked (normally three years). He would appoint outstandingly able men as soon as a vacancy occurred ; he might even create one for the purpose.

Republican precedents existed for these *legati pro praetore*. When Pompey was commissioned to suppress the pirates in 67 B.C., he was provided with *legati* to whom he delegated his *imperium* ; and again later, when he was appointed governor of the Spanish provinces in 55 B.C., he administered them through *legati* without himself leaving Italy.

The degree to which an imperial province was armed determined whether it was consular or praetorian. A province con-

---

[1] They usually held office for two years, sometimes longer.
[2] Achaea and Macedonia were imperial from A.D. 15 to 44.
[3] Baetica, Cyprus, Narbonensis became senatorial in 23 B.C. or later.
[4] Bithynia became an imperial province under Trajan.

taining more than one legion, as in the Late Republic, obtained
an ex-consul, not an ex-praetor.   An ex-praetor, however,
could be, and usually was, given the command of a legion in
one of these consular provinces ; as such he was a purely
military officer with the title of *legatus legionis*.   Thus a consular
imperial province contained two types of *legati*, who must be
sharply distinguished : the *legatus pro praetore* (or governor)
and the *legati legionum* (or legionary commanders).   In this way
the ex-praetor gained military experience that no doubt stood
him in good stead later on when, after holding the consulship
in his turn, he was in line for an appointment as governor of a
province of consular rank.   Before then, however, while still
only an ex-praetor, he might be appointed governor of one of
the praetorian imperial provinces ; these might contain forces
amounting to no more than one legion.

The armed forces were for the most part on the frontiers,
where the troops would be needed either to repel invasions or
to maintain order in districts imperfectly subjugated.   With the
lapse of time and the emergence of settled conditions the presence
of military forces in a province might become superfluous,
whereupon the Princeps would remove the soldiers from it :
Gaul is an example.   Augustus went even further than this :
he actually transferred three such demilitarized provinces to the
Senate, Cyprus in 23 B.C., Narbonensis in 22 B.C. and Baetica
at some unknown date.   The Princeps could well afford such
generosity, since he automatically obtained all new provinces,
e.g. Britain in A.D. 43.

Not infrequently such new provinces were small and did not
require large forces.   When this was the case they might be
assigned to governors of the equestrian aristocracy instead of
the senatorial.   Under Claudius such governors, originally
called prefects, began to be styled procurators.   These provinces
can be fairly described as equestrian.   They never contained
legions, but normally only auxiliary troops and local militia.
Judaea at the time of Christ's crucifixion was a province of this
type, its *praefectus* being the notorious Pontius Pilatus (26–36).
Pontius apparently was under the supervision of the *legatus
pro praetore* of the neighbouring province of Syria.[1]

[1] In this respect, however, he was probably a special case.   There is
no evidence that the procuratorial governors were invariably thus subordinated to the military command of a neighbouring consular province.

At Augustus' death the following were the imperial provinces :—*Consular* : Dalmatia [1] ; Lower Germany : Upper
Germany : Moesia ; Pannonia [1] ; Syria ; Tarraconensis.

Praetorian : Aquitania ; Belgica ; Galatia ; Lugdunensis ;
Lusitania ; Pamphylia (part of Galatia in his day ?).

Equestrian : Alpes Maritimae [2] ; Judaea ; Noricum [2] ;
Raetia [2] ; Sardinia-Corsica.[3] (See map, p. 299.)

§ 4. IMPROVEMENT IN PROVINCIAL ADMINISTRATION

Tacitus remarks that the provinces welcomed the change
from Republic to Principate ; and it is a fact that provincial
administration markedly improved under the Empire. The
first Princeps undoubtedly inaugurated this improvement, but
in this, as in so much else, he was content to make haste slowly,
possibly because he was unwilling to administer too drastic a
shock to the conceptions of the old nobility, who regarded the
provincial posts as the happy hunting ground of their class.
Augustus' successor Tiberius was the emperor chiefly responsible
for the distinct amelioration in provincial administration.

Various factors contributed to the improvement. In the
first place there was now something resembling a consistent and
well-thought-out frontier policy. Earlier volumes have revealed
how haphazard Rome's acquisition of provinces had been. It
is scarcely surprising that the methods of supervising them, once
acquired, were equally haphazard. Augustus introduced order
into a system that had been all too casual.

Secondly, the standard of governors undoubtedly improved.
The republican governors had not received a salary but only
an allowance. This latter was indeed usually on a lavish
scale, but it was not the most satisfactory method for remuner-
ating an official : unsalaried officials are not likely to feel any
twinges of conscience about accepting sums of dubious prove-

[1] Dalmatia and Pannonia as official names are not demonstrably
older than Flavian times. Originally the two areas formed the single
senatorial province of Illyricum. This became imperial and soon was
divided into two provinces : the Dalmatian part was called Upper
Illyricum and the Pannonian presumably Lower Illyricum.

[2] The Alpes Maritimae and Raetia were at first governed by *praefecti*,
not by procurators : the same is probably true of Noricum.

[3] Sardinia-Corsica were a senatorial province down to A.D. 6 and
again temporarily under Nero. The two islands were made separate
provinces under Vespasian.

nance. In fact, the republican governors were notoriously
venal; and their chief, although not their only, method of
amassing fortunes was by plundering their provinces. Even
when they resisted this temptation they were usually not much
better than well-meaning amateurs. The Principate altered
this. It might be overstating the case to say that the governors,
who now received a regular salary from the State, were experts,
but they were at least experienced men ; the prolonged *cursus
honorum* ensured this.

Thirdly, not only the governors, but also their staffs and
assistants improved. Under the Principate a regular civil
service gradually came into being, and as a result a provincial
governor now had at his disposal a staff of experienced officials ;
no longer was he almost exclusively dependent on the advice
of the *publicani* in his province. This dependence had been a
particularly vicious feature of the provincial system of the
Republic, for the *publicani,* not being state officials but only
the representatives of private corporations, considered primarily
their own private and selfish interests. Under the Principate
the imperial provinces were better served with officials than the
senatorial, although the latter were by no means neglected ; for
the quaestors, who were concerned with their finances, were not
amateurs but serious career men. In all his own provinces the
Princeps had his procurators, salaried men appointed for
indefinite periods.[1] They were almost imperial spies and
usually on bad terms with the governors. A governor had only
very limited power over the procurator in his province ; for
from very early times in the Principate the procurator had
supreme and independent authority in the financial affairs of
the province. Some procurators indeed had a kind of roving
commission over several provinces, in all of which they were
virtually independent of the governors. Imperial procurators
were also frequently stationed in senatorial provinces, the
Princeps no doubt relying on his *imperium maius* to despatch
them thither.[2]

Fourthly and most important, the governors were now
much more carefully supervised (thanks in part to the presence

[1] They are not to be confused with the governors of procuratorial
provinces.

[2] Under Augustus, however, they were responsible, and had authority,
only for the Emperor's private property (*patrimonium Caesaris*) in these
senatorial provinces.

of procurators), and could be much more quickly and certainly brought to book if they misbehaved. Human nature being what it is, maladministration and rapacity did not automatically disappear, but retribution did follow more swiftly and more surely and thereby act as a powerful deterrent. From the time of Tiberius onward, accused governors were brought before the High Court of the Senate. This latter was no doubt partisan, but we do nevertheless hear of defendants either anticipating the verdict by suicide or else being condemned. Condemnation might involve a fine, confiscation of property and exile ; at the very least, it entailed expulsion from the Senate and the ruin of the governor's career. Leading senators usually acted as prosecutors in such trials, although instances of provincial representatives pleading their own case in the senatorial court are not unknown. Most of the surviving accounts of extortion trials concern governors of senatorial provinces, the reason being that in the case of the imperial provinces the Princeps himself would immediately recall and punish the peccant governor ; moreover the standard of efficiency was higher in the imperial provinces, since the ex-consuls and ex-praetors selected by the emperor to govern his provinces had usually already shown their ability in senatorial provinces.

The control of the governors was tightened at both ends, both in Rome and in the province itself. In Rome the authorities were constantly getting reports on conditions in the provinces. Augustus regularized the courier service (*cursus publicus*)—a Postal Service as it is usually called—along the great arterial highways. Relays of post-horses were kept at fixed stages along the roads to enable the couriers to travel easily and swiftly. This system was no longer, as in republican times, at the exclusive disposal of senators. Nevertheless complaints that it was unfair were frequent : the burden of the upkeep of this essentially national service fell exclusively upon the local communities through which the couriers travelled, while imperial servants and even favoured private individuals were granted " free travel tickets " (*diplomata*).[1] But though the municipalities had reasonable grounds for complaint, the *cursus publicus* did greatly facilitate communications.

The Emperor Trajan's correspondence with the Younger

[1] Nerva remedied this somewhat by relieving Italian municipalities of these postal charges.

Pliny makes it clear that the imperial governors used these and other communications to consult the Princeps on all aspects of their charge. The senatorial provinces apparently were less closely supervised ; but their governors, too, were obliged periodically to send back formal reports, and in any event were encouraged to administer wisely by the hope that a successful term in the senatorial provinces would lead to one of the great posts in the imperial ones.

Besides the check at Rome there was also a control in the province itself. Augustus discouraged all organizations that might acquire a political character ; but, beginning with the three imperial provinces of Gaul in 12 B.C., he granted to the various provinces their own Councils. The *Concilium Provinciae* consisted of representatives from the various units composing the province, one of whom acted as its president with the title of Flamen or Sacerdos of the province.[1] Such a Council was not a parliament, since it lacked the power to legislate, although it did have the right to protest against legislation deleterious to the interests of its province. Its primary duty was to foster the loyalty of the province to the Roman government, and to that end it was largely concerned with Caesar-worship.[2]

A vicious governor, of course, would stultify any efforts the Council made to promote the welfare and loyalty of the province. Hence from the time of Tiberius onward, the Council of the Province was empowered to approach the Princeps or the Senate directly with a complaint against an irresponsible or incompetent governor, and such a protest would not be cavalierly disregarded. The Council likewise had the right, except for a short period under Nero, to pass a complimentary vote of thanks for a retiring governor.

§ 5.   THE CITIES OF THE EMPIRE

In some provinces, especially those which had formerly been under Greek or Carthaginian administration, the units which sent representatives to the Council were urban centres : such

[1] In the western provinces at least ; in the eastern, the president's title sometimes contains political implications, e.g. Asiarch. The president was usually a provincial who had held high local office and had acquired Roman citizenship.

[2] Caesar-worship was especially encouraged in the new provinces which stood in most urgent need of romanization. Hence, the new provinces got Councils quickly.

provinces were in fact collections of municipalities, each
municipality being responsible for the administration of the
territory immediately adjoining it and, in Roman parlance,
" attributed " to it. There were other provinces where local
conditions did not favour urbanization.[1]

The Romans, however, definitely preferred the urban type
of local government. The absence of a fully developed civil
service obliged them to use a system of local self-government.
In other words, the central government at Rome allowed its
subjects to manage their own affairs, while it devoted its
attention chiefly to safeguarding the Pax Romana, which alone
rendered such local self-government possible. The Roman
language, Roman religion and Roman customs were not imposed
upon the subject peoples, although—thanks in no small measure
to Rome's magnificent road system—they made their way over
increasingly large areas. Trade within the Empire was not
indeed free, but it attained a considerable volume, and it inevitably encouraged romanization. The widespread use of
Latin as a *lingua franca* must have contributed to the same end :
the ex-soldiers settled in the provinces helped to disseminate
it. The institutions of Rome also exercised a great attraction,
at any rate in the west ; this helped to romanize many areas.

In deliberately refraining from imposing their own ways of
life and in encouraging local customs, the Romans were wise.
Possibly they were not convinced of the desirability of tolerance
per se, but simply realized that, until they possessed a full-
fledged civil service, nothing else was practicable : once the
civil service was fully developed, the old tolerance disappeared
and local liberty became a thing of the past. But, in our period,
indirect rule through self-governing communities was the normal
Roman practice. The Romans did not usually force any particular kind of local government on these communities, although
they did encourage them to become urban, since Roman civilization could take firm root only in city life. Witness the case
of Spain. At the time when this volume opens Spain, excluding
the highly urbanized province of Baetica, had 179 towns or
cities and 114 non-urban communities ; at the close of our
period the number of non-urban communities had declined to
27, while the number of towns had increased to 248.

---

[1] Examples are Britain, Thrace (before Trajan's reign) and Gaul
which, despite its use of urbanized terms for its local government,
retained its well-defined, pre-Roman tribal organization.

Provincial cities might result naturally from the growth of trade and commerce ; or they might develop from the settlements (*canabae*) which came into existence about the legionary camps; or they might be foundations making provision for veteran soldiers ; or they might have been in existence from pre-Roman times.   Inevitably they all fostered the process of romanization.

The Empire thus came to present the inspiring spectacle of a grand panorama of flourishing cities, and we cannot but be impressed by the Roman achievement.   Nevertheless it is worth asking whether this policy of urbanization did not contribute greatly to the ultimate Decline and Fall.   A prime factor in the decay of the Empire was undoubtedly depopulation, and excessive urbanization may have helped to cause it : cities are notoriously bad breeders.

The cities of a province did not all enjoy equal status and privileges.   The Principate preserved the urban diversity of the Republic, but it did not preserve it entirely unchanged.   Under the Republic individual provincials could obtain the Roman citizenship, but not whole provincial communities : Narbo Martius in Gallia Narbonensis is an exception that proves the rule.   The republican government apparently found it hard to reconcile itself to the idea of a whole community of Roman citizens residing outside of Italy.   Julius Caesar was the first to depart from this narrow conception ; for him Roman citizenship and provincial domicile were not mutually incompatible, and he did not hesitate to organize communities of Roman citizens outside of Italy.   Under the Principate we find more and more provincial communities obtaining the citizenship, until finally in 212 the Emperor Caracallus made it universal throughout the Empire.

Although the ordinary Roman citizen had little real political power under the Principate, he did possess political privileges. The Roman citizen, if he resided in the provinces, had indeed to pay the usual provincial taxes, just like the provincials in general ; he even had to pay the inheritance tax in addition. But he was exempt from the caprices of local authorities, and he could " appeal to Caesar " even from the verdict of a provincial governor ; moreover he alone could aspire to governmental posts.   Presumably citizenship conferred economic advantages as well ; the path of a citizen in trade and industry must have been easier than that of a non-citizen.   The provincials consequently coveted citizen status, and the Roman emperors were able to exploit this fact to obtain provincial loyalty. Enfranchised provincials usually displayed staunch fidelity; many an inscription shows that they regarded the Emperor as a benevolent sovereign who, unlike the senatorial malefactors, did not fleece them. Even freedmen (who were allowed to become priests of *Roma et Augustus*) shared these sentiments. By A.D. 70 there was a provincial bourgeoisie devoted to the Princeps.

The result was that the provincial cities with the most favoured status were now no longer the *civitates foederatae*, the independent, non-citizen communities whose relations with the Roman Republic had been carefully defined by written treaties. Such treaty communities continued indeed to exist, but their independence of the governor's control gradually disappeared.

Under the Principate the privileged communities were those possessing the Roman citizenship with the title of either *colonia* or *municipium*. They were mostly in the western provinces: the eastern provinces contained no *municipia* and few *coloniae* until late in the Principate. We saw above (p. 58) how a *colonia* differed from a *municipium* in Italy. In the provinces, even though some *coloniae*, notably Augustus', were of the old military type and even though the title *municipium* did carry with it the suggestion of an alien derivation, it is scarcely true to say that the types of town differed from one another in that the former was Roman by origin and the latter by incorporation. Nor was a *colonia* in the provinces necessarily distinguished from a *municipium* by its internal constitution, as it was in Italy. In the provinces the difference was almost exclusively one of status,[1] the *colonia* owing to imperial favour ultimately becoming superior. The hierarchical principle, in fact, was applied to communities as well as to individuals. The inhabitants of a *municipium* were usually anxious for their community to obtain the status of a *colonia* with its higher prestige.

The number of Roman citizens in the provinces was certainly not small, and it was constantly increasing. Augustus enjoyed the reputation of being reluctant to bestow the citizenship on non-citizens; and it is doubtless true that he did not share Julius Caesar's liberal ideas about the right of provincials to hold magisterial offices. Nevertheless by the end of his reign the number of individuals and indeed of whole communities in the provinces that enjoyed citizenship was large, while under his successors it increased further. This is scarcely surprising,

[1] A *colonia* used the Latin language and Roman law; its chief officials usually obtained equestrian rank.

for apart from the worthy individuals upon whom the emperors were prepared to bestow citizenship there was the large class of ex-soldiers settled in the provinces.   Legionaries were citizens from the day they enlisted if they were not already such before, and auxiliaries automatically became citizens on their discharge. Time-expired veterans usually settled in the provinces, frequently in the area where they had served.   As their sons were also automatically citizens, the army must have been instrumental in greatly increasing the number of Roman citizens living outside Italy : [1] indeed by A.D. 70 the term Roman no longer denoted that an individual was of Italian origin, just as in Italy it had long since ceased to imply origin in the town on the Tiber. Manifestly the increasing number of Roman citizens living beyond Italy had to lead, inevitably if gradually, to the disappearance of the barriers separating Italy from the provinces. The final levelling of Italian with provincial status took place later than our period ; but the tendency even in our period is clear enough.

Besides the towns which enjoyed Roman citizenship, the provinces contained divers other communities.   Prominent among these latter were those that possessed Latin Status (*Ius Latii*), or, in other words, enjoyed the same rights which, in a much earlier period, the cities of Latium had enjoyed in relation to Rome.   Latin Status was, as it were, midway between citizenship and non-citizenship ; and individuals or whole communities usually obtained it as a preliminary to the full citizenship.   Thus under the Emperor Vespasian all the non-Roman towns of Spain became " Latin *municipia*." [2]   The local magistrates of such Latin towns automatically became Roman citizens.

In our period, however, the majority of provincial towns, especially in the eastern half of the Empire, were neither Roman nor Latin, and they exhibited considerable diversity.   They commonly enjoyed local autonomy (*libertas*).[3]

---

[1] Even under Augustus the army must have been creating new citizens at the rate of about 15,000 a year.   At any rate between 28 B.C. and A.D. 14 the number of adult male citizens rose from four to almost five millions, and natural increase alone can scarcely account for it.

[2] The title is a misnomer, since *municipium* strictly means a community of Roman citizens.

[3] Important exceptions are the communities on the African crownlands (*saltus*) and the Spanish mining areas : these were ruled by freedmen procurators.

There was great variety of local government. The central Roman government might lend its influence in favour of local aristocratic governments, since under the protection of the Empire large private fortunes flourished and their owners would naturally be loyal. But it did not as a rule impose aristocracies, preferring not to interfere with local customs. Undoubtedly the tendency was for the cities, including those that did not possess the Roman citizenship, to model themselves upon Republican Rome.[1] This was not so true of the eastern provinces, where the cities commonly retained their Greek constitutions. In the west, however, the civic institutions of Rome seem to have exercised the same attraction for provincial cities as they did for Italian.

This attraction was not confined to things political. The tendency to imitate all aspects of Roman life was very marked. Local languages tended to give way to Latin, local cults tended to become assimilated into the Roman pantheon, and above all the material civilization tended to become uniform thoughout the Empire. There is no mistaking a Roman building whether it be unearthed in Scotland or in Palmyra. The native inhabitants, who in many parts of the Empire were unsophisticated and primitive, naturally adopted the superior Roman civilization once they were brought into contact with it. As there was apparently no racial discrimination a genuine community of life naturally tended to spring up. This was reflected, especially in the western provinces, in an increasing standardization of life.

A municipal town would commonly have its own local assembly (usually organized in *curiae*, although occasionally in tribes), its own local senate, and its own local magistrates.

The local assembly was composed of the burgesses of the community, although not of the territory " attributed " to it. Non-burgesses resident in the community usually had a restricted right of voting. The assembly elected the local magistrates and pronounced on the desirability of proposals brought before it. Nevertheless the ordinary burgess probably participated but little in the actual direction of municipal affairs. Local government was effectively in the hands of the propertied classes which the Empire preserved and supp rted. Already in the first century A.D. local senates were appointing local magistrates, and ultimately there ceased to be any genuine political activity even at the local, municipal level.

It was not the local assembly that exercised power, but the

[1] There was some pressure from above, especially in the case of communities with Roman citizenship.

local senate (*ordo*). The *ordo*, in fact, was the most important body of men in a provincial city ; and they had to be men of wealth, since they could not become members of it without first paying substantial fees. Styled *decuriones*, they served for life and usually numbered one hundred, cooptation keeping them up to strength.

In the local magistracies the collegiate and annual principles were observed. The magistrates were subordinated to the *ordo* of decurions and normally deferred to their wishes. If they flouted them, they might be fined as much as 10,000 sesterces. Only in judicial matters do the local magistrates appear to have had any discretionary power of their own, and even then it was limited. The municipalities commonly had two *duoviri iure dicundo*, who, as their title implies, exercised jurisdictional powers in civil cases.[1] They also presided over meetings of the local assembly and senate, were responsible for public games, religious observances and the like, and every fifth year acted as local censors with the title of *quinquennales*, in which capacity they appointed ex-magistrates to fill up the gaps in the ranks of the decurions and let out public contracts. The *duoviri* were grouped with the two *aediles* (who supervised local streets, public buildings and food supply) to form the *quattuorviri*, who usually constituted the town's board of executive officials. The municipalities also had their own *quaestores*, who were concerned with the local finances.

The local magistrates all served without salary. On the contrary, they were expected to pay heavily for the privilege of serving. Clearly only men of wealth, leisure and status could act : a degrading occupation or servile birth normally excluded a man from local office. Despite these restrictions, there does not seem to have been undue difficulty in obtaining local magistrates in the first century A.D. Either local patriotism ran high or the propertied classes were anxious to serve in order to preserve their own predominance.

The result was that under the Early Empire there was a flourishing municipal life. There was, indeed, keen competition not only to obtain the local magistracies but even to bestow benefactions on one's city. Hundreds of inscriptions testify to the generosity of individuals in providing their cities with public buildings : aqueducts, baths, theatres, halls, etc. Freedmen, usually organized in the corporation of Augustales, apparently lavished their wealth on such local enterprises as much as men

---

[1] The provincial governor exercised jurisdiction over criminal cases. However, instances of criminal cases not handled by the governor occur.

of free birth.   No doubt many of these gifts were not altogether
spontaneous.   In some cases the local millionaires made their
gifts because they hoped thus to quieten discontent at the
glaring inequalities of wealth, or because their vanity was
flattered by the votes of thanks, the honorific statues, etc., with
which they were rewarded : a love of ostentatious display was
a besetting fault in the Roman Empire.   In any event men who
under the protection of the Empire had managed to amass large
fortunes could legitimately be expected to spend some part of
them on public projects.   But local patriotism as a motive should
not be entirely ruled out ; genuine loyalty and affection inspired much of the generosity.[1]   Civic self-government must
have engendered local patriotism ; municipal liberty resulted
in a vigorous municipal life.   The picture changed when the
central government began to interfere in local government.
Once bureaucratic despotism fastened upon the municipalities
they rapidly decayed.   That, however, was in a later age.

§ 6.   PROVINCIAL TAXATION

Owing to this generosity of private burgesses the cost of
municipal administration could not have been high ; and the
necessary menial jobs were performed cheaply by public
slaves.   On the other hand the cities usually had adequate
sources of income.   Their citizens did indeed pay some local
taxes,[2] and the rent obtained from municipally owned land,
monopolies, fines, decurions' and magistrates' fees, all contributed to the municipal revenue.   A water rate and octroi
dues were also not unknown.   Thus in our period the cities as
a rule were not hard pressed financially ; in fact they usually
could provide their inhabitants with admirable local services
without resorting to heavy local taxation.

Most provincial residents, however, Roman as well as non-
Roman, did pay direct taxes to the central government at
Rome : it was the revenue they contributed that enabled Italy
very largely to escape direct taxation.   This provincial taxation
might be said to have historical justification.   Under the
Republic the Romans made little or no attempt to rationalize
their imposition of provincial taxes ; if they thought about it

[1] It had its bad side.   Local pride and the effort of one city to surpass
another in brilliance led to municipal extravagance and sometimes to
financial ruin.
[2] Roman citizens *of Italian origin* apparently escaped these local
taxes.

at all, they probably argued that the provincials had been
accustomed to pay taxes in their pre-Roman days and might
just as well continue to do so, especially if they were not called
upon to perform military service or to pay more than previously
(actually in some provinces, Macedonia for instance, they paid
less [1]). Since there was no regular principle of provincial taxation, it is scarcely surprising that there was likewise no regular
method of taxation. This fact, together with the lack of a
regular civil service to supervise and collect taxes, had resulted
in the taxes varying widely from province to province.

Under the Principate method was introduced here as in
other aspects of provincial administration. We have seen that
Julius Caesar began the practice, which outlived him, of bestow-
ing Roman citizenship on whole communities in the provinces.
Now, if all these newly enfranchised communities had been
granted that exemption from tribute which Roman communities in Italy traditionally enjoyed the fiscal consequences might
have been disastrous. Accordingly the concept of " Italian
soil " was devised to ensure that provincial communities that
acquired Roman citizenship continued to pay taxes. Some
privileged communities, notably certain *coloniae* founded by
Julius or Augustus (which were all " military " and peopled
with citizens who had never paid tribute), were granted Ius
Italicum : that is, they were put on a par with Italy and escaped
the customary provincial taxes. All other provincial communities, specifically including Roman *municipia*, were regarded as
inhabiting land the legal status of which was different from that
of Italy and hence were tributary.[2]

The taxes which the inhabitants of the provinces paid were
indirect as well as direct. Of the direct taxes the most important was the *tributum soli* (a tax on land and fixed property)
which was extended to resident Romans in the provinces.
Further, there was the *tributum capitis*. In the poorer provinces
this might be, as its name implies, a poll-tax ; usually, however,
it was a charge on types of property other than land, its purpose
being to tax commerce and industry. It was not universal,
since communities enjoying *immunitas* did not pay it.[3]

[1] The Romans could scarcely regard their provincial revenues as
war reparations, since many of their provinces were obtained not by
conquest but by bequest from native rulers.
[2] The traditional view that the tribute which provincials paid was
really a rent for soil that belonged to the Roman People is untenable :
see A. H. M. Jones in *Journ. Rom. Stud.*, XXXI (1941), pp. 26–31.
[3] Under the Empire *immunitas* was rare ; nor did it imply general
exemption from taxation. Usually only Roman towns enjoyed it.

The principal indirect and occasional taxes were :—(i) *Portoria*, duties imposed for fiscal rather than protective purposes on all goods crossing frontiers. (This tax inside the Empire never amounted to more than 5 per cent *ad valorem*.) (ii) Taxes in kind, mostly grain which was supplied for the use of governors and their staffs. (Under this heading we might include the revenue from the mines.) (iii) *Aurum Coronarium*, the sum which a province paid at an imperial accession. (iv) The manumission tax on slaves. (v) The 5 per cent inheritance tax (paid only by Roman citizens).

The task of supervising taxation in a province belonged to the procurator (or, in senatorial provinces, to the quaestor). He was quite independent of the governor, who had little directly to do with the taxation and therefore had fewer opportunities for extortion than under the Republic. The evidence suggests that the direct taxes were usually collected by the procurator personally. Augustus, and still more Tiberius, took measures to curtail the republican system of tax-farming. It did not disappear entirely; indeed *publicani* are frequently mentioned throughout our period, but apparently their task was confined to collecting the indirect and occasional taxes, including the inheritance tax.

What sums were collected we cannot say; Augustus' revenues may have amounted to 400,000,000 sesterces a year. Nor can we say what happened to the taxes after they were gathered. The assumption that taxes from the imperial provinces went to the Emperor's treasury (*fiscus*), while those from the senatorial provinces went to the republican treasury (*aerarium*), is natural but untenable. All parts of the Empire must have contributed to the cost of defence; therefore the Emperor, who provided for the defence of both types of province, must have collected revenue also from the senatorial provinces ; indeed the latter, as the more stabilized, advanced and economically prosperous ones, were precisely the ones best able to contribute. Did then the *fiscus* get all the provincial revenues ? The frequent subventions the *aerarium* obtained (from Augustus and Nero amongst others) suggest as much. Yet before A.D. 69 the *aerarium*, as the official treasury (the *fiscus* being the Emperor's private affair), would seem a more logical recipient of taxes. After 69 the *fiscus* presumably monopolized them, since the Flavian Emperors merged the *aerarium* with the *fiscus* and their successors, although disentangling it, reduced it to a mere regional treasury.

Exactly what proportion of the total provincial income was taken in taxation is a matter for speculation, but the general level of economic prosperity throughout the Empire in our period suggests that it was not inordinately high.   Nevertheless, it was certainly onerous enough to oblige some provincial communities, even as in republican times, to resort to Roman money-lenders like Seneca, and for such loans interest rates were anything but low.   Seneca's admirable views on usury were not reflected in his own practice, and Boudicca's rebellion in Britain was partly caused by the depredations of the usurers. Unjust taxation is also said to have been partly responsible for the great Pannonian revolt of A.D. 6.   In this, however, as in other provincial matters, the Principate brought a great improvement.

Evasion of the taxes was not easy, since a close check was kept on the population and resources of the Empire.   The *breviarium imperii*, which was drawn up for Augustus in the last year of his life, was the most famous statistical compilation of the Empire, but it was not unique.   In the towns the chief local magistrates conducted a census every five years, bearing the title *quinquennales* for the occasion.   The non-urbanized districts could not be controlled with the same facility, but even in them the provincial governor seems to have undertaken a periodical scrutiny.   On the other hand the provincials got something substantial in return.   The central government took their money, but it gave them the Pax Romana.   The inhabitants of the Early Empire obtained comparative immunity from the armed conflicts which customarily characterize human activity : in the period covered by this volume they did obtain a greater measure of peace and protection from invasion than most human beings before or after them ; behind the sheltering cordon of the legions they could pursue their lives in security.   And besides protection from without, they enjoyed order within.[1]   We, no doubt, would not reckon their standard of living as very high ; indeed the vast majority of the inhabitants of the Empire probably lived a life not far removed from poverty, and social unrest was certainly not unknown.   In other words, the provincials enjoyed neither political power nor prosperity as we understand it.   On the other hand under Roman rule they did not live in personal fear.

[1] Some of the large provincial cities, e.g. Carthage and Lugdunum, even had Urban Cohorts modelled on those of Rome.

Nor did Roman rule normally reduce their living standards ; in fact, insofar as the huge private fortunes, which it made possible, were reflected throughout the population as a whole, it probably raised them. On the whole, therefore, it is not unfair to say that the taxes were not a stiff price for the security that the provincials enjoyed.

§ 7. EGYPT

Before leaving this account of the provinces a few words must be said about Egypt.

As a result of the defeat and death of Cleopatra the kingdom of the Ptolemies was added to the dominions of the Roman people by Augustus. It was not, however, organized as a regular province, but was an altogether exceptional equestrian one (see p. 78). The Princeps kept it under his own very close personal control, although it apparently did not form part of the *patrimonium Caesaris*, i.e. the Princeps' private property. It was assigned to a special Prefect of equestrian status, whose post was considered one of the choicest plums of the equestrian career.

So jealous an eye did the Princeps keep on Egypt that senators and *equites illustres* were not even allowed to set foot in it without special permission. Egypt thus occupied a unique position. Even its legions were unique, since they were commanded by men of equestrian, not senatorial, rank, who were granted *imperium* to permit them to do so.

The reasons for the Princeps' vigilance were the extremely strategic position occupied by Egypt at the eastern end of the Mediterranean and the importance of the country as a granary for Rome. In order to obviate the risk of food riots the Princeps had to maintain an adequate supply of grain in the capital ; and no less than a third of all Rome's grain requirements came from Egypt. Augustus laid down a grain quota, which the country had to meet every year. The quota was large and calculated on the assumption that the harvest would be bountiful. The greater efficiency of the imperial administration as compared with the Ptolemaic and in particular the extreme care bestowed on the dykes and canals on which the harvest depended may have led to this assumption. But of course there were years when the yield was low, and in such years Egypt itself was obliged to go short and was expected to recoup itself from later harvests. But each time that this happened recovery became more difficult. The inordinate demands of the capital made serious inroads even on the grain that would normally have been used for seed purposes, and the standard of living of the Egyptian peasant undoubtedly suffered.

Moreover, Egypt had to pay more than the annual grain quota.[1] Its heterogeneous population contained Roman citizens, Greeks and a large Jewish community at Alexandria,[2] besides the native Egyptians. The burdens and the privileges of these various groups differed very widely, and as Egypt did not, like other provinces, contain self-governing municipalities, the bureaucratic machinery needed there was large and complicated. Nevertheless it seems to have functioned only too efficiently. The various taxes were remorselessly collected. One of them was a poll-tax paid by all native male Egyptians between the ages of fourteen and sixty, which must have been a particularly grievous burden. Such a system of exactions was vicious, and it is no justification of Augustus to say that his taxation arrangements were in general modelled on those of the Ptolemies. Ultimately indeed the system led to economic ruin for the land of the Pharaohs.

[1] Apparently its inhabitants were regarded as *dediticii*, whereas provincials in general were usually regarded as *peregrini*.

[2] Officially, however, Alexandria was not a part of Egypt : see H. I. Bell in *Journ. Rom. Stud.*, XXXVI (1946), pp. 130–2.

CHAPTER IV

THE FRONTIERS AND BEYOND

§ 1. THE LEGIONS

THE Republic had always had men under arms. Military forces had been raised as required, either by conscripting citizens who had been chosen by lot or, under the Late Republic, by enrolling volunteers, usually from the proletariat. In the provinces, moreover, there were forces more or less permanently mobilized. According to a recent estimate the fourteen provinces existing *c.* 60 B.C., between them normally contained fourteen legions. Nevertheless, when serious trouble arose, armies literally had to be improvised even in the provinces. This was a makeshift method, adequate perhaps for the needs of a city-state but hardly for those of a world empire. Under the Republic there was in fact no regular military establishment such as would be needed to police and protect the Mediterranean basin. There was not even a commander-in-chief, a state of affairs that contributed not a little to the notorious difficulty of controlling ambitious generals. It was one of Augustus' greatest services to the Empire that he stopped the raising of emergency armies. No doubt the genesis of his system is to be sought in his determination never to relinquish that control over the armed forces which his defeat of Antony and Cleopatra had assured him. But the man who was bent on establishing order and regularity in all spheres of public activity would most certainly not have overlooked the army in any case.

The armies now obtained a generalissimo, *de facto* though not *de iure* : the Julian Emperor. When he had finally disposed of Antony and Cleopatra he found himself at the head of an army of sixty legions. He at once resorted to drastic demobilization of this excessive number, either repatriating the veterans or installing them in colonies. At least 300,000 men were demobilized in this way. *C.* 15 B.C. he decided on twenty-eight legions for the standing army, as against fourteen under the Late Republic. Each of these bore a number and in almost every case a distinctive title as well.[1] The full strength of a legion was

[1] This enabled the same number to be used more than once. Augustus made XXII the highest number in the army list, and later Emperors did not depart from this practice (except Trajan, who called one of his new legions XXX Ulpia).

about 6,000 men, since it comprised ten cohorts of six centuries each; thus the twenty-eight legions mustered 168,000 men. Roman tradition demanded that these legionaries should be Roman citizens and of free birth, and Augustus as usual was loth to break with tradition. Under the Empire conscription for service in the legions was constitutionally possible, but rare in practice, once the number of legions had been stabilized. The legionaries were volunteers, usually sons of the provinces, and they signed on, not for an indefinite period under a specific general as formerly, but for a fixed number of years.

In army matters, as in everything else, Augustus' policy was one of gradualness, necessarily so perhaps, for stabilization was impossible until the frontiers were secure. It was not until A.D. 5, when the frontiers acquired an aspect of permanence, that his military arrangements could take their final form. In that year, accordingly, terms of service were fixed. Henceforth legionaries remained with the colours for twenty years,[1] received ten *asses* a day,[2] and at the end were given an honourable discharge with a gratuity of 3,000 *denarii*. This system helped to keep generals out of politics, since they were no longer obliged to seek land-grants for their men at the end of every campaign. Discharged veterans were still occasionally settled as farmers in colonies; but the usual procedure was for them to be given a bonus from the Military Treasury (*aerarium militare*): this was established in A.D. 6 with the proceeds from the 1 per cent sales tax and the 5 per cent inheritance tax.

An army of twenty-eight legions was none too large to police and protect the provinces which Augustus organized. That it might perform its task more efficiently it was stationed in large camps on or near the borders of the armed, imperial provinces, which gradually developed into permanent stations.[3] Auxiliary troops (see below, p. 99) guarded the areas between the camps.[4] In general the legionaries must have led an unexciting life; many of them never took part in a war, and none of them

[1] Hitherto sixteen years, the traditional republican period of service, had been normal; but twenty years also had republican precedent: see Polyb. VI, 19, 2–4.

[2] Less than a third of what the Praetorians received.

[3] Each camp usually served as headquarters for one legion, but " double " camps containing two were occasionally established until A.D. 90.

[4] After Augustus' time detachments from the legions (*vexillationes*) were also so employed.

were allowed to marry, although naturally they found " common-law wives " among the native women.

Besides the legions thus stationed in their fixed camps, a central reserve, for service where required, would have been useful. Yet the army of the Empire did not possess one. Augustus, well aware that the army in the past had been a political menace, decided to exclude it from politics by keeping it busy with its military duties ; his army in the frontier camps was of a size nicely calculated to make sure that its hands were full. A central reserve, on the other hand, could easily have become a political nuisance : the behaviour of the Praetorians is instructive in this regard. The Princeps therefore dispensed with one. Whenever a frontier was threatened, it was usually strengthened, not with reserve forces, but with troops drawn from one of the other frontiers, which was thus weakened in its turn. If an attack came from more than one quarter at a time, the system would be subjected to very severe strain.

Augustus' reluctance to create reserve legions was probably reinforced by the consideration that it would have aggravated his problem of finding legionaries of the type he wanted. He was not eager to enrol non-Italians in the legions. But from the outset he had little option. Italians being reluctant he had to use provincials, and under his successor the legions contained a very large proportion of non-Italians, many of whom had undoubtedly been given the Roman citizenship to enable them to enlist. By posting the non-Italians to legions stationed far from their countries of origin, Augustus hoped to mitigate their influence on the army. But his own system of fixed camps largely nullified this attempt. A legion that was stationed for years, in some cases centuries, at the same frontier camp was bound to get its recruits from the sons either of its own soldiers or of the auxiliary troops stationed in the neighbourhood ; and the mothers of such recruits would normally be native women. The system of permanent camps undoubtedly developed an excellent *esprit de corps* in the individual legion, but it was also liable to breed local patriotism. By the year 70, although the legions in the west still contained a significant Italian core, largely recruited from Cisalpine Gaul, those in the east were mostly composed of non-Italians and were of an inferior quality.[1]

[1] When on active warfare these eastern legions always needed stiffening with Danubian units.

The Augustan army did not wholly lose its character as a field force. The definitive delimitation of frontiers, where these were not natural barriers such as rivers, was a task that Augustus left to his successors, along with an injunction not to enlarge the Empire's territories. The legions, moreover, had to be ready to keep the provincials in subjection as well as to repel external attack.

The officer class in the army of the Empire, although it no longer consisted of incompetent politicians, was nevertheless not quite so professional as the rank and file. For prudential reasons Augustus did not desire that the class which traditionally nursed political ambitions should become the repository of military experience, although he could not fail to observe that by assigning the highest military posts to senatorials he would make more plausible the fiction of a division of power between Princeps and Senate. The highest military posts, except in Egypt, were monopolized by men who had passed through the senatorial *cursus honorum*. But the evidence suggests that senators, who had had little or no military experience (see above, p. 40), were not used. High rank was reserved for senators of proved military capacity. They, needless to say, were never very numerous, and not infrequently special appointments had to be made, such as that of Corbulo in Nero's reign.

The commander of a legion (*legatus legionis*) was usually an ex-praetor, and it was rare for him to hold his position for more than three years. Then came the various gradations in military rank that one might expect in any army. Thus, below the *legatus legionis* came his staff-officers (*tribuni militum*): if these were equestrians they might have seen fairly serious service, although their duties as *tribuni* were largely clerical. Below them again were the commanders of the cohorts and centuries (*centuriones*): these were professional soldiers, who in many cases had risen from the ranks: on them clearly the higher officers must have depended very largely for advice.[1] Actually they were often of good family and some social standing. They might be members of the Equestrian Order or, if not, frequently became such on their discharge.

Thus it will be seen that the same hierarchical principle

---

[1] After A.D. 50 centurions were not commonly promoted to the rank of tribune: only one who had been *primus pilus* (i.e. first centurion in a legion) could normally achieve such promotion.

was observed in the Roman army as in Roman society : members of the Senatorial or Equestrian Orders could not serve in the ranks as common soldiers.

§ 2. THE AUXILIA

In Republican days, although occasionally some generals and notably Julius Caesar enrolled non-Italians in their armies, the provincials were not as a rule invited to perform military service. The Romans may have been reluctant to put weapons into the hands of subjects who might feel aggrieved. In any case the tradition was that only free-born Roman citizens could serve in the legions. But just as in former days the Romans had found it necessary to supplement their own man-power with that of their Italian allies, so under the Principate they were obliged to make increasing use of the resources in men of the provinces. In our period the non-Italian soldiers were for the most part obtained from inside the Empire.

Some of them, as we have seen, were enrolled in the legions. But as early as the reign of Augustus the legionaries were supplemented by the auxiliaries. These are to be distinguished from the local militias, who were called out as occasion demanded but were not part of the regular army. The auxiliary troops (*auxilia*) were organized either into battalions (*cohortes*) of infantry or wings (*alae*) of cavalry. These units normally contained about 500 men, and they were usually designated by a number and a special name indicating the man who first enrolled the unit, or the nationality of the troops that originally composed it, or the type of equipment it used. They were very numerous ; although their exact strength in Augustus' day is uncertain, the total number of auxiliaries is generally reckoned as hardly inferior to that of the legionaries.[1] The fact that they were inexpensive to raise and maintain recommended their use. Under the Julio-Claudian emperors they were mostly recruited in the armed imperial provinces where Roman citizens were rare, and from Tiberius' reign on they usually served in the areas where they enlisted.[2] In such areas they could conduct a reconnaissance or obtain supplies better than aliens

---

[1] In Augustus' day the cavalry probably played a more important rôle than the infantry in the *auxilia*.

[2] *Auxilia* might also be supplied by peoples like the Batavi, who were nominally only in alliance with Rome.

from far afield, and they would also be familiar with the enemy's fighting methods.

Down to A.D. 70 the *auxilia* were in effect national units. Their unit commanders (*praefecti*) were, it is true, Roman citizens of equestrian status ; but even they were often of the same nation as the men they commanded, having obtained the citizenship and equestrian status by imperial grant and not by birth.[1] The other officers in the *auxilia*, e.g. the centurions who commanded the subdivisions of an infantry cohort and the decurions who commanded the subdivisions of a cavalry wing, likewise possessed the Roman citizenship. The ordinary auxiliary soldier did not obtain it, however, until he received his discharge from the army, which after A.D. 50 at any rate normally came after twenty-five years' service. This, however, meant that his sons were citizens and hence could and did enlist in the legions in the vicinity.

Thus the military system of the Empire was based on long-term service, and the tendency to keep the same troops in the same province for years on end and to recruit even the legions on the spot led to a growth of local patriotism and even to particularism. In the case of the *auxilia*, indeed, there was the very real risk that, being national units, they would prove disloyal and make common cause with their kinsmen against Rome. Even their officers were not proof against this temptation, as is proved by the careers of men like Arminius and like Civilis, whose native troops were guilty of a serious uprising in 69. Thereafter the *auxilia* were usually obliged to serve in areas far from their homelands.

§ 3. THE IMPERIAL ROMAN NAVY

The navy of the Empire seems to have been a special branch of the *auxilia*. Under the Republic it had been even more of a makeshift force than the army. To the Romans sea-power always seemed of minor importance, largely because they had good land communications with nearly all parts of their Empire and were far less dependent than Britain on sea-borne supplies and raw materials. Ancient fleets were not well adapted to blockade and convoy uses since they could not remain long enough at sea. They were small and frail, and being adapted to ramming and boarding rather than to manoeuvring under

[1] They were mostly ex-centurions.

canvas, they required large numbers of rowers and marines ; consequently they had no room for large supplies of food and water, so that their cruising range was limited. Furthermore, if their scanty supplies did not restrict their range, then lack of navigational knowledge did so. Ships tended, especially at night time, to keep within sight of shore. It takes a long time to train a navy as compared with an army, and to the Romans the prospective results scarcely seemed to justify the effort. In republican times, when a need for warships arose, fleets were hastily improvised, largely by getting allied maritime cities to provide the ships.

But the war with Sextus Pompeius and the Battle of Actium had emphasized the need for a standing navy. Augustus accordingly proceeded to organize one, which he divided into two main fleets, the Tyrrhenian based on Misenum and the Adriatic based on Ravenna. Minor flotillas were at the service of the various provincial governors. But even for Augustus naval power was merely the handmaiden to military might. It is true that Mommsen's theory that he manned his navy for the most part with slaves or freedmen is demonstrably false ; [1] but he made no attempt to create a distinct class of naval officers. The Tyrrhenian and Adriatic fleets were each under the command of a Prefect, but these naval posts were not among the more highly valued of the great equestrian prefectures ; in fact down to A.D. 69 freedmen rather than knights were usually appointed to them, and it was not until the time of the Flavian emperors that the Prefecture of the Fleet became more esteemed.

Actually, the navy never became a really important member of the armed services, for it did not need to be. The indispensable link in the provincial system was Illyricum, but this could be held with land power. Thus mastery of the seas was not overwhelmingly important. In any case the Mediterranean was literally *mare nostrum*, and a comparatively small navy could carry out the necessary escort and convoy duties. The army and not the navy was the real instrument of empire, and in the period with which this volume is concerned no great naval battles were fought.

The garrison of the Empire, the force that kept out invaders and made the Pax Romana a reality, consisted therefore of the legions and the *auxilia*. At need these could be supplemented by the garrison of Italy which was by no means negligible.

---

[1] Dalmatians and Pannonians manned the Adriatic fleet.

§ 4. THE EASTERN FRONTIER

This standing army was mainly distributed over the provinces on the periphery of the Roman world. Augustus' policy for the garrisoning of these frontier provinces revealed itself only by degrees, and we do not know whether it determined the size of his standing army or vice versa. He abandoned the haphazard expansionism of the Republic and proposed to bring the Empire to what he considered its natural territorial limits and then to call a halt. Doubtless from the moment he obtained supreme power he had his plans for the ideal extent of the Empire, but he only disclosed them gradually : perhaps he could not do otherwise, for contemporary opinion undoubtedly favoured an imperialist programme. It was comparatively late in the reign that his proposed shape for the Empire emerged. For the conduct of his frontier wars Augustus, who was not himself a general of genius, had the supreme good fortune to be loyally served by men of great military ability, some of them men of quite obscure origin. The names of Agrippa, P. Sulpicius Quirinius, and the Emperor's stepsons, Tiberius and Drusus, will spring readily to mind.

At first the Princeps busied himself with the final subjugation of areas which, although nominally within the Empire, were actually still largely unpacified. Such areas existed at both ends of the Mediterranean.

In the eastern Mediterranean there were Asia Minor, Mesopotamia and Egypt, and the extent of Roman domination in these regions had to be decided. Asia Minor and Mesopotamia could not be disposed of easily. There was a very clearly defined demand at Rome that Parthia should be humbled : the disasters which had overtaken Crassus in 53 B.C. and Antony in 36 B.C. rankled as a national disgrace, and national honour demanded that they be avenged.[1] Augustus however thought that Rome lacked the strength to carry her standards beyond the Euphrates, although he prudently refrained from advertising his reluctance to undertake what most Romans regarded as their national mission. Accordingly he sought to restore Roman prestige and establish the Empire's security in this area without recourse to large-scale fighting. He regarded Parthia as an essentially oriental nation, and the propaganda which he had conducted

[1] Julius Caesar had bowed to this demand and was on the eve of departing for Parthia when the assassins' daggers struck him down.

against Cleopatra shows that he was not anxious to blend Rome's Mediterranean civilization with a cultural admixture from the east. Accordingly he tried to settle Rome's eastern question by diplomacy rather than the sword. Parthia was not a highly united state ; a careful fostering of rivalries within the royal house would render it too internally weak to threaten the Empire. Moreover, besides the Parthians, there was a multiplicity of other smaller kingdoms whose monarchs were mutually suspicious and hostile. A policy of *divide et impera* offered fair prospects of success.

Accordingly in 23 B.C. Agrippa, in 22 B.C. Augustus himself and in 20 B.C. Tiberius visited the east. Their diplomatic activity doubtless was designed to safeguard Rome's interests by keeping secular Asiatic rivalries alive. In 20 Tiberius recovered by negotiation the standards Crassus lost at Carrhae,[1] and Augustus carefully exploited this achievement for its full propaganda value : he represented it as that final settlement with Parthia for which public opinion at Rome had been noisily clamouring. This, however, did not bring the permanent peace one might have expected. Enmity between Rome and Parthia persisted. The Parthians could not forget the aggressions of Crassus and others, and they could not forgive Roman attempts to establish a suzerainty over Armenia, a country which the Parthians regarded as being in their own sphere of interest. Rome could not remain indifferent to Armenia : for one thing, too many natural routes ran across it to connect Syria and Asia Minor with India and China. But it posed a real dilemma. Was Augustus to annex it, to abandon it to the Parthians, or to make it a Roman protectorate ?

Outright annexation of Armenia would have been difficult from a military point of view. Troops could not be spared from Syria for the purpose, for this province was dangerously exposed to the Parthians and a strong military establishment had to be maintained at the camp of Zeugma. Moreover the conquest of Armenia would have also involved that of the intervening regions of Commagene and Cappadocia; indeed it would have involved even more. It was scarcely possible to move beyond the Euphrates without moving to the Tigris : thus the annexation of Armenia would inevitably have entailed the attempted annexation of Mesopotamia and probably of Assyria as

[1] In exchange the Parthian king obtained the extradition of the rebel Tiridates.

well—a task which Crassus and Antony and later Trajan vainly attempted. Rome was never strong enough to deal a mortal blow to Parthian strength ; [1] hence the policy of annexation of Armenia seemed unpromising.

Abandonment of Armenia to Parthia, on the other hand, would not only have had serious political repercussions at Rome : it would also have been interpreted as weakness by Parthia. Appeasement invites aggression ; and a strong Parthia could use Armenia as a base for operations against the Empire.

Appointment of a Roman nominee to the Armenian throne, the third possibility, would offend the Parthians and probably the Armenians as well. It might even lead to armed conflict. Armenia, as Augustus presumably realized, was scarcely amenable to western civilization ; like Parthia it was an essentially oriental state. Augustus nevertheless decided on the policy of a protectorate, and in 20 Tiberius established a Roman nominee on the Armenian throne. He hoped that this would mollify the vocal Roman chauvinists, while internecine strife in Parthia gave the plan a hope of success.

But when Parthia recovered its internal unity, it would be bound to dispute the Armenian settlement; hence Rome's frontier was only too likely to lapse into insecurity. To remedy this state of affairs as far as possible, Augustus resorted to a system of buffer states and established a chain of client kingdoms along the eastern frontier. The monarchs of these petty states saved the Romans the trouble of sending troops to maintain order in primitive and often unruly districts. The client kingdoms, even though they put their own military forces at the Empire's disposal, were indeed an element of weakness, and this sometimes in highly strategic localities : Commagene and Cappadocia, for example, controlled the important Euphrates crossings. Nevertheless it was more convenient to leave to native princes the task of raising the level of civilization in these areas than to attempt romanization by means of the usual provincial apparatus : until they had reached the stage where they were ready for incorporation such areas would be very troublesome to administer. The client kings were encouraged to foster urbanization and general economic improvement ; when their kingdoms had reached a level compatible

---

[1] The converse is also true : until late in the second century Parthian arms never succeeded in penetrating west of the Euphrates.

with that generally prevailing throughout the Empire, they could be and usually were incorporated so as to become provinces or parts of provinces.

Vassal states of this kind were the Bosporan kingdom on the north shore of the Black Sea, which, however, long retained its nominal independence; Galatia, which was annexed in 25 B.C.; Cappadocia and Commagene, both of which became provinces under Tiberius; Emesa; and Ituraea, which before its incorporation at the end of the first century A.D. was subdivided into the tetrarchies of Chalcis, Abila and Arca. In Judaea the able but unscrupulous dynasty of the Herods maintained a shrewd loyalty to their Roman suzerain until the annexation of the country in A.D. 6.[1]

Arabia Petraea retained its nominal independence for a hundred years longer. Augustus however was definitely interested in Arabia, and not merely in the more northerly parts of that huge country. In 25 B.C. Aelius Gallus [2] was ordered to lead an expedition into the country of the Sabaeans, that is the area now called the Yemen, Aden and the Hadramaut. Augustus may have been attracted by the wealth which the Sabaeans derived from their profitable but unilateral trade in spices with the Empire; or, more probably, he may have been mainly concerned to safeguard the ever more travelled route to India. Gallus' expedition was little more than a military demonstration.[3] In 24 he reached Arabia Felix (*Aden*), established friendly relations with that great mart and feudal kingdom, and then returned to Egypt. Thereafter Augustus apparently attempted no more eastern conquests.

§ 5. EGYPT AND AFRICA

Egypt presented no formidable defence problem, since the desert which flanks the Nile valley defines the frontier almost exactly. Only on the south would there be difficulty in determining the most suitable line. After the far from successful

---

[1] The Herods, however, did not become throneless. By imperial favour they ruled various client kingdoms which were not absorbed until *c.* A.D. 92.

[2] According to some he was Prefect of Egypt at the time.

[3] His reputed plan to sail to Leuke Kome on the Arabian shore of the Red Sea and thence march nine hundred miles across the desert to the Sabaean territory is fantastic.

expedition which the vainglorious governor Cornelius Gallus
led against the Ethiopians in 29 B.C., the First Cataract was
selected as the southern limit of Roman territory. At first the
Ethiopians were inclined to dispute this ; and Petronius, the
Prefect of Egypt, had to repel them in 25 B.C., at a time when
his garrison had largely been withdrawn for the expedition to
southern Arabia, and again in 22. *C.* 21, however, a definitive
peace was signed with the queen (Candace) of the Ethiopians,
and a military zone, the so-called Dodecaschoinos district, was
established between Egypt and Ethiopia. During the remainder
of our period Egypt was immune from attack from the south.
Here was one land frontier that never required elaborate defence
works of the *limes* type.

The province of Africa, which was along with Egypt the
chief granary of Rome, was the other important Roman area
in the dark continent. Although Africa contained legionary
troops and was therefore an " armed " province, it was senatorial. The main problem in Africa was to stablize relations
with the neighbours of the province, especially with Mauretania
on the west. The rugged, mountainous interior of Mauretania
deterred Augustus from attempting its conquest. Accordingly
at the death of King Bocchus (33 B.C.), who apparently bequeathed his realm to Rome, he established Juba, son of the
last king of Numidia, as a dependent king.[1] Mauretania
remained a client kingdom until *c.* A.D. 40, covering the western
frontier of the African province.

On the eastern and southern frontiers of Africa there was
sporadic fighting throughout the reign, and the proconsuls of
the province had to undertake punitive expeditions—Cornelius
Balbus against the Garamantes of Tripolitania in 19, P. Sulpicius
Quirinius against the Marmaridae of Cyrenaica some time before
12 B.C.,[2] and Cossus Cornelius Lentulus against those perennial
trouble-makers, the Gaetulian nomads of the south, *c.* A.D. 5.
But the province must have been reasonably well secured :
from A.D. 6 onwards it normally required no more than one
legion as its garrison (III Augusta).

---

[1] Juba's hereditary kingdom of Numidia was mostly incorporated in
the African province *c.* 25 B.C., although parts of it were merged with his
new Mauretanian domain.

[2] Sulpicius presumably was proconsul of the senatorial province of
Crete and Cyrene at this time. But it is more convenient to refer to
his exploit at this point.

§ 6.　SPAIN

Augustus' prolonged sojourn in Spain in 26 and 25 indicates how seriously that country needed his attention. Its many mountains and lofty plateaux were obstacles to military operations. Indeed the thorough conquest of the Iberian peninsula was a long drawn-out process ; it had been begun in the third century B.C. and was not completed until Augustus' day, and even then only after protracted operations, especially against the Cantabri, Astures and Gallaeci of the north-west. The Cantabri proved particularly recalcitrant enemies, but by 19 B.C., when Agrippa went to Spain, the subjugation of the peninsula was reasonably complete. By that time Baetica, the urbanized southern portion of Spain, did not need legionary troops, and it became a senatorial province shortly after, possibly in 15 B.C. on the occasion of Augustus' visit to the west. The rest of the country was divided into the two imperial provinces of Lusitania and Tarraconensis. These at first required a large military establishment, perhaps as many as five legions. Consolidation, however, proceeded apace. Roads were built to give the garrisoning legions greater mobility ; mountain strongholds were dismantled ; and many of Spain's turbulent fighting men were recruited into the Roman army and shipped to other provinces. These methods brought about more settled conditions, and the number of troops in Spain was gradually reduced. After A.D. 9 it contained three legions, by the middle of the first century only one.

§ 7.　THE ALPINE AREAS

It was, however, the northern frontier of the empire that caused Augustus the greatest concern. Even the areas immediately north of the Italian peninsula were still unpacified on his accession. In 25 B.C., for instance, his general Terentius Varro Murena had to march against the Salassi who dwelt in the region of the Great and Little St. Bernard Passes. Ruthless repression and the foundation of a large military colony, Augusta Praetoria (*Aosta*), secured the area.

But there still remained much work to be done. Augustus set his hand to this resolutely as soon as he had settled affairs in the east and in Spain. The first thing was to secure the Alps, which, despite the annexation of Gaul, had strangely been left in hostile hands. After P. Silius Nerva, the proconsul of Illyricum, had subdued the area of the eastern Alps *c.* 16 B.C., it was possible to incorporate the kingdom of Noricum (Tyrol) ; and in the next year (15) Augustus' stepsons, Tiberius and Drusus, successfully pacified the area between the Alps and the Upper Danube. In 14 B.C. the western or Maritime Alps were brought firmly under Roman control, a feat commemorated by the famous Trophy of Augustus which still stands above Monaco.

Henceforth there were no enemy threats to impede the development of the numerous cities of Lombardy. Indeed the sub-Alpine tribes which might have constituted a menace were now for the most part " attributed " to various Italian towns, while the mountain areas and the regions immediately to the north of them were organized as procuratorial provinces (Maritime Alps, Cottian Alps, Pennine Alps, Noricum, Raetia).[1]

§ 8.   THE DANUBE

All of this, however, was merely preparatory to the much more formidable enterprise further north along the rivers Rhine and Danube. Down to 13 B.C. Augustus' task everywhere had been chiefly one of consolidation in areas which were already nominally parts of the Empire. This is true also of Gaul, which, apart from the senatorial province of Narbonensis, still required legionary troops to suppress internal feuds. Augustus divided it into three imperial provinces, the *Tres Galliae* of Aquitania, Lugdunensis and Belgica. It soon became possible to move the legions from them.

Tacitus describes Augustus' work of pacification as a " peace stained with blood." But the modern student will feel that the Princeps was not unjustified in erecting his famed and beautiful Altar of the Augustan Peace in the Campus Martius. He had provided the Empire with an efficient and disciplined standing army and a broad territorial basis. But he had not yet provided it with a secure and defensible northern frontier ; and the rest of his reign was taken up with the search for this. The result is that after 13 B.C. his task becomes one of conquest rather than consolidation.

---

[1] Some of these were administered at first by prefects rather than by procurators (see above, p. 79).

His arms reached the Lower Danube in 29–8 B.C., and the imperial province of Moesia was subsequently organized here (*c.* A.D. 3). Nevertheless the area was not thoroughly pacified. *C.* 12 B.C. there was a fierce Thracian uprising, and about the same time the Dalmatians and the Pannonians, who dwelt along the Middle Danube, took to arms. It was probably this that decided Augustus to seek a firm line of demarcation for the Empire in the rivers of northern and central Europe. He selected the Elbe-Danube line, since it was short and therefore would require fewer troops to man it. He probably underestimated the difficulty of conquering the Germans beyond the Rhine : despite their interminable, internecine quarrels, they were to prove tougher foes than the Gauls.

In 13 B.C. the forward march to the Danube and the Elbe began. On the Lower Danube the Thracian uprising was suppressed, and some time within the next few years Cn. Cornelius Lentulus and Aelius Catus carried out expeditions beyond the river. The latter, indeed, removed a big menace to the tranquillity of the region by transporting 50,000 Getae, who were of the same stock as the Dacians, to Moesia.[1] The Lower Danube was the scene of recurrent Dacian raids, many of them led by a prince named Cotiso ; and the poet Ovid, in exile at Tomi, displays lively apprehensions for his personal safety. But apparently there was no major war here during the remainder of the reign.

Along the Middle Danube the Pannonian War (13–9 B.C.) was first entrusted to M. Vinicius and, within a few weeks, to Agrippa. But ill-health and death overtook the latter, and Tiberius was sent to the area in 12. The military situation was serious enough to terminate the career of Illyricum as a senatorial province : apparently it was at about this time that it was divided into the two imperial provinces that were later called Pannonia and Dalmatia. After some years of very hard fighting peace was imposed in 9 B.C.

Little is heard of the Upper Danube in these years, but along the Rhine Drusus, Augustus' stepson, was active. His ultimate objective was the River Elbe. The forces at his disposal, how-

---

[1] Both Getae and Dacians seem to have spoken a Thracian language. The former lived for the most part east and south of the Carpathian Mountains, and, as a separate nation, disappear from history early in the first century A.D. The Dacians mostly lived west of the Carpathians, the core of their strength being Transylvania.

ever, even though they amounted to five legions, were inadequate, and between 12 and 9 B.C. his trans-Rhenane expeditions could not have been much more than raids.   In 9 Drusus met an accidental death, and his brother Tiberius hastened from the Middle Danube to replace him on the Rhine.

By consolidating the Roman position on the east bank of this river in 8 and 7 B.C. Tiberius laid the foundations for the advance to the Elbe.   First, however, the Upper Danube had to be pacified.   This area was threatened by the Marcomanni, who had been driven out of South Germany by Drusus and had concentrated considerable power and even built up an empire in Bohemia under their able king, Maroboduus.   The pacification of this area was far from easy, and Augustus at once lost the capable services of Tiberius, who chose this time to go into retirement at Rhodes.   The Princeps thereupon was obliged to use other generals, L. Domitius Ahenobarbus and M. Vinicius, who met with only indifferent success.   It was not until after A.D. 4, when Tiberius had emerged from Rhodes, that substantial headway seemed likely.   After careful preparations Tiberius led a large expedition against Maroboduus in A.D. 6 ; it was at that precise moment that a revolt broke out in Pannonia.   Fortunately Tiberius managed to reach a settlement with Maroboduus, which recognized him as the friend and ally of the Roman people and was the basis for a later arrangement whereby Rome paid the Marcomanni to guard the Danube frontier.

Tiberius was now free to give his attention to the Pannonian revolt which, beginning with the Daesitiates under Bato in the south-east, soon spread to the Breuci under Pinnes and another Bato about the River Save.   Ultimately all Pannonia and Dalmatia became involved, and Roman losses were severe. The suppression of this great revolt occupied Tiberius for three years (A.D. 6–9), and only with the utmost difficulty did he succeed in quelling it.   He needed the aid of A. Caecina Severus, the legate of Moesia, before the reconquest was completed.[1]

It was with heartfelt relief that Rome learned in A.D. 9 that Tiberius had restored order in Illyricum, the key area of the Empire.

---

[1] The historian Velleius Paterculus and in the later stages Tiberius' nephew, Germanicus the son of Drusus, served in this war.   Suetonius (*Tiberius*, 16, 1) describes the Pannonian Revolt as " gravissimum omnium externorum bellorum post Punicum."

§ 9. THE RHINE ; THE VARIAN DISASTER

Immediately, however, the good tidings from Illyricum was offset by alarming news from Germany. The Roman commander there had as his *provincia* (that is, as his sphere of command) the whole area as far as the Elbe. To this responsible post Augustus had recently appointed one of his relatives by marriage, P. Quinctilius Varus. Whether the whole area as far as the Elbe could ever have been subjugated without the prior pacification of Bohemia is more than doubtful; and even if it could have been, Varus was not the man to do it. He only succeeded in provoking the tribes in the vicinity to oppose Rome in closer co-operation than they usually displayed, although even now they were far from unanimous. This fact has won for Varus' destroyer, a romanized German named Arminius, a reputation as a national German hero. Actually he was only the leader of a faction in his own tribe of the Cherusci, and he owes his fame more to the follies of Varus than to any merits of his own.

In the late summer of A.D. 9 Varus was enticed by the report of a rising some distance beyond the Rhine to lead Legions XVII, XVIII and XIX into the Teutoburg Forest. There they were trapped in an ambush and massacred ; Varus himself elected not to survive the annihilation of his three legions and committed suicide. The exact site of this famous disaster has never been discovered, although every year a new squad of industrious German scholars takes up the quest. The fact that Varus set out from somewhere near Minden on the Weser (Visurgis) and that six years later Germanicus reached the melancholy battle-field by marching north from Mainz indicates that it is to be sought somewhere between Osnabrück and Detmold.

Varus' defeat was a military disaster of the first magnitude. Trans-Rhenane Germany was lost. The three legions could not be replaced, for Rome simply lacked the man-power. Even in the years immediately preceding slaves had had to be enrolled to help in quelling the Pannonian revolt. Legions XVII, XVIII, XIX accordingly disappeared from the army list ; their ill-omened numbers were never subsequently given to any of the legions of the Empire.[1] Augustus' army was thus reduced from twenty-eight to twenty-five legions, and the Elbe policy was abandoned. Even before the Varian disaster the forces

[1] Thus arose the regular later practice of never resurrecting any legion that was annihilated with the loss of its eagle in battle.

available were not super-abundant; after it, the troops had to be rushed to the Rhine from Raetia, Spain and Pannonia and the strain on the Empire's military resources was extended to other frontiers.   Presumably *auxilia* could have been enrolled to make good the deficiency.   But Arminius had himself been an officer in the *auxilia* ; hence their services were suspect at this time.

Augustus made no public pronouncement, but the arrangements he now made, together with the fact that his successor, a scrupulous adherent to his policies, rejected the idea of trans-Rhenane conquests, show that he now abandoned the idea of advancing the frontier to the Elbe.   Varus' defeat might have had the even more serious consequence of the loss of the Rhine frontier as well, had the Germans whom Arminius was leading not fallen to quarrelling among themselves.   The competent work-horse Tiberius hastened to Germany and saved the Rhine frontier.   To safeguard it Augustus divided it into an Upper and Lower district,[1] each with a garrison of four legions,[2] and each consisting of a narrow strip of territory along the river. The ex-consuls who administered these districts were strictly military officers, Legates of the Army in Germany, not Legates of Germany.   It is usual to speak of these districts as the provinces of Upper and Lower Germany : actually they were not formally organized as provinces until eighty years later (A.D. 90).   Until then, for civil administration, they were placed under the governor of Belgica ; and even for fifty years after A.D. 90 they remained part of Belgica for financial administration.

§ 10.   THE DISTRIBUTION OF THE LEGIONS

The Pannonian Revolt and the Varian disaster revealed that the Empire had reached the limits of its military resources and therefore of its territorial expansion.   In Augustus' judgment it was time to call a halt.   His court poets might clamour for the annexation of Britain and, with one eye on public opinion at Rome, Augustus might choose not to dampen their enthusiasm.   Actually, as Tacitus makes very clear, he did not

---

[1] The boundary between them being at Brohl near Coblence.

[2] Now, if not before, began the practice of never having more than four legions in any one province.   For prudential reasons the Princeps would not want any one governor to have a larger army than this at his disposal.   If an area needed more than four legions, it was divided into two provinces.

seriously contemplate the conquest of the northern island. To
his successor he bequeathed the injunction not to advance the
Empire's boundaries, and Tiberius faithfully obeyed.[1]

The twenty-five legions were probably distributed as follows
for garrison and frontier duties : Syria four ;[2] Egypt two ;[3]
Africa one ;[4] Spain three ;[5] Moesia two ;[6] Illyricum (that is,
Pannonia and Dalmatia) five ;[7] Lower Germany four ;[8] Upper
Germany four.[9]

In times of crisis these legions could be shifted from one
province to another ; and it shortly became possible to reduce
the garrison in Spain. But it was not until after A.D. 70 that
a radical shift in the army strength was made. It was then
that the military might of the Empire began to be moved away
from the Rhine to the Danube and even further east.

[1] " Consilium id divus Augustus vocabat, Tiberius praeceptum."—
Tacitus, *Agricola*, 13, 3.

[2] III Gallica ; VI Ferrata ; X Fretensis ; XII Fulminata.

[3] III Cyrenaica ; XXII Deiotariana.

[4] III Augusta.

[5] IV Macedonica ; VI Victrix ; X Gemina.

[6] IV Scythica ; V Macedonica.

[7] VII ; VIII Augusta ; IX Hispana ; XI ; XV Apollinaris.

[8] I ; V Alaudae ; XX ; XXI Rapax.

[9] II Augusta ; XIII Gemina ; XIV Gemina ; XVI. On the disposition of the legions, see R. Syme, *Journ. Rom. Stud.*, XXIII (1933),
pp. 14–33.

CHAPTER V

THE LITERATURE OF THE AUGUSTAN AGE

§ 1. THE GOLDEN AGE

THE literature of the Augustan Age was both voluminous and of high merit. Augustus' achievement inspired men of letters. He had done more than make life and property secure, he had restored discipline and order in every field of human activity. Therewith a firm sense of values and ease of mind had returned ; men were no longer wandering about bewildered in a moral and spiritual vacuum, and their reassurance was reflected in literature. Troublous times usually breed strained and turgid writing ; but Augustan literature is the very reverse of this. Its mere externals make that sufficiently obvious, for Augustan verse exhibits a technical excellence, a mastery of form that results when poets are confident of their standards, and the prosodic uncertainties of the period of the Republic disappear. A comparison of Vergil's hexameters with those of Lucretius, of Horace's sapphics with those of Catullus, or of Tibullus' elegiac couplets with those of Catullus is instructive in this regard.   Nor is this certainty of touch confined to poetry : the prose writers, too, had mastered their medium.

In addition Augustus had unified Italy, so that the Roman State was no longer synonymous with the exclusive aristocracy of Rome, but had become definitely Italic. This was an achievement to catch men's imagination. The poets of the age are, indeed, above all things Roman : but in them Roman and Italian have become identical terms. Nothing attests the unification of Italy more triumphantly.

Towards the end of the reign, indeed, when the system of the Principate was firmly entrenched, the initial freshet of enthusiasm had largely spent itself. The life of the Empire proceeded smoothly, and the literary output became a product of routine. But in the early days of Augustus' supremacy, when he stood forth as the champion of Italy and things Italian against the pretensions of a handful of Roman nobles or against what he represented as the orientalizing threats from Egypt or Parthia, men of letters found themselves living in an atmosphere that stimulated their genius. Moreover the writers

114

received encouragement as well as inspiration. Men of wealth, who approved strongly of the régime but did not themselves possess the talent to give it adequate literary expression, fostered with financial as well as moral support men more gifted than themselves. For instance, both Gaius Maecenas and M. Valerius Messalla Corvinus became patrons of literary coteries.

§ 2.   VERGIL

The foremost poet of the age, P. Vergilius Maro (70–19 B.C.) was the protégé of Maecenas. Vergil did not hail from Rome ; he was one of those North Italians from the vicinity of Mantua who suffered cruelly in the confiscations of 41. Nevertheless he supported Octavian from the outset, being confident that the young man would work for the good of Italy as a whole. Vergil early caught the spirit of the Augustan régime. His first poems of any consequence, *The Eclogues*,[1] written between 43 and 39, exude a genuinely Italian flavour, even though modelled on the work of the Sicilian Greek, Theocritus. Their shepherds are genuine Italians, in some cases even actual personages, masquerading under Greek names. *The Eclogues* are not only the first attempt at pastoral poetry in Latin ; [2] they are also the first attempt to hymn the beauties of the Italian countryside. The Theocritean artificialities fail to hide Vergil's love and enthusiasm for the sights and sounds of the peninsula.

His next work, *The Georgics*, written between 37 and 30, is no less Italian in tone. Hesiod has now replaced Theocritus as the professed model : but the real inspiration is still Italy. In this work Vergil confidently takes the stability of the new order for granted—and this in a period before Octavian had yet become Augustus—and devotes himself to the task of teaching Italians how to make the most profitable use of their land. He was not the first or the last Latin poet to write with a didactic purpose : but the general pedagogical atmosphere does not prevent *The Georgics* from being a literary masterpiece.

After *The Georgics* Vergil was engaged upon his twelve-book epic, *The Aeneid*. Death, probably by tuberculosis, over-

---

[1] The much disputed question as to which of the poems in the *Appendix Vergiliana* are earlier than *The Eclogues* and which are by Vergil cannot be discussed here.

[2] They were to find inferior imitators : e.g. Calpurnius Siculus, in Nero's reign.

took him in 19 B.C. before he had revised this to his entire satisfaction. Nevertheless the work is to all intents and purposes complete ; and it must be regarded as the greatest literary achievement of the Augustan Age. As in the case of Vergil's other poems the influence of his predecessors is clearly perceptible. Verbal echoes of Lucretius and Catullus, and even of earlier writers like Ennius, abound in *The Aeneid* no less than in *The Eclogues* and *The Georgics*. Nor has the poet overlooked the Greeks : his indebtedness to Apollonius Rhodius and above all to Homer is most marked. Indeed the first six books of *The Aeneid* comprise a kind of *Odyssey*, just as the last six comprise a kind of *Iliad* ; even Homer's machinery is faithfully reproduced ; for this was a standard feature of epic poetry. The gods participate in the action ; there is a trip to the underworld ; there is a storm at sea ; there are epic similes and apostrophes. And all of these things are introduced in language that is frequently a translation or paraphrase of Homer's. This, however, should not be regarded as mere plagiarism or lack of originality. It is an extension of the Theory of Imitation from sculpture to poetry   Just as the perfect statue can be created by a harmonious blending of individually perfect parts taken from this work and from that, so the ideal poem can be composed by the writer who has the skill to take the inimitable parts of his predecessors' works and weld them perfectly together.

Vergil's aim was to produce a national poem describing the origin and achievements of the Roman nation. But for him the term Roman means Italian. It is Italy, the Saturnian land, prolific of crops and men, that receives his homage. The poet accepts the legend that Roman origins go back to a band headed by Aeneas who escaped from the sack of Troy. But Vergil insists on the Italian as well as the Trojan origin. Aeneas marries an Italian princess ; and it is from their union that there springs a race whose exploits are the poet's pride and inspiration. The poem probably contains allegory as well as national glorification. Readers of the episode in which Queen Dido of Carthage almost enmeshes the hero Aeneas would be irresistibly reminded of Antony's recent entanglement with Cleopatra, and the struggles of Aeneas to establish himself firmly in Latium are reminiscent of the efforts of Augustus to place the Principate upon a sound basis.

But *The Aeneid* does more than exalt the achievements of

the past in "the stateliest measure ever moulded by the lips of man." By his insistence that the mission of Rome is to bring order and the reign of law, by his sympathy for the unfortunate of no matter what class or creed,[1] Vergil with prophetic insight stresses what were to be the outstanding achievements of the Principate which Augustus founded, the Pax Romana and a growing humanitarianism. *The Aeneid* is truly representative of the spirit of the Empire in our period.

§ 3. HORACE

Vergil's close friend, Q. Horatius Flaccus (65–8 B.C.), was likewise a protégé of Maecenas and not a native of Rome. He too came from a part of Italy (the borderland of Apulia and Samnium) that had suffered severely in the Civil Wars. His father had been enslaved, presumably as the result of Sulla's harsh anti-Samnite measures, and Horace himself was apparently reduced to penury in the disorders following Julius Caesar's death. To judge from his earliest poems, *The Epodes* and *Satires*, which belong to the period before the Battle of Actium, he was not at first particularly impressed with Augustus' régime. As a matter of fact he had fought, without much distinction, against Octavian and his fellow-triumvirs at Philippi. Yet he soon came to appreciate Augustus' policies sincerely, even though his more matter-of-fact mind could never have been stirred to the same pitch of poetical enthusiasm as Vergil's. Horace realized that under Augustus Italy bade fair to acquire a new sense of well-being and self-respect; and by the year 23 he was a firm supporter of the Principate. The three books of *Odes* published in that year contain many an appreciative reference to the unification of Italy and, above all, to the restoration of order and discipline. The poems themselves are indeed perfect specimens of order and discipline : they are peerless examples of form in verse, in which Horace's earlier metrical crudities have been eliminated. With a deftness of touch, that is by no means so artless as it seems, Horace produces superb lyrics. Yet the thoughts for which they serve as the vehicle seldom rise above the ordinary ; they are common-sense maxims of universal application. This sanity of outlook, however, and the confidence with which it is expressed, are

---

[1] Herein Vergil's own early experiences may be reflected.

sure proofs that the State has found tranquillity. Horace's oft-repeated hedonistic injunction to take the days as they come surely results from his faith in the future. The *Odes* are the high-water mark of Horace's poetry.

In his later works, *The Epistles*, *The Carmen Saeculare* and a fourth book of *Odes*, there is an urbane mellowness that charms. But their atmosphere of comfortable certainty rather suggests that the Principate is becoming firmly entrenched in its smooth but essentially mediocre routine. One feature of these later poems is Horace's insistent protest against the habit of esteeming the ancient poets to the neglect of the moderns. This is of some significance. In the Early Empire there is manifest a distinct archaizing tendency. As men came to play less part in the shaping of the contemporary world, they tended to cast nostalgic eyes towards the past ; one observes this, for instance, in the preface to Livy's History. This was not simply an example of the eternal habit of regarding earlier ages as superior. Under the Principate definite attempts to turn back the clock were made in various fields. In literature, for instance, not only were the early writers admired ; archaic words and turns of expression were assiduously adopted. Some of the emperors, such as Claudius and Domitian, even passed legislation of an antiquarian character.

§ 4.   TIBULLUS AND PROPERTIUS

Of the lesser poets of the age Albius Tibullus, a member of Messalla's literary circle, has bequeathed two books of exceedingly mellifluous elegiac couplets,[1] a metre which, following the lead of Mimnermus of Colophon (*fl.* 600), Latin poets often used for love poems. Tibullus' elegiacs were written early in Augustus' reign,[2] and are in the main inspired by the author's two lady friends whom he describes under the pseudonyms of Delia and Nemesis. But they also reflect the peace and prosperity and recovery from the confiscations of the preceding period which Augustus' Principate brought to rural Italy in general, although apparently not to Tibullus personally (whose family estates seem to have shrunk). The rather languorous tranquillity of Tibullus' poetry suggests the stability which Augustus had brought to the troubled Roman world.

[1] The third book in the Corpus Tibullianum is not by Tibullus.
[2] Tibullus probably died in the same year as Vergil (19 B.C.).

Very different is Tibullus' fellow elegiac poet, the Umbrian Sextus Propertius (c. 50–15 B.C.).[1] He is rather representative of the uncertainty which it was Augustus' supreme achievement to terminate. His four books of elegies are curiously uneven in merit. At his best Propertius is a very fine poet indeed. Unfortunately he was prone to lapse into gross errors of bad taste. Even in its externals his verse is far from consistent, for it contains some of the finest elegiac couplets ever penned as well as some of the most incredible cacophonies. So long as his mistress Cynthia is his inspiration, as in the first two books, Propertius must be ranked with the greatest of poets. But, as was the case with the *affaires* of all the Latin elegiac poets, the romance was marked by neither felicity nor fidelity; and when Cynthia ceases to be the motif, Propertius is only too liable to flounder. He was intensely patriotic: nevertheless for him the idea of the Principate did not apparently bring complete spiritual comfort; at any rate his patron Maecenas vainly encouraged him to seek inspiration in its achievements. It is possible, however, that the Pax Augusta would ultimately have tranquillized Propertius also, had he lived longer. Certainly his last poem, for sustained elegance and good taste, is unsurpassed by anything else he wrote: it is " the queen of elegies."

§ 5.   OVID

P. Ovidius Naso (43 B.C.–A.D. 18), from Sulmo in Central Italy, is usually reckoned one of the elegiac poets, although his most considerable work is in hexameters. He began publishing in 20 B.C. or later, when the Principate was already well established, and the stirring events which had occurred in his childhood inspired him with no impassioned feeling. He wrote partly because it was fashionable to do so,[2] but largely because of his quite extraordinary facility. He has himself described to us the ease with which verses flowed from his pen. But these verses are not the result of a high moral purpose or deep emotion. Even the poems in which he celebrates his various love-affairs (*Amores*) are gracefully superficial: Corinna and the rest meant very little to him, even though, as he himself later insisted,

---

[1] He probably came from Asisium, the modern Assisi.
[2] Cf. Horace's famous " scribimus indocti doctique poemata passim " (*Epp.*, ii, 1, 117).

these amours were not just figments of his imagination. Ovid is pre-eminently the poet of the smart set at Rome, who in the security of the Principate idled their time away frivolously : brilliance rather than seriousness was what they demanded and what Ovid sought to provide. Of his skill there can be no question. Unfortunately he was prone to employ his un-doubted talents for trivial or unworthy ends. He was equally capable of producing adroit sketches of ancient heroines (*Heroides*), a clever dissertation on cosmetics (*Medicamina Faciei Femineae*), or scintillating pornography (*Ars Amatoria, Remedia Amoris*). The latter ran directly counter to Augustus' morality programme, and the Princeps noted it with grave displeasure. When a few years later Ovid committed a second offence by becoming tactlessly privy to some scandal that directly affected the imperial household, Augustus acted.[1] In A.D. 8 the poet was banished from Rome to Tomi (the modern *Constantza*), a dull and dangerous frontier station on the Black Sea. Thereafter Ovid wielded his pen industriously in the hope that the sentence of banishment might be revoked ; a flood of poems (*Tristia, Epistulae ex Ponto*) importuned the emperor and various influential friends. But it was all in vain : Ovid was never to see Rome again. He passed his life away in dreary exile and finally died at Tomi in A.D. 18. His fame, however, rests upon something more substantial than the im-moral trifles that led to his banishment or the lugubrious laments that followed it. In two long poems he shows that he is in the front rank of literary craftsmen. *The Metamorphoses*, in fifteen books of hexameters, is as its name implies, an account of magical transformations. *The Fasti*, in six books of elegiac couplets, is a metrical calendar of the Roman year much infected with the prevailing antiquarianism. In both works Ovid shows such unrivalled dexterity as a story-teller that he has always remained one of the most widely read of poets. But despite the artistry with which he relates episodes from the ancient myths or from Roman history, the impression remains that these works are examples of expertise rather than of genuine inspiration. They are the harbingers of the Silver Age of Latin literature.

[1] The exact nature of the poet's second indiscretion has been end-lessly debated, but remains a mystery.

§ 6. LIVY

The Augustan Age produced a large amount of prose as well as verse. Much of it, however, was of a technical nature, such as Vitruvius' work on architecture and the antiquarian writings of Verrius Flaccus and Hyginus. These, along with various writings in Greek like *The Geography* of Strabo, *The Roman Antiquities* and *Literary Essays* of Dionysius of Halicarnassus and *The Universal History* of Diodorus Siculus, prove that serious scholarship did not languish.[1] But the only prose work that can be considered as a contribution to world literature is Livy's Roman History.

Titus Livius (59 B.C.–A.D. 17), like the other important literary figures, was an Italian, not a Roman in the strict sense. He came from Patavium (*Padua*), a town which down to the time of his birth was Venetic-speaking. Livy himself presumably knew Latin as his mother tongue, his famed Patavinitas having reference to his accent rather than to provincialisms of style. His Latin does indeed differ from that of Caesar or Cicero, but it does not owe its grace, charm and somewhat poetical colouring to his Venetic origin.

Augustus' well-known remark that Livy was a Pompeian should not be taken to mean that he was a republican. Pompey in many ways anticipated Augustus.[2] He was not representative of the narrow circle of Roman aristocrats, who indeed disliked and distrusted him. Pompey's connexions were with Italy, with places like Picenum, rather than with Rome. If Augustus had regarded Livy as favouring a return to the senatorial rule that Julius Caesar overthrew, he would hardly have made him a teacher in the imperial household.[3]

Livy's masterpiece described Roman history from the foundation of the city down to 9 B.C. in one hundred and forty-two books, of which some thirty-five have survived virtually intact, together with summaries of all the lost books except two. Livy

---

[1] With these we might class a Hellenistic universal history in Latin by Pompeius Trogus which survives only in Justin's abridgement, and *The Universal History* of Nicolaus Damascenus in Greek which is not extant ; some fragments of a rather journalistic account of Augustus' education, also by Nicolaus, have survived however.

[2] See, for example, E. Meyer, *Caesars Monarchie und das Principat des Pompeius* ³ (1922).

[3] He taught the future emperor Claudius, son of Augustus' stepson Drusus.

devoted almost one hundred books to the last hundred and fifty years of the period he was describing ; the preceding six hundred years were described in much smaller compass. This enlargement of scale no doubt is partly to be ascribed to the greater wealth of source material for the later period ; but that is not the only explanation, for the annalists of Sulla's day had no difficulty in filling seventy-five or more volumes in their accounts of early Roman history.[1] Presumably Livy too, for all his admiration of the past, was specially interested in Augustus' unification of Italy.

Livy's use of source material is inexpert. Nevertheless his history is a work of art. He is not altogether free of the rhetorical tricks of the prose writers of the next hundred years : his prose style, like Ovid's verse style, anticipates the literature of the Silver Age, but his history was not a mere rhetorical exercise : it was a sincere tribute to Rome's great past and a lasting memorial of it.

[1] Aul. Gell., VI, 9. 17.

PART II

THE JULIO-CLAUDIAN EMPERORS

CHAPTER I

TIBERIUS

§ 1. THE SUCCESSION OF TIBERIUS

AFTER Augustus' death came the problem of effecting the succession. The consuls at once swore an oath of loyalty to his stepson Tiberius, and then administered this oath to the Senate, knights and People.[1] Apparently it was the Senate, acting on the consuls' motion, that actually proclaimed him Emperor. Tiberius professed great reluctance to assume the office; in fact it had to be pressed upon him. His motive in this is uncertain. The ancient sources make the not very subtle suggestion that he was merely playing the rôle of a dissembling hypocrite, a charge which they repeat time and again on other occasions during the reign. But the alleged duplicity of Tiberius does not carry conviction: it is wildly improbable that he was invariably a profound dissembler. Some other explanation must be sought for the curious scene in the year 14.

Perhaps he wanted the Senate to have an apparent freedom of choice, so that the precise method for transferring the imperial powers might be evolved; in other words, he may have been seeking to establish a precedent for the succession. Or it may be that in this, as in so much else, he was simply following Augustus' example: the scene in A.D. 14 is strikingly reminiscent of the scene in 27 B.C., when Augustus likewise had to be " persuaded " to accept the imperial powers.

But we should not dismiss the possibility that Tiberius was genuinely lukewarm about becoming Emperor. Once already he had retired from Rome in order to escape from the atmosphere of the imperial court, and later on he was to do so again. And besides such personal predilections, there were certain other considerations. In the first place, he was not a real Julian. By adoption he was the grandson of one *divus* and

---

[1] The taking of the oath by civilians is a significant departure. Hitherto it had been taken by soldiers as a gesture of loyalty to their commander.

the son of another : but no drop of Julian blood flowed in
his veins, and he probably shared Augustus' justifiable apprehension that the accession of a non-Julian might provoke
disorders.   In the second place, Tiberius may have been dis-
trustful of his ability to play the rôle of Emperor successfully.
The Principate, as Augustus had left it, was not explicitly
defined.   The boundary-line between the respective positions
of Princeps and Senate was not drawn openly, and it needed
considerable finesse to wield the velvet glove of the Emperor
without displaying the iron hand.   Augustus, the inventor of
the Principate, could do it tactfully enough ; as he remarked
on his death-bed, he knew how to act the comedy of life.   With
Tiberius it was otherwise.   He was a member of the old republican aristocracy, and it is quite possible that he was not particularly enamoured of the Principate.   He could not have relished
the prospect of trying to preserve the ill-defined, uneasy and,
in the last analysis, one-sided relations between Princeps and
Senate.   It was not that he feared comparison with Augustus ;
it was simply that he did not possess the master touch.   This
was revealed immediately when he accepted the Imperium
Proconsulare on the same terms as the Tribunician Power, for
life : Augustus had always gone through the formality of getting
it conferred for limited periods, at the end of which it was
invariably renewed.

Throughout his reign Tiberius found the task of reconciling
the old republican forms with the new imperial powers very
difficult.   He could, of course, always copy Augustus' procedure,
and this he did as closely as possible.   Thus, like Augustus after
23, he only assumed the consulship when he wished to introduce
his proposed successors to public attention, Germanicus in 18,
Drusus in 21 and Sejanus in 31.   His attitude to Caesar-
worship was likewise strictly Augustan ; that is, he discouraged
worship of himself, but sometimes found himself obliged to
permit it.[1]   His frontier policy likewise continued that of
Augustus, to an extent indeed that was almost servile.

But situations were bound to arise where there were no
exact Augustan precedents, or where Augustus himself had

[1] The Laconian inscriptions, published in 1928, reveal that he was
not everywhere as successful in suppressing worship of himself as he
apparently was in Further Spain : see Suet., *Tib.* 26.   Text of inscriptions, and commentary by M. Rostovtzeff, in *Revue Historique*, vol. 163
(1930), p. 1 f. ; see too G. Grether in *Amer. Journ. Phil.*, LXVII (1946),
p. 240.

deliberately bequeathed to his successors the task of establishing
the precedents, as in the interpretation of the law of treason.
In such cases Tiberius was no confident innovator. He tried
to take the line which he was convinced that Augustus would
have taken under similar circumstances. But he was still faced
with the difficulty of fitting it into the general scheme of the
Augustan Principate, and he never found this problem easy to
solve. It is this that has earned for him his undeserved reputation for vacillation. No doubt it was also due to this that at
times he had recourse to methods that seemed devious, and
consequently obtained a reputation for hypocrisy. The Senate
might have helped him with sage advice ; and he did genuinely
seek its aid. But it proved unhelpful ; usually he could expect
only servility from it, not independence of mind.

Already in 14 Tiberius, with his long experience, must have
foreseen the difficulties ahead ; hence his reluctance to accept
the imperial powers may not have been altogether feigned. He
actually did accept them because there was no other suitable
candidate at the time. But it is worth noting that he reserved
the right to abdicate later, when a suitable successor might be
expected to be available.

§ 2. MURDER AND MUTINY

Tiberius' reign suffered from a bad start ; it was ushered
in with murder and mutiny. The murder was that of Agrippa
Postumus, the loutish last-born of Agrippa and Julia. Augustus, clinging to a faint hope that even yet Julian blood might
succeed, had adopted him simultaneously with Tiberius. The
old Emperor could scarcely have had any illusions about
Postumus' character : he had himself banished him for brutish-
ness. Tiberius therefore may have been telling the truth when
he said that Augustus, realizing that he himself was at death's
door, had ordered Postumus' execution. The reason would be
obvious. He had obliged Tiberius to elevate Germanicus with
his close Julian connexions over his own son Drusus, a pure
Claudian. Here was potential trouble : each of these young
men, according to Tacitus, had his faction at court, and if
Tiberius suddenly died a struggle for power between them
might ensue. It is improbable that Augustus wanted to com-
plicate the situation still further by leaving Tiberius also with
a rival pretender : the story that Augustus was on the point

of being reconciled with Postumus in A.D. 14 is unconvincing.[1]

In view of all the circumstances, the decision to execute Postumus, while cruel and unjust, was certainly prudent. Even as it was, Postumus' slave Clemens almost succeeded in interesting the Rhine legions on his master's behalf; and two years later he caused Tiberius serious embarrassment by himself posing as Postumus. The murder, then, was carried out possibly at Augustus' order, and apparently without Tiberius' knowledge. Tiberius, however, had to bear the odium of the deed : Tacitus, without specifically accusing him, makes him responsible for it, and men generally noted that the reign commenced with an assassination. Postumus' mother, the profligate Julia, despairing of her banishment ever being revoked, now committed suicide.

Another change occurred almost simultaneously with Tiberius' accession : the Senate, instead of the People, henceforth elected the magistrates. This change had been foreshadowed during Augustus' last years, when consuls and praetors were " designated " by a special electoral college composed of senators and knights (above, pp. 39, 57).

By A.D. 14 the elections to the urban magistracies had become more and more of a formality, as Augustus made increasing use of his powers of control. The transfer of the elections to the Senate merely provoked a little " empty talk " and relieved candidates of the necessity for bribing the urban mob. The Emperor's control was not diminished by the change, though Tiberius did apparently use his right of *suffragatio* on a smaller scale than Augustus : in the elections for praetors his practice was to " commend " four (who were of course automatically elected) and to " nominate " twelve ; as twelve praetors were needed in all (before A.D. 33) the Senate thus obviously had to make some choice.

By making the Senate the sole electoral body Tiberius demonstrated that he was anxious to parade that co-operation between Princeps and Senate which Augustus had fostered. In fact throughout his reign Tiberius, despite his Claudian pride, usually showed great deference to the Senate. He steadfastly refused the *praenomen imperatoris*, which it might find offensive,[2]

---

[1] On the execution of Agrippa Postumus see also M. P. Charlesworth (*Amer. Journ. of Philology*, XLIV (1923), p. 145 f.) and E. Hohl (*Hermes*, 1935, p. 350 f.), who come to similar conclusions to those stated in the text.

[2] With him the title *imperator* was a military title, and not a name. He also refused the title of Pater Patriae ; but, contrary to what is often asserted, he did style himself Augustus. D. McFayden, *History of the Title Imperator*, p. 56.

he allowed it freedom of discussion and encouraged it to act independently. But even though it occasionally adopted proposals against his expressed desires, the Tiberian Senate usually behaved like a subservient but malevolent rubber-stamp.

But at the outset the army proved more of a danger than the Senate. The elevation of any but Julian blood might have been expected to touch off mutinies in the various provincial armies, each of which would seek to elevate its own general to the purple. This was to be demonstrated balefully in 69; but it was adumbrated now in A.D. 14 on the death of the first Princeps.

On the Rhine Tiberius' twenty-nine-year-old nephew and adopted son, the Julian Germanicus, held a proconsular *imperium* which Tiberius had asked the Senate to confer upon him immediately after Augustus' death. Serving under Germanicus were Gaius Silius, who commanded the four legions in Upper Germany,[1] and the veteran Aulus Caecina, who commanded the four in Lower Germany.[2] It was only the Lower army that mutinied, but some of its members even attempted to proclaim Germanicus Emperor. Germanicus' theatrical efforts to restore order do not excite our admiration;[3] but they were ultimately successful.

Meanwhile a revolt had also broken out among the three legions in Pannonia,[4] and their commander Junius Blaesus found the riot hard to quell. Tiberius' son Drusus, who was accompanied by L. Aelius Sejanus, finally brought the unruly soldiers under control by an admirable show of firmness: a timely eclipse of the moon (September 26) enabled him to play on their superstitious fears.

But although the soldiers thus revealed the fatal flaw in the Principate almost at its very beginning, it is only fair to add that these military mutinies on the Rhine and in Pannonia were not the result exclusively or even chiefly of the troops' desire to elevate their own nominee to empire. The legionaries had genuine grievances: they were underpaid, they were being

[1] II Augusta; XIII Gemina; XIV Gemina; XVI.

[2] I; V Alaudae; XX Valeria Victrix; XXI Rapax.

[3] He ended up by encouraging the mutineers to lynch their ring-leaders. He would have done better to copy the conduct of the camp prefect, M'. Ennius, who quieted some *vexillationes* by a determined display of resolution.

[4] VIII Augusta; IX Hispana; XV Apollinaris.

retained with the colours long after their term of service had expired, and they were the victims of bullying by their officers ; and all of this was in glaring contrast with the favoured status of the Praetorians.   It is possible that if the legionaries had not been of inferior human material, their patriotism and loyalty to the State would have restrained them from sedition.   But the legions had recently been brought up to strength from ex-slaves and the city rabble.   In the scare brought about by the Pannonian Revolt (A.D. 6–9) and the Varian Disaster (A.D. 9), Augustus had hurriedly taken his legionaries where he could find them.   The legions in Germany contained many freedmen, who usually were excluded from all the armed forces except the Vigiles ; while the mutineers in Pannonia were led by a former actor named Percennius and a common soldier named Vibulenus. On this occasion both mutinies were quelled when the men received assurances that their grievances would be redressed. But they were an uneasy portent for the future.

§ 3.   TIBERIUS' FRONTIER POLICY

After A.D. 9 Augustus' frontier policy was definitely one of non-aggression.   With Tiberius this policy (*consilium*) became a dogma (*praeceptum*).   He resolutely refused to countenance any extension of the Augustan frontiers or to embroil the Empire in war if he could possibly avoid it.   He was content to bring into a more settled condition areas which Augustus had annexed but had not had time to organize, Pannonia for instance.   Even so, the reign was not entirely devoid of foreign wars.

On the Rhine Germanicus was in charge.   Tiberius merely wanted him to restore Roman prestige, which Varus' defeat and the mutinies had greatly lowered, and firmly to re-establish the Rhine as the boundary between the Roman and the German worlds.   Tiberius' action in 28 in not reincorporating the revolted Frisians shows that his intention was not to re-conquer the trans-Rhenane Germans, but to leave it to their own internal quarrels to distract them from becoming a serious menace.   In this his judgment was vindicated a few years later when Germanic treachery removed the famous Germanic leader, Maroboduus, just as it had Arminius earlier.

Germanicus, however, had other ideas.   Perhaps he thought that active campaigning would restore discipline to legions lately mutinous. But, above all, he was avid of military glory. He certainly fancied himself as a general : his admirer Tacitus even suggests that he was the equal, if not the superior, of Alexander the Great. Between 14 and 16 Germanicus embarked on a series of forays across the Rhine, which Tacitus describes as remarkable, if not remunerative, campaigns. A critical reader, however, will not conceive any great respect for Germanicus' soldierly abilities. Tiberius witnessed these escapades with impotent anxiety. Germanicus had to be allowed some latitude ; he was after all the heir apparent, and he enjoyed great popularity, partly because of his own undoubted affability, partly because he was the son of the well-loved Drusus, but chiefly because of his Julian connexions, and the Julians were especially popular with the Rhine armies. Tiberius finally terminated his nephew's German adventures by recalling him to Rome and loading him with honours : he was granted a splendid triumph (May 26, 17), invested by the Senate with a *maius imperium* and despatched on an important mission to the eastern provinces. The Rhine remained the frontier and after Germanicus' recall the command of all the legions there was never again entrusted to a single person. We hear of barbarian border raids across its upper reaches in Tiberius' last years, but in general it was a firm frontier during his reign.

In central Europe the watch on the Danube was kept by certain Suebi and Marcomanni under a native chieftain Vannius, who were hired for the purpose—a practice which later emperors were to imitate.

In south-eastern Europe Tiberius sought to consolidate the frontier by combining the senatorial provinces of Achaea and Macedonia with Moesia in 15 and putting the whole area under an imperial legate, Poppaeus Sabinus. Greater economy and efficiency of administration probably resulted, and Tiberius' arrangement lasted until 44, when Achaea and Macedonia were restored to the Senate by Claudius.

On the Lower Danube the frontier areas were in the hands of the unreliable Thracians. Augustus had divided Thrace into two client kingdoms, but in 19 one of the kings murdered the other. Thereupon the two Moesian legions [1] moved on Thrace, the surviving king was quickly captured and taken to Rome, and a Roman Resident was sent to the country to keep an eye on the two new kings. For the remainder of Tiberius' reign there

[1] III Scythica ; V Macedonica.

was sporadic but gradually decreasing trouble in Thrace. Romanization proceeded apace as more and more of the natives were recruited into the *auxilia*. It was not until 46, however, that the territory was formally incorporated into the Empire as a province.

Some of the eastern client kingdoms had already undergone absorption. Both Cappadocia and Commagene were formally annexed early in Tiberius' reign, and Cilicia was incorporated in the province of Syria. This scarcely contravened the Augustan policy on frontier extensions, for he had made it unmistakably clear that the client kingdoms possessed no more than an interim status : annexation was always intended as soon as they were sufficiently romanized. Tiberius' object in annexing was to make the eastern frontier as defensibly strong as possible.

In North Africa the Roman territory was beset by the semi-nomadic, semi-civilized tribe of the Musulamii, whose migrations in search of pasturage were liable to provoke clashes with the Roman authorities. The Musulamii were usually more of a nuisance than a menace ; they even had their uses, for auxiliary troops could be recruited from their ranks. In the reign of Tiberius North Africa was the scene of serious trouble. A certain Tacfarinas who, like Arminius before him and Civilis after him, had seen service in the Roman army and was thoroughly conversant with Roman military methods, worried the Romans over a period of seven years (17–24) by repeatedly raiding the senatorial province of Africa. Although invariably worsted in pitched battles Tacfarinas scored numerous successes in guerrilla actions. So serious did his depredations become that in 21 the command in Africa was not given to a senior ex-consul in the usual way but to the Pannonian commander, Junius Blaesus. With one of his own legions [1] and the African legion (III Augusta), he succeeded by scientific and methodical soldiering in shattering Tacfarinas' forces in 22. For this he won the title *imperator*, since officially he was the Senate's general, not the Emperor's. But it was the last time that anyone outside the imperial house was permitted to receive the appellation. Two years later a Roman force surprised and slew Tacfarinas, and Africa obtained peace.

In Gaul meanwhile a rebellion had broken out in 21. It was caused in the first instance by the exactions of Roman

---

[1] IX Hispana.

financiers, but was probably fanned into bigger proportions by
the fanatical Druids. Like every other national religion in
antiquity Druidism was an integral part of the State, and
Gallic resistance to Rome centred about it. As usual, however,
the Gauls were not united. It was the Aedui of Lugdunensis
and the Treveri of Belgica who gave most trouble. Two Roman
citizens, Julius Florus and Julius Sacrovir, the latter possibly
a Druid, headed the rebellion. It would not have been regarded
very seriously if it had not been for the smallness of the Roman
military establishment in Gaul, which normally consisted of some
twelve hundred men. Finally the legions of the Upper Rhine
under Gaius Silius came down and helped the urban cohort of
Lugdunum to crush Sacrovir and his rebels. Silius used his
victory immoderately, and Tiberius was obliged to exile him
three years later for extortion.

§ 4.　TREASON TRIALS

Tiberius, indeed, always strove to promote efficient government in the provinces : even Tacitus, a hostile witness, is
emphatic on that point. It was he who was chiefly responsible
for the improvement in provincial administration under the
Principate. He rendered extortion more difficult and more
dangerous by further suppressing the system of tax-farming and
by encouraging the provincial *concilia* to prefer charges against
peccant governors. He was usually careful to select good
governors : L. Vitellius in Syria (A.D. 35) is an instance. And
his regular practice was to keep them in their provinces for
long periods, an arrangement which increased their experience
and hence their efficiency, and at the same time lessened their
temptation to get rich quick. The most extraordinary instance
of a governor being thus retained was C. Poppaeus Sabinus,
who held Achaea-Macedonia-Moesia for twenty-four years.[1] If
in spite of everything the governors (and this is truer of those
in the senatorial than of those in the imperial provinces) still
proceeded to plunder the provincials, the legal machinery was
relentlessly set in motion. As early as A.D. 15 we find an ex-
governor being condemned for extortion, and others shared his

[1] Other examples of long tenure are : C. Calvisius Sabinus in Pannonia (almost the whole reign) ; P. Cornelius Dolabella in Dalmatia
(14–19) ; L. Apronius in Lower Germany (28–37) ; Lentulus Gaetulicus
in Upper Germany (29–39).

fate before the reign was out. Tiberius' severity became proverbial : justice and efficiency were indeed the twin goals of the reign.

But if the trials of misbehaving governors attest a praiseworthy determination on Tiberius' part to obtain good government, other legal proceedings of his reign have from ancient times evoked a chorus of indignation. These were the trials resulting from Augustus' legislation, and above all from his revised law of treason. Tacitus describes how the reign of Tiberius gradually degenerated owing to the way in which the laws of treason were invoked and to the growth of the accompanying evil of the professional informers (delatores). He implies that Tiberius' interpretation of the law of treason was tantamount to judicial murder. But a study of Tacitus' own account of the treason trials will scarcely support this view.

Although Augustus had passed laws defining the crime of treason more exactly, he had been hesitant to invoke them. It was left to his successor to do that, and thus to determine exactly how the laws should be interpreted : and Tacitus makes it pretty clear that many of the treason trials were test cases, the primary object of which was to establish precedents. It is difficult to understand otherwise why so many of them were quashed as frivolous, or why Tiberius frequently intervened either to mitigate the sentence or even to pardon completely. There may be some basis of fact for Tacitus' picture of a gradually developing reign of terror, in which the delatores, at first suppressed,[1] ultimately were allowed to run amok and procure condemnations on trumped-up and irresponsible charges : the two years in which there were certainly no treason trials at all are both comparatively early, 18 and 27. Tiberius' Claudian pride might have grown increasingly resentful of lampoons ; yet it is impossible to prove that any person in the whole reign was ever punished merely for slandering the Emperor; indeed Tiberius ruled that derogatory remarks against him and his mother were not to be considered grounds for punishment. Even if acquittals did become rather less frequent as the reign progressed, there is a simpler explanation for this than to assume that despotism was becoming more marked : once test cases have established the exact application of a law, it is

[1] Tiberius took very strong measures against them ; he systematically punished false accusers.

inherently probable that prosecutors will make sure of their ground before instituting proceedings. And even for the latter part of the reign Tacitus' picture is exaggerated, for the convictions were not as numerous as he implies. It is not easy to determine exactly how many treason trials there were, since often the accused had to face other charges simultaneously : Tacitus regards them all indiscriminately as treason trials. Recent research, however, has shown that in the whole twenty-two years of Tiberius' reign not more than fifty-two persons were accused of treason, of whom almost half escaped conviction, while the four innocent people to be condemned fell victims to the excessive zeal of the Senate, not to the Emperor's tyranny.[1]

This, of course, did not render the system any less censurable, since the practice of encouraging private citizens to initiate prosecutions against their fellows for pecuniary gain inevitably leads to abuses. Tiberius, of course, was not responsible for it, for it derived from the fact that there was no Crown Attorney or official state prosecutor in ancient Rome. In default of some other system Tiberius had to use the *delatores*. The informer system was not confined to the treason trials ; violations of Augustus' social legislation were prosecuted in the same way. But it was in the treason trials that the personal advantage which the informer could hope to gain was greatest. If his prosecution was successful, he was given a portion (usually one-fourth but sometimes more) of his victim's property. The prospect of such rewards inevitably tempted unscrupulous men to trump up charges against the wealthy, and the *delatores* became one of the great scandals of the Empire.

Usually the trials were conducted before the Senate. In fact, it was in Tiberius' reign that the jurisdictional powers of the Senate first manifested themselves on a big scale ; the Senate gradually replaced the praetorian *quaestio* as the court where treason trials were heard.

The trials began quite early in the reign, and in 16 one of more than ordinary interest came up. Libo Scribonius Drusus, member of a great Roman family, was accused of resorting to

---

[1] Of the twelve executed, Tiberius expressly ordered the deaths of eight (all obviously guilty). The latest trials probably incurred particular odium because the property of the condemned, less the informers' share of it, sometimes went elsewhere than to the public *aerarium* : see Tac., *Ann.*, IV, 20 ; VI, 2 ; VI, 19.

supernatural magic in order to achieve treacherous ends.[1] He committed suicide to avoid certain condemnation. Other condemnations were to follow ; Tacitus draws a picture of " cruel orders, continuous prosecutions, treacherous friendships, the ruin of the innocent." His words have given rise to the suggestion that Tiberius began that systematic extermination of the old Roman nobility and its substitution by a new one, which by the year 70 was virtually complete. This view is untenable. Tiberius was, in fact, continuing the policy of Augustus : [2] so far from initiating the process, he did not even accelerate it, for his own prejudices were aristocratic and in favour of the republican nobility. We know of more than one instance where he gave money grants to members of the old aristocracy and thus enabled them to remain in the Senatorial Order.

No doubt the old nobility were not disposed to regard Tiberius, any more than Augustus, as superior to themselves. They resented his pre-eminence as they had that of his step-father before him. Some indeed felt that they, rather than he, should be Princeps ; and they engaged in conspiracies against him, just as they had against his predecessor—in fact there were more conspiracies against Tiberius than there had been against Augustus. Treason trials and condemnations were the inevitable result, and they may have become more numerous as the reign progressed. But they were not directed exclusively against the old republican families, although some of these were embroiled, with the result that the old nobility lost some of its members.

§ 5. GERMANICUS AND PISO

The most famous trial of the reign was that of Cn. Calpurnius Piso, which was closely connected with the career and death of the Emperor's genial but obstreperous nephew, Germanicus. After the latter's recall from the Rhine in 17 he was sent as a virtual plenipotentiary to the east. The Armenian question had suddenly become acute again, since the Parthian king

[1] Tiberius, despite his association with Chaldaean seers during his sojourns on Rhodes and Capreae, frowned on foreign superstitions : in 16 he banished astrologers and magicians from Italy, and in 19 Jews and Isis-worshippers.

[2] See above, p. 48.

Artabanus had expelled the Roman nominee from the throne
of Armenia in order to elevate his own brother, Orodes.
Germanicus' task was to instal a Roman appointee in Armenia
without endangering pacific relations with Parthia. He was
given authority commensurate with his princely rank, being
invested with a *maius imperium*, which made the governors of
the eastern provinces technically his subordinates.

Tiberius had to entrust this mission to his nephew : to give
it to some one else would have been too direct an affront to
the heir apparent. Moreover it was desirable for the destined
successor to familiarize himself with frontier conditions in the
east as well as in the west. At the same time, however, Tiberius
had no high opinion of Germanicus' capacities. After his
performances on the Rhine he was only too likely to involve
the Empire in war with Parthia. Tiberius decided therefore
to send to the east simultaneously a man who might keep an
eye on the prince and, so far as possible, restrain him from major
indiscretions. The man selected was Cn. Calpurnius Piso, who
came from a very old and very proud Roman family and had
once been Tiberius' colleague in the consulship ; the natural
determination of his character was stultified by an arrogant
hotheadedness that made him appear merely obstinate. Piso
was now appointed governor of Syria (with secret instructions,
according to Tacitus), in place of Germanicus' friend, Creticus
Silanus.[1]

Whatever Tiberius may have intended it to be, Germanicus'
mission developed into a kind of triumphant but leisurely grand
tour through the east. His appearance at Athens with only
one lictor emphasized his respect for the rights of that " allied
city." He travelled through the Aegean, redressing grievances
and manifesting an appropriate interest in the local antiquities.
He established a popular king, Artaxias, on the Armenian throne.
He conciliated the newly established provinces of Cappadocia
and Commagene by empowering his legates to remit their
tribute. In 18 he met Artabanus of Parthia on the Euphrates
and arranged a compromise which was to endure throughout
Tiberius' reign except for some temporary trouble in 34, when
Artaxias of Armenia died. Germanicus also established a
Roman Resident in the desert caravan-city of Palmyra. Then
he went on to Egypt, where his behaviour was much the same

[1] Creticus' daughter had recently been betrothed to Germanicus'
son, Nero.

as it had been in the Aegean : he evinced a lively and even excessive interest in Egyptian antiquities and redressed grievances ; he opened the state granaries and reduced the price of grain in Alexandria.

In all this there was obviously much that was praiseworthy. Unfortunately it was coupled with much that was highly imprudent. Germanicus' headstrong vanity was not content with the extravagant honours which were everywhere showered upon him, he was eager to make an ostentatious display. He may not indeed have issued the silver coins with his own head on them which celebrate his Armenian settlement ; his son Gaius, when Emperor, probably struck them. But there were other undoubted actions of his that were injudicious. He was, for instance, over-anxious to parade Rome's military might in Armenia. Above all there was his visit to Egypt. This action was definitely illegal, since members of the Senatorial Order were expressly forbidden to set foot on Egyptian soil. The Prefect of Egypt, Gaius Galerius (?), could hardly have refused admission to one of his rank. If Germanicus thought about the matter at all he probably argued that, as a Julian and as a holder of *maius imperium,* he, like Gaius Caesar years before, needed no special permission to enter Egypt. Tiberius strongly criticized in the Senate an action which had occurred before he could stop it.

Piso meanwhile interpreted his commission to restrain the prince as authority to counteract Germanicus' arrangements. His position was undoubtedly difficult. Technically he was the subordinate of Germanicus, so that the most he should have done was tactfully to offer advice. Actually what he did was to refuse Germanicus military support, without which Germanicus' authority was liable to be undermined. Moreover, the relations between the two men's womenfolk exacerbated the situation. Germanicus' wife Agrippina, acutely conscious that she was Augustus' only surviving grandchild, had already shown on the Rhine that she was as opinionated as her husband ; and Piso's wife Plancina, the intimate of the Empress-mother Livia, was no model of humility. The two women quarrelled bitterly.

The upshot was that "Piso determined to leave Syria," apparently at Germanicus' order.[1] The order was of doubtful legality, but Piso's attempt to prejudice the Syrian troops

[1] Germanicus significantly had Cn. Sentius Saturninus ready to fill Piso's place the moment he left.

against Germanicus was also an egregious *faux pas*; for it was quite unlikely that the soldiers would stir against the most popular member of the imperial household, especially when he was Piso's superior. But hardly had Piso left his province than Germanicus fell sick and died (October 10, 19), accusing Piso on his death-bed of having poisoned him.

Piso now seems to have lost his head completely. He attempted to recover Syria by force, but at the same time he did not prevent Germanicus' wife and friends from preceding him to Rome, where they, of course, at once accused him of murder. Piso was recalled to Rome and put on trial. At first the proposal apparently was to charge him in the regular *quaestio de sicariis*; but ultimately he was brought before the High Court of the Senate. There Piso easily cleared himself of the charge of poisoning Germanicus. But he was also accused of misconduct in and out of his province. Of this he was undoubtedly guilty. By inciting the troops against his superior and subsequently attempting to recover his province by force he had put himself outside the pale of even the Emperor's intervention, though presumably Tiberius would have liked to save him. Foreseeing his certain condemnation the unhappy man committed suicide. His aim presumably was to save his family and estate; but his action convinced many men that he might have been guilty of poisoning Germanicus after all, and Agrippina encouraged the rumour that he had done so at the orders of Tiberius, who wanted his real son, Drusus, to be his successor. No responsible student to-day believes this wildly improbable story. In antiquity, however, it was otherwise. Tacitus records a rumour that Tiberius had promised to save Piso but subsequently had him executed to prevent him producing documents compromising to the Emperor. Moreover both Tiberius and his mother Livia, or Julia Augusta as she was now called, rather tactlessly stood aloof from the widespread mourning for the popular Germanicus. Tiberius, indeed, seems to have made little effort in the way of counter-propaganda to the slanders of the waspish Agrippina.

§ 6.   THE RISE OF SEJANUS

From the outset Tiberius had not been enamoured of his imperial responsibility. He had not resigned it, possibly because he was anxious for his heir to obtain the maximum experience before becoming Emperor. There is no evidence that Tiberius planned to depart from Augustus' arrangement whereby a Julian (Germanicus) would ultimately become Princeps. He doubtless felt that only a Julian could command the unquestioning loyalty of all the provincial armies : the elevation of any other family would provoke revolts from rival pretenders. But with Germanicus now dead, the succession seemed destined to pass to someone who had no Julian blood at all. Tiberius' own son Drusus was almost of an age with Germanicus and his wife Livilla, Germanicus' sister, was of Julian ancestry ; she bore him twin sons in 19 (Tiberius Gemellus and another Germanicus). Drusus may not have been exactly a model character : his morals apparently were not unexceptional, and his bloodthirsty delight in gladiatorial shows was not the happiest augury for his probable behaviour if he should ever reach a position of unbridled power. But it was his non-Julian blood rather than his character that had caused Augustus to insist that Tiberius should prefer Germanicus to him for the succession. The only honour conferred upon Drusus during Augustus' lifetime was the quaestorship in A.D. 11. Tiberius had loyally obeyed Augustus' orders in the matter of the succession, but he scarcely shared Augustus' anti-Claudian bias. Hence shortly after his succession he had made Drusus consul (15) and began to employ him for various official duties which he discharged competently enough. In A.D. 20 Drusus was destined for the highest post of all, although it seems that, like his father before him, he was obliged to recognize the prior rights of the Julians (Germanicus' sons) over his own sons for the future succession.

Beginning with the year 21 Tiberius' absences from the capital became both frequent and prolonged. Perhaps he was leaving the way open for Drusus to obtain administrative experience. In 21 Drusus was named consul for the second time, and in the next year was formally marked out for the succession by the grant of Tribunician Power. He did not, however, find co-operation easy with his father's most trusted adviser. This was L. Aelius Sejanus, the son and colleague of a Prefect of the Praetorian Guard and since 17 himself the sole Prefect. Sejanus had already displayed his talents under Augustus, and Tiberius reposed the same unbounded confidence in him that Augustus had done in Agrippa. Drusus' antipathy ultimately no doubt would have foiled Sejanus' ambitions. But

Drusus died suddenly on September 14, 23, and one of his twin sons [1] quickly followed him. Sejanus' wife Apicata later asserted that he had seduced Drusus' wife Livilla and induced her to poison her husband. The story may be true, for Livilla presumably resented her husband's recognition of Germanicus' sons instead of her own as next in line for the succession, and Sejanus certainly divorced his wife and in 25 sought Tiberius' permission to marry Livilla (unavailingly, as it happened). Livilla's suicide after Sejanus' death would also seem to support the story.

The death of Drusus seems to have increased Tiberius' natural moodiness : Tacitus, indeed, emphatically asserts that it was now that the really marked and rapid degeneration in the reign began. For the ensuing tragedy the direct responsibility is usually attributed to Sejanus. But Tiberius connived at, if he did not actually encourage, it. Nor are Agrippina and her friends, by their plots and slanders, altogether free from blame. They, however, were to be the victims. What appears to be a regular persecution of the friends and family of Germanicus soon began. Sejanus, so it is said, was the actual agent of persecution, since he was aiming at the succession. [2] Germanicus' children would obviously constitute obstacles in his path. He therefore cleverly exploited the latent rivalry between the Julian and Claudian houses.

Tiberius allowed Sejanus to excite his jealous fears of Agrippina and her children, since he was tired of her venomous tongue and disapproved of the excessive enthusiasm of the Senate and People for her sons. The two eldest of these sons [3] would be the heirs apparent, at least until Tiberius' remaining grandson (Tiberius Gemellus) grew up. They in fact would be Gemellus' guardians. Sejanus decided to supplant them, and Tiberius does not seem to have been unwilling for the change. Apparently it was only later that he decided that Sejanus' intrigues against Germanicus' family were anything but disinterested.

In the year 23 Sejanus concentrated the Praetorian Cohorts, which hitherto had been stationed throughout Italy, in a single

---

[1] The so-called Germanicus.

[2] He came of a family, which while not distinguished was not altogether obscure : on his mother's side he was descended from the old nobility ; his father was a wealthy equestrian.

[3] Nero and Drusus.

camp on the outskirts of Rome. Tiberius probably acquiesced in this move at the time in question because of the menacing attitude of Agrippina and her party; prior to 23 Drusus had opposed it. The move increased the power of the Praetorian Prefect, who also obtained many other honours and powers from Tiberius, especially after he had saved the Emperor's life at the risk of his own in a collapsed cave (26).

§ 7. THE FALL OF SEJANUS

After that year Sejanus' intrigues, which hitherto had been directed chiefly against Agrippina's influential friends rather than against her immediate family, became bolder, and were doubtless facilitated by her own tactlessness, by the ambiguities of the treason laws and by the Emperor's permanent withdrawal from Rome. In 26 Tiberius left the capital for ever. He went to the lovely island of Capreae in the Bay of Naples, where memorials of his presence can still be seen. His motive, according to the ancient sources, was to indulge in lustful excesses. But the presence of serious scholars on the island with him is conclusive : Tiberius did not go there to practise vice. Nor is it likely that he went there to escape his mother's attempts to influence him unduly. Nor was he trying to escape work : he still laboured as hard as ever for the Empire. Possibly his aims were, first, to enable his successor to obtain experience and, secondly, to escape Agrippina's intrigues on a natural island fortress. But the retirement was an error of judgment. If it did nothing else, it advertised the craven dependence of the Senate upon him. This was all the more glaring since Tiberius had now apparently dispensed with the advice of a Senate Committee. On Capreae he does not seem even to have availed himself much of the counsel of his official " friends," something which the emperors regularly did.

Sejanus' intrigues now had greater scope. He is even said to have played successfully upon the ambitions of Agrippina's second son, Drusus, in order to plot the ruin of the elder, Nero. But the full ruin of Agrippina was not encompassed until after the death of Empress-mother Livia in 29.[1] She did not care much for Agrippina : in fact the personal relations of the two women were marked by considerable acrimony. Livia, however, was contemptuous rather than fearful of her grandson's widow, and she did not permit the younger woman's folly to

[1] She was now officially Julia Augusta, Augustus having made her a Julian to facilitate her son's succession.

bring her to disaster. But with Livia gone, disaster soon struck.
In the very year of Livia's death (29) Agrippina and her elder
son Nero were banished. Apparently they were not actually
charged with conspiracy, although they may well have been
guilty of it. Agrippina's foolish tongue was in itself enough to
get her into trouble, as indeed her dying husband had foreseen ;
he had warned her not " to provoke the stronger by jealousy
of their power." Her eldest son, Nero, was hounded to suicide
and her second, Drusus, imprisoned in Rome in 30.[1]

Sejanus now seems to have overreached himself. The surviving records are fragmentary and by no means explicit, but
they imply that the favourite, waxing impatient, was now
plotting to expedite his own accession. The powerful position
he had attained is proved by his matrimonial connexions with
the imperial house : himself betrothed to Tiberius' granddaughter, his daughter had been engaged to the future Emperor
Claudius' son. Tiberius himself may have been the object of
Sejanus' plot. But it was the younger males of the imperial
house who stood in the more immediate peril. These were
Tiberius Gemellus, Tiberius' grandson, and Germanicus' remaining sons, Drusus and Gaius. With Drusus incarcerated, Gaius
was now the heir apparent. Whatever Sejanus' designs against
Gaius may have been they were foiled. Tiberius' suspicions
were aroused by his sister-in-law Antonia, Germanicus' mother,
with whom he had always been on good terms. In 31, when he
ostensibly honoured Sejanus by granting him Imperium Proconsulare and becoming his colleague in the consulship, he acted.
Gaius was called to Capreae, and in October Tiberius sent
Naevius Sutorius Macro to Rome with the secret commission to
replace Sejanus as Praetorian Prefect. The Emperor had to act
clandestinely, since he had little armed force at his disposal on
Capreae, while Sejanus at Rome had the Guard. Macro brought
with him a despatch which, after a long and vague preamble,
suddenly denounced the favourite. What followed was vividly
described by the satirist Juvenal writing about a hundred
years later.[2] Sejanus at once found himself virtually friendless
and universally detested. He was hurried to prison and executed the same day. His partisans naturally shared his fate :
they included, however, only one ex-consul.

[1] The latter is said to have become mad and was executed in 33, the
year which also witnessed Agrippina's death.
[2] Satire X, 71 : verbosa et grandis epistula venit a Capreis.

§ 8. GOVERNMENT FROM CAPREAE

After the fall of Sejanus Tiberius' fears of revolt or assassination increased. He continued to avoid Rome, mostly living on Capreae.[1] He did not, however, neglect matters of state. Increasing weariness may explain why in his last years he retained governors on the Rhine who certainly left something to be desired. But it is equally possible that his fear of conspiracies explains his reluctance to send really strong men to the armies that were notoriously the most pro-Julian. Most emphatically he neglected neither Italy nor the Empire. Even Rome, a place for which he entertained an obvious dislike, was efficiently administered by him to the very end.

Like Augustus before him, he became personally responsible through his *curatores* for some of the essential services of the city proper. Apparently it was he who separated the *curatores riparum et alvei Tiberis*, whose main task was to take flood precaution measures, from the *curatores locorum publicorum*, who reclaimed public property which had passed into private ownership. Nor did he depart from Augustus' practice of appointing a City Prefect. Indeed under Tiberius this official was not just an occasional appointment ; possibly as a result of the Emperor's lengthy absences from the capital, the City Prefect became a permanent and very important official. The Urban Cohorts were put at his disposal, and he thus became responsible for maintaining law and order in the city. This entailed the exercise of wide jurisdictional powers over the urban mob, such as we find the Prefect wielding in Nero's reign. In other words, the City Prefect, who was responsible directly to the Emperor, became more authoritative than the urban magistrates proper : his court gradually supplanted the *quaestiones*.

In Italy, apart from Rome, Tiberius was mindful of his responsibilities to the very end of his reign. In 19 he provided large subsidies to permit the price of grain to be lowered. In 27 he took energetic relief measures, when the collapse of an amphitheatre at Fidenae killed or wounded the incredible number of 50,000 spectators. In 33 he vigorously attempted to alleviate the financial crisis brought about by a currency shortage : [2] he lent the treasury 100,000,000 sesterces, interest free, to put in

---

[1] In 32 he visited his gardens on the Tiber bank ; in 33 he came within four miles of Rome ; in 34 he was at Tusculum. But he never entered the city proper.

[2] The coins were being drained off to the provinces and the Far East.

circulation. In 36 he disbursed a similar sum to repair the ravages of a disastrous fire on the Aventine. Such acts of generosity, which were by no means confined to Italy, were rendered possible by his efficient supervision of the Empire's resources. He was particularly careful to eliminate all unnecessary public expense. Heavy military disbursements in the last years of Augustus' reign had bequeathed a depleted treasury to Tiberius. Perhaps it was this that enjoined measures of the strictest economy upon him : at any rate his reign was anything but financially extravagant. By avoiding wars, by largely eliminating public gladiatorial shows, and by embarking on few public building projects in the capital,[1] he kept expenses down. His own personal habits were frugal and austere, his court entailed no costly upkeep. Thus he was able not only to afford generous gestures but also to reduce the unpopular sales tax from 1 to $\frac{1}{2}$ per cent temporarily. The fortune he bequeathed to his successor amounted to 2,700,000,000 sesterces (some sources say 3,300,000,000).

His provincial administration manifested the same anxious care. In 17, when a severe earthquake ravaged the east, all Roman taxes were remitted for the senatorial province of Asia for a period of five years. Sardis and other cities received similar aid after earthquakes in 24 and 29, and the Emperor gave sorely stricken Sardis a liberal relief grant from his own purse. The Roman authorities settled internal disputes in the provinces rigorously but impartially : thus in 22 the abuse of asylum rights in eastern temples was terminated, and in 25 the secular quarrel of Lacedaemonians and Messenians was finally settled. Provincial communications were carefully supervised. Perhaps Tiberius should not be credited with road improvements in the senatorial provinces of Africa and Narbonensis, but he was certainly responsible for the building of roads and bridges in Syria, Spain, Moesia, and above all in Dalmatia and Pannonia. Moreover, in marked contrast with Italy under Tiberius, the provinces witnessed a good deal of public building, including even the establishment of whole cities. The provincials showed their appreciation of his scrupulous government : more than one province, despite official discouragement, attempted to worship Tiberius as a god.

[1] The restoration of Pompey's theatre and the languid construction of a temple to the Deified Augustus and the erection of a huge palace on the Palatine are the reign's principal building activities in Rome.

§ 9. TIBERIUS AND THE SUCCESSION

Nor did Tiberius neglect the problem of the succession. But after the deaths of Germanicus, Drusus and Sejanus it was not an easy problem to solve when Tiberius gave it fresh attention in 35. His own grandson Tiberius Gemellus, Drusus' son, was really too young, being only sixteen. The other possibility was his great-nephew, Germanicus' son Gaius, nicknamed Caligula, from the fact that his childhood had been spent in a soldier's camp where he had been arrayed in baby military boots (*caligae*). He was rather older than Gemellus, and was of Julian blood.[1] These twin advantages normally would have settled the issue in his favour. At the very least they meant that Tiberius dare not pass him by, even though he wanted to do so. Tiberius was well aware of the grave defects in Gaius' character : Suetonius implies that he regarded him as a potential murderer capable of ruining the Empire.

Tiberius tried to solve the problem by naming both Gemellus and Gaius as his co-heirs. He knew that, if he himself were to die soon, Gaius as the Julian and the elder would succeed. But he probably hoped to live long enough for Gemellus to grow up, when he might find some means for ensuring his succession : he could hope for Gemellus to become disembarrassed of Gaius in somewhat the same way that he himself had ultimately become disembarrassed of Agrippa Postumus. Meanwhile, distrusting Gaius, Tiberius did not give him any responsible office or administrative post to fill, but kept him at Capreae, possibly to shield him from conspiratorial intrigues, but more probably to keep an eye on him.

However, if the seventy-eight-year-old Tiberius hoped to live long enough to train Gemellus and ensure the relegation of Gaius, he was doomed to disappointment. In 37, feeling that his last illness had come upon him, he left Capreae for the mainland. But death quickly overtook him at Misenum on March 16. Gaius was with him at the end and obviously profited from his death. There is, however, no evidence to substantiate the rumour that he hastened the old man on his way.

---

[1] His father, Germanicus, had been the grandson of Augustus' sister ; his mother, Agrippina, had been the actual granddaughter of Augustus ; and he himself had been born at Antium, the site of the sanctuary of the Julian *gens*.

§ 10. APPRAISAL OF THE REIGN

Tiberius was a man of very considerable abilities.[1] On many an occasion, both before and after his accession, he demonstrated his capacity. Yet neither in ancient nor in modern times has his character won whole-hearted approval. Tacitus' picture of him is no doubt coloured by that historian's experience of life under an autocrat who made Tiberius' memoirs his favourite reading and who was consequently thought by Tacitus to have made Tiberius his model. But it should be remembered that Seneca and the Elder Pliny, both of whom lived through Tiberius' reign, give some support to Tacitus.

The Senate's point-blank refusal to accord him divine honours posthumously indicates that he had inspired no great affection in the hearts of the upper classes. The soldier historian, Velleius Paterculus, seems to be an exception to this. But Velleius was writing in 30 and probably missed the last and gloomier years entirely : in any event his enthusiasm for Tiberius was little more than calculating flattery.

But if he inspired no great enthusiasm among his contemporaries, Tiberius was not universally hated. If he had been, his memory surely would have been condemned ; whereas the evidence suggests that it was not : his head would hardly have appeared among the coin types of Titus, Domitian and Trajan, and his name would hardly have been mentioned in Vespasian's *Lex de Imperio*, if he had anticipated Nero in suffering *abolitio memoriae*.

But the reserved, austere Emperor evidently suffered from serious faults of temper. Nor can he be entirely absolved of grievous errors of judgment. The appointment of Piso, the reliance first on Sejanus and subsequently on Macro, the retirement to Capreae, the retention of the worthless Pilate as a provincial governor for ten years, must all be classed as mistakes.[2] In some instances Tiberius may have noted his own error in time : this may explain the curious cases of L. Arruntius and Aelius Lamia, who were appointed governors respectively of

[1] His virtues : Liberalitas, Providentia, Clementia, Moderatio (see R. S. Rogers, *Studies in the Reign of Tiberius, passim*).

[2] Some of the things that happened in Judaea under Pilate's régime probably never reached Tiberius' notice : the crucifixion of Christ, for instance. But it is impossible that he remained completely in the dark about Pilate for ten years. Perhaps he had difficulty in finding a successor : competent men were notoriously reluctant to go to Judaea.

Spain and Syria, but by an afterthought were not allowed to leave Rome.

Some of these errors of judgment derived perhaps from the Emperor's own unhappiness.[1] His personal life had been sad before he became Princeps, and it became even sadder afterwards. The folly of Germanicus, the death of Drusus, the treachery of Sejanus, the evil promise of Gaius, were cumulative blows. There is no need to doubt that Tiberius became increasingly gloomy, and a judgment that is clouded by sorrow is only too likely to be faulty. Besides this, he was conscious of the inner contradiction in the Principate. He was called upon to preside over a delicately balanced system in which one party (the Princeps) possessed the real authority and another party (the Senate) the semblance of it.[2] The system was not of Tiberius' making, and probably not to his liking. Yet he was the one who had to direct its further development. And development there certainly would be : the old order always changes and yields place to something new. Tiberius did not shirk the task of direction : but is it surprising if he was guilty of occasional errors of judgment in discharging it ?

[1] *Tristissimus homo :* Pliny, *H.N.*, XXVIII, 231.
[2] Cf. Seneca, *de clem.*, I. 4. 3.

CHAPTER II

GAIUS

§ 1. THE BEGINNING OF THE REIGN

THANKS largely to the good offices of Macro, Gaius succeeded his great-uncle without incident (March 18, 37). The Senate apparently voted him the imperial honours ; but it probably had some qualms about him because of his youth. His age normally admitted one only to the lowest major office in the senatorial *cursus* ; as he had not even assumed the *toga virilis* until A.D. 32, the general impression of his youthfulness must have been very strong. Nor was he experienced : he had merely been made a pontifex in 31 and been named quaestor in 33.   However, Augustus' desire for a successor of Julian blood now materialized.   Gaius was far more truly a Julian than his father Germanicus and himself insisted on his Julian connexions ; he had even married into the family, his wife being the daughter of Junius Silanus, a descendant of Augustus.

The senatorial nobility, however, was not favourably disposed towards him, partly because of his youth and partly because Sejanus had got rid of most Julian partisans in the Senate. The Equestrian Order, on the other hand, seems to have supported him throughout his reign. And the populace in general throughout the Empire, as numerous inscriptions testify, welcomed the accession of a son of Germanicus with enthusiasm.

At first, probably on the advice of his grandmother Antonia, the young Emperor tried to conciliate the nobility. He abruptly curbed the activities of the *delatores* and quashed all impending treason trials. Gaius also showered honours on the Claudian family, which, although not generally popular, was preferred to the Julian by the old nobility. He adopted Tiberius Gemellus and made him Princeps Iuventutis ; and he dragged his uncle, the forty-seven-year-old Claudius, away from his antiquarian pursuits to make him his colleague in the consulship and to marry him into the Julian family : Claudius took as his wife, his third, Valeria Messalina, who was related to Augustus on both sides. In effect, Gaius was proclaiming Gemellus as his successor, with Claudius as Emperor-regent in case of necessity.

To the populace at large he paid out the legacies of Tiberius and Livia, distributed largesse twice within four months, imitated Tiberius in having the unpopular sales tax reduced, and provided spectacular games and shows : he even temporarily restored the *comitia* to the people.

He also attempted to gain universal popularity by a vigorous foreign policy. Ever since Julius Caesar visited it, Roman sentiment had expected and even demanded the annexation of Britain. Augustus prudently conveyed the impression through his court poets that the conquest was always imminent. Actually, remembering Julius' difficulties with Gaul, he never seriously contemplated it.[1] Tiberius, of course, followed Augustus' example : but during his reign there was much peaceful penetration of the island and Roman influence became very marked.[2] Gaius knew that a British expedition would fire the popular imagination. There was also the consideration, natural for a Julian, that it would enable him to get to know the army. His northern expedition was planned early in the reign. And he had a pretext : he could allege that a renegade British prince Adminius (Amminius), son of Cunobelinus,[3] had handed over the island to him. But he could not move immediately owing to a serious illness in 37.[4]

After his recovery the character of the reign changed for the worse, for Gaius decided henceforth to be an absolute monarch. It may be that, realizing how a malicious Senate had manoeuvred him into accepting extravagant honours,[5] he determined to live up to them; but it is more probable that his natural inclination was towards despotism, for Gaius was eccentric ; his successor, indeed, called him mad. This possibly is abuse of the type Emperors frequently employed in order to contrast their own reigns favourably with those that preceded. But Gaius did suffer from epileptic fits ; nor are all of the curious

[1] Dio mentions abortive British expeditions in 34, 27, 26. Strabo (IV, 5, 3, p. 200) says Augustus thought conquest unprofitable. Gaius knew that the average Roman regarded *virtus* (i.e. bravery as displayed in successful war) as an emperor's most laudable quality : cf. M. P. Charlesworth in *Journ. Rom. Stud.*, XXXIII (1943), p. 3. Cf. too *Odes* I, 35, 29 f. ; Verg., *Georg.*, III, 25.

[2] The coins of Southern British tribes bear representations of Greco-Roman divinities and are inscribed in Latin.

[3] The Cymbeline of Shakespeare.   [4] Probably a nervous breakdown.

[5] E.g. he, a mere youth, was ultimately induced to accept the title of Pater Patriae, which Tiberius had steadfastly refused. Such giddiness demonstrated that he was a worthy object for conspiracy.

actions attributed to him susceptible of a really rational explanation.

§ 2.　THE DIVINITY OF GAIUS

Gaius' exercise of the imperial power was independent, not to say irresponsible. The vagueness of the boundary line between imperial and senatorial authority conveniently suited his purposes. Of his two illustrious great-grandfathers he chose Antony rather than Augustus as his model. He quickly made it evident that he would dispense with the services of the Senate. The respect he at first prudently paid it had evoked flattery and servility but no genuine attempt to be helpful. Under similar circumstances Tiberius had displayed a weary patience; the more youthful Gaius could not conceal his contempt. From the end of 37 on he either completely ignored or else deliberately humiliated the Senate. He openly asserted that he would overthrow it rather than co-operate with it. He put an end to the Senate's exclusive right of coinage in Rome by himself issuing coins there.[1] He did not bother to use a Senate Committee, and he even made senators prostrate themselves before him. Beginning with the year 39, to parade his supremacy still more openly, he regularly became one of the annual consuls.

Apparently he justified this behaviour by a theory of divine right. He had Julian blood, and the Principate belonged to the Julian branch of the imperial family. The house whose continuing welfare was the object of Caesar-worship was the Julian: it was the *domus divina*. And Gaius emphasized the Julian connexion with divinity. Very early in his reign (August, 37) he dedicated the Temple of the Deified Augustus with great *éclat*; he stressed his relationship with the deified Julians (Julius and Augustus) and dissociated himself from the undeified Claudians. Then he claimed divinity for himself by announcing himself a god-ruler, a veritable Hellenistic monarch. Perhaps he planned to convert the Principate into an oriental monarchy. His intimate adviser, the oriental prince Herod Agrippa I, may have given him these notions : that is, if the direct descendant of Mark Antony needed a councillor in such matters. Just like an oriental monarch, Gaius is said to have committed incest with his sisters, and the charge may be true. Romans

[1] The gold and silver issues which hitherto had been minted at Lugdunum.

normally established themselves politically by marrying into the right house, which Gaius would regard as the Julian ; and many Hellenistic monarchs married their own sisters. Gaius certainly attached great importance to the female side of his house : otherwise he would scarcely have made his sister Drusilla his heir or have ordered extravagant honours to be paid to her when she died in 38.

The theatrical tendency Gaius had inherited from his father helped him to advertise his godhead. The story that he built a bridge from the Palatine to the Capitol to enable him to commune more easily with his " brother " Jupiter may be apocryphal. But apparently he did build a bridge of ships across Baiae's bay in 39 and ride over it wearing the breastplate of Alexander the Great : godlike he was riding the waves and, like Alexander, he was contemplating great military adventures.

§ 3.   THE EXPEDITION TO THE NORTH

By early 38 Gaius' attempt to establish an absolute monarchy had already provoked plotting among the senatorial nobility, the class that traditionally claimed a share in the government and was now not even allowed to tender advice ; men who presumed to give it were executed, even men like Junius Silanus, Gaius' father-in-law, and Macro, who had a claim on his gratitude. The Claudian house was the most convenient rallying point for this opposition, although we may suspect that the nobles did not seriously plan to elevate the youthful Tiberius Gemellus but nursed ulterior designs of a republican restoration.

Gaius reacted ruthlessly. Gemellus was executed in May 38, and throughout the remainder of that year and the next the aristocratic partisans of the Claudian family were sought out under the laws of treason, specially revived for the purpose, and executed. In Philo's words, Gaius became the enemy of the whole Claudian house. Meanwhile he used the full treasury left by Tiberius to keep the populace amused with shows and to go ahead with military preparations.

In the event, the situation on the Rhine forced him to begin his expedition very suddenly and unexpectedly in September 39. Gaius would have gone to the Rhine in any case, since it was traditionally the scene of Julian exploits and the place where the son of Germanicus could reasonably hope to find

unswerving loyalty among the troops.¹ He stood in need of
this, for the fidelity of some of the other provincial armies was
suspect : he had already had to put the governor of Pannonia,
Calvisius Sabinus, on trial for treason.

Officially Gaius could say that he went to the Rhine to
strengthen the frontier. This sounded plausible since Tiberius
had not maintained strong governors there in his last years,²
and the resultant weakening of military discipline had enabled
the German tribes to make occasional raids across the Upper
Rhine. Actually Gaius seems to have gone there when he did
because one of the Rhine commanders was involved in a plot
against him. The plot was a serious one, since the conspirators
planned to exploit against him his own action in emphasizing
the value of matrimonial relationships with the imperial family.
The chief conspirator, Aemilius Lepidus, was the widower of
one of Gaius' sisters (Drusilla) and the paramour of another
(the Younger Agrippina), and he also succeeded in implicating
the third (Julia Livilla). Military support was promised by
Lentulus Gaetulicus, commander on the Upper Rhine. Gaius,
however, reached the Rhine before Gaetulicus could move ;
the two men were executed and the princesses banished.
Gaetulicus' army was then assigned to a stern disciplinarian,
Ser. Sulpicius Galba, the future Emperor ; and it is not without
interest that another future Emperor, T. Flavius Vespasianus,
who was praetor in this year, likewise helped Gaius to stamp
out the conspiracy.

The ancient writers make merry of Gaius' exploits on the
Rhine : they say that he celebrated them with a triumph in
which provincials were disguised as German captives. Actually
he celebrated not a triumph but an ovation, which was no
abnormal method for marking the suppression of a conspiracy.
The Emperor passed the winter of 39–40 in Gaul, while his
Rhine legions, whose number he had apparently increased by
two,³ put a stop to German border forays.

¹ The ancient sources naively say that the need to recruit Batavians
for his bodyguard took Gaius to the Rhine.

² As a Claudius Tiberius may have been reluctant to strengthen
the armies which were traditionally the most pro-Julian and therefore
potentially the most opposed to himself.

³ However the next Emperor may have been responsible for the
creation of these two new Rhine legions, XV Primigenia and XXII
Primigenia. They brought the army list up to twenty-seven legions :
the final Augustan figure was twenty-five.

In the spring of 40 Gaius was at last ready to undertake the invasion of Britain. Once again the ancient sources, attributing incredible naiveté to his soldiers, represent his expedition as a mere farce : the troops were marched to the Channel and ordered to collect " the spoils of Ocean "—sea-shells (*musculi*). It seems more probable that, when the troops reached the Channel, they behaved as did those of Claudius two years later and refused to embark. Gaius, unlike Claudius, could not wait for them to recover their nerve for fear of what might be developing back in Italy. The most he could do, therefore, was to issue a political manifesto formally announcing the annexation of Britain ; but the actual military occupation he could not attempt. He ordered the troops to repack their engineering equipment (*musculi*) and returned to Italy.[1] He arrived there in August with his mind a prey to the suspicions and fears which the conspiracy of his nearest relatives had engendered.

§ 4. TYRANNY

Perhaps not unnaturally he now took exaggerated precautions for his own safety. Treason trials became increasingly common, and in them baser motives began to manifest themselves. Gaius used the trials, as Tiberius had not, to raise money. His privy purse was now short of funds. His personal habits were expensive ; he squandered money on luxurious banquets and doted on the horse races and other spectacles of the Circus : he is even said to have appeared himself occasionally as a singer, gladiator or charioteer. By gratifying his own instincts in these matters, he could also hope to win the popularity of the mob, and thereby make up for the hatred of the nobility. But shows cost money, and his extravagances had already exhausted the Tiberian surplus. Accordingly he exploited the treason laws to procure the condemnation of the wealthy and the confiscation of their property.

These methods, however, although they might fill his privy purse, hardly sufficed for the treasury. So he resorted to other expedients. He charged exorbitant fees for entrance into the college of priests to his own godhead. He introduced drastic taxes, using his troops to enforce payment of levies on lawsuits,

[1] Thus J. P. V. D. Balsdon (*Journ. Rom. Stud.*, XXIV (1934), p. 13 f)., interprets Suetonius' absurd story that Caligula bade his troops collect sea-shells (*musculi*) in their helmets (*Caligula*, 46, 1).

foodstuffs, porters, panders and prostitutes. The sales tax was probably re-imposed at the old rate.

These draconic measures apparently filled the treasury, for Claudius on his accession found funds to make some very large disbursements. But they destroyed Gaius' popularity even with those classes which had previously favoured him. The terror now became complete. He could trust no class of the population, and anyone who showed the slightest eminence in any sphere was liable to fall victim to the imperial jealousy. An ever present danger threatened all prominent senators, jurisconsults, literary men, and especially orators, for Gaius was inordinately and not unjustly proud of his own oratorical skill. Philosophers also were not immune, which is an interesting anticipation of later developments.[1] Even a name could excite his envy : he compelled Pompey the Great's descendant to drop the title Magnus.[2]

§ 5. GAIUS' PROVINCIAL POLICIES

In his provincial policies he was no less autocratic. He was not, indeed, completely lacking in constructive vision : in Spain, Gaul and Dalmatia he continued Tiberius' road-building programme, and in Achaea he planned a Corinthian Canal. But in general his behaviour in regard to the provinces was erratic.

In the east he favoured the client kings who were his teachers in despotism. Thus he restored Commagene, which Tiberius had organized as a province, to its king, Antiochus ; and he granted other kingdoms to Thracian princes. He especially favoured Herod Agrippa I by presenting him with the tetrarchies of his uncles, Philip and Herod Antipas, an action that contributed not a little to the subsequent disorders in Judaea. At the same time he apparently allowed Parthian influence to become supreme in Armenia. Gaius thus reversed Augustus' policy, which had been to strengthen the frontier against Parthia by gradually incorporating the client kingdoms in the vicinity of a Roman-controlled Armenia. Gaius' motive may have been his desire to pose as a Great King with numerous dependent vassals : in this, as in his proposed visit to Alexandria, Antony

[1] See below, pp. 186, 220 f., 235.
[2] It is still used, however, in an inscription of the year 40. Dessau, *Inscr. Lat. Sel.*, 9339.

was his model. Gaius probably preferred client kings, bound to himself personally by ties of gratitude, to provincial governors who were members of the conspiratorial Senate and might build up armies.

In Africa he reduced the senatorial proconsul to the status of a civil authority in Carthage and assigned his troops to an imperial legate. He also deposed Ptolemy, the client king of Mauretania, whose territory he proposed formally to annex. These actions, however, may not be so capricious as they at first appear. In Tiberius' reign the province of Africa had only been indifferently protected by the army of its senatorial proconsul against the attacks of the neighbouring semi-nomads under Tacfarinas : it had finally been a special imperial appointee, Junius Blaesus, who restored order. Gaius, while no doubt finding it congenial to strip the Senate of its remaining military power, may also have been seeking to prevent any repetition of this state of affairs. Actually the by no means uncivilized inhabitants of Mauretania, whom Tacfarinas had numbered among his supporters, were shortly afterwards once again in arms, possibly because they resented the deposition of their king.

§ 6. GAIUS AND THE JEWS

Gaius' policy towards the Jews was equally provocative. Despite his friendship with Herod Agrippa, Gaius, like his father before him, was an anti-Semite.[1] At Alexandria in Egypt there was a large Jewish community, which was not only persistently denied local citizenship by the Alexandrian Greeks, but was also periodically the object of anti-Semitic outbreaks. The arrival of Gaius' favourite, Herod Agrippa, there in 38 led to unusually turbulent disorders, which spread even as far as Syria. To score off the Jews the Greeks demanded that the Emperor's statues should be displayed in all the Alexandrian synagogues and even in the Holy of Holies at Jerusalem. As Gaius officially regarded himself as a god he was not likely to oppose such a demand. To plead their cause the Alexandrian Jews in 40 sent an embassy to Gaius headed by Philo, and his account of the interview reveals the eccentricity of the Emperor. The Princeps led the embassy a merry

---

[1] It is significant that the Jewish communities were the only ones in the eastern Mediterranean which did not vote high-sounding honours to Germanicus and his family.

dance through the rooms of his villa near Rome, and ultimately
dismissed them unsatisfied with the contemptuous remark :
" Men who think me no god are more unfortunate than criminal."
Obviously, however, he intended to insist on his statues being
displayed in the synagogues, for Petronius, the governor of
Syria, received instructions to that effect. Gaius' death
occurred in time to prevent this rash order from being carried
out, although not in time to prevent the seeds of the later big
Jewish revolt from being sown.

§ 7.   THE MURDER OF GAIUS

Had Gaius lived longer, his policies might have involved the
Empire in disaster.   Fortunately his early death and the firm
foundations laid in the provinces by Augustus and above all by
Tiberius prevented really irreparable damage from being done.
By the end of 40 Gaius had managed to alienate most groups
in the population.   Only the Praetorians still bore him some
goodwill : he had given them a donative on his accession, he
had increased their numbers, and he had otherwise pampered
them to compensate for his execution of their Prefect Macro.
But finally he was foolish enough to make enemies even in their
ranks, and a group of them struck him down on January 24, 41.
The leader of the assassins was a Tribune of the Guard, Cassius
Chaerea, who thus avenged repeated gross insults heaped upon
him by Gaius.   A group of senators, headed by the ex-consul
L. Annius Vinicianus, was almost certainly behind the plot.
The Senate as a whole, which he had so arrogantly bullied,
now obtained a measure of revenge ; it was prevented by Gaius'
successor from officially damning his memory, but it did
rescind all his acts.
While modern apologists have sought to find some kind of
logic in Gaius' behaviour as a whole, it must be admitted that
many of the actions recorded of him seem tyrannically irresponsible.   Witness the oratory contest at Lugdunum, in which
he obliged unsuccessful contenders to lick out their own com-
positions, and his dismantling of an aqueduct at Rome before
adequately providing for its rebuilding.   Perhaps he was
endeavouring to advertise that his autocratic will was law.
Certain it is that his short reign brought into startling relief
the despotism inherent in the Principate.   Already the hopeless
dependence of the Senate on the Emperor had been made

manifest during Tiberius' long absence from Rome. Under
Gaius its inferiority was demonstrated to a far greater degree,
and his reign helped to change the composition, as well as the
rôle, of the Senate, for his use, or rather misuse, of the treason
laws extirpated still more of the noble senatorial houses. Thus,
the elimination of the old republican aristocracy, which began
with the Principate, went on apace.

CHAPTER III

CLAUDIUS

§ 1. A SHAKY BEGINNING

GAIUS, like Julius Caesar, was struck down by men who fondly imagined that, with the death of the tyrant, the Republic would automatically return. The Senate, although some of its members were realistically proposing potential candidates for the purple, actually discussed the feasibility of a republican restoration. Meanwhile the Praetorians did not stand upon ceremony. They acclaimed Claudius, the brother of Germanicus and hence Gaius' uncle. The Senate thereupon tamely conferred the imperial powers upon Claudius.[1]

Thus began the reign of a man who is variously depicted in the ancient sources as a fool, a weakling and a bloodthirsty tyrant. The truth is far otherwise. It is usually said that he had survived amid the imperial intrigue to the ripe old age of fifty because he had deliberately chosen a life of prudent obscurity and allowed himself to be regarded as a simpleton. Claudius' antiquarian studies had no doubt taught him that a certain Brutus had once avoided assassination by simulating imbecility ; and Claudius could have acted such a part with verisimilitude, since an attack of paralysis in his childhood had left him with a grotesque appearance—palsied head, slobbering mouth, shaking hands, shambling gait, spindly legs and pot belly. But feeble-mindedness had not saved Agrippa Postumus. Nor had Claudius' life up until 41, although lacking in administrative experience, been quite so obscure as is usually believed. He had been fairly prominent in the Equestrian Order. He had presided occasionally at the games. Under Augustus he had been an augur and a *sodalis Augustalis* ; under Tiberius he obtained the insignia of a consular ; under Gaius he had actually been the Emperor's colleague in a two-month consulship ; the Senate had honoured him more than once.

Probably he owed his escape chiefly to the fact that he was a Claudian rather than a Julian. He had, indeed, inherited some Julian blood from his grandmother Octavia, Augustus' sister ; but above all he was a Claudian and, unlike Germanicus, had never been adopted into the Julian *gens*. As only the Julian

[1] In legal theory the soldiers should have had no say in the choice of an emperor.

house could count on the support of the provincial armies, his chances of becoming Emperor must always have seemed remote, and by exercising discretion and devoting himself to learned pursuits he escaped the executioner.

Immediately on his accession he took pains to identify himself with the Julian house. He assumed the name of Caesar which, though hated by the Senate, was popular with the army, city mob, Italian bourgeoisie and the provincials, and he insisted that Augustus would be his model. (Actually many of his policies were to differ from those of Augustus). Still further to demonstrate his solidarity with the Julian family he executed the actual murderers of Gaius.[1] But merely to advertise his relationship, real or assumed, with the Julian family did not seem enough. He won over the soldiers by bribery : the Praetorians each received 15,000 (or possibly 20,000) sesterces, and their numbers were probably increased.[2] Such donatives were nothing new, but this was a particularly large one and obviously set a dangerous precedent for later reigns. But Claudius had no choice.

To win over the nobility he displayed an exaggerated respect towards the Senate : he even refused to take action against the senators implicated in Gaius' murder. The magistrates were treated with courtesy, the treason trials in the court of the Senate were abruptly broken off, and exiles, including Gaius' two sisters, were recalled. The people were also put into good humour. Gaius' new taxes were abolished and gladiatorial shows and other magnificent spectacles were provided, the Circus ·actually being flooded to stage a realistic mock naval engagement.

Nevertheless one of the provincial governors thought Claudius' Julian relationship too remote to impress all the soldiers. In the second year of the reign, the commander of the army in Dalmatia, Furius Camillus Scribonianus, attempted a revolt. His troops, however, refused to respond to his republican cry of " liberty," and his conspiracy was suppressed without much difficulty. Among his supporters was Caecina Paetus, whose

---

[1] He personally disapproved of Gaius : he rescinded his acts and publicly branded him a lunatic, thus repaying the contempt Gaius had heaped upon him during the preceding three years.

[2] There were nine praetorian cohorts under Augustus and twelve under Nero. Either Gaius or Claudius or, more probably, both were responsible for the increase.

wife Arria has won immortality for showing him how to face
suicide with fortitude. Thereafter Claudius always carefully
cultivated the troops. The Praetorians received an annual
donative, the other soldiers were given opportunities for booty,
and various honours were showered upon different army units.
This explains, perhaps, why he survived at least six plots during
his reign.

We are told that in all Claudius executed no fewer than thirty-
five senators and either two or three hundred equites. He
always had to take exceptional precautions against senators :
for the first thirty days of his reign he did not enter the senate-
house, and he forbade soldiers to enter senators' houses at any
time. The senatorial conspirators, men like Statilius Corvinus
and Asinius Gallus, were as usual intriguing to replace the
imperial principate with a truly senatorial one. The large
number of knights in this list is more surprising, since the
Equestrian Order was usually loyal to the Principate, and
Claudius moreover previously had been closely associated with
it. Perhaps the equestrian conspirators, the most notable of
whom was Cn. Nonius in 47, resented the pre-eminence which
certain of Claudius' freedmen came to obtain.

§ 2.   THE CONQUEST OF BRITAIN

To popularize his régime Claudius at once decided, like
Gaius, to pursue a bold foreign policy and resumed his plan
to annex Britain. But first came some unfinished business
from the previous reign. Remembering Tacfarinas, Claudius
ordered his generals, Suetonius Paulinus and Hosidius Geta, to
restore order in Mauretania, where a rebellion had broken out.
This accomplished, Mauretania was organized into two procuratorial provinces, Caesariensis and Tingitana, which, however,
were never perfectly subjugated.

Claudius was now free to move against Britain. Pretexts
were plentiful. Besides the one which Gaius had used, Claudius
could also plead that he was fulfilling a civilizing mission :
Druidism with its human sacrifice and other savage rites must
be suppressed, and it could scarcely be suppressed in Gaul if
its fount and origin across the Channel continued unchecked.
Indeed Gaul would never be romanized so long as Britain
remained independent : even Roman deserters as well as
recalcitrant Gauls could find refuge there. No doubt economic

motives—the desire to safeguard Roman traders and to exploit Britain's greatly exaggerated resources in metal, timber, cattle and slaves—were also mentioned as reasons for the attack. Even the wish to remove Germanic *auxilia* far from their homeland may have been a contributory reason. Undoubtedly, however, Claudius' chief motive was his conviction that national Roman sentiment strongly favoured the adventure.

In 42 his preparations were complete. Three Rhine legions [1] and legion IX Hispana from Pannonia were placed under the able command of A. Plautius Silvanus, who was later granted an ovation.[2] Auxiliaries and detachments from other legions [2a] brought the expedition up to about 50,000 men.

After some delay at the Channel these forces crossed to the Kentish coast in 43 and rapidly advanced towards the Thames. The passage of the river did not take place until Claudius himself arrived with reinforcements. Then Cunobelinus' capital Camulodunum (*Colchester*) quickly fell, and Claudius was able to return to Rome and announce the addition of a new province to the Empire. Senate and People received the news with delirious enthusiasm, thereby vindicating his belief that a British conquest would strengthen his régime. The Emperor was voted a triumph and larger constitutional powers. He himself shrewdly gave publicity to Britain rather than to his territorially bigger conquest of Mauretania.

During the remainder of his reign the area of Britain under Roman control was systematically expanded. Legion II, commanded by the future Emperor Vespasian, headed westward and conquered the Isle of Wight (Vectis); Legion IX pushed north; while Legions XIV and XX advanced north-westward. The mutual hostility of the various British tribes facilitated the Roman conquest: it ultimately delivered the most redoubtable British chieftain, Caratacus, into the hands of Claudius, who, however, spared his life at a celebrated interview. By 47, when P. Ostorius Scapula succeeded Plautius as commander in Britain, the Roman frontier was marked by the famous Fosse Way, a road, for the most part straight, running from a point just east of Exeter (Isca Dumnoniorum) to Lincoln (Lindum), the headquarters of Legion IX. In 51 Colchester became the first city

---

[1] II Augusta; XIV Gemina; XX Valeria Victrix: they were replaced on the Rhine by the two new legions, XV Primigenia and XXII Primigenia.

[2] He was the last person not of the imperial house to celebrate one.

[2a] Notably legion VIII Augusta.

ROMAN BRITAIN

Names of Modern Towns underlined

Scale

0   20   40   60

English Miles

Dunkeld

Perth.

R.Forth

R.Clyde

HADRIAN'S WALL

R.Tyne

Solway Firth

MONA
(I. of Man)

BRIGANTES

EBURACUM
(York)

MONA
(Anglesey)

LINDUM
(Lincoln)

DEVA
(Chester)

ICENI

Lichfield

VIROCONIUM
(Wroxeter)

RATAE
(Leicester)

TRINOVANTES

WATLING STREET

CAMULODUNUM
(Colchester)

SILURES

GLEVUM
(Gloucester)

VERULAMIUM
(St.Albans)

ISCA
(Caerleon)

DUROCORNOVIUM
SIVE CORINIUM
(Cirencester)

LONDINIUM

R.Thames

FOSSE WAY

AQUAE SULIS
(Bath)

VENTA BELGARUM
(Winchester)

REGNI

ISCA DUMNONIORUM
(Exeter)

VECTIS
I. of Wight

Land's
End

in Britain to obtain the status of *colonia*. It was the centre of administration and of the official Caesar-worship, although the great port of London (Londinium) was easily outstripping it in size and soon became the seat of the imperial procurator. When Claudius died in 54 Roman troops were at the borders of Wales and were advancing to attack the last vestiges of Druidism on the island of Anglesey (Mona). Roman capital was pouring into the island, and although urbanization did not make rapid headway,[1] some cities were springing up : Bath (Aquae Sulis), Cirencester (Durocornovium), Leicester (Ratae)—these three were all on the Fosse Way—Winchester (Venta Belgarum) and St. Albans (Verulamium), which obtained the charter of a *municipium*.

Thus by 54 the Romans controlled virtually all of England (but not Wales) south of a line drawn from east to west through Lincoln. Within this area there were the autonomous client kingdoms of the Regni (in Sussex) under King Cogidubnus (*legatus Augusti in Britannia*), and of the Iceni (in East Anglia) under King Prasutagus.

§ 3. FRONTIER POLICY

Claudius himself shared the popular wish to which he responded by attacking Britain. An erudite, if somewhat pedantic, pupil of the historian Livy, and himself a voluminous writer on antiquarian subjects, he had a keen sense of Rome's historical mission. He saw no reason why the process of expansion and assimilation, which so impressed him, should stop at the Channel. Why should it not embrace Britain as well ? Later, by solemnly performing the symbolic ritual of extending the city's *pomerium*, he demonstrated that this was a cardinal feature of his whole reign ; he coveted the title " Extender of Empire."

This motive can be seen underlying most of his work on the frontiers. His twenty-seven imperial acclamations show that he was anxious to stress that his was a reign of military achievements. Thus besides annexing Mauretania and Britain, he extended Roman influence in Palmyra and around the shores of the Black Sea. He annexed Lycia (43) and the eastern client

[1] So far as is known Britain never had more than one *municipium* and four *coloniae*.

kingdoms of Judaea (44), which had been restored to Gaius'
friend Herod Agrippa in 41, Thrace (46) and Ituraea (49), which
was incorporated into Syria.　This does not mean that he disapproved of the Augustan policy of client kingdoms, for he actually established some on the borders of his new British province,
and he gave Commagene to Antiochus IV.[1] Claudius rather
was reversing Gaius' policy of weakness towards Parthia : he
insisted on a Roman nominee when the throne of Armenia became
vacant in 49 and, like Augustus, he tried to keep Parthia internally divided by internecine strife.　This policy is sometimes
said to have been responsible for the trouble with Parthia in
Nero's reign ; but trouble with Parthia surely would not have
been avoided by appeasement.

On the Rhine Claudius departed somewhat from Tiberius'
policy.　The Lower Rhine had been weakened by Tiberius'
action in allowing the Frisii to secede in 28.　Claudius therefore
sent his able general, Domitius Corbulo, to establish the frontier
firmly on the northern mouth of the Rhine, although he
prudently removed Corbulo once the task was done.

But Claudius' historical studies had taught him that Rome
assimilated as well as expanded.　Therefore he established
numerous *coloniae*, chiefly in the imperial provinces in order to
raise them nearer to the level of romanization prevailing in the
senatorial ones.　There were at least five such foundations in
Mauretania, many more in the Danubian provinces, and the
famous ones in the western provinces, Camulodunum in Britain,
and Colonia Agrippinensis and Augusta Treverorum in Germany.
As further aids to romanization, he incorporated numerous
municipia and built numerous roads in Spain, Gaul, Asia Minor
and elsewhere.

§ 4.　ROMANIZATION AND ASSIMILATION

In the interests of assimilation he also extended the citizenship or Latin rights to individuals or groups that were ready
for it, for instance to the Anauni, Tulliassi and Sindunes, who
lived in a valley in the Tyrol.　Although " attributed " to the
Italian city of Tridentum, their exact status had never been
clarified.　They regarded themselves as Roman citizens, but

---

[1] He did, however, stress their relationship to himself : in his reign
the client kings frequently style themselves *legatus* (or *procurator*)
Augusti.

no earlier Emperor had ever given a ruling to that effect. Claudius did not hesitate to do so.

Of greater interest and importance is the case of the nobles of Gallia Comata.[1] The leading men of the romanophil Aedui enjoyed the Roman citizenship but not the right of holding Roman magistracies or of entering the Senate. Claudius in a partly extant oration " persuaded " the Senate to permit him to adlect into the Senatorial Order Gallic noblemen who, while being Roman citizens, did not hail from Roman communities (i.e. either *coloniae* or *municipia*), hardly any of which existed in the Three Gauls at that time. Hitherto the handful of provincial Roman citizens to become senators had in almost every instance possessed *municipalis origo*, as it was called. Claudius now ruled that Gallic noblemen, of tribal as well as municipal origin, were eligible for Senate membership so long as they were Roman citizens. This step, potentially far-reaching since the privilege could hardly be restricted to Gauls, did not nevertheless flood the Roman Senate with tribal chieftains. Admittedly, in the next generation non-Italian senators became common ; and before the end of the century a provincial actually became Emperor. But the sons of the provinces, who thus made their mark in Rome, were citizens who could claim municipal origin.

He also readily conferred Roman citizenship upon provincials—even an ex-enemy Mauretanian chief obtained it— and some individuals thus honoured were recruited into the Equestrian Order. The census figures reflect this policy. Between A.D. 14 and 48 the number of adult male Roman citizens increased from five to six millions, which cannot be attributed solely to natural causes. Presumably the ancient sources are right in saying that Claudius was to some extent responsible for it, but they are wrong in suggesting that he bestowed the citizenship recklessly : the very moderateness of the increase proves otherwise. Actually Claudius insisted on romanization as a prerequisite to citizenship : he deprived a Greek, whose Latin was poor, of his citizen status.

Just as Augustus narrowed the gap between Rome and Italy, so Claudius narrowed it between Italy and the provinces. The *urbs* was being replaced by the *orbis*. Doubtless under a monarchy, where all men are alike subjects, the inevitable tendency is for them all to find the same level. Under Claudius

[1] That is, Transalpine Gaul apart from Narbonensis.

the assimilated provincials begin to play their full part in the
Empire. He himself obtained his officials from them, and the
army was being increasingly recruited from their number.

§ 5. CENTRALIZATION ; THE CIVIL SERVICE

In his policy of combined expansion and assimilation
Claudius' model, whatever his public professions might be, was
not Augustus but Julius ; but he resembled both in his desire
for efficiency. Tiberius had also aimed at this ; but, unlike
Tiberius, Claudius realized that new conditions, new stresses
and new conflicts demanded modifications in the Principate.
His historical studies had taught him that life does not stand
still : the problem was to decide in which direction to steer the
Principate. Gaius had, in fact, shown the way when he had
carried the Principate to its logical despotic conclusion. But
Gaius, like Julius before him, was moving too fast in advance
of contemporary Roman opinion, and Julius' fate counselled
evolution rather than revolution. Claudius accordingly reverted
to Augustus' policy of making haste slowly and of not gratu-
itously parading his pre-eminence. He did not monopolize
the consulship, only holding it four times during his reign.
He did not demand divine honours, although, like Augustus and
Tiberius, he found it hard to refuse permission to provincials
to worship him, especially in Britain, where the natives were
only too prone to deify their conqueror.[1] Claudius also imitated
Augustus' attitude of outward respect and deference to the
Senate : he insisted, for example, that senators be given their
special seats in the theatre. Indeed he vigorously upheld
Augustus' hierarchical division of society, re-enslaving freedmen
who posed as knights and executing men who falsely claimed
Roman citizenship.

It is, therefore, not surprising that when he took measures
which strengthened the powers of the Princeps at the expense
of the Senate and accelerated the trend towards a centralized
autocracy, he did not openly avow that this was his intention,
but justified his actions by an appeal to ancient precedents.
Coming from him this sounded plausible : for he was notorious
for his antiquarian interests. He tried to add three letters to

[1] The Egyptians had been similarly eager to deify their conqueror,
Augustus.

the Roman alphabet; [1] he reorganized the ancient college of *haruspices* ; he restored *fetial* practices ; he created patrician families ; he celebrated the Secular Games (in 47); he disapproved of new-fangled foreign cults ; he legislated through the *comitia*.

In actual fact his policies were due, not to his desire to revive ancient practices, but to his realization that the State had developed since Augustus' day and could no longer be efficiently administered by a system which left the relations between Princeps and Senate somewhat anomalous. This does not mean that Claudius' antiquarian revivals were merely an hypocritical attempt to pull the wool over contemporary eyes. Like Augustus, he saw that new institutions cannot be entirely divorced from ancient traditions ; his measures, like those of Augustus, had a conservative basis. But seeing the necessity for change, Claudius allowed greater scope to the reforming element than the conservative. The reform he proposed was greater centralization under the strong hands of the Princeps. [2]

Even the reluctant Tiberius had been obliged to take some hesitant steps in this direction : he had appointed a secretary for petitions at Rome, a secretary to supervise the inheritance tax, extra officials to supervise the steadily growing imperial estates, and possibly even an imperial treasurer. Tiberius found these clerks and secretaries in the traditional fashion of the great Roman houses, by recruiting them among his freedmen and slaves. Yet his civil service, while growing, was still small. Under Gaius this tendency had proceeded even further ; under Claudius it ceased to be a tendency and became a system : it is he who is chiefly responsible for the Imperial Civil Service, and his reign witnessed the organization of a secretariat, the growth of a centralized bureaucracy.

Thus, evidently with the idea of effecting economies, public finance was completely overhauled. It was perhaps now that the various *fisci* were united : at any rate the Emperor's financial secretary (*a rationibus*) is henceforth spoken of as if he supervised one central *fiscus* or imperial treasury. The public treasury (*aerarium Saturni*) was also brought largely under the Emperor's control. For in 44 Claudius took it away from the control of ex-praetors and restored it to the quaestors, who, however, were his personal nominees and served for three years

[1] An inverted digamma ⅃ to represent consonantal *u* ; an antisigma Ɔ to represent *bs* or *ps* ; and Ⱶ to represent vocal *y*. (Tacitus, *Annals*, XI, 14, 5.)

[2] The republican magistracies never recovered from the effects of his reign.

instead of the traditional one. Moreover it was an imperial procurator that henceforth controlled the inheritance tax, while the proceeds of the manumission tax also seem to have been transferred to the imperial treasury. Simultaneously a procurator of the Emperor's personal property was appointed. The procurators now emerge much more clearly as state officials and not just as personal agents of the Princeps.

Great offices of State were organized, unofficially at least. A secretary-general (*ab epistulis*) was in charge of all official correspondence, being helped by officials resembling attorneys-general who dealt with petitions and legal dossiers (*a libellis, a cognitionibus*). The Emperor likewise had a kind of privy seal and librarian (*a studiis*) and a variety of lesser officials. Some of these were taken from the ranks of the equites, but not an exceptional number of them; the most important posts of all were monopolized by imperial freedmen. Claudius' financial secretary was Pallas, his secretary-general Narcissus, his legal secretary Callistus, and his privy seal Polybius. In this there was, of course, nothing new. But the increase in centralization meant that these freedmen wielded far more power and influence than they would have done in similar positions under Augustus and Tiberius. They are alleged to have occupied important places on the boards of advisers, which Claudius consulted from time to time, and they were actually allowed to sit in the Senate House on occasions. As this was furthering his policy of assimilation, Claudius did not object to important posts being thus occupied by men whose background was non-Roman. But that is far from saying that he allowed his freedmen to dominate him. Although he was prone to seek advice and counsel from others—his advisory boards being exceptionally large for that very reason— he did not permit his freedmen to twist him around their fingers. All his decisions, all his recorded sayings bear the stamp of his own personality. He created the new system, and he dominated it. No doubt there were abuses in the new centralized bureaucracy, for the organization of a new department of state is only too likely to be accompanied by nepotism, favouritism and even corruption, until the system for obtaining career-men has become regularized.

Claudius was, in fact, elaborating the machinery of imperial autocracy. The direction of imperial affairs obtained a new unity. Inevitably it meant an increase in the personal powers of the Princeps and a diminution in that of the old magistrates and the Senate. The fourth Emperor had his bureaucratic officials and could afford to dispense with the administrative experience of the old senatorial aristocracy in a way that Augustus could not. Actually this resulted in an increase of efficiency.

For example, when Claudius abolished the *quaestores classici*, one of whom, the *quaestor Ostiensis*, had important duties in connexion with Rome's grain supply, he removed a certain amount of overlapping and obtained a more competent grain commission supervised by the *praefectus annonae*. Even the burden of distributing the free grain to its 300,000 recipients was taken away from the Senate ; the senatorial Prefect of the Grain Dole (*praefectus frumenti dandi*) was replaced by an imperial procurator, and the service was financed from the imperial treasury.[1]

By assuming the censorship in 47 and 48, ostensibly in order to revive some obsolete customs, Claudius revealed the diminished rôle of the Senate, for although his tenure of the censorship did not exceed the historical eighteen months, it was the office that traditionally controlled the Senate ; for that reason Augustus had avoided it.

Claudius' interference in senatorial provinces likewise demonstrated the Senate's inferiority. According to Dio he appointed governors to such provinces : Galba's appointment to Africa is one example of this and there may have been others. In 53 his procurators actually obtained jurisdictional powers over financial matters in senatorial provinces.

Nevertheless the Emperor's primary aim was to obtain administrative efficiency, not to humble the Senate and urban magistrates. Unlike Gaius, he did not wish to dispense with the Senatorial Order. On the contrary, he eagerly availed himself of any prestige or experience it possessed. He always preferred to enact his measures by means of senatorial decrees rather than imperial fiat. In 44 he restored to the Senate the provinces of Achaea and Macedonia which Tiberius had made imperial. He allowed to the Senate its ancient right of issuing copper coins. Probably it was through him that the Senate recovered the right to conduct the elections which Gaius had given to the People. He tried to impress senators with the

[1] A near risk of famine, caused apparently by Gaius' thoughtlessness and itself the cause of riots in the city, taught Claudius the importance of the grain supply, and he distributed it more efficiently. Possibly, however, he retained the *praefectus frumenti dandi* (G. E. F. Chilver in *Amer. Journ. Phil.*, LXX, 1949, pp. 7–21).

importance of their position by strictly enforcing their attendance at meetings and controlling their absences from Italy. It is true that he granted the Senate very little power in essential matters ; but he was not averse to its wielding power where it did not interfere with efficiency.

While the uneasy partnership of Princeps and Senate was thus dissolving and the Principate was becoming more like an avowed monarchy, the Emperor's house presumably came to resemble a royal palace replete with courtiers, ceremonies and camarillas. Even so, Claudius was none the less genuinely interested in good and honest government for its own sake. This can be seen especially in the provinces. Peccant governors were prosecuted, and order was maintained by the suppression of piracy, brigandage, raiding and rioting : for instance, at the very beginning of his reign he ordered the Alexandrian Greeks to drop their anti-Semitism and the Alexandrian Jews to drop their agitation for the citizenship. He tried to raise the level of material prosperity. To that end he expanded the Empire's shipping, both mercantile and naval ; he improved ports and waterways ; and built roads and aqueducts. He tried to lighten the excessive cost of the Cursus Publicus, and he granted a lengthy immunity from taxation to cities that had been stricken by earthquake and the like.

Such solicitude for the provinces is perhaps not surprising in an emperor who, although of an old Roman family, was actually born in one of them.[1] But Claudius was equally interested in good government for Italy. There, too, he built roads (the Via Claudia Valeria to the Adriatic and roads over the western and the eastern Alps) and aqueducts (the Aqua Claudia and Anio Novus, both serving Rome). There, too, he improved the ports : his ambitious harbour works at Ostia can still be seen. There, too, he tried to raise the level of material prosperity. To promote trade he increased the monetary circulation, using the metal from imperially owned mines for the purpose, and he tried to foster Italian agriculture by discouraging absentee landlordism and by reclaiming the bed of the Fucine Lake.[2]

[1] Claudius was born at Lugdunum in Gaul.
[2] To drain this lake Claudius employed 30,000 men for eleven years and excavated a three-mile-long *emissarium* from the Lake to the River Liris. The cost in money and men was enormous ; and the attempt ultimately proved futile.

Clearly the measures taken by Claudius were practical. But they were also humanitarian. Thus, he forbade usurers to make anticipatory loans to sons preliminary to their fathers' deaths, or masters to recover sick slaves whom they had abandoned. In his reign we see that feature of the Roman Empire which is so attractive : a concern for the humblest subject anywhere and a desire to deal fairly by all.

§ 6. CLAUDIUS AND THE SENATE

This desire for equity caused Claudius to display unwonted interest in jurisprudence and legal procedure, an interest which was further fostered by his antiquarian studies. In the field of litigation, too, he sought for efficiency : he abolished unnecessary holidays and festivals and he made the Emperor's private court more easily accessible to Roman citizens everywhere.   This court had its origin in the fact that Roman citizens in the provinces naturally claimed the right to appeal from a governor's judgment to that of the governor's chief. In Claudius' time this would especially be the case owing to his particular concern for the provinces : people outside of Italy, even in the senatorial provinces, would regard him as the person to whom they could have recourse.

This expansion of the Emperor's court enabled Claudius to keep his promise not to force the Senate to condemn its own members to death.   Presumably his court, sometimes held *intra cubiculum principis*, condemned the thirty-five senators allegedly executed during his reign.   The jealous nobles disapproved of such a court anyway, since it made inroads on some of their cherished powers.   But they came to hate it bitterly when it condemned some of their own number and when it was alleged to be under the influence of ambitious imperial freedmen and women, who for motives of greed or envy hastened innocent victims to their doom.[1]

§ 7. THE FALL OF MESSALINA

The excessive influence of Claudius' freedmen and womenfolk has been exaggerated.   It can undoubtedly be admitted that in his last years he may have depended rather more heavily

[1] It is significant that, at the beginning of the next reign, trials *intra cubiculum* were temporarily abandoned.

on their advice, but he himself was a prodigious worker to the very end.

At the time of his accession he was married to Messalina, a union that Gaius had arranged for political motives.[1] Messalina bore Claudius two children, a daughter, Octavia, and a son, whom he called Britannicus in celebration of his British conquest. The story that Messalina was a monster of cruelty and sexual depravity presumably has some truth in it. Married while young to an exceptionally ugly man almost thirty years her senior and coming from an arrogant house and a class whose morals were traditionally lax, it would indeed be surprising if she did not give rein to her passions. That the Emperor should have been as ignorant of her scandalous conduct as the ancient sources imply seems unlikely; he probably tolerated it for the same reason that he married her, because she was of Julian stock. Finally, however, in 48 she had the hardihood to go publicly through a form of marriage with the consul elect, Gaius Silius. Claudius thereupon ordered her and Silius to be put to death, obviously because this was a senatorial conspiracy : the affair resembles that of Aemilius Lepidus and the Younger Agrippina in Gaius' reign.[2] Silius' political connexions belonged to the Julian faction of Germanicus ; with Messalina he planned to obtain military support for their plot from the Prefect of the Vigiles and from the head of the imperial school of gladiators.

§ 8. AGRIPPINA

Claudius now decided to take unto himself another wife, his fourth. The woman selected was his niece, the Younger Agrippina. That he was infatuated with her charms, as the ancient sources suggest, is improbable. He could not have been ignorant of her character. While not as promiscuous with her favours as Messalina—outwardly indeed she was a model of decorum—she was no paragon of female virtue. She had been the mistress of Lepidus in Gaius' reign and of Pallas in the days of Claudius. She had already been twice married, the first time to the scion of a dissolute but powerful Roman family, which at one time after Julius Caesar's death seemed to have a chance of obtaining the Principate. By this first husband,

[1] See above, p. 147.
[2] See the vivid account of the conspiracy in Tacitus, *Annals*, XI, 26–38.

Cn. Domitius Ahenobarbus, she was the mother of a son, Lucius. From her mother, the wife of Germanicus, she inherited an imperious and ambitious temperament ; she was prepared, if necessary, to wade through slaughter to a throne.

In marrying Agrippina, Claudius acted as the result of consultation and deliberation rather than of passion. The Senate, his intimate friend L. Vitellius (his colleague in the censorship), his financial secretary Pallas, all advised in favour of the marriage, making light of the fact that according to Roman Law it was incestuous. Agrippina was a direct descendant, a great-granddaughter of Augustus ; it was her close ties with the Julian house that decided Claudius.

Inscriptions suggest that it was also her Augustan blood, not her domineering personality, that led him to the arrangements he now made for the succession. Her son by her first marriage, L. Domitius Ahenobarbus, was at once betrothed to Octavia, Claudius' daughter by Messalina, and in 50 Claudius adopted the youth with priority over his own son Britannicus : henceforth L. Domitius is known to history as Nero. This seemingly unnatural conduct was not due simply to the fact that Nero was five years older than his stepbrother, but rather to the fact that he could be regarded as more of a Julian. Claudius could cite the example of Tiberius who had similarly adopted the Julian Germanicus ahead of his own son Drusus. There is other evidence to show that Claudius had Tiberian precedents in mind. Just as Macro was appointed Praetorian Prefect in 31 and subsequently ensured the succession of Gaius, so Burrus was appointed Praetorian Prefect twenty years later to safeguard Claudius' successor, Nero. Moreover, Claudius had noted how Tiberius' failure to train Gaius for the responsibilities which would one day be his had led to unfortunate results when the inexperienced youth became Emperor. Claudius did not propose to repeat Tiberius' mistake.

Young Nero was pushed on at a speedy pace. In 51, when only fourteen years old, he assumed the *toga virilis*, was named consul elect for the year 58, and was given the title of Princeps Iuventutis. In the next year he was made Prefect of the City. One year later he appeared in the Senate and married Octavia ; as in Augustus' reign the stepson and destined successor married the reigning Princeps' daughter.

Agrippina, at first at any rate, must have watched her son's rapid preferment with gratification. Her ambitions were indicated by the appearance of her head on the reverse of Claudius' coins, an honour which she was the first Empress to receive. Undoubtedly she was hoping one day to rule the world through her son. The coins make this unmistakably clear : in the first months of Nero's reign her head appears on the obverse and not merely on the reverse.

But in 54, when her son's succession was absolutely assured, she contrived Claudius' murder. The story that she suborned a notorious poisoner named Locusta to doctor a dish of mushrooms, which proved fatal to the Emperor, derives ultimately from the Elder Pliny, her arch-enemy, and has accordingly been regarded with suspicion. But it does seem quite probable that she was responsible for Claudius' assassination on September 13, 54, either by this or some other means. At first glance the murder seems pointless, since Nero was certain to succeed in any case. Possibly she was afraid that Claudius might change his mind, for we are told that Narcissus, the secretary-general, was urging the Emperor to designate Britannicus rather than Nero as his successor. But it seems more probable that she had a baser motive. Claudius was now in his sixty-fourth year : in other words, although old, he was not of really advanced years. It could be reasonably expected that, like Tiberius, he would live another ten or fifteen years. In that length of time Nero would be able to obtain so much experience in the duties of the imperial office that when his turn came to become Emperor he would have no need of his mother's advice. If Claudius had taken careful note of Tiberius' reign, so had Agrippina. When Tiberius became Princeps he was already fully familiar with his administrative and military duties, and hence he had been able to dispense with the advice of his mother, Livia. In fact Tiberius had firmly refused to allow Livia to participate in any way in the government, and she had passed her last years in comparative obscurity. Agrippina had no intention of sharing the lot of Livia. She preferred to have her son become Emperor at an age when he was still amenable to her influence, when she would be able to establish a firm hold over him and through him become mistress of the world. Such probably was Agrippina's motive in procuring Claudius' death in 54 when Nero was just sixteen years of age.

All things considered, it is hard to feel much compassion for the fate that subsequently overtook this woman, for the man she killed, despite his physical infirmities, is worthy of respect.

The Roman world, indeed, paid him more than respect; it accorded him divine honours after death. He was the first Emperor since Augustus to be so distinguished. It is true that a group of disgruntled senatorial nobles, whose spokesman was Seneca, sneered at his apotheosis and represented it as a cheapening of godhead.[1] The Roman world in general, and least of all the provinces, did not agree with them. Many an inscription shows that the provincials were genuinely grateful to Claudius for his disinterested efforts to provide them with a government that was at once efficient and humane, in other words, good. Indeed many provincials had been eager to deify Claudius even during his own lifetime, and he had not always been successful in dissuading them.

[1] See below, p. 264, and cf. the remarks of W. H. Alexander in *Proc. Roy. Soc. of Canada*, XXXVII (1943), pp. 33–5. He is not, however, called *divus* in the surviving portions of the Vespasianic *Lex de Imperio*.

CHAPTER IV

NERO

§ 1. A YOUTHFUL PRINCEPS

NERO succeeded his stepfather smoothly enough. As anticipated, Burrus played the rôle of Macro. The Praetorian Guards
proclaimed the youth Emperor, and a compliant Senate voted
him the imperial powers. None of the provincial armies protested the accession of one who was the great-great-grandson of
Augustus. To make assurance doubly sure, however, a donative
of Claudian dimensions was paid to the Praetorians (15,000
sesterces per man). Nero at once made the customary speech
in the Senate, promising that he would model his Principate
upon that of Augustus. The odious trials *intra cubiculum*
would be dropped, an end would be put to the venality and
power of the court favourites, especially the freedmen, and in
particular the privileges, prerogatives and powers of the Senate
and individual senators would be respected. As Nero was only
sixteen, it is scarcely surprising that this speech was written
for him by Seneca.

Agrippina now thought that her day had arrived. She at
once set to work to consolidate her position by eliminating
possible family rivals. Nero's aunt, Domitia Lepida, and
Augustus' great-grandson, M. Junius Silanus, the proconsul of
Asia, were hounded to death. Narcissus, reputedly the supporter of Britannicus, seems to have been executed at once;
Callistus was probably removed from office. Agrippina's head
on the obverse of the coins shows that she did in fact almost
become the regent.

But Seneca and Burrus, even though they had been her
supporters in Claudius' lifetime, were not enamoured of the
prospect of a woman ruling the Roman world. They set to
work to undermine her influence by suggesting to the Princeps
that he was the master of the world and did not need to share
his power with anybody.

Nero, indeed, was quite content to leave serious and tiresome
matters of state to someone else, while he surrendered himself
to self-indulgence. From his early youth he had shown an
interest in things aesthetic : literature, music, the fine arts—

all caught his fancy. Nor was he indifferent to the more sensual pleasures. In the company of young bloods such as Otho the future Emperor, Annaeus Serenus the commander of the Vigiles, and Claudius Senecio, he went on nocturnal " jewel-hunts " through the streets of Rome, in search of unwary members of the opposite sex ; and although married to Octavia, he was known to have a freedwoman concubine, Acte.

Agrippina, meanwhile, had the mortification of seeing her dreams of empire fade. Her obvious eagerness to be invested with the trappings of authority played into the hands of Seneca and Burrus. In the competition to indulge the youthful prince's vanity she was at a disadvantage from the start. Her head returns to the reverse side of the coins, and then disappears entirely. Her attempt to sit at her son's side at a reception of some Armenian ambassadors was disallowed. Pallas, the financial secretary who had been her steady supporter, was relieved of his office and replaced, probably by another freed-man, Phaon.

Agrippina accordingly resorted to intrigue. She began to champion the cause of Claudius' own children, Britannicus and Octavia. But hers was the kiss of death. Throughout his reign Nero showed a morbid fear of possible rivals inside the royal household, so that it is hardly likely that Britannicus, or even Octavia for that matter, would have permanently escaped assassination. But Agrippina's new-found interest in them precipitated their doom. The skill of Locusta was invoked to get rid of Britannicus in 55 ; Octavia's turn did not come until some years later. Agrippina herself was accused of treason, but escaped by boldly facing her son. She was, how-ever, compelled to remove herself from the palace, and her influence disappeared entirely. The government of the Roman world rested effectively in the hands of Seneca and Burrus.

§ 2.   QUINQUENNIUM NERONIS

Owing to a remark which the Emperor Trajan later let drop, Nero's reign for a five-year period, the famous *quin-quennium Neronis*, is traditionally regarded as one of the better periods in human history. Trajan's words actually refer to Nero's achievements in public architecture, which came late in the reign. Nevertheless, those scholars are more probably right who think that, if any five-year period in Nero's reign is to be regarded as a period of general happiness, it is the five years following the elimination of Agrippina's influence (56–61), when Seneca and Burrus were chiefly responsible for the government. That is not to say that the government was perfect. Seneca was a leading spirit in the senatorial group that was bitterly opposed to Claudius and his policies. Nero, so long as his vanity was flattered and he was allowed to sow his wild oats without tiresome interruptions, was content to let Seneca's senatorial group manage affairs. He followed Seneca's advice and adopted an outward attitude of deference, of submissiveness even, to the Senate. He was indeed consul in 55, 57 and 58, but he made the gesture of refusing a perpetual consulship. Even coins in the precious metals were issued, nominally at any rate, on the Senate's authority. It almost looked as if a senatorial Principate had at last become a reality.

However, Seneca and Burrus, who had only attained to their position of influence by encouraging Nero to insist on his untrammelled power, could not make it obvious that they had merely substituted themselves for Agrippina as the power behind the throne; they necessarily had to tread warily. To satisfy Nero's conceit they had to pretend that everything was being done by his divine beneficence. If happy days were there again, then it was because the Princeps had graciously allowed them to return : it was thanks to the imperial *clementia* alone that there was some semblance of good government throughout the world. The adulation fell little short of adoration, and many an inscription, in the west as in the east, is couched in terms almost as extravagantly worshipful as those demanded by Gaius. Thus the spirit of the reign was really absolutist, even in the days when Seneca and Burrus were directing affairs.

Nor was absolutism confined to the spirit. Seneca, himself a financier, was interested in the Empire's economic life. To obtain the maximum financial efficiency, Claudius' reform was carried a step forward. In 56 imperial *praefecti* replaced the quaestors at the senatorial *aerarium*. As this put control of the revenue even more firmly in the Emperor's hands, he could easily afford the gesture whereby he willingly turned over forty million sesterces of his own funds to the Senate's treasury.

Something was also done in the interests of trade in the provinces. Measures were taken to keep a closer control over the *publicani*, and extortionate governors were promptly brought to trial before the court of the Senate. The Emperor himself even suggested the abolition of all indirect taxes throughout the Empire in an effort to stimulate trade.[1] But this drastic proposal was dropped when the serious practical difficulties it would involve were realized.

§ 3. MATRICIDE

Nero presumably tolerated the supremacy of Seneca and Burrus because of his conviction that it was not they but Agrippina who was seeking the indirect control. Whether they deliberately fostered his resentment against her we cannot say. He certainly came to conceive the liveliest hatred for her, so that he determined to put an end to her ambitions for ever. Perhaps he was egged on by his new mistress, the beautiful Poppaea Sabina, whose husband, the Emperor's friend Otho, had been conveniently sent to Lusitania as governor. Poppaea went even further than Seneca and Burrus in encouraging Nero to get rid of anything or anybody that hampered his freedom of action. Agrippina foiled a first attempt to drown her (a fishing-smack rescued her) ; whereupon Anicetus, the freedman Prefect of the Fleet at Misenum, had her assassinated by his sailors (59).

So odious a crime would normally excite universal detestation ; and when the victim came from Julian stock, she being the great-granddaughter of Augustus himself, there might be even more serious repercussions. Accordingly Nero, in doubt as to how the Roman world would take the matricide, had retired to Naples. He need have had no apprehensions. Seneca and Burrus, who even if they were not accessories before the fact certainly were after it, helped to spread the version that he had barely escaped from his mother's murder plot. The Senate proceeded to pass extravagant votes of thanks to the Gods for delivering the Emperor, and Nero returned to the city in triumph.[2]

---

[1] Perhaps direct taxes were also involved in the proposal (T. Frank, *Econ. Surv. of Rome*, V, p. 42, n. 23).

[2] Tacitus' account of the matricide (*Annals*, XIV, 1–13) is one of the best examples of his power of conveying a great deal of meaning in a few words.

§ 4. CAPRICIOUSNESS ENTHRONED

The servility of the Senate, while it reassured the Princeps, also imbued him with the heartiest contempt for the Senatorial Order. If he could with impunity murder his own mother, who had Julian antecedents, he need not stop at anything. He could shake off all restraints, and, if he felt like it, safely coerce any member of the aristocracy. Of popular support he was assured : he had won over the urban mob with two separate donatives of four hundred sesterces a head, and he also kept them amused with games and shows. In the very year of his mother's murder he instituted some informal but lavish games called *Iuvenalia*. Moreover, he noted that Gaius' personal appearances, although distasteful to the nobility, had been welcomed enthusiastically by the populace. Nero accordingly did not hesitate to appear in public as a charioteer and as a musician, and he forced knights and senators to follow his example and descend into the arena. One group of knights, indeed, was organized into a claque known as the Augustians, whose task it was to hymn the Emperor's praises, and especially his singing and playing. However, even Nero did not yet venture to flout the stigma attaching to the acting profession ; his appearance on the stage was reserved for some years later (at Naples in 64). His performances were popular, even though attendance at them had its perils, for he had bullies in the gangways to flog people who applauded either too languidly or too inopportunely. The future Emperor, Vespasian, indeed, almost lost his life when he was caught taking a nap through one of the Emperor's efforts. Such coercion was probably reserved for the more aristocratic members of the audience.

The success of his matricide, the first act he had taken on his own responsibility, filled Nero with self-confidence. Seneca and Burrus were now hoist with their own petard. They had indulged their pupil's vanity not wisely but too well : Nero now became as impatient of their advice as he had formerly been of his mother's. No doubt Poppaea encouraged him in this attitude. Henceforth the Princeps went his own wilful way, and it was the way of licentiousness, extravagance and vice. A kind of luxurious sensualism became a feature of his court.

He did not share the Roman passion for the brutal gladiatorial sports ; his passion rather was for things Greek. But it was the Hellenistic rather than the fifth-century Greeks who excited his admiration. From his boyhood he had evinced extraordinary interest in their activities, and he was now able to put this interest to practical use. Buildings where Greek exercises could be carried out were constructed : an amphi-theatre in the Campus Martius, a circus in the Vatican Valley, a Gymnasium with Public Baths nearby. In 60 he inaugurated a quinquennial festival called the Neronia and entirely modelled on Greek contests : Nero himself won first prize in poetry and oratory, graciously allowing others to win the prizes for athletics, chariot-racing and music.[1]

Meanwhile his programme to free himself from all restraints made steady progress. In 62 Burrus died. The story that Nero had him poisoned is untrustworthy,[2] but Nero did avail himself of the occasion to demonstrate that he was freeing himself of Seneca's influence. To succeed Burrus he appointed as Praetorian Prefects Ofonius Tigellinus, the Prefect of the Vigiles, a sinister figure of whom Seneca could not possibly have approved, and Faenius Rufus, the Prefect of the Grain Supply. Seneca took the hint and retired into private life.

Nero's conduct now became unbridled. The treason law was revived, even though its first victims, Antistius Sosianus and Fabricius Veiento, were exiled rather than executed. Octavia was eliminated, probably at the urging of Poppaea : at any rate Poppaea profited, since she took Octavia's place as the lawful wife of the Princeps. The unfortunate Octavia, deprived as she now was of Burrus' support, was charged with adultery and, when she refuted this, was accused of sterility, divorced and banished to Campania. Subsequently she was found guilty of a second trumped-up charge of adultery and was removed to Pandateria. Public pity for her misfortunes proved fatal to her, for she was murdered shortly afterwards (62).

Octavia, however, was not the only victim. Any person, who was closely related to the imperial house, could easily excite the Emperor's jealousy. Rubellius Plautus, Tiberius' grandson, and Cornelius Sulla, Claudius' son-in-law (both of whom had been banished in 60, the former to Asia and the latter to Gaul), were murdered in 62. D. Junius Silanus, a descendant of Augustus, was obliged to commit suicide in 64. These

[1] The Neronia were celebrated again in 65 : they lapsed after Nero's death.
[2] He probably died of cancer.

barbarities completely alienated the senatorial class, and soon the urban mob was given cause for offence by the great fire of Rome.

§ 5. THE FIRE AND THE CHRISTIANS

This conflagration, which broke out on the bright moonlight night of July 18, 64, and raged unchecked for over a week, totally destroyed three of Rome's fourteen regions and partially destroyed seven others. The rumour spread that Nero had deliberately fired the city. He was away at Antium when the blaze started, and the alibi appeared suspiciously convenient, especially as he was reported to have declaimed his own composition on the Sack of Troy while he watched the home fires burning from Maecenas' Tower. No responsible student to-day believes that Nero was an incendiary; nor did he fiddle while Rome burned. He took the most energetic measures both to bring the fire under control and to provide relief for the homeless and destitute. He may have been indiscreet enough to remark that the fire was a godsend in that it presented an excellent opportunity for rebuilding and redesigning the congested city : but that is far from saying that he ordered the torch to be set to it. Actually fire was an ever present hazard at Rome, as was proved again one generation later when Nero's wise building regulations had done something to mitigate the peril.

Nevertheless, so acute were popular suspicions that Nero thought it prudent to direct public resentment elsewhere. The natural target, those eternal scapegoats, the Jews, were protected by Poppaea, who, although not a Jewess herself, undoubtedly entertained a considerable sympathy for them. Nero accordingly picked on the Christians. They were by now generally recognized to be distinct from the Jews, but were no more popular than the latter, and the rabble scarcely needed any rousing against them. It cannot be demonstrated that there was now a general persecution of Christians, but there certainly was a local persecution in Rome, the first recorded official persecution by the Roman government of the new religion, traditionally the persecution in which Saints Peter and Paul lost their lives.[1] The task of persecution seems to have

[1] Some Christians may have been banished from Rome in Claudius' reign (Suetonius, *Claudius*, 25, 4 : Iudaeos impulsore *Chresto* assidue tumultuantes Roma expulit). But there is no need to assume that " Chrestus " is a corruption or misspelling of " Christus." It was a common name for slaves. Cf. *Acts of the Apostles*, XVIII. 2.

been entrusted to the City Prefect.   The precise charge against
the Christians may have been that they had illegally formed an
organization ;   but whether they were specifically accused of
arson or not, the authorities certainly encouraged the public
to believe that the Christians could have been responsible for
the recent holocaust.   Many of them were consequently given
an appropriate punishment : they were smeared with pitch, tied
to stakes and set on fire to act as torches for nocturnal games in
the imperial gardens and Vatican Circus.   Others were fed to
wild beasts in the arena.   In the end, if the ancient sources
can be believed, the public was nauseated by such brutalities.

§ 6.   EXTRAVAGANCE ;   CURRENCY DEPRECIATION

Nero at once proceeded to the rebuilding of Rome, and his
artistic propensities were now allowed full scope.   The most
spectacular, although by no means the only grandiose, new
building was his famous Golden House, remains of which can
still be seen.   Replete with lakes, gardens, springs, colonnades
and a colossal statue of the Emperor, it was planned to cover
an extensive area between Caelian and Esquiline.

This and similar building enterprises cost large sums, and
henceforth Nero was hard-pressed financially.   He had recourse
to forced contributions from both Italy and the provinces.
Greece was thoroughly ransacked for *objets d'art* of all kinds.
But these methods did not suffice.   At any rate it was at about
this time that Nero depreciated the gold coins and debased the
silver ones ; it is hard to believe that the two events were
unconnected.   Nero, in fact, reformed the mint-system.

In reducing the weight of the *aureus* by about ten per cent
and the silver content of the *denarius* by slightly less, Nero
may have been trying to stabilize the two precious metals at
their correct ratio to one another ; just as it is fairly certain
that both his gold and silver coins were brought into relation
with the new bronze coins which he now proceeded to strike.
It may also be the case that Nero was anxious to issue an entirely
new series of coins, so that in them he might display his artistic
capabilities ;   certainly no Roman issues are more beautiful
than his.

But it is also most unlikely that he overlooked the consideration that a reduction of the precious metal content of the coins
would help him to make ends meet.   However, it is only fair

to add that, apart from his own personal extravagance, there
were other causes at work that rendered currency devaluation
inevitable. The drain of precious metals to the east to pay
for oriental luxuries had already commenced. The amount
of currency in circulation had either to be greatly curtailed,
or else kept at its existing level by a reduction in the size
of the coins. The former course would have involved drastic
deflation, which is always unpopular. It is hardly surprising
that the Roman Emperors, who always thought it advisable to
keep the mob in good humour, preferred the easier path of
inflation. Even in the gold coins of Gaius and Claudius some
slight reduction in weight is observable. But it was Nero who
took the first big step in this direction.

Whatever Nero's motive, he established a precedent. After
him few Emperors could resist the temptation to meet their
expenses by debasing the coins. By the second half of the
third century A.D. the currency was in a chaotic state.

§ 7. THE CONSPIRACY OF PISO

Nero, however, was still not obtaining all the funds he
needed. Accordingly, like Gaius, he now began to murder
individuals whose wealth he coveted. Hitherto the nobility,
apart from relatives of the imperial house, had not gone in fear
and trembling for their lives, although some of them had been
banished. From 65 on, however, Nero was openly at war
with them. The traditional picture may be exaggerated, but
it is basically trustworthy: the days of Gaius seemed to have
returned. The headstrong wilfulness which had led Nero to
repudiate the advice and influence, first of Agrippina and subsequently of Seneca, now manifested itself as a ruthless absolutism,
a kind of oriental despotism.[1] Senators from the eastern part
of the Roman world became not uncommon, while the Emperor's
oriental freedmen were installed in places of power and influence,
even in the army. This in itself, apart from any acts of petty
tyranny, earned the hatred of the upper classes. Even those
members of the nobility who were not desirous of a republican
restoration became anxious to replace Nero with someone else.

Matters came to a head in 65. The consul designate

[1] The oriental monarchies were practically the only ones known to the
Romans; in any event the philhellene Nero naturally directed his eyes
to the Near East.

Plautius Lateranus, one of the Praetorian Prefects Faenius
Rufus, the poet Lucan, and a large number of senators and
knights formed a plot. The aim of most of the conspirators
was to replace Nero with C. Calpurnius Piso, and for that reason
the affair is usually called the Conspiracy of Piso. Rumour had
it that some preferred Seneca to Piso ; nevertheless it seems
unlikely that Seneca was privy to the plot. The scheme proved
abortive, for the night before the conspirators were due to
take action, the authorities got wind of the matter, made
some arrests, and by inducing some of the culprits to turn
King's Evidence, uncovered the whole affair. The hearings
were not conducted in any public court, and the trials *intra
cubiculum principis* grimly reappeared. At least nineteen
persons, including Seneca and Lucan, who is said to have
betrayed his own mother's complicity, were either executed or
driven to suicide. Another thirteen and probably more were
exiled.

Nero thus escaped. But his fears for his personal safety
became more lively, and the terror increased in consequence.
Tigellinus, the other Praetorian Prefect, seems to have been
liberally provided with secret agents and given his head to
conduct a ruthless purge. The purge, to be really effective,
would have had to be widespread, for Nero's unpopularity with
all classes in the capital was growing. Besides those nobles
who hated him for personal or political reasons, there were
those who disapproved of him on moral grounds.

In the general cynicism which the closing years of the
Republic had produced, the more serious and thoughtful minds
at Rome had sought solace in philosophy. But despite the
endeavours of Lucretius, it was not Epicureanism that attracted
them : Roman *gravitas* rejected a system which could only too
easily be interpreted as advocating momentary gratification
and the selfish pursuit of pleasure. The finer minds at Rome
found a refuge in Stoicism. The egalitarian tenets of this
philosophy need not necessarily have made its adherents
opponents of the Principate. Indeed Stoicism might even have
been expected to endorse a system which reduced all men to
the one common level of subjects of the Empire ; and this
actually came to pass in the second century, when the Emperors,
although thoroughly autocratic, sought to be benevolent rulers.
In the first century, however, it was otherwise. The fact that
Brutus and the Younger Cato had professed Stoicism inclined

Stoics to be republican in sentiment. Moreover in the tyrannical nature of Nero's autocracy they sought in vain for any conception of their own belief in the brotherhood of man. Accordingly they gravely paraded their disapproval of the tone of the feckless Emperor's court, if not of his actual government. Early in the reign, before the year 62, the satires of Persius and the attitude of Annaeus Cornutus, the famous tutor of Lucan, implied strong criticism of the régime. Thereafter a small group of Stoics, headed by the ex-consul P. Clodius Paetus Thrasea, although apparently not guilty of actual conspiracy, made their uncompromising disapprobation of the matricide Nero unmistakably clear. In 63 Thrasea ostentatiously withdrew from all participation in public affairs and refused to attend meetings of the Senate. He and his fellow Stoics began to present the appearance of a regular "opposition."

In addition to disaffection in the ranks of the nobility, there was also growing opposition to Nero in the army. In general Nero was careless about the troops. He did indeed increase the number of legions to twenty-eight by enrolling Legion I Italica, and so long as Seneca and Burrus were directing affairs, colonies to make provision for veterans were established, not a few of them in Italy. But unlike Gaius, Nero did not exhibit himself to the armies. He avoided military camps, and he was even indiscreet enough to appoint his oriental freedmen as army officers. The soldiers began to hate Nero. He was also losing his hold on the Roman mob. The fire of Rome had already put it in an ugly mood; and it was not likely to be mollified when pestilence followed the fire.

Nero countered his growing unpopularity with increased despotism. The terror tried to eliminate all opposition elements. The grim and dreary list of victims cannot be given in full. It includes soldiers as well as civilians. Poppaea's name should not be included among the purged : her death in 65 was the result of an accidental kick by Nero when she was already advanced in pregnancy.[1] But the year 66 witnessed the execution of Annius Vinicianus, who headed a rather obscure conspiracy : it may have aimed at replacing Nero with Vinicianus' father-in-law, the celebrated general Corbulo. The witty and sophisticated author of the *Satiricon*, Gaius Petronius, also was hounded to death : he fell victim to the jealousy of

[1] Nero next married, in 66, the beautiful, witty and profligate Statilia Messalina.

Tigellinus. Nor did the Stoic philosophers escape : Nero had
not failed to note that Seneca had publicly claimed to be a
Stoic. Thrasea Paetus was condemned to death by the subservient Senate in 66. The young tribune Arulenus Rusticus
would probably have shared his fate, had Thrasea not restrained
him when he proposed to invoke his obsolete power of veto.
Helvidius Priscus, Thrasea's son-in-law, and Paconius Agrippinus
were both banished, while Barea Soranus and his daughter
Servilia were executed.

The Neronian reign of terror practically wiped out what
remained of the old nobility, and Nero's successors were obliged
virtually to create a new nobility.

The soldier victims met their fate a few months later when
Nero had already left Italy : they included the celebrated
Corbulo and Scribonius Rufus and Scribonius Proculus, gover-
nors respectively of Upper and Lower Germany.

§ 8. THE TRIP TO GREECE

Nero now began to insist on his own divinity, identifying
himself with various gods and having coins struck that show
him wearing a radiate crown, a distinction hithero accorded
only to Emperors who had been deified. Months and places
were named after him, and according to one version he even
planned to re-name Rome Neropolis.

Like Gaius he decided to journey to that part of the Roman
Empire which would be most receptive of an oriental god-king.[1]
His growing unpopularity may have contributed to his desire
to get away from the capital : it will be remembered how he
avoided Rome immediately after his mother's murder. But this
was not his only or even his main reason for leaving Italy in
September of 66. He had long planned a trip to the east, for
its traditions of absolute monarchy and emperor-worship
appealed to him. Moreover Greece was the home of the arts
and accomplishments which he particularly admired. Accordingly he made straight for Greece, where he entered on a dizzy
whirl of artistic and athletic competitions.

As a competitor he took himself very earnestly and was
anxious to be awarded first prize in every contest either as

[1] Also like Gaius he planned to cut a canal through the isthmus of
Corinth.

harpist, tragedian or charioteer. But it is not easy to explain his mental quirks except on the theory that he was eccentric, to use no stronger word. One would have thought that a really serious competitor would be satisfied with nothing less than genuine competitions. Some of those in which Nero appeared in Greece may have been such, but many more undoubtedly and obviously were not. This fact does not seem to have troubled Nero; he did not even object when the Greeks awarded him first prize in competitions which he did not even enter. Nor did he go to Athens, the home of the arts, the one place where he might have been expected to be eager to display his aesthetic accomplishments. In any case Nero was greatly impressed by the good taste of the Greeks in awarding him no fewer than eighteen hundred and eight first prizes. They obligingly celebrated all of their various national games in the one year (67) in order to enable him to win first prize in all.

Whether it was because of this flattering reception or because he had long planned to do so, Nero on November 28, 67, solemnly proclaimed the liberation of Greece[1]; in other words, Achaea was emancipated from the control of the governor of Macedonia. This does not mean that Greece was made independent of the Empire, but merely that the country as a whole obtained the wide autonomy and immunity from taxation already enjoyed by free cities like Athens and Sparta. The Senate was given Sardinia to compensate it for the loss of the Achaean part of its Macedonian revenue. Incidentally this step did not prevent him from plundering the wealth of numerous moneyed Greeks.

§ 9. THE REVOLT OF VINDEX AND GALBA

From Greece Nero planned to go further east where a would-be oriental monarch would feel still more at home. He was deterred from doing so, partly because a big revolt had flared up in Judaea, and Nero did not relish the idea of visiting military camps, partly because trouble had broken out in Rome itself.

When Nero departed for the east he had not appointed a City Prefect, but had left his freedmen to administer the government in Rome. Their rule in 67 bred discontent, and this was

---

[1] The speech he delivered on this occasion is extant: Dessau, *Inscr. Lat. Sel.*, 8794. Perhaps Lycia was similarly " liberated."

exacerbated when faulty organization led to a breakdown in the grain supply. The unceasing activity of *delatores* in Rome also contributed to the growing unpopularity of the régime. Trouble was brewing, and Helius, the freedman governor of Rome, entreated the Emperor to return. Nero arrived in Italy at the beginning of 68, and the storm broke immediately.

The governor of one of the Gallic provinces, probably Lugdunensis, C. Julius Vindex, raised the standard of revolt in March. His battle-cry was " Freedom from the tyrant." What his real aim was is doubtful. He himself was a romanized Gaul, a brave, intelligent and generous officer ; and he may have been intending to lead a Gallic national movement with the aim of winning for Gaul the same, or perhaps an even greater, degree of liberation than Nero had bestowed upon Greece. The local militia and some of the Gallic tribes, notably the Arverni, Aedui and Sequani, flocked to his standard, until ultimately he had a force of 100,000 men. However, internecine strife was the besetting fault of the Gauls ; like others before him, Vindex did not win over all of them. Lugdunum remained loyal to Nero, probably because neighbouring Vienna had declared for Vindex. The Treveri and Lingones also opposed Vindex. Within a few months his host was overwhelmed at Vesontio (*Besançon*) by the three legions [1] of the vigorous and able governor of Upper Germany, L. Verginius Rufus. Vindex committed suicide.

Meanwhile Ser. Sulpicius Galba, the governor of Hispania Tarraconensis for the past eight years, had associated himself openly with Vindex' movement on April 6. Galba apparently suspected that Nero was plotting his death. Accordingly he proclaimed himself " Legate of the Senate and Roman People " and announced his intention of overthrowing Nero. His soldiers actually saluted him as Emperor, but for the time being he professed to be striking only in the name of the Republic. Otho, Poppaea's former husband and now the governor of Lusitania, supported Galba ; and so did A. Caecina Alienus, the quaestor of Baetica, a worthy of whom we shall hear much.

Resolute action by Nero might have saved the day, since preparations for an eastern expedition were well forward in Rome and troops were therefore available. Moreover Galba had only one legion in his province,[2] although he at once started

---

[1] IV Macedonica ; XXI Rapax ; XXII Primigenia.
[2] VI Victrix.

to enrol another. Actually the Senate, although equivocal in its attitude, at first prudently pronounced against Galba.

Nero did make himself sole consul to deal with the emergency; but he lost his nerve when Tigellinus, the Praetorian Prefect, left him in the lurch by disappearing, and when Clodius Macer, the governor of Africa revolted, like his predecessors, " in the name of the Republic."

Verginius Rufus meanwhile, perhaps because he was only the son of an eques, resolutely refused to strike for the purple himself. But since he also entertained republican feelings, he placed himself at the disposal of the Senate, and its attitude was now determined by Nero's own irresolution. That irresolution probably originated from the Emperor's knowledge that he had alienated all classes in Rome. Moreover, owing to Tigellinus' defection, he could not count on the Praetorian Guard. When Nymphidius Sabinus promised the Praetorians a donative of 30,000 sesterces per head in the name of Galba, Nero's fate was sealed. Nero now paid the penalty for neglecting to cultivate the soldiers. The various provincial armies renounced their allegiance, and on the night of June 8 he fled fearfully from Rome and was promptly proclaimed a public enemy by the Senate, which now joined the Praetorian Guard in recognizing Galba as Emperor.

Nero, hiding in the villa of his freedman Phaon near Rome and bemoaning the fact that in him the world was losing a real artist,[1] determined on suicide. But he lacked the courage to administer the fatal stroke himself and needed the help of a loyal freedman, Epaphroditus, to plunge the sword into his throat (June 9, 68). His nurses and his mistress Acte buried him on the slopes of the Pincian Hill.

Thus passed away in his thirty-first year the last of the Julian stock. Like Gaius he paid with his life for his attempt to establish an undisguised absolutism of the oriental type. An absolutist policy ill becomes a weakling, and such Nero was. No doubt he had considerable amateurish talents as an aesthete ; but the avidity with which he collected undeserved honours in Greece, and the cowardice with which he met his end, alike stamp him as an imperial charlatan. His reign no doubt accelerated the trend of the Principate towards autocracy, but its more irresponsible and unbridled features perished with him.

[1] Suetonius, *Nero*, 49, 1 : qualis artifex pereo.

§ 10.   THE PROVINCES UNDER NERO

It has often been remarked that it was chiefly Rome, and only a comparatively narrow circle there, that suffered from Nero's wilful caprices, whereas the provinces enjoyed good government in his reign.   The fierce strife that broke out in certain parts of the Empire, so it is argued, was really a legacy from his predecessors.   If this is true, it can with equal justice be argued that the quiet and orderly prosperity of certain other provinces was likewise due to his predecessors, who by their wise provision had established the Empire on a firm basis.

Actually we are not as well informed about Nero's government in the provinces as about his performance in Rome.   The evidence rather suggests that, except for Greece, he was not particularly interested in them.   Some of them were lucky enough to obtain able imperial officials, while to others poltroons worthy of their master were sent.   Apparently the Emperor did not devote sustained attention to the needs of the Empire, or carefully seek the right man for the right position. He was content to leave much to the haphazard chances of routine.   Even so, he merely had to let well alone and allow the normal machinery for dealing with peccant governors to take its course.   Where it is possible to discern a piece of provincial policy which he himself initiated and for which he alone was responsible, as in Greece, we are not impressed. Vespasian, significantly, reversed Nero's policy in Greece immediately.

Nero planned a tour in Egypt, as well as in Greece, but it never materialized.   Otherwise little is heard of the African continent in his reign.   Nor do we learn a great deal about the western provinces.   The fact that it was precisely in them that the movement to get rid of him began indicates that the soldiers of the west thought poorly of his performance as Emperor. Undoubtedly the romanization of the west continued steadily, as is indicated by the granting of Latin rights to the Maritime Alps and the transformation of the client kingdom of the Cottian Alps into a procuratorial province (c. 58).   This process, however, presumably went on independently of the Emperor.

§ 11. BOUDICCA'S RISING

The western province about which we hear most in Nero's reign is Britain. On Nero's accession Roman Britain extended as far north as Lincoln. C. Suetonius Paulinus, the conqueror of Mauretania, then became the commander in Britain, and in 60 and 61 he moved against Anglesey to settle accounts with Druidism once and for all. In the very moment of victory, however, trouble broke out in his rear. (See map, p. 161.)

In the conquered south disaffection against Roman rule came to a head, partly as a result of the avarice of the imperial procurator, Catus Decianus, and of Roman usurers, among whom Seneca's name conspicuously appears, but above all as the result of an outrage perpetrated in the client kingdom of the Iceni. On the death of King Prasutagus, his widowed queen Boudicca (*Boadicea*) was despoiled of her kingdom *c.* 60 and flogged, while her daughters were raped. Boudicca raised the standard of revolt. Her people sprang to arms, and other British tribes such as the Trinovantes quickly joined the movement. Boudicca has become a legendary British heroine, and one cannot help but sympathize with her attempt to avenge her wrongs, even though we deplore the savage excesses by which it was marred.

The rebels quickly fired the unwalled colony of Colchester and then threatened St. Albans and London. Q. Petilius Cerealis at once marched bravely south from Lincoln, with a detachment from his legion,[1] but it was caught and annihilated before he reached London ; the commander and some cavalry alone escaped from the battlefield. Meanwhile the governor, Suetonius Paulinus, ordered all the legions in Britain to concentrate at Wroxeter. Legion IX, however, was already crippled, and Legion II never reached the rendezvous. Thus when Suetonius reached London, the only troops at his disposal were the two legions he had brought with him (XIV and XX), and these were insufficient to defend the metropolis. So he withdrew to more suitable ground, leaving St. Albans and London to the tender mercies of the rebels, who quickly stormed and sacked both places, slaughtering 70,000 people in the process. But Suetonius' decision, though hard, was militarily sound. He and his two legions now fought the decisive battle on ground of their own choosing, somewhere between St. Albans

[1] IX Hispana.

and Wroxeter, probably near Lichfield. The terrain enabled
them to extirpate Boudicca and her followers with comparatively
small losses to themselves. With the aid of reinforcements
sent by the central government, Suetonius proceeded to stamp
out the last sparks of the rebellion. He suffered, however,
the fate which the imperial jealousy usually reserved for Nero's
successful generals : he was recalled to Rome, unhonoured, in
61. His successors, P. Petronius Turpilianus and M. Trebellius
Maximus, at once set to work to rebuild the ravaged cities,
and by a policy of caution and moderation they removed the
vestiges of discontent.

§ 12. THE NORTHERN FRONTIER

The Rhine frontier during Nero's reign appears to have
presented no serious problems. The Danube frontier, too, was
safely preserved under Nero ; the Dacian princes across the
river gave homage, and possibly hostages, to Rome. Nevertheless the action of Ti. Plautius Silvanus, the governor of Moesia,
in transporting 100,000 of the Transdanubian peoples to the
Roman side of the river, was a straw in the wind : the Danube
frontier was soon to assume critical importance.

Nero generally reversed Claudius' policy of having client
kingdoms. Those in the Alps and Britain were annexed,
and Pontus had reached the stage of romanization where
its incorporation within the Empire was adjudged feasible
in 63.

§ 13. CORBULO'S PARTHIAN CAMPAIGNS

But the real danger spot in the east was Armenia, the old
bone of contention between Roman and Parthian. Claudius
had abandoned Gaius' policy of appeasing Parthia, but in 51
Parthia had obtained a new and able king, Vologases (Arsaces
XXII) ; and shortly after Nero's accession it was learned that
he had established his brother Tiridates on the throne of
Armenia in place of the pro-Roman Radamistus. For the
moment the imperial government acquiesced, but in 55 Vologases
found himself faced with a revolt inside Parthia, headed
apparently by his own son Vardanes. Here was Rome's
opportunity, and Nero's advisers, Seneca and Burrus, decided
to use force in Armenia. (See map, p. 251.)

For the task they appointed Corbulo, the general who had already displayed his military skill on the Lower Rhine in Claudius' reign. Corbulo had been appointed to Galatia Cappadocia late in 54, and C. Ummidius Durmius Quadratus, the governor of Syria, was now ordered to transfer to him some of the four legions under his command.[1] Corbulo found these Syrian troops ill-disciplined and badly trained, and lost precious time knocking them into shape at his base in Cappadocia. Simultaneously he recruited additional troops both in Cappadocia and Galatia.

It was not until 57 that Corbulo crossed the Euphrates at Melitene. He advanced far enough to spend the winter in the Armenian uplands, probably at Erzerum. In 58 he sought to persuade Tiridates by means of guerrilla operations to recognize Roman suzerainty, but herein he met no success. Accordingly Corbulo decided to teach Tiridates a stern lesson.

Campaigning in the difficult terrain of Armenia is never easy. Corbulo, however, was a competent master of war. Late in 58 he captured the Armenian capital, Artaxata, 200 miles due east of Erzerum, and levelled it to the ground. In the next year he marched on Armenia's second city, Tigranocerta, 300 miles to the south-west. On its surrender Tiridates fled to Parthia.

That the Roman victory might not prove illusory, Corbulo in 60 was set up in place of the recently deceased Ummidius as governor of Syria. He at once proceeded to instal Tigranes, grandson of the former Cappadocian king Archelaus and of Herod the Great, on the Armenian throne. As Vologases had by now quelled the revolt of Vardanes, he was free to challenge this arrangement. Actually Tigranes took the initiative and rashly provoked the Parthian monarch. Vologases' reply was to threaten the province of Syria in order to tie down the Roman troops there. Corbulo dared not send more than two legions to Cappadocia to support Tigranes, while he retained three legions with himself in Syria.[2] Simultaneously Corbulo asked the authorities in Rome to send a commander to take charge of the expeditionary force planned for Armenia. The commander,

---

[1] III Gallica, VI Ferrata, X Fretensis went to Corbulo; XII Fulminata stayed with Ummidius and was soon reinforced with Danubian legions: IV Scythica c. 57, V Macedonica c. 61, XV Apollinaris in 63.

[2] IV Scythica and XII Fulminata went to Cappadocia ; III Gallica, VI Ferrata and X Fretensis remained in Syria.

who was sent early in 62, was an incompetent braggart named Caesennius Paetus.

Meanwhile Corbulo, who had been negotiating with Vologases during the winter of 61–62, as a *beau geste* withdrew both Tigranes and the Roman troops from Armenia. But Nero, who was now ridding himself of the advice of Seneca and Burrus, had already adopted the unwise policy of annexing Armenia. In the spring of 62 Caesennius Paetus, taking the two legions which Corbulo had sent to Cappadocia, and without waiting for Legion V Macedonica, which was coming from Moesia to reinforce him, crossed the Euphrates, after first formally proclaiming the annexation of Armenia by Rome. He had not got very far when Vologases laid siege to his base camp at Rhandeia. Corbulo reluctantly took the risk of leaving Syria and marched to his rescue, but Paetus cravenly surrendered with the great general less than fifty miles away. The capitulation of Rhandeia restored Armenia to the Parthian sphere of interest.

Corbulo was now invested with a *maius imperium*, and in 63 he made vigorous use of his troops, reinforced by the Pannonian legion XV Apollinaris. He taught the Parthians respect for Rome's arms and persuaded Tiridates to regard Rome as his nominal suzerain.

This arrangement, whereby the King of Armenia was actually appointed by Parthia, but nominally installed by Rome, may have satisfied the *amour propre* of both nations. At any rate, after Tiridates came to Rome in 66 and received his crown formally from Nero amid splendid and imposing ceremonial, peace reigned between Rome and Parthia for half a century. Yet it is arguable that this peace should be attributed not to Nero but to his successors, who gave the eastern frontier their close attention.

Corbulo for his part had to pay the usual price for eminence under a tyrant. As soon as it was apparent that trouble no longer threatened from Parthia, he was ordered to commit suicide (67). Possibly he was accused of complicity in the plot of his son-in-law, Annius Vinicianus.

§ 14.   THE JEWISH REVOLT

The troops in Syria were intended to serve, if need be, anywhere in the Eastern Mediterranean, in Judaea no less than in

Armenia or against Parthia. The Romans had never found
Judaea easy to govern. The Jews, with their intolerant and
aggressive monotheism, were unassimilable and presented a
permanent problem to the Roman authorities. The Romans
were tolerant of this, as of other strange religions, and allowed
the Jews local autonomy and jurisdiction. They might despise
Jewish rites such as circumcision and the observance of the
Sabbath, but they gave the Jews the legal right to practise
them. Nevertheless it was not easy to maintain order and
good government in Judaea. The frequent changes in administrative methods there no doubt represented efforts by the
imperial government to find the right formula for governing it.
But such changes were unsettling.

Under Nero Judaea was a procuratorial province com-
prising the four regions of Galilee, Samaria, Judaea proper and
Transjordanian Peraea. The nationalist patriotism of its
Jewish population, which the follies of Gaius had done much
to inflame, cannot be regarded as unworthy. Unfortunately
it was often mingled with a bigotry that manifested itself in
bloody sectarian strife between Sadducees and Pharisees.
Furthermore, others than Jews inhabited the area and complicated the situation. Jews and Greeks were fierce enemies, in
Judaea no less than in Alexandria ; and the presence of a
Christian population, which since the days of Christ's ministry
in Tiberius' reign had been steadily growing, was anathema to
the Jews. At the first sign of a weakening in Roman authority
communal rioting flared up. Thus in 62, when the province
was temporarily without a procurator, the Sadducee High
Priest had James, " brother of the Lord," stoned to death.
Disturbances in fact were endemic in Judaea : it was the most
uncomfortable province that any imperial governor could
obtain. Good men were unwilling to go to the unwelcome post,
with the inevitable result that the procurators were often
conspicuous for their incompetence. Even so, though like
jesting Pilate they might be impatient in their quest for truth
and scornfully unsympathetic towards Jewish customs, some
of them did try to use tact and justice.

But the task was not easy. The governor of Judaea at Nero's
accession, although personally unpopular, was not altogether incompetent. This was Tacitus' *bête noire*, the rapacious Antonius
Felix, brother of Claudius' financial secretary Pallas.[1] During

[1] Tacitus, *Histories*, V, 9, 5.

his eight years there (52–60) he was skilfully aided by his Jewish wife Drusilla, the sister of Herod II Agrippa, the ' Agrippa ' of *Acts*. Felix had inherited a legacy of poor administration from his predecessor Ventidius Cumanus (48–52). Moreover there had sprung up in Jerusalem a particularly violent group of Jewish chauvinists, the so-called Zealots, led by Eleazar, the son of the High Priest Ananias. In 60 there were wild disturbances between Greeks and Jews in Caesarea, and Felix only managed to save the Christian St. Paul from the Jews by placing him in protective custody.[1] Considering that the garrison in Judaea seldom exceeded 3,000 men, Felix must be reckoned to have discharged his duties with some ability.

The procurators who came after him held their offices for much shorter periods. We know nothing particularly to the discredit of Porcius Festus (60–62). But Albinus (62–64) has left an unenviable though possibly undeserved reputation for avarice; while the misgovernment of his successor, Gessius Florus, is said by Josephus to have been responsible for the great rebellion which broke out in 66.

The exactions of this petty procurator may have contributed to, but they hardly caused, the rebellion. The basic cause was the not unnatural Jewish desire for national independence and the calculation that recent events in Armenia had so weakened Rome as to give the rebellion a chance of success. Rioting in Caesarea and a refusal by the High Priests to sacrifice to Jehovah on Caesar's behalf marked the beginning of the movement. The feeble Florus at once invited the governor of Syria, Cestius Gallus, to restore order; and Cestius marched on Jerusalem from Antioch with an army of 30,000 men, including Legion XII Fulminata. But with winter coming on he quailed at the thought of a frontal attack on the city, and returned through guerrilla-infested country to his province.

In the ensuing winter (66–67) the Jews busily organized their defence. The fortifications of Jerusalem were immensely strengthened, while a rogue named Josephus, the future romanophil historian, was entrusted with the defence of Galilee and raised a force of 60,000. The imperial government for its part was not idle. It appointed C. Licinius Mucianus to replace Cestius as governor of Syria (67) and entrusted the forthcoming

---

[1] St. Paul, a Roman citizen, somewhat rashly " appealed to Caesar " against his detention under Felix' successor (*Acts of the Apostles*, XXV. 11–12).

expedition in Judaea to a soldier who had proved his worth in Britain and had served as governor of Africa, the future Emperor T. Flavius Vespasianus. The core of his army were Legions V Macedonica, X Fretensis and XV Apollinaris, and his plan was to reduce the country piecemeal, reserving the assault on Jerusalem till the last.[1]

In 67 Galilee was overrun; its wily defender Josephus, who finally surrendered at Jotapata, became Vespasian's friend. Meanwhile in Jerusalem the terrors of sectarian strife were now added to the horrors of war. After a series of bloody massacres, rival factions of the Zealots obtained control in different quarters of the city. In 68 Vespasian overran Transjordanian Peraea and Samaria, and moved into Judaea proper. But the death of Nero then interrupted the work of drawing the net closer about the doomed city of Jerusalem.

In 69 Vespasian departed in quest of the Principate, and left over to his son Titus the task of investing the city.

Finally in 70, after a resistance of stubborn heroism, Jerusalem fell and was levelled to the ground. Titus was either unable or, more probably, unwilling to restrain his soldiery.

The " abomination that maketh desolation " fell upon Jerusalem, and for the next three years Roman troops were engaged in stamping out the last sparks of the great rebellion. Some, but by no means all, of the Jewish population was scattered over the face of the earth. The destruction of Jerusalem contributed only a little to the great Dispersion of the Jewish nation, which was already well under way long before 70. But Judaea did henceforth cease to be a specifically Jewish state, not so much because its juridical status was changed,[2] but because the Sanhedrin and High Priesthood were abolished and worship at the Temple in Jerusalem was forbidden.

[1] This left four legions with Mucianus in Syria: IV Scythica, VI Ferrata, XII Fulminata and III Gallica. But the latter was posted almost immediately (in 68?) to Moesia.

[2] Instead of an equestrian governor the province now obtained a legate and was garrisoned by a legion (X Fretensis).

PART III

THE ITALIAN EMPERORS

CHAPTER I

ANARCHY

§ 1. GALBA

NERO, who resembled Gaius in so much else, was also like him in failing to make provision for the succession. This omission was to prove more serious, however, in 68 than it did in 41, for on this occasion no male member of the Julio-Claudian household could be conveniently found and elevated to the purple by the Praetorians. Nor were the provincial armies likely to give their unanimous allegiance to anyone but a Julian. Even the two Claudian emperors, Tiberius and Claudius, both of whom were closely associated with the Julian house, had encountered disaffection in some of the provincial armies at their accession.

The generals, who moved against Nero in 68, Vindex, Galba, Clodius Macer and ultimately Verginius Rufus, all realized this. They all, therefore, prudently announced that they were not striking for their own hand but were acting on behalf of the Senate. Such a claim, however, was not likely to inspire the various provincial armies, and would be viewed with positive dislike by the Praetorians who, with the disappearance of the Emperor, would lose their own *raison d'être*. The various armies might be reluctant to give their allegiance to any individual but a Julian, but they were equally unwilling to give it to the Senate. Therefore in mutual jealousy they began a ruinous competition for the elevation of their respective generals, and Nero's death ushered in the so-called Year of the Four Emperors, when civil wars and their concomitant horrors stalked through the Empire.

When it was obvious that a republican restoration was no more feasible in 68 than it had been in 41, the Senate bowed to the inevitable and recognized Galba as Emperor. His troops had already saluted him as such, and he had set out for Rome immediately after Nero's death with his newly enrolled legion

VII Galbiana, which he was soon to send to Pannonia.[1] By
appropriating the name Caesar Galba proclaimed himself heir
of the defunct Julian house.   The Praetorians, won over by the
promised donative, supported him.   Thus, as Tacitus puts it,
" the secret of empire was revealed :   an Emperor could be made
elsewhere than at Rome " : [2] by which he means that the
Principate was no longer the exclusive prerogative of the Julio-
Claudians at Rome, acting with Praetorian support, but could
be won by anyone with a provincial army to back up his claim.

Verginius Rufus, who was apparently a genuine republican,
acquiesced in the Senate's pronouncement.   Clodius Macer did
not ; but he disposed of only one legion (III Augusta), and
Galba quickly procured his murder.   Thereafter Africa plays
but a small part in the events of 69.

By October of 68 Galba was in Rome, the officially recognized
Princeps.   But from the commencement of his reign things
went badly.   He himself was seventy-three years of age,[3] and
his advanced years as well as the habits of a lifetime and the
traditions of the old Roman aristocracy, to which he belonged,
made it almost impossible for him to follow a course of flexibility
and expediency.   His motives may have been of the best, but
the soldiers were in no mood to tolerate the disciplinary strictness
of an aged martinet.

When Galba discovered that Nero's extravagances had
virtually bankrupted the State, he resolutely set to work to
rehabilitate public finances.   He appointed a commission of
thirty knights to undertake the futile task of trying to recover
the monies which Nero had lavished on his favourites.   At the
same time a rigid economy in all public expenditures was
instituted : the People had to go without shows and the soldiers
without bribes.   Even the donative which Nymphidius Sabinus
had promised to the Praetorians was not paid.   Such parsimony
punctured Galba's popularity.

Moreover men noted that privately the new régime was by
no means so virtuous.   Favours to the Gallic supporters and

---

[1] Vespasian subsequently renamed it VII Gemina, the title probably
signifying that it was amalgamated with Legion I which joined Civilis'
revolt.

[2] Tacitus, *Histories*, I, 4, 2.

[3] He had been governor of Upper Germany as long ago as the reign
of Gaius.   Tacitus' characterization of Galba (" omnium consensu
capax imperii, nisi imperasset "—*Histories*, I, 49, 0) is perhaps the best
known of all his *mots*.

punishments for the Gallic opponents of Vindex were perhaps to be expected.[1] Galba had after all been Vindex's associate. But there was no similar explanation for the unbridled licence allowed to such rapacious rascals as T. Vinius, Galba's consular colleague, Cornelius Laco, his new Praetorian Prefect, and Icelus, an imperial freedman who had been elevated to equestrian status. Nor was Galba's cruel severity distributed impartially. The marines whom Nero had enrolled to oppose Galba's entry into Rome were cut down. Some of Nero's appointees such as Cingonius Varro, consul designate, and Petronius Turpilianus, were summarily executed; and the unlovely Nymphidius Sabinus met the fate he deserved. Yet Tigellinus, the most notorious of Nero's creatures, was permitted to live in luxury at Sinuessa; it was left for Galba's successor to make an end of him.

It is possible that these faults might not have been sufficient in themselves to bring about Galba's overthrow. But he also laboured under another and more fatal defect. Despite his assumption of the name Caesar, his pretext that he was the heir of the Julii did not convince the troops. He was obviously a typical member of the senatorial nobility. More than any previous Emperor he seemed to represent the old republican element in the State. One of his direct ancestors was Mummius, the destroyer of Corinth in 146 B.C.; another was one of the liberators who slew the first great Julian. The soldiers, least of all the soldiers of Germany who could not forget his association with Vindex, would not give him their allegiance. The army of Upper Germany had acquiesced only with the greatest sullenness when their commander Verginius Rufus pronounced in Galba's favour, and they were completely alienated when Galba at once recalled Verginius and replaced him with the aged Hordeonius Flaccus. The soldiers of Lower Germany became openly mutinous when the governor, Fonteius Capito, was murdered on Galba's behalf by Fabius Valens, the commander of Legion I. The fifty-five-year-old Aulus Vitellius was appointed to Capito's place.[2]

Matters now came quickly to a head. At the beginning of the year 69 the legions of Upper Germany refused to take the

[1] The favours would take the form of citizenship grants, tax exemptions, etc. The punishments would be loss of territory or revenue.
[2] He was the son of Claudius' intimate friend, and had himself served not discreditably as proconsul of Africa under Claudius.

customary New Year's oath of allegiance to the Emperor, and
two days later they supported the legions of Lower Germany
when these latter saluted their new commander Vitellius as
Emperor. Valens hastened to side with Vitellius; so did
Galba's old associate, the quaestor of Baetica, A. Caecina
Alienus, whom Galba had made commander of Legion IV
Macedonica in Upper Germany. All those Gauls who had
opposed Vindex naturally supported Vitellius; Raetia, Britain
(nominally at any rate) and ultimately Spain followed suit.

Galba met the threat by adopting a younger man, who might
be expected to support as well as succeed him. On January 10
he announced that his choice had fallen on L. Calpurnius Piso
Licinianus. The choice was unfortunate, since Piso, although
himself of the highest personal character, was likewise a typical
representative of the old senatorial nobility, a descendant of
Crassus and Pompey and the brother of the most notorious
conspirator against the Julian, Nero. The soldiers would have
been most reluctant to accept such a man in any case, but Piso
was doubly displeasing to them because of his military and
political inexperience. The clandestine way in which the
adoption was made shows that Galba was not unaware of
Piso's unpopularity.

There was not lacking a man at Rome to exploit the soldiers'
discontent. This was M. Salvius Otho, who as Galba's earliest
supporter had confidently expected the appointment. Otho
had nursed his resentment against Nero for stealing his wife
Poppaea for ten years; he was not likely to be less resentful
of what he considered Galba's ingratitude. Five days after
Piso's adoption, while Galba was sacrificing at the Temple of
Apollo, Otho hurried away to the Praetorian camp. The other
soldiers in the capital proclaimed him Emperor, and finding the
venerable Galba in the Forum, they murdered him; Piso, Vinius,
Laco and Icelus shared his fate (January 15). The Senate
hastened to ratify the choice of the troops.

§ 2. OTHO

Otho at once made it clear that he, like Galba, claimed to
be the heir of the Julii. He too assumed the name Caesar;
he even allowed himself to be hailed as " Nero," and he caused
that last Julian's statues to be restored. The Praetorians
and soldiers in the capital actually did regard him as the

successor of the Julii and not as a senatorial noble attempting to capitalize on the Julian name, so that he became very popular with them.   Their attitude to the Senate, on the other hand, is revealed by the fact that only with difficulty were they restrained from massacring the whole body.

The German legions had already saluted Vitellius as Emperor on January 3, and their advance forces under Galba's former supporters, Caecina and Valens, were already moving south by the end of the month.   Otho should have moved north at once to close the Alpine passes to them.   Perhaps he was reluctant to disperse the comparatively small forces he had available among the various passes ;   perhaps he was waiting in the hope that the German troops would abandon their hostility now that its chief object, Galba, was dead.   This hope proved vain ;   to the German armies Otho was just another member of the hated Vindex-Galba combination.   Whatever the reason, Otho dallied two fatal months in Rome.   His rule there was characterized by tact and moderation, just as his ten-year governorship of Lusitania had been ;   among his acts of prudence we might count his appointment of Verginius Rufus to the consulship.   Despite his personal vices Otho might have made a good emperor.   The legions on the Danube and Euphrates recognized him at once, and even though the two Spanish legions, VI Victrix and X Gemina, did not, he could claim in all the allegiance of some seventeen legions.   These, however, were unfortunately scattered throughout the Empire and not immediately available.   Meanwhile the west as a whole, together with Africa, had declared for Vitellius.[1]

§ 3.   THE BATTLE OF BEDRIACUM

Vitellius, unlike Otho, did have most of his legions immediately available.   Those of Britain could not indeed be employed,[2] but in the Germanies there were seven legions with their auxiliaries ready to march.[3]   In addition Vitellius could count on Legion I Italica stationed at Lugdunum in Gaul.   In all, he could send about 100,000 men into Italy, and enlistments *en route* might increase these to half as many again.

---

[1] Thus the ultimate division of the Empire into two halves was clearly foreshadowed.

[2] II Augusta ;   IX Hispana ;   XX Valeria Victrix.

[3] I ;   V Alaudae ;   XV Primigenia ;   XVI (in Lower Germany) ;   IV Macedonica ;   XXI Rapax ;   XXII Primigenia (in Upper Germany).

He split his forces into three groups. Caecina, with some 30,000 men mostly drawn from the army of Upper Germany, set out from Vindonissa and, after plundering the territory of the Helvetii *en route*, crossed the Pennine Alps into Italy by way of the Great St. Bernard; by the second week of March he was at Cremona on the River Po. Valens, meanwhile, with about 40,000 men mostly from the Lower German army, had a much longer route by way of the Cottian Alps and the Mont Genèvre Pass. His advance was marked by the same disgraceful scenes as Caecina's. Vitellius himself, with the rest of his forces, was following more slowly.

To oppose these armies Otho did not have strong forces immediately to hand, for the legions of Syria under Mucianus [1] and those in Judaea under Vespasian [2] were too far distant to hope to participate in the campaign. Otho could reasonably hope that the Danubian legions with their *auxilia* would ultimately see action.[3] But for the time being he had to rely on the Praetorian Cohorts under Licinius Proculus, a recently enrolled legion of marines (I Adiutrix) and some 2,000 recruited gladiators under Martius Macer; in all about 25,000 men. He did, however, have experienced generals at his side.

Having failed to block the Alpine passes, Otho decided in March to hold the line of the Po and to keep open his communications with the Danubian provinces. His general Vestricius Spurinna garrisoned Placentia on the Po and successfully resisted Caecina's efforts to dislodge him, while Annius Gallus, establishing himself at Bedriacum, a road centre and river crossing, safeguarded the communications with Pannonia and Dalmatia, whose legions were moving west to a rendezvous with Otho in North Italy.[4] Otho dispersed his scanty forces still further by sending some of them on a futile errand by sea to Gallia Narbonensis: his intention may have been to create a diversionary move against Valens. The remainder of his troops under Suetonius Paulinus, the hero of Britain, and P. Marius Celsus, followed Vestricius and Gallus to the north on March 14, Otho himself accompanying them.

[1] IV Scythica; VI Ferrata; XII Fulminata.
[2] V Macedonica; X Fretensis; XV Apollinaris.
[3] VII Galbiana; XIII Gemina (in Pannonia); XI Claudia; XIV Gemina (in Dalmatia); III Gallica; VII Claudia; VIII Augusta (in Moesia).
[4] The Moesian legions were temporarily detained by Roxolani raiding across the Danube.

Caecina on April 6 made an ambitious attempt to ambush Suetonius and Celsus at Locus Castorum, midway between Cremona and Bedriacum, but they turned the tables on him: indeed the Othonians came very near to annihilating Caecina's force on this occasion. If Suetonius had only shown greater alacrity the issue might have been decided in this skirmish, but he either could not or would not show the dash he had once displayed in Mauretania and Britain.[1] Suetonius and Celsus now joined their forces with those of Gallus at Bedriacum.

But in April Valens, foiling Otho's diversionary move in Narbonensis, joined Caecina at Cremona, and Otho was in a position of grave numerical inferiority, even though some of the Pannonian and Dalmatian troops, including Legion XIII Gemina, had reached Bedriacum and some of the Moesian ones Aquileia. Under the circumstances he would have been well advised to follow Suetonius' advice and await further Danubian reinforcements. But apparently both he and his troops were impatient to wipe out the enemy before Vitellius with his force could arrive. He therefore seems to have decided on the following plan: while Vestricius at Placentia contained the Vitellians at Cremona on the west, and Martius Macer and the gladiators held them on the south across the Po, Otho's brother Titianus with Proculus, Suetonius and Celsus was to attempt to encircle their whole army by a march from Bedriacum round the north of Cremona. The Danubian legions meanwhile were to move up to Bedriacum. Otho himself, as commander-in-chief, retired with a strong force of Praetorians to Brixellum, whence he could supervise and direct the whole intricate operation.

It is doubtful if his forces were large enough for such a complicated manœuvre. In any event it required precise timing, and the division of command of the main effort (the encircling movement from Bedriacum) prevented this from being achieved. Titianus, Proculus, Suetonius and Celsus engaged the Vitellian army prematurely near Cremona on the night of April 14 and after a bitter fight were routed. Their troops were chased back to Bedriacum, which gave its name to the battle, and surrendered the next day.

The battle of Bedriacum need not have spelled the end for

---

[1] His behaviour during and after the campaign makes one suspect him of treachery.

Otho. He still had command of the sea ; he still had some troops with him at Brixellum who were willing and indeed anxious to fight for him ; he still held the capital and all the prestige it carried ; and he still had his supporters outside Italy. But he refused to inflict upon the world a struggle which he feared would be protracted and bloody. He preferred to bring civil war to an end by getting rid of one of the pretenders, and with this noble motive he committed suicide (April 16) after urging his followers to make peace with Vitellius. Thus perished one of the strangest mixtures of vice and virtue ever to wear the imperial purple.

§ 4. VITELLIUS

To his own partisans Vitellius had been Emperor ever since January. By now he himself had reached Lugdunum in Gaul, and the Othonian generals, Suetonius and Proculus, hastened there to make their peace with him. The Senate at once extended official recognition to him. He himself, although he refused to be called Caesar until the last days of his reign, was not unaware of the magic of the Julian name : like Otho he claimed to be Nero's successor. After Bedriacum, he marched swiftly to Cremona and confidently concluded that he was now the undisputed master of the Roman world. Some of his own troops, including Valens' rowdy Batavian cohorts, he sent back to Germany. Of Otho's defeated legions he sent I Adiutrix to Spain, XIV Gemina to Britain, and the Pannonian and Dalmatian legions ultimately back to their respective provinces. He unwisely took no measures against the three Moesian legions, which were now concentrated on Italy's northeast frontier. Otho's Praetorians, however, he disbanded, replacing them with sixteen cohorts of his own recruited from his German troops.

He left Cremona about the end of May, and as he moved south he was either too weak or too lazy to restrain his men from putting into practice the habits of plunder they had learned when marching earlier through Helvetian and Gallic territory with Caecina and Valens. Indolence was his besetting fault ; he rarely bestirred himself except at the sight of food. He is said to have been the most voracious glutton ever to become Emperor, squandering no less than nine hundred million sesterces on the pleasures of the table in his few months of rule. When he reached Rome, he shocked public opinion by entering the city like a conqueror clad in the garb of a field-general and accompanied by 60,000 troops.   His subsequent rule, despite a certain porcine geniality and outward respect to the Senate, did little to remove this first impression.   He allowed his troops and their camp followers to run amok in the capital.   Moreover, though Vitellius himself was too lazy to be personally very brutal (he was merciful to Otho's partisans and relatives, just as he was later to Vespasian's), the generals who had elevated him to the throne, Caecina and Valens, abused their power in the most shameless way, and his freedman Asiaticus seemed a reincarnation of Icelus.   The execution of wealthy nobles on suspicion soon became a common event.

But Vitellius' position was precarious.   Even before he reached the city, rumblings could be heard in the east.   Flavius Vespasianus, the commander in Judaea, had indeed administered to his own three legions the oath of allegiance to Vitellius, as soon as the news of Otho's death reached him.   But the soldiers received the oath in sullen silence, for there was little love lost between the army of the east and the army of the Rhine. Mucianus, the governor of Syria, who also had three legions behind him, now urged Vespasian to claim the purple for himself. The able Prefect of Egypt, an apostate Jew named Tiberius Julius Alexander, and Vespasian's own son Titus supported Mucianus.   It would not be the first time that a victorious general had returned from the east to impose his will on Rome. At first, however, Vespasian hesitated and seemed inclined to imitate Pompey rather than Sulla, possibly because the Syrian legions on which he would have to rely were notoriously inferior, whereas those of Germany enjoyed an excellent military reputation.   Finally, however, he yielded to the urging of his advisers and the enthusiasm of the troops, and allowed the two legions of Egypt (III Cyrenaica and XXII Deiotariana) to salute him as Emperor on July 1 : subsequently he reckoned this date, rather than the day when the Senate recognized him, as the day of his accession.[1]   His own three legions in Judaea followed suit on July 3, and the three legions of Syria a fortnight later.   The eastern client kings also supported him.   Ultimately he was able to count on at least fourteen legions, since the Danubian legions supported him.

The governors of the Danubian provinces, L. Tampius Flavianus (Pannonia), M. Pompeius Silvanus (Dalmatia) and M. Aponius Saturninus (Moesia), were opportunist nonentities

---

[1] On the significance of this, see A. H. J. Greenidge, *Roman Public* p. 359.

who at first preferred to remain prudently non-committal.
The decision to support Vespasian was made by their subordinates—Cornelius Fuscus, the procurator of Pannonia, who was
later to be the Praetorian Prefect and to die in battle against
the Dacians in Domitian's reign ; Annius Bassus, the commander of Legion XI Claudia in Dalmatia ; Vipstanus Messala,
a tribune of Legion VII Claudia in Moesia ; and above all the
commander of Legion VII Galbiana in Pannonia, M. Antonius
Primus. It was Antonius who really won the purple for
Vespasian, aided by a capable senior centurion named Arrius
Varus, a former soldier of Corbulo, who admired the army of
the east ; he too subsequently became Praetorian Prefect. At
a meeting of Vespasian's Danubian supporters at Poetovio it
was decided to attack Italy at once without waiting for the
troops which Mucianus was bringing from the east.

Energetic action could still have saved the day for Vitellius,
for although the Spanish army would not and the German army
in the upshot could not support him, and although the British
army only managed to send him token aid, he had at hand the
troops he had brought with him to Rome. Numerically these
were a match for the Danubian legions, and Vespasian's eastern
legions could not arrive until some months elapsed. At the
very least Vitellius should have blocked the Alpine passes.
But, like Otho before him, he failed to do so. In other respects,
too, the coming campaign was to resemble the one that had
just preceded it.

Possibly Vitellius was overcome with his customary inertia.
At any rate he simply left matters to Valens and Caecina ;
and Valens was ill, while the rascally Caecina was once again
planning to play the traitor, possibly in order to score off Valens
of whom he was insanely jealous.

§ 5. THE BATTLE OF CREMONA

Meanwhile the Flavians, as Vespasian's party may now be
called, were moving methodically. Vespasian himself had gone
to Egypt, probably to cut off Rome's grain supply. His son
Titus had assumed the command in Judaea, and Mucianus had
commenced to march westward with Legion VI Ferrata and
13,000 assorted troops.

Simultaneously the Danubian troops moved on Italy.
Antonius Primus and Arrius Varus rushed forward with a

recklessly small force and won the race for the passes over the
Julian Alps ; pressing on beyond Aquileia, they actually seized
a bridgehead over the Athesis (*Adige*) before they made contact
with the Vitellians under Caecina.   This traitorous ruffian had
marched north from Rome with some 40,000 legionaries, but
had been in no hurry to reach and hold the Alpine passes.
He garrisoned Cremona with two legions and with the remainder
of his troops was occupying a position in front of Hostilia,
covering the line of the Po.   Together with the Prefect of the
Ravenna Fleet, Sex. Lucilius Bassus, he now began to negotiate
secretly with the Flavians.   Bassus managed to persuade his
men, ex-Othonians mostly, to declare for Vespasian ; but
Caecina could not, and his troops seized him and put him in
irons.   This left the Vitellian troops without a commander,
since Valens, although he had by now left Rome, did not take
over.   He preferred to imitate Otho's futile diversionary move
of six months earlier and made for Transalpine Gaul, probably
in search of reinforcements.   He fell into Flavian hands not
long afterwards.

With the defection of the Ravenna fleet Antonius Primus
would be able to turn the Vitellian position along the line of
the Po, once he obtained more men.   These were soon forthcoming, for the two Pannonian legions [1] met him at Patavium
and were quickly led to Verona, where they were shortly joined
by the three Moesian legions.[2]

The forward position of the Vitellians at Hostilia was now
clearly untenable.   Consequently the subordinate officers, who
were now in charge, decided to fall back on Cremona where
they had two legions in garrison.   Antonius' obvious move was
to stop them if he could, so that the Vitellian army from Hostilia
and the Flavian army from Verona engaged in a race for
Cremona.   The Vitellians won, since the two legions garrisoning
the town sallied forth on a diversionary move against Antonius'
troops, and although defeated in the ensuing skirmish (the
so-called " second battle of Bedriacum "), enabled the troops
from Hostilia to reach the city safely.   Thereby the Vitellians
obtained a concentration of troops capable of holding their own.
It was now, however, that the absence of an experienced commander made itself felt.   Instead of resting comfortably within
the city walls for the night, impatience got the better of them,

---

[1] VII Galbiana ;   XIII Gemina.
[2] III Gallica ;   VII Claudia ;   VIII Augusta.

just as it had of the Othonians earlier in this same vicinity, and they rushed out to engage in the crucial struggle the same night (October 27).

The ensuing Battle of Cremona was desperate, but the Flavians gained the upper hand and then closed in on the city. Although the Vitellian officers surrendered both it and Caecina, who was sent under guard to Vespasian, the city did not escape destruction. For four days the Flavian army sacked the venerable Roman colony with every conceivable form of horror and outrage. Fifty thousand people are said to have been slain.

§ 6. THE FLAVIAN TRIUMPH

By the Battle of Cremona Vitellius had lost the north and west beyond repair. The legions on the Rhine could not come to his aid, for they were busy suppressing a German rebellion which Antonius had instigated to keep them out of Italy. Britain, Gaul and Spain all took the oath to Vespasian. The defeated Vitellian troops were distributed throughout the Danubian provinces.

Nevertheless Vitellius still held peninsular Italy. Antonius Primus could expect no immediate reinforcements from Mucianus, who was busy repelling a Sarmatian attack on the Danube, and to Antonius' force Vitellius could oppose his devoted Praetorians. He also had a newly enrolled legion of marines (later called II Adiutrix) and the four Urban Cohorts, although the latter were a doubtful quantity since their commander, nominally at any rate, was the City Prefect, Vespasian's brother.

Vitellius' troops were at least adequate to block the passes over the Apennines, and Antonius' rather leisurely advance down the Via Flaminia encouraged Vitellius to make the attempt. He himself with fourteen of his Praetorian Cohorts took up a position at Mevania. But when he heard that the fleet at Misenum had revolted he ordered these troops to fall back to Narnia, returned himself to Rome and further dissipated his strength by sending troops to Campania to deal with the insurgent sailors. Antonius was thus able to cross the Apennines unopposed.

By now Vitellius' officers were deserting to the Flavians, and the force at Narnia soon followed their example. Antonius advanced his forces to Ocriculum and despatched a cavalry force to the very walls of Rome under Vespasian's kinsman, Q. Petilius Cerealis.[1] Vitellius himself now tried to desert, and opened negotiations with the Flavians. A parley was easily arranged, since Vespasian's brother Flavius Sabinus, curiously enough, still held the office of City Prefect to which Otho had appointed him. The meeting was held in the Temple of Apollo, among the intermediaries being the well if not favourably known epic poet, Silius Italicus ; and on December 18 Vitellius agreed to abdicate and retire to Campania with a princely pension.

But the weary Roman world, even now, was not to obtain peace. Vitellius' soldiers, made of sterner stuff than their doltish master, would hear of no such settlement and attacked Sabinus. He sought refuge in the Capitol in company with the eighteen-year-old Domitian, the younger of Vespasian's two sons. In the ensuing fracas the Temple of Jupiter Optimus Maximus, symbol of Rome's dominion, was burned ; men noted the omen with dismay. With the temple destroyed, Vitellian troops had a short-lived moment of triumph ; Domitian managed to escape but Flavius Sabinus was caught and killed. Vitellius was thus obliged to renounce his abdication.

The Flavian army, however, was just outside the walls and now, thirsting for revenge, it attacked the city. It was desperately engaged by Vitellius' German veterans, while the Roman mob looked on indifferently as the Flavians gradually gained the upper hand. Vitellius himself was caught and killed (December 20), and the Flavian troops proceeded to repeat the atrocities of Cremona, for Antonius could not restrain them, and Domitian did not even try. On December 22 the Senate, outdoing the well-known Vicar of Bray, hastened to recognize Vespasian just as it had recognized Galba, Otho and Vitellius before him. We are indeed particularly well informed about the powers voted to Vespasian by the Senate and ratified by the People, since they are enumerated in the extant Lex de Imperio Vespasiani, the earliest known example of the imperial powers and prerogatives being conferred *en bloc*. They included an unlimited power of *commendatio*.

Order was not fully restored until Mucianus arrived in January of 70. He acted as regent until Vespasian reached Rome some six months later to usher in an era of peace after ten dreadful months of civil war.

[1] He had audaciously resisted Boudicca's rebel Britons in 60 ; for his later exploits see below, pp. 240, 245.

CHAPTER II

VESPASIAN

§ 1.   DISCIPLINE RESTORED

WITH the accession of Vespasian the weary Roman world found peace.   For this the success of Flavian arms was primarily responsible ;   but a general weariness of the chaos which rival pretenders had provoked was also a factor.   Men were prepared to support Vespasian for the same reason that they had been prepared to support Augustus :   he bade fair to put an end to the tribulations of the State and promised some sort of order and security.

The new Emperor was a sign and a portent.   The year 69 had emphasized the increasingly prominent rôle that Italians, as distinct from Romans in the most literal sense of the word, were playing in the State :   Otho came from Etruscan Ferento, Caecina from Venetian Vicetia, and Valens from Hernican Anagnia.   It was, therefore, appropriate that the man who managed to establish himself permanently as Emperor should be an Italian.

Vespasian was born in A.D. 9 at Reate in the Sabine country. Although of an undistinguished family, he had received a good education :   he could read, quote and jest in Greek.   He had held a number of important offices, especially in the military sphere, and he had distinguished himself as a soldier in Thrace, Germany, Britain and Judaea.   Entering Rome as Emperor at the age of sixty-one, he brought with him the native shrewdness of the Central Italian husbandman rather than the intellectual brilliance of the city-dweller.   Even his wit, more marked though it was than that of any other Emperor, was rustic rather than urban.

He now found himself at once faced with pressing problems over and above the normal cares and duties of a Princeps. There was a universal lack of confidence ;   the Roman world had barely escaped the later chaos of the third century.   Thanks to his calm courage and dogged determination, Vespasian eventually healed the wounds of the State.   Early in his reign he was able to close the Temple of Janus, and before he died he ceremoniously extended the *pomerium*.   He inaugurated a century of stability ; but at the outset, with trouble in both the west and the east, his prospects were anything but favourable.

In Germany and Gaul a native German named Civilis was leading a most dangerous rebellion.[1] Vigorous action finally succeeded in suppressing it, but not before it had made clear the necessity for some sort of army reform. Vespasian would no doubt in any case have given the army his close attention. He had noted that it was Nero's failure to remain on intimate terms with the soldiers that had led to his overthrow. Vespasian was not going to make this mistake ; he cultivated the troops and thereby won their loyalty. Indeed, he and his sons must be given credit for reconciling the provincial armies to the idea of the Principate. Hitherto only the Julian house or, failing that, their own commanders, had been able to win their allegiance. For the next century and a quarter they obediently supported the reigning Princeps. It was the achievement of the Flavians that they won the soldiers' acquiescence in a definite theory and practice of succession.

But Vespasian needed to do more than merely spend a good deal of his time with the soldiers. The revolt of Civilis showed that a neglected army was a danger to the Empire as well as to the Emperor. Civilis largely owed his success to the widespread support he found among the nominally Roman troops quartered in Germany and Gaul. These troops were mostly natives of the region, recruited on the spot and sympathetic with the nationalist aspirations of the rebels. This was particularly true of the auxiliaries ; but the system of fixed legionary camps made it also true in large measure of the legionaries as well. They, no less than the auxiliaries, had been recruited in the vicinity, and they too joined Civilis. Once the revolt was suppressed, Vespasian took measures to prevent its repetition. He made the *auxilia* serve in areas far from their countries of origin. Moreover their units were probably no longer homogeneous but composed of troops coming from widely separated localities. Nor were they any longer allowed to serve under native officers. Thus the danger of another sepoy rebellion was obviated, and in fact the *auxilia* were never again guilty of nationalist ambitions.

The same measures could not be taken against the legions without abandoning the system of fixed camps, and that was far too dangerous a step to take in 70. Vespasian struck the

[1] See below, p. 238.

names of the mutinous German legions from the Roman army list,[1] but he did not abandon the recruitment of non-Italians. On the contrary, partly owing to the growing difficulty of finding suitable legionary material,[2] he actually admitted larger numbers of non-Italians, mostly from the western provinces and especially Spain. But it is going too far to say that he anticipated Septimius Severus and banned Italians from legionary service altogether.

§ 2. THE NEW NOBILITY

The provinces, especially those of the west, had attained such a degree of romanization and development generally that they were capable of making valuable contributions to the cultural and political as well as to the military life of the Empire ; and they possessed sufficient native energy to desire to play a prominent part. So far, despite Claudius' action in opening the Senatorial Order to Gallic nobles, provincials had on the whole not been granted very much scope for their talents : Seneca is an exception to prove the rule. There was, therefore, a danger that their energies and talents might be canalized in other directions, towards separatism for instance. That seemingly was the lesson of the movements headed by Vindex and Civilis.

Vespasian decided to enlist provincial abilities for the Empire rather than let them drift away. This probably was his principal motive in increasing the proportion of non-Italians in the legions. But he wanted to avail himself of provincial political and administrative capacities in addition. Claudius had begun this process by seeking Gallic participation in the counsels of the State ; Vespasian sought Spanish collaboration

---

[1] Under the Flavians, as under Nero, the legions apparently numbered twenty-eight. But I, IV Macedonica and XVI Gallica disappear. In their places we find I Flavia Minervia Pia Fidelis (after 82) and IV Flavia Firma and XVI Flavia Firma. The two latter probably contained veterans from the disbanded legions. They were, significantly, not sent to Germany : the former went to Dalmatia, the latter to Cappadocia.

[2] This difficulty, however, should not be exaggerated. Nero had recruited his new legion in Italy, as indeed its name implies (I Italica). Galba is said to have enrolled only Italians when he mobilized Legion I Adiutrix in 68 ; and Marcus Aurelius, a century later, was able to find enough Italians for his two new legions, II Pia Italica and III Concors Italica. Vespasian's action, therefore, was chiefly the result of deliberate policy.

as well. *C*. 73 he conferred Latin rights on the province of
Baetica, at the same time encouraging extensive urbanization
throughout the whole peninsula ; between 74 and 84 no fewer
than three hundred and fifty Spanish towns received municipal
charters.[1] Such urbanization had the same effect in Spain as
elsewhere in accelerating romanization ; the Latin language and
Roman customs penetrated into the farthest corners of the
peninsula. Caesar-worship, which hitherto had been confined
to the north, was established at Corduba in the south, and
Roman institutions were copied in the remotest villages ; and
the ports of Tarraco and Gades became exceedingly busy.
Once a community was organized as a Latin *municipium*, its
local office-holders automatically acquired Roman citizenship
and the chance to advance to high positions within the Empire.
The Spaniards, in other words, were being taken into the
imperial partnership. Nor were they the only ones so honoured,
for Vespasian founded numerous *coloniae* and encouraged
municipia throughout the provinces. Herein he showed that
he had a thorough appreciation of Rome's historical mission.

§ 3. VESPASIAN AND THE CENSORSHIP

It was possible that, even now, the prejudices of the nobility
might seek to stultify the Emperor's programme. It could not
have escaped Vespasian's observation that, even though the
municipal aristocracy had been making its way into the Senate
at Rome on a fairly substantial scale during the past hundred
years,[2] the tone of the Order remained very much the same ;
the newcomers identified themselves with the ancient senatorial
tradition of exclusiveness. To this, of course, the Princeps
could oppose his power of *adlectio*. But that was an indirect
procedure whose results would take some time to manifest
themselves, whereas Vespasian needed men immediately.
Therefore he preferred not to stand on ceremony, and in 73,
abandoning Augustan precedent, he assumed the office of censor.[3]

[1] The two most famous being the partly extant Domitianic ones of
Malaca and Salpensa (both Latin communities).
[2] It has been calculated that in Flavian times only thirty of the
old republican families were still represented in the Senate.
[3] Inscriptions suggest that he held it every year, as an annual office,
as did his son Titus. It was left to his younger son Domitian to become
censor perpetuus.

It was the office that traditionally controlled the list of the aristocracy ; and Vespasian used it to fill the gaps caused by imperial persecution and civil war with a new aristocracy drawn chiefly from the municipal towns of Italy and the western provinces, although the east and Africa were also represented.[1]

By assuming the censorship he openly proclaimed his intention to obtain an obedient rather than a co-operative Senate of the Augustan type. Thus the fiction that the senatorial nobility was the Emperor's equal partner now came to an end. The autocracy, implicit in the Princeps' position from the beginning, was now hardly disguised. That is not to say that the Principate now became an absolute despotism of the type envisaged by Gaius and Nero. The Senate was still treated with respect. Vespasian, for all his notorious parsimony, did not hesitate to keep deserving men within the Order by giving them financial help ; and he preferred to promulgate his new legislation, most of which was in the puritanical tradition of Augustus or the humanitarian tradition of Claudius (these being the Emperors whom he chiefly admired), by means of senatorial decrees.

Neither was Vespasian's reign a naked military dictatorship.[2] It did, of course, possess the ultimate backing of armed force ; but the Principate had had that from the outset. But Vespasian, although careful to retain the goodwill of the soldiers, cannot be described as parading their weapons in order to win a cowed obedience from all sections of the population. The Principate had not yet become a dominate. For the next hundred years and more most of the Emperors used methods of suggestion and persuasion rather than of brute force ; and most of them were tactful and courteous in their dealings with the Senate. For all that, they were undoubtedly autocrats. Vespasian, for instance, did not hesitate to insist on his nominees being appointed to senatorial provinces : thus Eprius Marcellus became governor of Asia. This, needless to say, did not endear Vespasian to the Senate. It despised the Italian municipal parvenu.

[1] Under him we find the first African ever to hold the consulship : Q. Pactumeius Fronto in 80. By 96 fifty per cent of the senatorial families of A.D. 65 had died out ; and by 135 only one of the forty-five patrician families restored by Julius Caesar still survived.

[2] But it is significant that Imperator now replaces Princeps as the designation of the supreme ruler.

§ 4. VESPASIAN'S ADMINISTRATION

Nevertheless Vespasian did not use his autocratic power irresponsibly. His new aristocracy was sober and industrious : it included men like M. Ulpius Trajanus, father of the future Emperor, Cn. Julius Agricola, the famed governor of Britain, and M. Annius Verus, the ancestor of Marcus Aurelius. So far as possible, Vespasian tried to select men of like mould to himself, and they, being his nominees, felt a loyalty to him. In general they served him and his family well.[1] Their respect for him is clearly shown in the improved tone of the imperial court. The luxurious sensualism and licentious frivolity of Nero's day made way for an almost mid-Victorian respectability to conform with the simple habits of the Princeps.[2] It was this serious and loyal new aristocracy that provided the devoted servants of the Empire, who were responsible for the good government that generally prevailed during the next century and a quarter. It is significant that there was only one recorded trial for provincial misgovernment in Vespasian's reign, and even in this case the accused was acquitted.

As there was now scarcely even the appearance of equality between the Princeps and the Senate, Vespasian saw no reason for following Augustus' example and avoiding the consulship : he held the office, and as ordinary not suffect consul, in every year of his reign except 73 and 78. And he not only held it himself : he had his elder son Titus with him as his colleague on no fewer than six occasions.[3] His object was obvious enough : he was training Titus for the succession ; for Vespasian was determined to prevent any recurrence of the events of 68 and 69. By cultivating the troops he avoided any rebellion against himself ; and by carefully providing for the succession he prevented any outbreak of anarchy after his death.

---

[1] L. Antonius Saturninus, who rebelled against Domitian, being almost the unique exception.

[2] After the death of his wife Flavia Domitilla, some time before 69, Vespasian did indeed maintain a concubine Caenis, whom scandal accuses of selling honours ; but he treated her as if she were his legal consort.

[3] His other son, Domitian, held it with him only once

§ 5. TITUS CO-REGENT

Besides making Titus consul on six occasions, Vespasian
invested him in 71 with the Imperium Proconsulare and the
Tribunician Power. Vespasian went even farther than this.
He had noted the rôle of the Praetorians in installing Gaius and
Claudius and in unseating Nero and Galba. Therefore to make
assurance doubly sure he made Titus his Praetorian Prefect.
And in addition to all this Titus was his colleague in the censorship and was officially styled Princeps Iuventutis (as was his
brother Domitian).[1]

There is no reason to doubt Suetonius' assertion that Titus
was very useful to his father in these offices. He certainly
signed edicts and the like in his father's name, and seems to
have served as his father's quaestor in the Senate.[2] Vespasian's
main object was undoubtedly achieved, for when he died in
79 no year of anarchy ensued.

§ 6. VESPASIAN AND THE FINANCES

The various actions and policies of Vespasian, which we have
considered so far, all provided carefully if imperiously for the
future welfare of the State. He was equally attentive to its
present needs. As we shall see, he gave not a little of his
attention to the frontiers.

But it was his work in the financial sphere that has contributed most powerfully to his fame. The extravagances of
Nero and the civil wars of 69 had thrown the public finances
into a chaotic condition. If one ancient text can be believed,
Vespasian found on his accession that forty milliards of sesterces
were needed to restore the financial situation. More than a
mere liquidation of past debts was needed. There were urgent
tasks awaiting completion that would require large sums:
frontier defences and war damage had to be repaired, and
gratuities had to be paid to retiring Praetorians.[3]

Early in his reign Vespasian addressed himself to the

[1] Henceforth, if not before, the title Princeps Iuventutis indicates
the successor to the Principate.

[2] The scandal that he was ambitious to overthrow his own father can
be dismissed for the nonsense that it is ; while the Emperor Hadrian's
belief that Titus poisoned Vespasian merely shows how curiously
Hadrian's mind worked on occasions.

[3] Vespasian reduced Vitellius' sixteen Praetorian Cohorts to nine, the
Augustan figure. Domitian subsequently raised them to ten.

financial problem with energy and shrewdness.   His assumption
of the censorship in 73 enabled him to make a careful census,
and this record of the Empire's resources revealed that bankruptcy could be avoided.   The provinces had reached a point
of prosperity where they could provide much larger revenues
than in Augustus' day.   Egypt alone could raise five hundred
million sesterces a year, a larger sum than the whole Empire
was providing three quarters of a century earlier.[1]

Vespasian's methods were divers and varied.   Any taxes
remitted by his immediate predecessors, for example by Galba,
were re-imposed.   The tribute payable by the provinces was
increased and in some cases even doubled.   Undoubtedly, too,
he imposed new taxes, although all the details are not certain.
Some " free " cities, that is cities which escaped certain taxes,
were now assigned to provinces and forced to pay : this happened to Rhodes, Samos and Byzantium.   Achaea, the province
to which Nero had granted immunity from taxation, was
abruptly put back on the paying list.   Provincial mining areas,
like those of Spain, were now if not before obliged to contribute
to the imperial revenues.   In fact, not only mines but all lands
owned by the State and the Emperor were placed under strict
imperial control and made to yield a profit.   For example,
Vespasian began to sell the so-called *subsiciva*, the marginal
land of colonial foundations, which had been originally un-
allotted and subsequently appropriated by squatters.   The
ancient sources even make the wildly improbable charge that
he raised money by the sale of offices and similar corrupt
devices.   There is, however, no reason to doubt that he employed methods which can fairly be described as unsavoury.
His tax on urine is a notorious example, even though we do
not know exactly how it was levied.[2]

Besides trying to increase revenue he was equally careful to
restrict expenditure as much as possible.   Retrenchment
undoubtedly eliminated much wasteful extravagance.   The
simplicity of his court and his new and as yet relatively un-
corrupted officialdom helped to keep expenses down.   Indeed
his reorganization of the administration may have been partly
dictated by the need for economy.

[1] Currency depreciation no doubt partly explains the higher figures.
[2] Vespasian's lack of squeamishness on this subject is illustrated by
an anecdote of Suetonius (*Vespasian*, 23, 3) which is condensed into the
pungent but unauthentic phrase, " pecunia non olet."

Vespasian's thrifty handling of the finances has always been a subject of jokes and even of derision. His stinginess has become a byword. But even though it is true that he left a full treasury behind him, he does not deserve so strong an epithet. Vespasian did not waste money; but when a job needed doing, neither did he hoard it. In every province he spent money freely to build roads, provide public works, regulate boundaries and strengthen frontiers; he even granted taxation immunity to some deserving communities. In Italy he undertook a programme of building and repair of civil war damage; even before his arrival in Rome the rebuilding of the Capitoline temple had been begun in token of Rome's resurgence. He also commenced the Flavian Amphitheatre (or Colosseum as it has been called since Medieval times) in the space between the Caelian and Esquiline hills. The end of civil war was celebrated by the erection in 75 of a Temple of Peace in a large piazza which soon came to be popularly known as the Forum of Vespasian. The spoils of the Jewish campaign were deposited in this temple.

In the field of education especially Vespasian spent money generously. The first professor to be paid a salary from public funds was appointed in his reign, the celebrated Quintilian. Men of letters were also encouraged with money grants.[1] Schools were built and endowed, and wealthy citizens like the Younger Pliny were soon inspired to follow this Emperor's example.

A new era, a new life for the Empire was commencing; and in the new order the Emperor's watchword would be public service instead of a wilful self-indulgence. The Flavian Amphitheatre was symptomatic of the Emperor's intention in this respect. The fact that Augustus had planned an amphitheatre for this site no doubt influenced him, but it was also the site which was to have held the Golden House, symbol *par excellence* of Nero's apolaustic selfishness. It now obtained a building which over 80,000 citizens could use simultaneously.

§ 7.   THE OPPOSITION TO VESPASIAN

The peace and prosperity which Vespasian restored were marred only by a plague which ravaged Italy towards the end of his reign. But the termination of internecine strife was not

---

[1] The poet Seleius Bassus is said to have received half a million sesterces.

Vespasian's only achievement : his other services to the Empire were many and great. Despite this, and despite the universal longing for tranquillity, his reign was not free from opposition.

His own nominees to nobility were usually loyal to him, but the Senate as a body was not. Many senators, particularly those from Cisalpine Gaul, were implacably opposed to this *novus homo*. His well-nigh continuous consulship did ennoble his house, but along with his censorship it also advertised his autocracy, which now bade fair to remain permanent by his careful provision for Titus' succession. No doubt the Senatorial Order was also coldly furious at his evident determination to fill its ranks with upstarts from the Italian municipalities and the provinces of the west and even of the east. By Vespasian's day the Senatorial Order was no longer a well of romanism pure and undefiled, but it still cherished the old tradition of noble privilege.

To what extent such considerations swayed the Stoic philosophers we cannot say, but they certainly shared the dislike of many senatorials for Vespasian. Some of them, as in the reign of Nero, were apparently still bemused by a nostalgic longing for the Republic ; it was not until a later day that they realized that their egalitarian teachings were much more likely to be put into practice under the benevolent paternalism of a solitary autocrat than under the republican system of class privilege. Some of them preferred the Stoic ideal of Kingship, namely the rule of the best man chosen from an aristocracy of the educated ; whereas Vespasian unhesitatingly demonstrated that he relied on a loyal army rather than on any well-intentioned theory of government to maintain his position. The Cynic philosophers gave even more trouble than the Stoics. They assailed the social and legal barriers by which the Principate enabled the upper classes to maintain their privileged position ; in effect they preached political anarchy. Whatever their motive, the philosophers made their opposition to Vespasian's régime unmistakable, and they were punished in consequence. Helvidius Priscus now found the fate he had so narrowly escaped in Nero's reign. His family connexions were suspect : his wife Fannia was the daughter of Thrasea Paetus and the granddaughter of Caecina Paetus, and his friends, Arulenus Rusticus and Junius Mauricus, were notorious republicans. At the beginning of the reign Priscus had tried to exalt the Senate at Vespasian's expense, and when the Emperor refused to countenance this, he had recourse to a kind of boorish obstructionism. His refusal to co-operate in public administration, his openly paraded discourtesy to the Emperor, and above all his publication of a subversive pamphlet provocatively entitled *In Praise of Cato*, led first to his banishment and ultimately to his death. In general, however, Vespasian refrained from executing the philosophers; he even tried, belatedly as it happened, to countermand the order for Priscus' death. As he put it, " I shall not kill dogs that bark at me," and he was content to remove them out of harm's way. In 71 he issued a general order expelling the vagrant Stoic and Cynic philosophers from Rome, including the well-known Cynic Demetrius and C. Tutilius Hostilianus. An exception was made in the case of Musonius Rufus, a Stoic who knew how to bridle his tongue. Even exile did not cure the others : they continued their wordy sniping even from across the sea.

The philosophers, with their impractical yearning for a dead and gone Republic, Vespasian could simply regard as nuisances. But amongst the senatorial nobility there were opponents whom he was forced to take more seriously. The plotters, who had no illusions about a republican restoration, usually planned to replace the Emperor with a nominee of their own. According to Suetonius, " continual conspiracies " of this sort were formed against Vespasian, and Dio records a plot in 79 in which the ex-consul Eprius Marcellus and the Vitellian traitor, A. Caecina Alienus, were implicated ; Caecina was at once executed and Marcellus forced to commit suicide. Details concerning the other conspiracies have not survived, but presumably Vespasian suppressed them vigorously, even though, as Suetonius insists, he condemned no innocent person to death. At any rate he did not fall victim to any plot : he died of natural causes at his native Reate on June 24, 79. His opponents could not even obtain the posthumous revenge of systematically blackening his memory, dearly though they would have liked to do so. His son Titus at once succeeded him and ensured his deification. The grim old Emperor, indeed, foresaw this : on his very deathbed he had jested, " Methinks I am becoming a god." [1]

---

[1] Suetonius, *Vespasian*, 23, 4.

CHAPTER III

TITUS

§ 1. HIS POPULARITY

THE meticulous care which Vespasian had devoted to the question of the succession ensured Titus' elevation. Although only forty, Titus was well and widely known for his services to the Empire. He had served in Germany, Britain and Judaea, and the impressive " triumph " which he celebrated in Rome after his capture of Jerusalem in 70 engendered confidence in his military capacity and endeared him particularly to the army of the east. His administrative ability had been demonstrated during his partnership in the Principate with his father. Neither was he lacking in tact : his charm of manner was famous. In 75 he had made it plain that he respected Roman prejudices and traditions by putting aside a beloved mistress whom men suspected of aspiring to be another Cleopatra, the Jewess Berenice, sister of Herod Agrippa. In his youth he had indeed been extravagant, and in Judaea he had earned a reputation for ruthlessness ; hence his accession was at first viewed with some apprehension. The Senate especially would not be disposed to welcome another Flavian very enthusiastically. But Titus' succession was not disputed : there was no desire anywhere to precipitate a repetition of the evils of 69.

§ 2. ERUPTION AND FIRE

Immediately he became sole emperor, Titus proceeded to increase his popularity. He gave splendid shows and games, at which the spectators frequently received opulent presents. The ancient sources indeed suggest that his brief reign of twenty-six months was one unbroken succession of open-handed gestures of this sort : he reckoned that day lost on which he did not bestow a princely gift on someone. His lavish generosity and urbane geniality made him universally beloved, and his reign would have seemed like the return of the Golden Age had it not been marred by two serious disasters.

The first of these was the famous eruption of Mt. Vesuvius on the Bay of Naples on August 24, 79, which buried Pompeii,

Herculaneum and some neighbouring villages. The Younger Pliny, who witnessed it, has left a graphic description of the catastrophe and of the heroic efforts of his uncle, the Prefect of the Misenum Fleet, to rescue as many victims as possible and simultaneously satisfy his own scientific curiosity.[1] Systematic excavation of the ruins of Pompeii and Herculaneum has also thrown much light on the disaster. Titus immediately appointed a commission of outstanding men (*curatores rei publicae restituendae*) and provided them with public funds to take whatever steps they could to relieve suffering and restore damage.

The other disaster in Titus' reign was a huge fire in Rome, probably in 80, which consumed the new Capitol, the Pantheon and Agrippa's Baths among other buildings. Titus once again set relief measures in motion promptly. He even sold some of his private furniture to raise funds, asserting that if possible none should suffer but himself. This may explain why his private life during his reign was simple to the point of frugality.

Apart from the two major calamities that occurred, Titus' reign is largely a record of benevolence. There were no executions and no treason trials, even though his reign was not free from conspiracies : the Senate would resent Titus' Flavian habit of monopolizing the consulship. In general he continued his father's policies, and not least in his building activities. It was he who dedicated the Flavian Amphitheatre with sumptuous shows lasting one hundred days. Nearby he also constructed his luxurious Baths, and celebrated their opening with lavish gladiatorial shows.

§ 3. THE DEATH OF TITUS

Titus' health, however, was poor, and death overtook him at Reate on September 13, 81. He left no son ; nor had he made any formal provision for the succession. Apparently he distrusted or was jealous of his younger brother, Domitian. He was heard to remark that Domitian was his appointed successor, but he never conferred the Imperium Proconsulare or Tribunician Power upon him. Manifestly there was little love lost between the brothers ; that, however, is no warrant for believing the rumour that Domitian procured Titus' murder. Fortunately

[1] *Epistulae*, **VI, 16.**

the Roman world was spared another year of anarchy, for the Praetorians at once proceeded to proclaim Domitian Emperor.

The handsome Titus was perhaps the best loved of all Rome's Emperors.[1] Modern critics point out that this favourable estimate derived from his lavish spending and his short reign. Gaius and Nero had likewise started out well and then changed for the worse once the money had run out. Might not Titus have behaved similarly ? Might not his cruel streak, which is suggested by his fondness for the bloody sports of the arena and by other signs, have led him into acts of tyrannical oppression like those of the two predecessors whose early careers so strongly resemble his ?

We have no means of knowing to what extent these speculations are justified. Some of his acts of generosity were urgently needed after the eruption and fire. Others, if correctly reported, appear giddily heedless ; for example, his dispersal of vouchers among arena audiences entitling the finders to gold, food and horses at the expense of the *fiscus*. What sums such gestures involved we cannot say ; probably Titus should not be charged with extreme wastefulness. Even so, much of the surplus which Vespasian's thrift had built up was dissipated, and this bequeathed a serious problem in imperial finance to Titus' brother and successor.

There was, of course, never any doubt about his deification. If his own popularity had not assured him of the posthumous honour, Domitian, eager to be the son of one *divus* and the brother of another, would have made sure that he obtained it.

---

[1] Suetonius, *Titus*, 1, 1 : amor ac deliciae generis humani.

CHAPTER IV

DOMITIAN

§ 1. THE CHARACTER OF DOMITIAN

THE thirty-year-old Domitian had not been formally marked out for the succession. As Vespasian's son, respect had been shown to him from the year 69 onward ; he had been made a member of various sacred colleges and had even held the consulship several times, once with Vespasian as his colleague. Along with Titus he had been styled Princeps Iuventutis and Caesar, and his name is found coupled with his brother's on inscriptions. Nevertheless he had not held any post that would give him real experience and thoroughly prepare him for the duties of an emperor. Vespasian had not given him as good an education as he had given Titus, and he refused Domitian's request to be allowed to lead an expedition against the Alans in the Caucasus. Domitian, in fact, seems to have been kept in the background of the Flavian family in somewhat the same way that Claudius had been in the Julio-Claudian. It was even proposed that, like Claudius, he should marry his own niece, Titus' daughter Julia. Domitian rejected this proposal, even though Titus made it. He might be treated like Claudius, but in temperament he resembled Tiberius. He resented the slights to which he was subjected and spent a good deal of time in semi-retirement studying the *Acta* of Tiberius, his favourite reading, and interesting himself in Greek studies and poetry, of which he wrote some himself.

But even though he had not been officially designated, the succession of Vespasian's remaining son was not likely to be disputed. The other armies acquiesced when the Praetorians proclaimed him Emperor on September 13, 81, and the Senate ratified their choice the next day. This did not mean that the senatorial nobility liked him. On the contrary, they hated Domitian far more than Vespasian, not only because he quickly made it evident that he was bent on furthering his father's policies, but also because they regarded him as even more of an upstart. Vespasian had at least earned his elevation by terminating civil war, and Titus had suppressed a revolt in Judaea. Domitian had done nothing, not even enough to earn recognition from his own father and brother. In short, he merely had the good fortune to be the son of Vespasian and of a woman who, so it is said, for a long time had not even been a Roman citizen.

Domitian was not followed by a successor who was anxious to safeguard his memory, and the Senate was able to damn it officially the moment he died. Furthermore, the régime that came after his, in an effort to establish itself more securely, fostered the systematic denigration of Domitian : it sought to convey the impression that the bad old days had ended and a new Golden Age was beginning. The Senate was eager enough to disparage Domitian in any case ; when it was officially encouraged to do so, virtually no limits were set to its vilification.

The ancient writers, on whom we depend for our knowledge of the reign, for the most part shared the senatorial outlook, and they depict Domitian as a monster of cruelty and wickedness. The Christian writers also join in the hostile chorus, since some Christians may have lost their lives in the reign. They describe Domitian as the Second Persecutor.

This picture undoubtedly contains a kernel of truth. There was a streak of cruelty in Domitian as in the other Flavians : the many friends and servants who fell into disgrace during the reign prove that. Domitian probably had other defects too. How otherwise are we to explain the failure of Vespasian and Titus to designate him formally for the succession ? Presumably neither his father nor his brother had full confidence in him. Yet it is by no means certain which is cause and which is effect. Had he been allowed by the two earlier Flavians to gain some real political and administrative experience early in life he possibly might not have been guilty of some of his later actions. His inflated sense of dignity and other pieces of tactlessness at the very least might have been avoided.

The traditional representation of Domitian's reign as a period of unmitigated terror is no doubt an exaggeration. But his reign obviously was not a happy period for certain sections of Roman society. Domitian was not a genial figure ; at the end, even his wife, Corbulo's daughter, of whom he was very fond, turned against him.

§ 2. INCREASE IN AUTOCRACY

One thing can be said with certainty of the reign of Domitian :
it was even more autocratic than that of Vespasian. Domitian
scorned partners, he merely wanted servants, and he did not
hesitate to parade his autocracy. For the first eight years of
his reign he was consul every year ; [1] in all he held no fewer
than seventeen consulships during his lifetime, far more than
any of his predecessors. In other words, while copying his
father in this, he was also going beyond him. The same is
true of the censorship. Instead of holding it as an annual
office, as Vespasian seems to have done, Domitian in 85 proclaimed himself *censor perpetuus*. His intention to dominate
the Senate completely could scarcely have been more openly
proclaimed, and dominate it he did. Vespasian had sought to
pack it with municipal and provincial elements who would
collaborate with him, Domitian was more impatient. He did
not at first actively persecute it : indeed, at the outset, he
tried to win its approval by attending its meetings and forcefully
suppressing the *delatores*. However, he was tactless enough to
appear in the Senate in his triumphal robes and to insist on
voting first, and he refused the customary promise to put no
senator to death. Soon he began to ignore the Senate completely
and to carry out his policies in a thoroughly dictatorial way.
His policies in themselves were not bad, but his high-handed
methods evoked bitter resentment. When, for instance, the
Senate was arbitrarily deprived of its revenue from the aqueducts, it was hardly likely to reflect that the Emperor's Fiscus
paid for their upkeep, and that there was therefore a certain
degree of equity in the change.

Domitian readily availed himself of the services of individual
senators who were loyal and willing to serve him. But his
impatience with the Senatorial Order as a whole is shown by
the increased importance he gave to the Equestrian Order. He
did, indeed, seek to lessen the consequence of one of the
equestrian prefectures. As he did not, like Vespasian, have a
son to serve as his Praetorian Prefect, he was not anxious for
this officer to be a person of power. Therefore his usual practice
was to have two Praetorian Prefects, and he took care to change
them frequently.

[1] In his last years he usually avoided the office : perhaps he had
become contemptuous of so senatorial an office.

In other respects, however, he gave the knights far more influence than his predecessors had been disposed to do. Claudius, the great organizer of the imperial bureaucracy, had not been eager to use equites; he had rather relied on freedmen from his own household. It was Vitellius who, in an effort to court aristocratic support, began to take the big positions away from the freedmen. Domitian, although not entirely dispensing with the services of freedmen, continued this tendency. Henceforth the great state secretaryships are no longer an exclusive libertine preserve; indeed on at least one occasion Domitian raised the rank of his freedman Secretary of State,[1] so that the office might be held by a person of equestrian status.

In thus honouring a class whose abilities and capacities richly deserved it, Domitian showed sound common sense. Unfortunately he was tactless enough to use knights in positions that were hitherto reserved for senators, and this gave mortal offence to the Senatorial Order. Thus he appointed knights to his judicial *consilium*, which sat in judgment on senators. In an emergency he made C. Minicius Italus, a procurator (that is, a knight), proconsul of the senatorial province of Asia; and he placed his Praetorian Prefect, likewise a knight, in charge of the war against the Dacians.

Domitian did not assume his perpetual censorship merely in order to advertise his own autocracy; he hoped as censor to improve the tone of Roman society. To this end he purged the Equestrian as well as the Senatorial Order: wealthy upstarts who posed as knights in the theatre were quickly put in their place. Like Vespasian, he encouraged the old Italian virtues, and as usual went farther than his father. Vespasian had sought to bring about a return to simpler ways and a healthier outlook by himself setting an example; Domitian tried to legislate men into morality. Licentiousness on the stage was suppressed and disabilities were placed in the path of actors, and he tried to curb prostitution. Being Pontifex Maximus as well as censor, he was especially concerned to restore religion to its pristine purity. The dread archaic punishment of death by starvation was revived for unchaste Vestals. The spread of oriental religions was checked, severe measures especially being taken against proselytizing Jews or

[1] Claudius, who had started his career under the Emperor of that name.

judaizing Gentiles.[1] Christianity, too, may have come under the ban, although it is by no means certain that any Christians who lost their lives in his reign were executed because of their Christianity. If any Christians were executed, the charge against them was probably one of atheism. The old Roman cults, on the other hand, were greatly fostered. New temples were erected to Jupiter Capitolinus and Jupiter Custos, the former being a magnificent affair with a roof of gold; and old temples to Janus, Castor and Apollo were rebuilt. The worship of Minerva was particularly supported, since Domitian regarded her as his special protecting deity,[2] much as Augustus had had a partiality for Apollo. Quinquennial Capitoline games were instituted in 86 and the Secular Games were celebrated in 88, although with so much Hellenic ceremonial that they probably offended instead of conciliating the nobility. The Emperor encouraged family life by vigorously enforcing certain provisions of Augustus' Leges Iuliae which had fallen into desuetude. He refused to accept legacies from testators who had children and heavily taxed legacies from testators who had not.

§ 3. DOMITIAN AND THE FINANCES

The new temples were only part of a very ambitious building programme. Domitian completed the Flavian Amphitheatre which Vespasian had begun and Titus dedicated. In the Campus Martius he built special structures for his Capitoline games, an Odeum, Stadium and Circus. He built a temple to his deified father and brother, and further honoured Titus by erecting the surviving arch that celebrates his capture of Jerusalem. He was also responsible for buildings of a more utilitarian character : for himself a grandiose mansion on the Palatine and a villa overlooking the Alban Lake, and for the public a shopping centre in the Saepta, granaries and water works.

His principal motive for this frenzied building activity may have been to do honour to the gods and perhaps to add to the grandeur of Rome. He was certainly fond of pompous ostentation, as is shown by the fact that he tried to have two months

[1] The worship of Isis, however, was not frowned upon. By now it had become so widespread—Domitian himself was a devotee—that it could fairly be regarded as naturalized.

[2] Domitian may have derived his predilection for Minerva from his native Sabine country, where she was held in special esteem.

of the year named after him and caused numerous statues of himself, some of them equestrian, to be erected throughout the city. As a thorough-going autocrat Domitian presumably felt it necessary to impress the populace with such monuments. Undoubtedly he was touchy about his dignity : when he found men ready to address him as Lord and God (*dominus et deus*), he was nothing loth. He did not indeed have these titles conferred upon him officially and at first was chary about using them publicly, but before the end of his reign they were customarily used, even by the Emperor himself. Apparently he was anxious for deification in his own lifetime, but proceeded rather cautiously because of the fate that had overtaken the similarly minded Gaius and Nero. It is significant that towards the end of his reign a refusal to worship his genius was regarded as a proof of atheism, and the number of men charged with this was steadily growing when death overtook him. Needless to say, this supplied the senatorial aristocracy with an additional reason for hating him.

His building projects, which were not confined to Rome,[1] required vast sums. He had other expenses to meet as well, for he fought several costly wars, and he provided the populace with spectacular gladiatorial shows and beast-baitings. Since he had inherited a rather bare treasury from the open-handed Titus, he must have had difficulty in making ends meet. Domitian cannot be charged with spendthrift recklessness : if he spent money freely in some directions, in others he was very careful and displayed some of his father's noted hard-headedness. He was much less lavish with donatives than his immediate successors,[2] and he seems to have left the public finances in order at his death ; certainly his successor Nerva on his accession was able to disburse fairly large sums. How Domitian accomplished this feat is far from certain. He did not resort to debasement of the coinage; indeed he seems to have restored it to a pre-Neronian standard of purity. Efficiency in administration and in the collection of taxes was presumably responsible. It is specifically asserted that the men who served him were good, and the fact that his successors kept many of them in office, his secretary Cn. Octavius Capito for instance, substantiates the assertion. At the beginning of his reign he

---

[1] Cf., for example, the road he built to link up Sinuessa with Cumae.
[2] His three separate donatives to the citizens of Rome amounted in all to 225 denarii a head.

cancelled bad debts to the State of over five years' standing, and he confirmed in their holdings the occupiers of marginal land in Italian *coloniae*, whom Vespasian had proposed to evict. These were preliminary regulatory steps of an equitable nature, but in general he was not prepared to lose sources of revenue. Taxes, the Jewish poll-tax for example, were rigorously and promptly collected ; this indeed caused the uncivilized Nasamonians of North Africa to stage a short-lived revolt *c.* 85.

Domitian presumably used his censorial powers to obtain an exact knowledge of the Empire's economic resources. Undoubtedly he was interested in them ; in 91, to stimulate wheat production throughout the Empire, he forbade the planting of new vines. But this attempt failed ; and it was left to his immediate successors to devise a better method for aiding agriculture.

According to the ancient sources, Domitian acquired funds by methods of confiscation and judicial murder. And there is some evidence to support this charge : it is significant that under him the lighter form of banishment (*relegatio*) involved the forfeiture of one's property. Pliny even suggests that it was greed for money that was chiefly responsible for his attacks on the nobles ; but he exaggerates when he makes avarice Domitian's principal motive.

Nevertheless his reign was undoubtedly marred by numerous treason trials and by the reappearance of the hated *delatores*. It is probable that the unpopularity of this last Flavian resulted in plots by senatorial malcontents. Domitian reacted violently, for he was suspicious by nature, as his temporary divorce of his wife Domitia in 83 [1] and his execution of his cousin Flavius Sabinus at about the same time show. Once convinced that his suspicions were not unfounded he became merciless. The testimony of Pliny and others make it clear that the last years of his reign were a period of terror. The immediate cause for this probably was the rebellion of a military commander in one of the provinces in 88.

§ 4.   THE REBELLION OF SATURNINUS

Domitian diligently supervised the provinces for reasons of military security and of efficient administration. Only one

---

[1] For a time his niece Julia replaced her as his concubine : cf. **Vespasian and Caenis.**

case of provincial misgovernment is recorded in his reign, and
the peccant governor was condemned. Domitian lavished
particular care on Greek cities. But he saw to it that provincial
appointments everywhere went to men of ability, who for the
most part served him loyally and well. Some of them were
members of Vespasian's new aristocracy and were themselves
of provincial origin. Among the more illustrious were Cn.
Julius Agricola, the governor of Britain, L. Javolenus Priscus,
the well-known jurist, Julius Frontinus, the noted writer on
technical subjects, and M. Ulpius Trajanus, the future Emperor.
The latter was a Spaniard, as were L. Licinius Sura and Marius
Priscus, while Julius Quadratus who held several provincial
governorships came from Asia Minor. Some of the armed
provinces did indeed witness considerable frontier fighting
during Domitian's reign. But from the point of view of civil
administration the provinces generally were happy and contented under him, and the routine of Empire functioned smoothly.
We should have many tangible memorials of this prosperity,
had not his successors systematically sought to destroy his
memory and rob him of the credit for much of his work.

In one province, however, serious internal trouble did
develop, in Upper Germany. In 88 L. Antonius Saturninus,
commander of Legions XIV Gemina and XXI Rapax stationed
at the " double " camp of Moguntiacum, raised the standard
of revolt.[1] What caused his burning hatred for the Emperor is
uncertain. Presumably he was not merely one of the disgruntled senatorials, since he was one of Vespasian's new
nobility. He may have been provoked by the rebuke publicly
administered to him by Domitian for his scandalous life, or
possibly the proposal to eliminate " double " camps offended
him since it would have resulted in the halving of his command.
Certainly after his rebellion Moguntiacum ceased to be a
" double " camp, and XXI Rapax went to Pannonia ; but it
is obvious that this could have been the result rather than the
cause of Saturninus' rebellion. The revolt demonstrated the
unwisdom of having large military concentrations ; Domitian
therefore put an end to " double " camps (except in Egypt).[2]
Probably the simplest explanation of Saturninus' hatred of

___

[1] Vespasian had had I Adiutrix at Moguntiacum, but Domitian had
sent it to Pannonia c. 85 and replaced it with XXI Rapax from Bonna
in Lower Germany. His new Legion I Minervia took its place at Bonna.
[2] III Cyrenaica and XXII Deiotariana were together as late as A.D. 119.

Domitian is the truest, that he coveted the imperial power for himself. The time seemed ripe for his attempt : Domitian was heavily involved in a war on the Danube, and in Rome senatorial circles were in a state of alarm mingled with fury owing to Domitian's recent ruthless suppression of a conspiracy.[1] Saturninus obviously thought that he had widespread support ; when he began his rebellion he did not hesitate to proclaim himself Emperor. By seizing the savings bank in which his legionaries' pay was deposited he was able to blackmail his two legions into supporting his cause. He may have used the money thus criminally acquired to bribe the Chatti to take up arms on his behalf. They needed little urging in any case, for they had an old grievance against Domitian,[2] and they took the field.

Domitian, however, had followed his father's example in carefully cultivating the provincial armies, and his popularity with them now stood him in good stead. Although the Danubian legions were unavailable, he was able to muster overwhelming forces against the insolent pretender : the other two legions of Upper Germany,[3] the four legions of Lower Germany under L. Appius Maximus Norbanus,[4] and the Spanish legion which the future Emperor Trajan rapidly transferred.[5] Domitian himself hurried north with some of his Praetorians in January 89. But before he arrived Saturninus had already been defeated and killed by Norbanus somewhere north of Moguntiacum on the left bank of the Rhine. An unseasonable thaw prevented the Chatti from participating in the battle : the ice broke up, so that they could not cross the river.

Saturninus' was not the first conspiracy against Domitian, but it was the most dangerous. Domitian's fears may even have magnified it, for he could not discover its ramifications. Any papers that might have implicated others were destroyed by Norbanus in the rebels' camp.

----

[1] The conspiracy to which allusion is made in the records of the Arval Brethren for 87.

[2] See below, p. 242.

[3] VIII Augusta at Argentorate ; XI Claudia at Vindonissa.

[4] This most probably was Norbanus' position, but the matter is disputed.

[5] Spain now enjoyed an excellent road system : hence one legion, VII Gemina, with headquarters at Leon, was sufficient to maintain order there.

§ 5. THE TERROR

In fear for his own safety, the Emperor henceforth had recourse to spies and *delatores*. These included M. Aquilius Regulus, a notorious informer from Nero's day; Catullus Messalinus, whose blindness did not prevent him from encompassing the ruin of many an excellent man; Mettius Carus, who aspired to be informer-in-chief; Fabricius Veiento, the terror of Roman society. There may be some exaggeration in the surviving accounts of Domitian's last years. The story of the imperial freedmen and favourites running amok is not very credible, for the imperious Domitian was not the man to surrender authority to such creatures. Nevertheless the prevailing atmosphere of terror is so vividly described by Pliny, Tacitus and Juvenal, all of whom lived through it, that the substantial accuracy of the picture can hardly be doubted.

The victims were given the formality of a trial. That, however, did not save them, and the Senate was forced to condemn some of its own members. The dreary list of unfortunates contains some notable names. Mettius Rufus, the Prefect of Egypt, was disgraced, while C. Vettulenus Cerealis and Sallustius Lucullus, governors respectively of Asia and Britain, were executed *c.* 90 : M. Arrecinus Clemens, a former Praetorian Prefect, apparently shared their fate. M'. Acilius Glabrio, a prominent senator, was first forced to fight in the arena and was then sent into exile, where he was subsequently executed. Trumped up, trivial charges proved fatal to many, since the suspicious Domitian, unlike Tiberius, did not discourage the officious zeal of *agents provocateurs*.

The chief sufferers under the Terror were not the ordinary People, who were kept in good humour with lavish shows, much less the common soldiers, who received a $33\frac{1}{3}$ per cent increase in pay. It was the Senatorial Order more than any other that felt the Emperor's heavy hand. Some of its members, such as Frontinus and Agricola, sought safety in retirement from public life. The Younger Pliny implies unconvincingly that this was the policy which he too adopted, but that it failed to secure him immunity : Domitian, at the time of his death, had an accusation against Pliny on file—at least that is what Pliny says.

Senators, however, were not the only group singled out for persecution. Domitian entertained an intelligible dislike for the philosophers who had so plagued Vespasian. In 89 he expelled them from Rome and in 95 from Italy. Two of the most illustrious, Epictetus and Dio Chrysostom, were thus banished from Italy by a decree of the Senate. A sterner fate befell the remnants of the Stoic opposition. *C.* 93 Herennius Senecio, eulogist of Helvidius Priscus, was executed; Priscus' son and Arulenus Rusticus, pupil of Thrasea Paetus, shared his fate; Priscus' widow Fannia was sent into exile. Actors and freedmen also felt the iron fist. The well-known Paris fell out of favour and was murdered, while Epaphroditus was executed for having helped Nero to commit suicide a quarter of a century earlier.

The stories that Domitian filled his privy purse by confiscating the property of his victims or by accepting bribes to hold his hand or by forging last wills and testaments have some truth in them. A respectable person like the Younger Pliny vouches for their accuracy; but it should not be forgotten that Pliny was anxious to ingratiate himself with a régime that was concerned to blacken Domitian's.

There is much solid evidence to show that Domitian's last years were years of tyranny and cruelty, if not of downright sadism.[1] The manner of the Emperor's death in itself proves it. The allegation that the tyrant, himself subject to the dread tyranny of fear, had recourse to astrologers and took elaborate precautions for his own safety may or may not be true.[2] In any case, all his precautions proved unavailing once his own household began to feel insecure.

This happened after 95, when he executed his two Praetorian Prefects and his slothful cousin, Flavius Clemens, the latter being charged with atheism, in other words with conversion to a foreign religion (probably Christianity). Clemens' wife Domitilla, who was also the Emperor's niece, was simultaneously exiled. This proved the Emperor's undoing, for if a harmless sluggard like Clemens could not escape, then no one could feel safe. A palace plot, which reckoned among its members his wife Domitia, his chamberlain Parthenius and apparently his new Praetorian Prefect Petronius Secundus, was accordingly formed against him. The conspirators arranged for him to grant an interview to a certain Stephanus, Domitilla's steward,

[1] The story of the senators who by a grim jest were forced to attend a feast that seemed to be their own wake readily springs to mind.

[2] He is said to have covered his palace walls with mirrors, so that no one could stalk and slay him.

who pretended to have an injured arm but actually had a dagger concealed among the bandages. Even then Domitian might have successfully resisted his attacker, had not Parthenius' servants aided Stephanus to overwhelm the Emperor (September 18, 96).

The Flavian dynasty died with him. He was far from being its most genial member, and he doubtless suffered from serious faults of temper. But he governed the Empire well, even if despotically. He may not have been the " greatest of the Flavian princes," but he had a keen eye for the needs of the Empire and showed great capacity in caring for them. The fact that the Senate immediately proceeded to damn his memory and officially to abolish his acts should not blind us to his achievements. Indeed if he had had a son or brother to succeed him he almost certainly would have been deified. But unfortunately for him he did not ; in fact, one of the gravest charges that can be brought against him is that he had failed to make provision for the succession. Not that he had neglected this problem. Since his own son died young, he had marked out the succession in 90 for his second cousins, the sons of Flavius Clemens and Domitilla, and made the illustrious Quintilian their tutor.[1] But when he executed their father in 95 he apparently abandoned all thought of the succession for them, and before he had made any other arrangement the hand of the assassin struck him down.

In consequence the State at his death faced the same situation as in 68. But it had the good fortune to escape a repetition of the evils that followed the death of Nero. Domitian's murderers, before they struck, had taken the precaution of obtaining a candidate for the Principate, an old, respected jurist and senator, M. Cocceius Nerva.

[1] Like Vespasian, Domitian was interested in education. He provided Rome with splendid libraries.

CHAPTER V

FLAVIAN FRONTIERS

§ 1. THE GENERAL FLAVIAN POLICY

ON the frontiers the aim of the Flavian emperors was not so much to add fresh territories, although they did that also, as to render Roman soil inviolable. Augustus had not delimited the frontiers strictly ; on occasions he had used his legions as a field force instead. Their task was to maintain internal order as well as to repel external attacks, and for this purpose their fixed camps were usually of earth and easily transferable. In general Augustus had sought natural boundaries such as rivers, mountains, oceans and deserts. Where these were lacking, his frontiers had not been firmly demarcated. Thus in the Germanies, in Raetia and in Syria the exact extent of Roman territory not bounded by rivers was left somewhat uncertain. Yet clearly defined and, if possible, short frontier lines were an urgent necessity in order to facilitate administration, and above all to enable the none too many legions to discharge their wide-flung duties efficiently. The Flavians sought to mark out such frontiers.

Their method was to bring and keep the military establishment up to full strength. It was now that the sequence and hierarchy of military appointments attained the precision and regularity described above (pp. 55 f., 98 f.). The Flavians made sure that army formations actually had the personnel and weapons laid down in the establishment. The legions thus fully equipped became genuine garrison armies stationed in permanent camps that were henceforth built of stone. From these stone camps, thanks largely to the network of military roads which Augustus' successors had been industriously building, and thanks to the shortened frontiers which the Flavians themselves established, it was possible to despatch legions, or more usually parts of legions, to wherever they were needed. The extensive use of legionary detachments (*vexillationes*) is a notable feature of Flavian military activities and is a direct consequence of having the legions permanently at full strength.

§ 2. THE REVOLT OF CIVILIS

One of the fortunate and surprising features of the terrible year 69 was the lack of more serious repercussions in the barbarian world beyond the frontiers. This was due to a variety of circumstances. Despite the fact that it was a Spanish legion that inaugurated the series of ephemeral emperors, the troops of that province as well as of Britain hardly participated in the civil wars, and were able to perform their usual frontier duties in consequence. Nero's understanding with Parthia kept the eastern frontier tranquil. Disturbances did occur along the Danube, but they were kept within bounds, partly by the fact that the legions there did not get into the actual fighting in Italy until late in 69, and partly by the agreements which the Flavian leaders made with various kings and chieftains across the river. Things were different on the Rhine. Its legions were among the first to depart to Italy to struggle for Empire, and with frontier vigilance thus relaxed, the Germans and some of the Gauls seized the opportunity and attempted to throw off the Roman yoke.

The movement was actually instigated by the Flavian leader Antonius Primus, who was anxious that the Roman troops in Germany should have their hands full and be unable to send help to Vitellius. The rebels in fact did at first claim to be acting in support of Vespasian ; it was not long, however, before they dropped the mask.

The rising of Vindex in 68 had already revealed the existence of discontent in Gaul, but there was far more among the German tribes living along the Rhine. Between this river and the Meuse lay the so-called Island of the Batavians, a region which Corbulo had brought under Rome's dominion in Claudius' reign. Its German inhabitants, the Batavi, and their less numerous kinsmen, the Canninefates, did not pay tribute to Rome but did supply troops. The Emperor's personal bodyguard indeed consisted of Batavians.

When the Flavian troops entered Italy, the Batavians were incited to rise by one of their chieftains, a brave and eloquent barbarian named Julius Civilis who, despite his protracted service in the Roman army and possession of the Roman citizenship, had long been planning rebellion. In the latter half of 69 he saw his opportunity. The Roman commander on the Rhine was Galba's aged and feeble appointee, Hordeonius

Flaccus, who secretly favoured Vespasian and, like Antonius, urged Civilis to revolt. Civilis scarcely needed any urging. He must have been sorely tempted to revolt by the paucity of troops at Hordeonius' disposal ; the soldiers that accompanied Vitellius to Rome had not been sent back and had been only partially replaced. Instead of its normal garrison of eight legions with their corresponding *auxilia*, the Rhine was defended at this moment only by detachments from six legions,[1] in all some fifteen to twenty thousand men, whose auxiliaries were largely recruited from local tribes and were ready to join the rebellion. It was a most formidable threat to the whole Empire and might well have proved irretrievably disastrous, had not the fissiparous tendencies of Germans and Gauls once again manifested themselves. Most of the German peoples on both banks of the Rhine joined Civilis ; but the Cimbri and Cherusci did not move, and the Ubii had to be coerced against their will ; even Civilis' own nephew fought fiercely against him. In Gaul fidelity to Rome or indifference to the rebel cause was much more widespread ; the powerful Remi and Sequani remained loyal. The Treveri, Lingones and Nervii were the principal Gallic tribes to revolt, their leaders being the romanized Julius Classicus, Julius Tutor (both of the Treveri) and Julius Sabinus (of the Lingones).

The rebels, at first claiming to be acting in Vespasian's interest, cleared the Island of the Batavians of Vitellian troops. But after the Battle of Cremona, when Vespasian had won universal recognition—even from the soldiers on the Rhine— Civilis still refused to lay down his arms. He now made his real aim clear : national independence. He and his troops laid siege to the legionary camp at Castra Vetera. Hordeonius Flaccus sent Dillius Vocula, commander of Legion XXII Primigenia, to raise the siege, and this he ultimately succeeded in doing ; he even saved Moguntiacum for a time. This success, however, was only temporary ; for unfortunately Vocula had to disperse the comparatively few legionaries at his disposal too widely ; and in addition they, like the auxiliaries, were in great part of German origin. Three of the legions[2] proved mutinous and Vocula was murdered at Novaesium. It was at

---

[1] V Alaudae and XV Primigenia at Castra Vetera ; XVI Gallica at Novaesium ; I at Bonna ; IV Macedonica and XXII Primigenia at Moguntiacum.
[2] I, IV Macedonica, XVI Gallica.

this stage that the Gauls joined the rebellion, influenced no doubt by the symbolic interpretation they gave to the Capitol conflagration at Rome and by simultaneous Dacian and Sarmatian attacks across the Danube. It seemed as if all Gaul and Germany would be lost. All the Roman camps and forts, except Moguntiacum and distant Vindonissa, were burnt. At Vetera Legion XV Primigenia was apparently wiped out: at any rate its name disappears from the Roman army list. The Imperium Galliarum was almost an accomplished fact.

But now in the spring of 70 Mucianus, who was ruling Rome pending Vespasian's arrival, was in a position to take vigorous counter-measures; he could even count on the defeated Vitellians being eager to pay off old scores against the Germans. In fact, it was two Vitellian legions [1] that were sent north under Petilius Cerealis, who was later joined by VI Victrix from Spain and XIV Gemina from Britain. With these forces he proceeded to pacify the Lower Rhine and the adjacent parts of Gaul. After subduing the Treveri and their fanatical boy leader Valentinus, Cerealis recovered successively Colonia Augusta Treverorum (*Treves*), Colonia Agrippinensis (*Cologne*), Vetera and the Island of the Batavians. Meanwhile Otho's old general Annius Gallus with three Flavian legions [2] and the recently enrolled I Adiutrix was defeating the Lingones and restoring order in Upper Germany.

Thus the great rebellion was suppressed and the German and Gallic provinces saved for the Empire. The chief credit for this belongs to Cerealis. It was to him that Civilis made submission, and he received as a reward his appointment as governor of Britain (71–74).

§ 3.   CONSOLIDATION OF THE RHINE FRONTIER

Vespasian prudently restored the number of legions along the Rhine to eight.[3] But he did more than merely restore the military establishment, for he and his sons made important

---

[1] II Adiutrix; XXI Rapax.

[2] VII Claudia; VIII Augusta; XI Claudia.

[3] Four in Lower Germany: X Gemina (at Noviomagus), XXII Primigenia (at Vetera), VI Victrix (at Novaesium), XXI Rapax (at Bonna); four in Upper Germany: I Adiutrix, XIV Gemina (at Moguntiacum), VIII Augusta (at Argentorate or more probably farther west near Dijon), XI Claudia (at Vindonissa).

changes along the Rhine frontier. The mainly anti-Flavian literary sources are silent about their work, but it has been revealed by archaeological discoveries.

Had Augustus' original plan of an advance to the Elbe been permanently accomplished, the northern frontier of the Empire would have been considerably shorter. After Varus' defeat the Elbe-Danube line had to be abandoned, and it was left to the Flavians to effect such straightening of the frontier as was still possible.

Between the Upper Rhine and the Upper Danube there is a triangle of land which is mostly occupied by the Black Forest. This area, so Tacitus implies, was called the Agri Decumates, a title, possibly obsolete and native, that has never been satisfactorily explained.[1] In 73 Vespasian instructed Cn. Cornelius Clemens, legate of Upper Germany, to annex the region. Frontier rectification was presumably his main motive : the boundary would thus become shorter and straighter, and intercommunication between Rhine and Danube camps would be facilitated. In the process Vespasian would safeguard the growing civil life on the left bank of the Rhine and would also obtain land on which to settle his veterans. He may even have hoped to derive a large revenue from the area, a consideration to which the thrifty Flavian would certainly not be indifferent. To find a pretext was not difficult. The area was sparsely populated and of uncertain ownership : if Rome did not claim it, somebody else probably would. The annexation was achieved without undue difficulty, although it did not proceed very rapidly. With each step forward fortresses were established to consolidate gains; some of these ultimately grew into towns and cities. By 79 Roman arms had at least reached a line that stretched from Argentorate (*Strasbourg*) by way of Arae Flaviae (*Rottweil*), where a centre of Caesar-worship was instituted, to Lake Constance ; and they may even have got as far north as the line that runs from Baden to Günzburg on the Upper Danube. This would seem to be the area of the Agri Decumates proper.

Vespasian also strengthened the Roman position on the Lower Rhine. In 75–78 Rutilius Gallicus and Vestricius Spurinna conducted successful operations against the Bructeri.

Although Roman forces were operating in the sector immediately north of the Agri Decumates (the so-called Taunus

[1] See F. Hertlein, *Klio*, XXI (1926), pp. 20–43.

district) in Vespasian's reign and have left traces of their forts, it was Domitian who really consolidated this more northerly region. It is situated on the right bank of the Rhine immediately north of Mannheim. Domitian's motives were mixed. He wanted to continue his father's policies and he wanted to become known to the troops; unlike Vespasian and Titus he had had little chance for military distinction before his accession.

The Chatti, a powerful, warlike and barbarous German tribe dwelling in the Taunus district, gave Domitian his opportunity. In the past they had often clashed with Rome. As recently as 69 they had joined Civilis' movement and had actually plundered Moguntiacum. In 82, incited perhaps by Domitian's forcible recruiting methods among the neighbouring Usipi, they tried to repeat the performance by advancing through the country of the Mattiaci to attack Roman territory. But this time they were to pay heavily for their temerity. Domitian headed north in person, ostensibly to conduct a census in Gaul, but actually to chastise the Chatti. At the same time he exploited the mutual hatred existing among the German tribes : he bribed the Cherusci, ancient enemies of the Chatti, to menace their rear.

Thanks to Tacitus, who apparently regarded Domitian's German war as responsible for the curtailment of his father-in-law Agricola's operations in Britain, Domitian's German campaign was belittled in antiquity and indeed was depicted as a joke. Modern research, however, has revealed a different story. At Moguntiacum, together with his accompanying Praetorians, Domitian mustered strong detachments from nine legions : the four in Britain,[1] the four in Upper Germany,[2] and XXI Rapax.[3] C. Velius Rufus was placed in charge of these troops, and he proceeded to expel the Chatti from the valley of the Main. They were gradually driven back into the forests of the Taunus and disappeared into the obscurity of the wild hinterland of the Hercynian forest, while Domitian's arms were probably carried right into Lower Germany. The Emperor then traced a new frontier, some hundred and twenty miles in length, which presumably ran north of the Taunus and was strengthened with earthen forts, wooden watch-towers and roads

[1] II Adiutrix ; II Augusta ; IX Hispana ; XX Valeria Victrix.
[2] I Adiutrix ; VIII Augusta ; XI Claudia ; XIV Gemina.
[3] This legion was now permanently removed from Lower Germany.

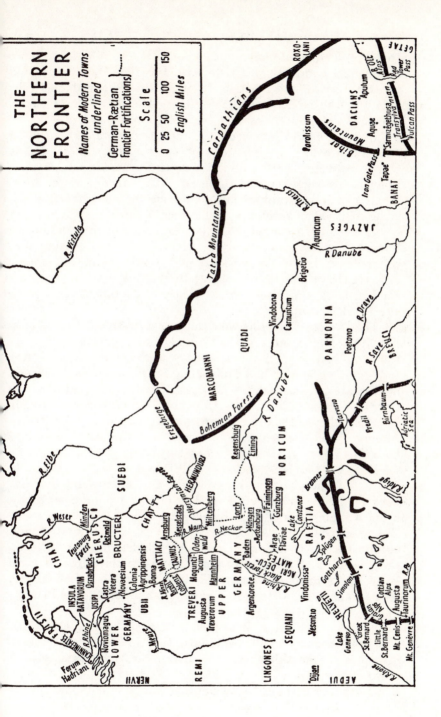

THE
NORTHERN
FRONTIER

Names of Modern Towns underlined
German-Rætian frontier fortifications ------

Scale

0 25 50   100   150

English Miles

that provided good communications with the " double " camp at Moguntiacum. By his two-year campaign Domitian added the territory of the Mattiaci (that is, the Odenwald and the valley of the Neckar) to the Empire. He surely deserved his five imperial salutations and his title of Germanicus.

In 85 Domitian returned to Rome and celebrated a splendid triumph which was featured by spectacular games. He is chiefly responsible for consolidating the new German annexations, as his coins not unfairly insist. The line of forts between Brohl and Kesselstadt, each accommodating one cohort, and a series of wooden watch-towers between Köngen and Faimingen on the Danube, are apparently his work, and the fort at Rottenburg on the Neckar certainly is. It was left to later Emperors to construct the defence works of the renowned Limes Germanicus : Hadrian built the wooden palisade, while the continuous earthen bank and ditch (the so-called Pfahlgraben) belongs to the third century.[1]

The Flavian Emperors were concerned to strengthen not only the Upper Rhine, but also the Upper Danube which since Augustus' day had formed the boundary to Raetia. The earthen forts which Claudius had built along its southern bank seemed inadequate to Vespasian, who constructed another at Regensburg and crossed the river. Here too Domitian continued his father's policy. He drew a new northern boundary for Raetia running from Köngen to Faimingen, and towards the end of his reign he may have advanced this.

Thus the Flavians, and above all Domitian, were responsible for the addition to the Empire of the triangle of land that lies between Rhine and Danube and is bounded on the north by a line running from Brohl by way of Arnsburg and Lorch to Eining on the Danube. Domitian also gave some kind of civil administration to Roman Germany. Under him for the first time we hear of a legate of Germany as distinct from a mere legate of the army in Germany.[2] The first of these new legates seems to have been the well-known jurist, L. Javolenus Priscus, in 90.

From now on the Roman hold on the left bank of the Rhine was not seriously challenged until the time of the Frankish invasions in the third century. Even the right bank settled down into a peaceful condition. In fact so tranquil did the Rhine frontier become, that Domitian was soon able to transfer

[1] See below, p. 304.   [2] See above, p. 112.

two of its legions (I Adiutrix and XXI Rapax) to an area where far more serious danger threatened, the Lower Danube.[1]

§ 4.   PETILIUS, FRONTINUS AND AGRICOLA IN BRITAIN

The Flavian governors of Britain were men of renown.   The first of them, Petilius Cerealis (71–74), the conqueror of Civilis, defeated the Brigantes, a confederation of tribes inhabiting Yorkshire and Lancashire, and transferred the camp of the ill-fated Legion IX Hispana, which he had commanded against Boudicca in 61, from Lincoln to York (Eburacum).

His successor, Julius Frontinus (74–76), the well-known writer on military tactics, pushed west rather than north and gained successes over the Silures.   Apparently it was during his governorship that Caerleon (Isca) became the permanent camp of Legio II Augusta.[2]   Meanwhile Legion XX Valeria Victrix moved to Chester (Deva), where it was to remain for centuries.

Frontinus was succeeded by Cn. Julius Agricola (77–84), who had already seen extensive service in Britain.   Thanks to the biography of him by his son-in-law, the historian Tacitus, he is the most famous of the governors of Britain.   He was an able administrator, a skilful soldier and an excellent engineer. Whether his conception of the strategic potentialities of the Empire was sound is another matter.   He proposed to bring the whole island, from John o' Groats to Land's End, under Roman dominion, and in five campaigns, the exact details of which cannot be discovered owing to Tacitus' geographical and chronological uncertainties, he did achieve some striking military successes.   After completing Frontinus' subjugation of Wales he moved north.   As he progressed, his practice was to secure the ground won by a chain of forts.   He established such a chain between the Tyne and Solway, and linked them with a road, the so-called Stanegate, which like Ostorius' Fosse Way a generation earlier, served to mark the frontier.[3]

---

[1] Domitian's final arrangement of legions on the Rhine seems to have been as follows : in Lower Germany, X Gemina (at Noviomagus), VI Victrix (at Vetera), I Minervia (at Bonna) ; in Upper Germany, XXII Primigenia (at Moguntiacum), VIII Augusta (at Argentorate), XI Claudia (at Vindonissa).   See R. Syme, *Journ. Rom. Stud.*, XVIII (1928), p. 43 f.

[2] Previously it may have been at Gloucester (Glevum).

[3] The Stanegate may be pre-Agricolan.

From here Agricola pressed into Scotland, erected another chain of forts between the Forth and Clyde, and penetrated to a point north of Perth, where he won the celebrated battle of Mons Graupius somewhere near Dunkeld. At this point Domitian summoned him to Rome. Tacitus, reflecting the embittered view of his father-in-law, suggests that the recall was due to imperial jealousy. This, however, is not very probable. Domitian had already once extended Agricola's term of office, and probably felt that the time was ripe for a change, more especially as Agricola was contemplating campaigns that would have overtaxed the military resources of the Empire. He proposed to conquer not only all of the Highlands but Ireland as well. No doubt it would have been strategically an excellent plan to round off Rome's conquests in this part of the world, and it is just barely possible that Agricola was not over-sanguine in thinking that he could do so with the troops available ; one legion might, as he said, have sufficed for the conquest of the emerald isle. But the course of the fighting had indicated that the swift conquest and rapid romanization of south-eastern Britain would not be repeated in the north and west. In fact, those prime romanizing agents, towns and villas, of which the latter are very plentiful in the south-east, seldom made their appearance in the north or in Wales. Hence Agricola would have needed strong forces to hold the areas in subjection after subduing them ; but the Empire simply did not have the troops to spare for such an enterprise. Actually some of the forces already in the island were urgently required elsewhere ; in 86 Domitian was obliged to transfer one of the British legions, II Adiutrix, to the threatened Danube frontier.[1]

§ 5.   THE DACIAN WARS

Of the tribes that lived north of the Danube, Germans, Scythians and Thracians, the Germans were not consistently hostile to Rome. The Hermunduri, who lived opposite Raetia, were usually friendly ; but the Marcomanni and Quadi, Suebian tribes living opposite Regensburg and Carnuntum respectively, had frequently clashed with Rome, though recently they had recognized Roman suzerainty and accepted pay to act as frontier guards.

[1] Petilius Cerealis had brought it to Britain in place of XIV Gemina which, after Civilis' defeat, had stayed in Germany.

The Scythians, on the other hand, who dwelt farther down the river, were a recurring problem. The Sarmatian Jazyges indeed, who lived between the Theiss and the Danube, had not of recent years been particularly unfriendly ; but the Roxolani, farther to the east in Moldavia and Bessarabia, were continually giving trouble with their dreaded, armour-clad cavalry.

Between the Jazyges and Roxolani lived the Dacians, a by no means uncivilized people who seem to have been of Thracian stock. As early as Julius Caesar's day a Dacian emperor named Burebista gave cause for foreboding, and in Augustus' reign mention is made of Dacian raids under a native prince, Cotiso. More recently the Dacians had been quiescent ; they had been weakened, partly by Plautius Silvanus' transportation of some 100,000 of them south of the Danube in Nero's reign,[1] but chiefly by the mutual feuds of their twenty or more loosely-knit tribes and by their quarrels with their kindred, the Getae.[2]

The year 69 revealed the weakness of the Danube frontier. A horde of Roxolani swept over the river into Moesia. They were repulsed indeed by Mucianus ; but as their action had gravely prejudiced Vespasian's chances for Empire he was not likely to forget the incident or the frontier where it occurred, more especially as in the next year the Roxolani again breached this frontier and slew Fonteius Agrippa, the legate of Moesia.[3] After Vespasian became Emperor, he gave the Danubian defences some attention : he rebuilt Claudius' fort at Carnuntum and constructed another at nearby Vindobona (*Vienna*). Vespasian, however, was more preoccupied with Germany and Britain than with the Danube. Under him the key Danubian province of Pannonia had a garrison of only two legions,[4] while Moesia contained only three.[5] It was Domitian who really reinforced the Danubian defences. Early in his reign he seems to have sent Legion V Alaudae from Germany to Moesia.

It may be that Vespasian's military measures in the area,

---

[1] Included in this total are some Bastarnae, a people whose ethnic connexions are uncertain. Originally their territory was extensive, but by Domitian's day they seem to have been confined to an area well north of the river.

[2] See above, p. 109.

[3] His successor Rubrius Gallus restored the situation.

[4] XV Apollinaris at Carnuntum and XIII Gemina at Vindobona, whither it had been transferred from Poetovio.

[5] VII Claudia at Viminacium (?), V Macedonica at Oescus, I Italica at Novae.

minor as they were, provoked the Dacians.   In any event, in
Domitian's reign they found national unity under a powerful
and ambitious king named Decebalus and were in a pugnacious
and aggressive mood.   The core of their strength was in the
mountain-girt, natural fortress of Transylvania, and they were
formidable enemies.   In 85 they invaded Moesia, penetrated far
to the south and slew the legate of the province, Oppius Sabinus,
probably at the modern village of Adamclisi in the Dobrudja.
Domitian at once hurried to the Danube with his Praetorian
Prefect, Cornelius Fuscus, whom he put in charge of operations.
At the same time Legion IV Flavia Firma was transferred from
Dalmatia, bringing to five the number of legions in Moesia,
which was now divided into two provinces, an Upper with three
legions and a Lower with two ; [1] the River Ciabrus (*Tzibritza*)
may have been the boundary between the two.   Lower Moesia
was further protected by the so-called *vallum*, or greater earth
wall with thirty-five hastily constructed forts about a mile
apart, which was built across the Dobrudja, apparently at this
time.[2]

When Moesia had been thus cleared of the enemy, Cornelius
Fuscus, probably with Legion V Alaudae and detachments from
the other Moesian legions crossed the Danube in 86 and
made for a gap in the Transylvanian Alps (probably the Vulcan
Pass) with the intention of invading Dacia.   He was chased
back, however, across the Wallachian plain and pursued over
the Danube.   He and his army were caught and, as Legion
V Alaudae now disappears from the Roman army list, they
were presumably wiped out.

Domitian spent the year 87 in making preparations to
retrieve the disaster.   In 88 his general Tettius Julianus,
advancing from Viminacium towards the Iron Gate Pass, the
western approach to Transylvania, inflicted a severe defeat on
the Dacians at Tapae.

It was at this moment that Antonius Saturninus broke into
rebellion in Germany and, to add to Domitian's difficulties,

[1] II Adiutrix at Singidunum (?), VII Claudia at Viminacium, IV
Flavia Firma at Ratiaria (?), in Upper Moesia ; V Macedonica at Oescus,
I Italica at Novae in Lower Moesia.

[2] The " altar ", or more properly cenotaph, at Adamclisi behind this
wall was also probably built at this time, presumably to commemorate
Oppius Sabinus and the men who fell with him.   For the Tropaeum
Traiani, which was erected 200 yards from this cenotaph in 109, see
below, p. 277.

Jazyges, Marcomanni and Quadi, who had hitherto recognized Roman suzerainty, turned ugly and began to threaten Pannonia. Domitian, therefore, prudently made peace with Decebalus, who allowed a force under C. Velius Rufus, Domitian's commander against the Chatti, to cross his territory and carry out a successful flank attack on these new aggressors. It was to meet this new threat that Domitian, having successfully disposed of Saturninus, transferred to Pannonia two of the eight legions which Vespasian had left on the Rhine (c 89).[1]

Under the terms of peace with Dacia Decebalus surrendered all his prisoners of war and in return was recognized by Domitian as king of the Dacians. Domitian also lent Decebalus a number of Roman engineers to help him build defence works and paid him an annual subsidy in money. We can hardly share the view of Domitian's court poets who flatteringly regard this as a famous victory. But neither can we subscribe to the view of Tacitus, who, resenting the fact that his father-in-law Agricola was not put in charge of the operations, represents the peace as a grievous humiliation. Domitian was not paying the Dacians Danegeld, he was resorting to the old Roman policy of hiring peoples outside the Empire to act as guardians of the frontier. Possibly he was influenced in favour of such a policy by the fact that his favourite predecessor, Tiberius, had also adopted it along the Danube. Tiberius had hired the Suebian Marcomanni and Quadi for this task; since they proved hostile, Domitian not unnaturally transferred the task to the Dacians. Under the existing combination of circumstances this may have been the only practical policy. The obvious disadvantage of it was that the Dacians were likely to construe it as a sign of weakness and be encouraged to aggression; but for the time being the position was re-established along the Danube. This was shown in 92, when Marcomanni and Quadi attacked Pannonia and annihilated one of its legions (XXI Rapax). The Dacians did not support them but watched Domitian's counter-measures unmoved. The Emperor replaced XXI Rapax with XIV Gemina.

Domitian however took no particular pride in his Danubian achievement. It is significant that although he himself was present in person at a great part of the action in this area he did not take the title Dacicus as he had the title Germanicus in 85. At his death the Danube was strongly guarded with

[1] I Adiutrix went to Brigetio and XXI Rapax to Aquincum.

nine legions, four in Pannonia and five in the two Moesian provinces. Domitian had thus shifted the military centre of gravity from the Rhine to the Danube; under him there were more legions in Pannonia than in any other province, and they were reckoned the best in the Empire.

§ 6. THE EASTERN FRONTIER

Vespasian was commanding in the east when he made his bid for Empire. Naturally, therefore, he paid particular attention to that frontier.

In the absence of a " natural " boundary in the Asia Minor—Mesopotamia area the usual policy was to establish a Roman nominee on the throne of Greater Armenia, to maintain along the frontier a chain of client kingdoms, which as time went on were gradually incorporated, and to rely on the military establishment of the province of Syria. This arrangement was not an ideal one. Some three hundred miles of virtually undefended frontier stretched from Syria to the Black Sea in Asia Minor. There were, indeed, the two vassal kingdoms of Commagene and Lesser Armenia, and between them lay Cappadocia, which Tiberius had incorporated as a procuratorial province. But the real defence of Asia Minor would have to be provided, not by the scanty local militia of Cappadocia, but by the four legions from distant Syria, whose military reputation was not high. In the case of a sudden attack the Syrian legions would hardly be able to arrive in time, and the chances of a sudden attack were considerable. The peoples of the Caucasus were already becoming restless, especially the Alans, a Scythian tribe who raided Armenia in 69, thus giving a foretaste of the serious trouble they were to cause in the next century.

To remedy this state of affairs, Vespasian stationed Roman troops in the vassal state of Iberia immediately south of the Caucasus to contain the Alans, and in 72 incorporated the client kingdoms of Lesser Armenia and Commagene, the former shortly afterwards obtaining a seat of Caesar-worship at Nicopolis. Lesser Armenia and Cappadocia were added to the area administered by the governor of Galatia, thus forming a large Anatolian province that contained legionary troops.[1] It may have been now that Satala, the centre of a network of military roads that the Flavians built in Asia Minor, became a legionary

[1] There also seems to have been some reorganization of the provinces of Cilicia and Lycia-Pamphylia.

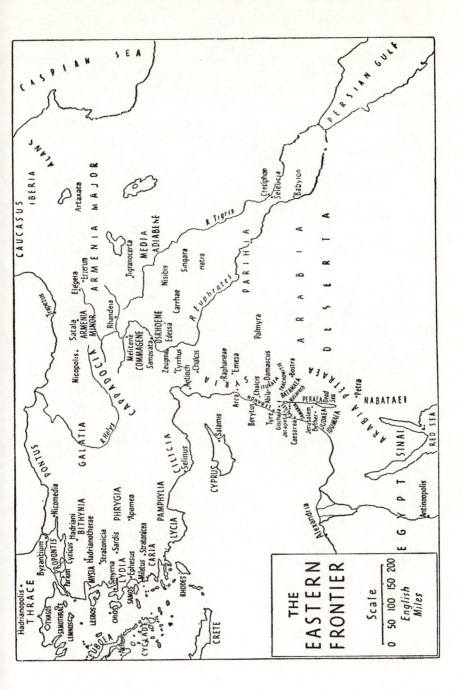

THE
EASTERN
FRONTIER

Scale

0   50 100 150 200

English
Miles

camp.[1] Melitene in Cappadocia, which controls an important crossing of the Upper Euphrates and the approach to Southern Armenia, certainly became a permanent camp at this time.[2]

Commagene was added to the province of Syria, whose governor was specifically charged with the defence of Zeugma and Samosata, where there are crossings over the Euphrates into Mesopotamia. No doubt in an extreme emergency the governor of Syria would still have to provide the protection for the whole of the eastern frontier. His army was now reduced from four legions to three ; [3] but his burden was eased because he had the two supporting legions to his north in the Anatolian province and the one to his south in Judaea.[4]

Vespasian thus followed Augustus' policy of gradually incorporating the local dynasties of the east. He also imitated Augustus in favouring the dynasty of Herod II Agrippa, whose territory lay east of the Jordan and included the areas of Batanea, Trachonitis and Abila ; Vespasian actually increased the territory of this client kingdom. Ultimately, however, its fate was no different, for Domitian logically continued the process of annexation and incorporated it, along with the client kingdom of Chalcis in the Lebanon and the principality of Emesa in Syria, c. 92. Palmyra also seems to have been annexed in Flavian times, so that only Arabia Petraea remained as a buffer state between Roman and Parthian territory. Whether this Flavian reorganization of the eastern frontier provoked or temporarily stilled Parthian restlessness is a moot point ; but the succeeding régime felt it necessary to attempt a very different policy. [5]

[1] Its first garrison may have been Legion XVI Flavia Firma, which was undoubtedly in the east at about this time. Satala, however, may not have become a camp until later. Certainly it was not until towards the end of Trajan's reign that XV Apollinaris was brought here from Pannonia.

[2] It obtained Legion XII Fulminata.

[3] VI Ferrata at Samosata, IV Scythica at Zeugma or Cyrrhus, III Gallica at Raphaneae (?).

[4] X Fretensis at Jerusalem.

[5] Flavian policies brought some changes in status for imperial provinces. Consular provinces were now ten (as against eight under Nero) and praetorian eight.

CHAPTER VI

THE ECONOMIC LIFE OF THE EMPIRE

§ 1.   THE GROWTH OF TRADE

TRADE and industry played very much less significant roles
in the Roman Empire than in the modern world : inevitably so,
since technology was backward and transportation primitive.
Ships sailed only between April and September, and as the horse-
collar had not been invented, the ox, the donkey and the camel
had .to be used as the beasts of burden.   Agriculture rather
than commerce was the great source of wealth, and its methods
were wasteful of land and labour.   The alternate year of fallow
was normal ; handmills, rather than water mills, ground the
grain.   Nevertheless there had been a great burgeoning of
economic activity under the Principate, and by A.D. 100 the
Empire may have been exchanging goods and services on as
large a scale as Europe ever attained before the later Middle
Ages.
   There were good reasons why this should be so.   The life
of the Empire for the most part was not disrupted either by
serious invasions from without, or by vast civil wars from
within.   (The year 69 was quite abnormal.)   The Pax Romana was
a reality making for stable conditions and consequently fostering
economic growth.   Other aids to economic expansion were the
standard and as yet scarcely debased currency and a considerable freedom of movement of both men and goods.   Nationality
was no bar to migration ; indeed merchants and craftsmen from
the ·Hellenized east made their way all over the Empire, and
more than held their own in competition with Italians.   In the
big transit and distributing centres such as Lugdunum there
must have been a brisk hotel business catering to the needs of
these travellers.   Goods did indeed have customs tariffs and
tolls to surmount at provincial boundaries and ports of entry,
but such charges were for fiscal rather than protective purposes :
usually they were not imposed with the deliberate intention of
either throttling trade or canalizing it in certain directions.
   The official policy of urbanization must also have had the

effect of intensifying trade, since economic activity is invariably on a higher level in cities than in country districts.

§ 2.   COMMUNICATIONS

The basis for economic activity anywhere is a system of communications ; and the better and more extensive the communications, the more intense and complex the economic activity will become.   In this respect the Empire by *c.* A.D. 100 was particularly well provided, for its network of roads literally stretched to the farthest corners of the Roman world.   By modern standards they were indeed narrow, but they were solidly built, with sound beds, good drainage and durable surfaces.   Primarily they served military needs, facilitating the movements of legions, or more usually detachments and auxiliaries, rapidly from place to place, for the Roman government's chief concern was with military and political problems, and economic matters did not monopolize its attention to the same degree that they do in modern states.   Nevertheless, measures taken primarily for military reasons could incidentally serve civilian needs, and in fact the government did occasionally build roads for the express purpose of opening up backward areas.   Agriculture provided the overwhelming bulk of the revenue ; but trade helped and the Emperors were not averse to it.

The great arterial roads provided excellent thoroughfares for traffic.   And the rivers and oceans performed an equally important service.   Inland waterways, although not fully exploited, were certainly very busy, and in the summer months there must have been a large volume of shipping at sea.   There was reasonable security from piratical attack, even though journeys by land as well as by water were not without their hazards.

There were regular trade routes, and passengers could be fairly sure of finding passage.   The ships were relatively large, up to 1,000 tons register ; the ship that was carrying Josephus to Rome had 600 persons on board.   Many of them came from Gades in Spain, the biggest shipbuilding centre and one of the biggest ports in the Empire.

By modern standards voyages were slow.   It took almost three weeks to get from Alexandria to Ostia, and over a week to go from Ostia to Gades.   As much as a year might be needed for the round trip to India.   On land a speed of about 50 miles a day was achieved for the Cursus Publicus.[1] Commercial traffic, usually much slower than this, might sometimes have moved as swiftly but not often.

§ 3.   PRIMARY PRODUCERS

The imperial government, although eager that trade should flourish, in general pursued an attitude of *laissez faire*. But in the case of certain raw materials it was itself the biggest consumer. It needed metals for army equipment and coins, and stone for its vast building enterprises. Therefore it naturally kept a very close eye on these resources : mines and quarries throughout the Empire were usually imperial monopolies,[2] and they were intensively worked. The Romans, like the ancients in general, did not realize the economic value of coal;[3] but the gold, silver, copper, mercury, iron, tin and lead of Spain, the lead and to a lesser extent the tin of Britain, and the iron of Gaul (except the phosphoric ore of the Lorraine field), were put to good use. The central government, with one eye on the monthly grain dole in the capital, also controlled large tracts of agricultural land, especially in North Africa. With these notable exceptions, however, the exploitation of the Empire's natural resources was mostly left to private enterprise, and private enterprise seized the opportunity.

In the first half of the first century A.D. the Empire presented a curious contrast to Modern Europe, for in those days, as distinct from now, it was western Europe that supplied raw material and the eastern half of the Empire that housed most of the secondary industries. This was because the Hellenized east had had an ordered civilization for considerably longer than the west. It was the great ports of Alexandria in Egypt, the centre of the world's trade, and of Antioch, Tyre and Ephesus in Syria, that cleared the great volume of manufactured exports, prominent among which were : textiles, papyrus, metal and glassware, jewellery, perfumes, and drugs.

Down to A.D. 50 Italy was practically the only western land

---

[1] See above, p. 81.

[2] The actual mining operations, however, were normally conducted by middlemen working under government contract : the extant mining law from Vipasca in Spain shows that they paid royalties of as much as 50 per cent of the ore recovered.

[3] They did, however, use it freely in Britain.—See R. G. Collingwood— J. N. L. Myres, *Roman Britain and the English Settlements*, pp. 231–2.

which could boast of secondary industries manufacturing for distant, and not merely for local, markets. Indeed the general production of Italy exceeded that of any other country. The red-glazed table-ware of Arretium, the *terra sigillata*, was shipped very far afield, even as far as Britain, in the time of the Julio-Claudians. Puteoli manufactured pottery and jewellery ; Capua produced valuable metal objects, Aquileia articles of amber and iron. At Rome the discovery of the technique of blowing glass (recently made at Sidon), instead of moulding it, led to the development of a large glass industry. Even Italian agriculture was, as it were, industrialized : large quantities of Italian wine were sold all over the Roman world, while attar of roses from Pompeii was famous.

§ 4. INDUSTRIAL DEVELOPMENT

But as settled conditions came to prevail, the western provinces gradually developed industries of their own. Even before the days of the Empire Gaul had had a rudimentary iron industry, which now expanded rapidly. As a pottery-making centre the La Graufesenque district of south-western Gaul surpassed Arretium before the first century was out, and shortly afterwards the Lezoux potteries in central Gaul were developed. Important glass factories sprang up in the neighbourhood of Cologne. As Italy's manufactured exports had found their chief markets in the west, this growing industrialization of the west affected the Italian economy adversely. The products of Gallic industry began to replace those of Italian.

Manufactured exports, thanks to the excellent system of communications, sometimes travelled very long distances. This might be expected of luxury articles. It is hardly surprising if Belgian brooches found their way to the Caucasus, and Capuan bronzes to Sweden. Specialized products will always find their way to areas which lack a supply of experienced technicians. In the Empire there was a large two-way traffic in specialities.

But even very cheap commodities might be transported right across Europe : rough textiles manufactured in Flanders were sold to the poor in Italy. Primary products, too, performed long journeys. The pottery whose fragments have built up the huge mound called Monte Testaccio at Rome once conveyed oil, wine and grain to the capital from Gaul and distant parts of Spain. However, transportation costs were high.

Of course the goods that travelled long distances were the exceptions not the rule, for the vast mass of goods was consumed locally. Indeed many of them did not leave the estate where they were produced, for what is generally called house-economy was extensively practised and the big estates tried to be as self-sufficient as possible. And in any event in ancient times, as in modern, there were many things which would not normally be shipped very far afield : bread would scarcely be sold outside the city where it was baked.

Nor, when we speak of industry, should we visualize the large-scale, mass production methods of to-day, although the Gallic potteries clearly must have been fairly big establishments. Industry on the whole remained in the hands of small masters. If conditions at Pompeii are any criterion, it was housed, as often as not, in single work-rooms. In other words, though the volume of production and exchange was far from small, industries did not become giant corporations. The big warehouses at Ostia show that there were indeed large export and import firms ; nevertheless, organization and the technique of distribution did not develop as rapidly as the volume of trade and the extensive range of goods might have led one to expect. Retail trade, despite the existence of shopping centres like those in the Saepta or on the north side of Trajan's Forum in Rome, was largely in the hands of peddlers and hawkers, and street fairs were very common. The large department store was unknown.

The relative backwardness of commerce, as compared with industry, is rather surprising, since as early as republican times the equestrian tax-farming companies had shown that the Romans were capable of organizing large businesses. Under the Empire, however, trade for the most part was not in the hands of joint stock companies but of individual merchants and small partnerships engaging their personal capital. Rents rather than dividends were the normal source of investment income. The consequence, or more probably the cause, of this state of affairs was that banking operations, on the whole, remained comparatively simple : business in the Roman Empire did not rest on a vast foundation of credit.[1]

[1] Nevertheless devices resembling our Letters of Credit and Bankers' Orders were quite well known.

§ 5.   DECLINE IN THE ECONOMIC IMPORTANCE OF ITALY

As the western provinces became more industrialized, Italy gradually ceased to be the economic centre of the Empire, and her trade balance became increasingly passive.   It is significant that in the first century A.D. the great exporting port of Puteoli declined, while Ostia, through which passed the vast volume of imported goods consumed by Rome, handled an ever-growing traffic.   Claudius found it necessary to enlarge the harbour works at Ostia, and Trajan shortly after A.D. 100 followed his example.   Incidentally other ports besides Ostia were the object of imperial concern both in Italy and the provinces ;   they were dredged and provided with installations.

Italy's excess of imports came in large part from the east, for despite the growing industrialization of the west, the Hellenized part of the Roman world was still a large supplier of secondary products.   And in addition there were the products that came from far beyond the eastern portions of the Roman world.   Italy, and especially Rome, was a great consumer of silks, spices and other oriental luxuries that might come indirectly from as far away as China.   According to Strabo, even in Augustus' day a hundred and twenty ships cleared the Red Sea port of Myos Hormos every year for India.   Nor was India the only country with which direct trade relations were established.   Ships were plying the sea to Zanzibar, Ceylon and Malaya before the end of our period.   Besides such direct routes there were indirect ones, by land as well as by sea ; many of the goods which China supplied travelled right across the continent of Asia by land.

Though this traffic was not entirely unilateral, the exports of Italy, the great consumer of oriental luxury goods, were inadequate to pay for the mass of imports.   That in itself need not have entailed serious economic consequences.   In the last analysis what matters is not the balance of trade but the balance of payments ;   and Italy had very considerable invisible exports in the form of provincial tribute and the capital brought to Rome by provincial senators and returning administrators.   The serious fact was that the balance of payments of the Empire as a whole, and not merely of Italy, was adverse.   The Empire could indeed supply all its vital necessities, but it wanted luxuries as well : the Elder Pliny caustically remarks that the object of conquests was to obtain expensive perfumes.   Despite its immense resources, the Empire could not pay for such things by exchanging its own goods and services for them; therefore it became necessary to export increasing amounts of bullion to the Far East to pay for oriental imports. The drain of the precious metals to the Orient was well under way.

This almost certainly was a contributing factor to the subsequent vicious debasement of the imperial coinage. Two things can cause monetary inflation : an unbalanced budget and an adverse balance of payments. Both causes operated in the Roman Empire. If the primary urge to debase the coins came from spendthrift Emperors, a second and very powerful factor was the growing shortage of the metals from which the coins were made. The precious metals were literally disappearing down the oriental sink at a time when the great volume of trade required a plentiful supply of coins. The seeds for the future currency chaos were sown in our period.

When the western provinces became more industrialized, agricultural and pastoral pursuits did not languish. The secondary industries, being normally small affairs, did not employ huge numbers and the vast majority of the population continued to get its living from the soil. Western Europe in fact was intensively cultivated, and this is particularly true of Italy, which did not witness any important industrial growth. The spectacle of the swollen city of Rome heavily dependent on food imports from abroad should not blind us to the fact that Italy was the garden of Europe, and that Italian cities in general did not require huge grain imports. Columella's work on husbandry indicates the important rôle of farming in the Italian economy of the first century A.D. The famous remark of the Elder Pliny that large estates had been the ruin of Italy [1] should not be taken to mean that the agricultural conditions which the Gracchi sought to remedy had returned. Large estates worked by gangs of slaves for absentee landowners do not seem to have been the rule; nay, rather, the system of tenant-farmers prevailed. The failure of big-scale foreign wars to supply slaves in huge numbers may have been in part responsible for this. Whatever the reason, the landowners apparently found the métayer system more profitable.

Pliny's statement implies, however, that all was not well with Italian agriculture. Exactly what was wrong it is not easy to say. Pliny's nephew, the Younger Pliny, tells us that

[1] *Hist. Nat.*, XVIII, 35 : latifundia perdidere Italiam.

there was a certain amount of grumbling at agricultural conditions, but this is a perennial phenomenon in farming communities everywhere. The probabilities are that Italian agriculture lacked working capital. The drain of money to the east may have been partly responsible for this. Money was indeed invested in Italian land : the Younger Pliny makes it clear that this was the main source of senatorial incomes. But apparently wealth was no longer concentrated in the hands of a few senatorial families as it was under the Republic. Down to A.D. 50 Italy had her multi-millionaires, but after that date, although she had numerous moderately wealthy individuals like the Younger Pliny himself, the really large fortunes were in the provinces, as in the case of Opramoas of Lycia, Eurycles of Sparta and Herodes of Athens. The average small farmer in Italy seems to have had difficulty in finding working capital,[1] and he seems to have found provincial competition severe. Domitian *c.* 91 found it necessary to encourage grain growing by forbidding any increase of the acreage under vines in Italy. At the same time he protected Italian viticulture by ordering the elimination of half the provincial vineyards, and this drastic order was actually carried out in Africa and elsewhere.

It cannot be positively asserted that Italian agriculture was suffering from a shortage of population as well as capital, but it seems probable. The Younger Pliny's lack of concern at threatened depopulation is an *argumentum e silentio* that is not cogent. On *a priori* grounds it is probable that when Italy ceased to be the economic centre of the Empire, emigration in search of more favourable opportunities abroad would have occurred. Besides this, the falling birth-rate already observable in Augustus' day and the large export of officials and administrators must have been reflected in the Italian population figures by A.D. 100. It is significant that Domitian's successor, Nerva, found it necessary to establish numerous colonies of small farmers throughout Italy ; while Nerva's successor, Trajan, may have gone even further and sought to remedy both the shortage of working capital and the threatened depopulation, for he ordered provincial senators to invest one third of their capital in Italian land, and there are grounds for thinking that he forbade emigration from Italy.

---

[1] The emperors who succeeded the Flavians sought to remedy this by an ingenious scheme. See below, p. 269 f.

§ 6.   ECONOMIC ACTIVITY THROUGHOUT THE EMPIRE

Thus not all parts of the Empire benefited equally from the generally increased tempo of economic activity. Nor did all classes benefit equally from it. The labouring class was in a depressed condition, and it did not have any trade unions to agitate for social amelioration. The guilds of craftsmen and traders, which were such a common feature of Roman industry and commerce, did not normally concern themselves with questions of wages, prices or working conditions ; they resembled rather our friendly societies and clubs. The presence of slave labour undoubtedly helped to keep the living standards of the free workers down. Many of these slaves were highly skilled craftsmen, who were reasonably well treated simply because they were not easily replaced. That, however, is not to say that they were well paid. Workers' wages could hardly have risen much above the subsistence level. But then in Europe they never did do so before the Industrial Revolution.

The upper classes were, of course, incomparably better off. Obviously for them the economic activity of the empire provided an adequate base for the continuation of a fairly high material civilization. But even for them there was something lacking. Their material standards were probably better than any that the world had hitherto seen, but they tended to become stereotyped. The official tolerance of local customs, languages and religions did not prevent widespread imitation of Rome. In externals especially, empire-wide uniformity manifested itself, particularly among the well-to-do. The ease of communications meant that the ideas and methods of one area quickly became known in, and were adopted by, other areas. The material remains of Roman civilization, wherever they are found, bear the stamp of sameness. This is not due simply to the materials with which buildings were made. There was some export of building materials from Italy : Carrara marble is found in Britain and bricks and tiles from Ariminum turn up in Dalmatia ; but usually buildings were made of the diversified local materials. Nevertheless there was less variety in architectural plans and methods than the varying climes would have led one to expect. Slave labour is not likely to be industrially inventive : it has no incentive to devise new methods. The mingling of nationalities which the volume of trade of course encouraged was also a powerful factor favouring standardization : the Roman Empire was a real melting pot.

When we remember further that spiritual outlets were not abundant, it is not surprising that life in the Empire tended to be essentially banausic. Such a life of standardized materialism was not intellectually stimulating. The Empire, despite its countless memorials of public-spirited private munificence, did not stir its masses to enthusiasm. Men were eager and proud to obtain its highest form of citizenship (the Roman), since it conferred material advantages. They were less zealous, however, in aspiring to the real Roman spirit, and exciting adventures in the world of ideas were rare. In this respect the Roman Empire of the first century A.D. cannot compare with the Athenian Empire of the fifth century B.C. A world that is not intellectually vibrant already contains the seeds of its own decay. The outwardly imposing structure which the Roman pursuit of materialism erected was substantial enough to prevent any sudden Fall of the Roman Empire. But the sterility of its intellectual life foreshadowed inevitable Decline.

CHAPTER VII

LITERATURE BETWEEN A.D. 50 AND 100

§ 1. PROSE : SENECA

THE lack of real intellectual vigour is well attested by the
literature that was produced after *c.* A.D. 50. Its abundance
distinguishes the period from that immediately following the
death of Ovid (A.D. 18). The latter merely produced such
minor works as Manilius' poem on astrology ; the rhetorical
exercises of the Elder Seneca ; the collection of historical anecdotes by Valerius Maximus ; a sketch of Roman history by
Velleius Paterculus ; the highly rhetorical Greek works on
Biblical exegesis by the Alexandrian Jew, Philo ; the metrical
paraphrases of Aesop's fables by Phaedrus ; a biography of
Alexander the Great by Curtius Rufus ; and the technical
writings of Celsus, Pomponius Mela and Columella on medicine,
geography and agriculture respectively.

About the middle of the century works of greater consequence
began to appear. But on the whole this literature is shallow,
and its practitioners, finding their intellectual horizon circumscribed, aim at brilliance rather than excellence.

Nero's adviser Seneca (A.D. 3–65) is typical. His *Tragedies* [1]
display a real mastery of words. The gruesomeness of his
descriptions of scenes of blood and terror, and the gratuitous
addition of choral odes merely for the sake of display do not
prevent us, any more than the early Elizabethans and even
Shakespeare himself, from being impressed with the meretricious
glitter. Similarly in the numerous prose essays which he wrote
on philosophical themes, mostly in the reign of Claudius, and in
the *Quaestiones Naturales, Dialogues* and *Epistulae Morales,*
which were mostly written under Nero, Seneca shows no real
depth or originality of thought ; he merely sets forth the
practical rules for good living of the conventional Stoic philosopher. But he does so with such skill and ability that, despite
his own failure to practise what he preached and his consequent
widespread reputation for hypocrisy, he has been more widely

---

[1] The present writer accepts the Senecan authorship of nine of these
plays. The *Octavia* is certainly not by Seneca : it obviously belongs to
the Flavian epoch.

read and has exercised a greater influence than practically any other Latin author. Great literature, however, is the outcome of passionate conviction, and this Seneca did not feel. In one work attributed to him, the satirical skit on the posthumous deification of Claudius, the passion is indeed beyond question. This, however, may not be by Seneca ; and in any event, despite its genuineness of feeling, it must be regarded as a slight and savage thing.[1]

Some of Seneca's contemporaries did set forth the tenets of the fashionable Stoicism with undoubted sincerity. The youthful Aulus Persius (34–62) of Etruscan Volaterrae, produced six *Satires* in verse. But these are so involved in obscurities as to give the impression of learned lucubrations rather than of enjoyable literature. Among Stoic prose-writers were the Greek authors, Musonius Rufus (*fl.* 65) and somewhat later Epictetus (*c.* 50–120). The former is extant only in fragments ; the latter's vigorous exposition is as earnest as Persius' but far more practical : there is nothing bookish about Epictetus.

§ 2. POETRY : LUCAN, VALERIUS FLACCUS, SILIUS ITALICUS, STATIUS

In general the poetry of this age, like Seneca's prose, is brilliant but superficial. For example, the epic on the Civil War between Caesar and Pompey by the youthful Lucan (39–65) contains some marks of genius. After some early flattery of Nero the poem develops a genuinely republican atmosphere, and its sustained grandeur of language is truly remarkable ; but the whole composition is overstrained and intolerably repetitious. The metallic clangour of Lucan's *tour de force* impresses for fifty lines but becomes wearisome when kept up unremittingly throughout ten books. The *Argonautica* of Valerius Flaccus, an eight-book epic produced under the Flavians, shows less genius but more moderation ; among some very fine passages it describes Jason and Medea's love-affair with true psychological insight. On the other hand Flaccus' contemporary, Silius Italicus (25–100) is a dullard, who describes the Second Punic War with tiresome monotony throughout seventeen books of stodgy hexameters. The twelve-book *Thebais* and unfinished *Achilleis* of the Neapolitan P. Papinius Statius (*c.* 60–96) exhibit the same characteristics as the other Silver Age epics.

[1] On the title of this work, see F. A. Todd in *Class. Quart.* XXXVII (1943), pp. 103–7.

All these writers pay lip-service to Vergil, but their imita-
tions of him border on the grotesque. The conventional epic
similes and storms at sea are introduced with frequency, fidelity
and an utter lack of proportion, and the epic apostrophe de-
generates into interminable ranting. And although Vergil is
their professed master, they have been more influenced by
Ovid with his tendency to revel in blood-curdling descriptions
and abstruse allusions. With a humourless lack of restraint
these authors out-herod Herod. Gruesome accounts of gory
horrors vie with inappropriate displays of erudition, and to
impress the reader with the writer's cleverness the whole story
is told in language on which every rhetorical trick and artifice
are lavished.

The *Institutio Oratoria* of Quintilian (*c.* 35–90) shows that
higher education in those days aimed at producing accomplished
orators. As Quintilian points out, such a rhetorical training is
capable of producing real eloquence ; in some admirable chapters
of literary criticism he suggests the best models. The contemporary Greek pamphlet *On the Sublime* by an unknown
author, but bearing the name of ' Longinus,' also indicates that
this kind of education should not necessarily result in bizarre
and usually prolix bombast. Unfortunately, however, oratory
was not free and untrammelled. In Tacitus' immortal expression, it had been " pacified." The professional informers
obliged orators to watch the contents of their speeches carefully.
The sense of restraint varied under different emperors ; those
that permitted reasonably unrestrained speaking were said to
have restored " liberty." (Under the Principate *libertas* means
little more than this.) But even in the periods of greatest
libertas tact and circumspection were required, and the number
of things that a person could say was limited. The inevitable
result was that the content of a speech came to be of minor
importance ; instead, care was lavished on its form. Every
rhetorical trick, every literary artifice was exploited to the full,
so that even though men had nothing to say, they might say
it in a dazzling way. Men were systematically trained to produce
oratorical masterpieces of pretentious emptiness—the influence
of such a training is apparent everywhere in the literature.
Balanced antitheses, witty epigrams, over-clever paradoxes,
ingenious figures of speech, incessant attempts to be arresting,
in fact any exotic device calculated to contribute to display,
mark the writings of this period. This is observable not only

in prose and drama and epic, but even in occasional poems like
Statius' *Silvae*, which are not without some real poetical gems.
It is significant that in this age poetry was normally published
by declaiming it in public.

§ 3.   SATIRE : PETRONIUS, MARTIAL

Great writing in the form of positive contributions of the
human mind was scarcely possible, even though the Flavian
Emperors and especially Domitian sought to encourage it.
Conventions, whether of ordinary life or of thought, could be
defied only with peril; for prudential reasons one dared not
try to be a leader of thought or to advance ahead of his times.
The only field which allowed an original genius any scope was
satire, and in fact the greatest literary productions of the age
were satirical. In Nero's reign Petronius wrote his *Satiricon*,
a prose work interlarded with passages of quite able verse.
The surviving fragments, from its fifteenth and sixteenth books
only, reveal it to have been a picaresque novel describing the
disreputable adventures of a couple of rascals in Southern Italy.
It is a most realistic reproduction of the shadier side of contemporary life told with remarkable verve and skill. The
vivid account of a dinner-party given by the freedman Trimalchio
and attended by other parvenu upstarts, all of whom speak in
character, is writing of genius. Petronius is one of the great
names in literature.

His counterpart in verse, although on a lower level, is M.
Valerius Martialis (*c.* 40–104), whose twelve books of *Epigrams*
are essentially satires on life in the capital. Indeed it is largely
thanks to Martial that the word ' epigram ' has come to acquire
its modern meaning of a pointed reflection on a given situation :
the surviving Greek epigrams of the first century rarely show
such wit. Martial himself was an unlovely character who
courted the favours of the great with the grossest flattery;
his work constitutes a lively and frequently bawdy protrayal of
Roman society. His picture of arrogant opulence on the one
side and of grinding poverty on the other, of millionaires and
of schemers seeking to share in their wealth, is not pleasant :
and the general impression of a city where only the unworthy
can get ahead is no doubt false. But then satirists invariably
exaggerate. Martial's satire unfortunately has not even the
saving grace of moral indignation.

§ 4.   TECHNICAL WRITERS :   ELDER PLINY, FRONTINUS

One form of mental activity that was relatively safe and not so unsatisfying as the usual preoccupation with empty rhetoric was the study of technical subjects. But the language of authors concerned with these was also liable to be rhetorical when it was not technical. Besides Quintilian's work on education, we might mention the *Natural History* by the Elder Pliny (23?–79), a work of immense, universal and uncritical erudition in thirty-seven books, and Frontinus' treatises on military tactics and the Roman water supply. These works, although scarcely literature in the true sense of the word, are not unimportant as an indication of men's interests in that age : minor writers always have such an historical value. Numerous allusions to natural phenomena in the Silver Age epics and a work like Seneca's *Quaestiones Naturales* indicate that the Elder Pliny was not unique in his interest in such things. Greek writers, for instance, wrote on technical subjects : works on botany by Dioscorides and on medicine by Soranus and Archigenes are extant.

One aspect of the literature of this period is deserving of emphasis. The increasing projection of Italy into the provinces and the tendency of the provinces to come to Italy is made clear. The Greek writers naturally were of provincial origin. For example, besides those already mentioned, there was the romanized Jew, Flavius Josephus (*c.* 37–100), who came from Judaea ; he is the only contemporary historian whose work has survived in quantity, Tacitus' writing being produced somewhat later. But even the Latin writers often came from the provinces, especially Spain. Columella, Seneca, Lucan, Quintilian, Martial and possibly Valerius Flaccus [1] were Spaniards. Literature thus reflected the growing cosmopolitanism of the Empire as well as its declining energy of mind.

[1] He came apparently from Setia, but whether from the Italian or Spanish town of that name is unknown.

PART IV

THE NON-ITALIAN EMPERORS

CHAPTER I

NERVA

§ 1. THE SENATORIAL NOMINEE

THE death of Domitian without an heir almost plunged the Roman world into another civil war. His assassins had indeed already selected his successor, a sixty-six-year-old senator named Cocceius Nerva, who had held the consulship twice and was distantly related to the Julio-Claudians on his mother's side. But even though on family grounds he was probably the best available choice from among the senators, it was still painfully obvious that he was a senatorial nominee. This is shown not so much by his promise to execute no senator— many Emperors gave this assurance at their accession—nor even by the fact that he kept his word, but rather by the fact that the ancient tradition, which derives mostly from senatorial sources, is unfeignedly favourable to him. Tacitus and Pliny speak of him in effusive terms, and the Senate regarded his accession as a triumph for itself.

Galba's career, however, had shown that a candidate who was acceptable to the Senate was not necessarily so to the soldiers. At first his régime was not much more secure than Galba's had been. The popularity-seeking character of practically everything he did shows how precarious was his position. But he was careful not to repeat Galba's mistakes : he avoided alike unyielding stinginess, misplaced severity and indulgent favouritism. Above all, although he imitated Galba in quickly adopting a younger man to succeed him, he wisely chose a man whom the soldiers would accept.

But despite his prudent and tactful behaviour Nerva had to step warily to escape disaster. The Senate might rejoice over Domitian's death, and the People might remain more or less indifferent. With the troops it was otherwise : the Flavian family was popular with them, Domitian was no stranger to their camps, and they bitterly resented his murder. In Syria

and on the Danube there were mutterings of mutiny, although
the troops finally accepted Nerva's elevation with a bad grace :
so well had the Flavians taught the troops to acquiesce in the
idea of the Principate.   In Rome the Praetorians would probably
have moved against this second Galba as they had against the
first if they had only found another Otho to organize their
discontent.

The regular donatives were immediately paid to the troops
and to the populace of Rome.   The people of Italy were courted
in various ways which the fiscus found expensive ; exemptions
from the inheritance tax were increased and the cost of the
Cursus Publicus abolished for Italy.   Economic distress was
alleviated by land-grants to the indigent.   Nerva imitated
certain of his predecessors and sold his private property, furniture
and jewels to obtain some of the sixty million sesterces which
this measure required.   It is a matter of interest that the
distribution was enacted by an Agrarian Law passed by the
Comitia, the last recorded legislative act of this body.

§ 2.   THE ALIMENTA

Above all, in Italy the famous *alimenta* were instituted.
Under this scheme small farmers, after pledging their land as
security, could borrow one twelfth of its value from the fiscus.
On this loan they paid a low rate of interest, almost certainly
five per cent, not to the fiscus but to their own municipality.
Their municipality used the funds thus acquired to give maintenance grants to parents of poor children within its territory
until they reached the age of puberty.   The scheme as a whole
was administered by a central office at Rome, directed by a
Praetorian *praefectus alimentorum* (i.e. a senatorial), who had a
staff of *procuratores alimentorum* (i.e. equestrians).   The local
supervision was carried out by *quaestores alimentorum*.   As these
are found in at least forty Italian towns, the scheme must have
been widespread.   It intended to make provision chiefly for
legitimate offspring of male sex, although girls and even bastards
were not entirely overlooked.

Various students have seen in this measure an attempt to
prevent the disappearance of small farms from Italy, the need
to alleviate the prevailing poverty, a plan to arrest the decay of
country towns, the beginning of that paternalism that contributed so markedly to the decline of the Empire.   Probably it

had two main purposes : to stimulate the Italian birth-rate and to find working capital for small farmers, a perennial problem for South European peasants. Nerva also was not oblivious to the propaganda value of the scheme. The small farmers would welcome it, while the public at large would be impressed by the picture of well-fed, healthy children. The *alimenta*, in short, would win support for his régime. Therefore he made a display of the *alimenta* : references to them were even stamped on his coins.

Actually the scheme was not entirely original with Nerva. In the fifties A.D. a philanthropist, T. Helvius Basila, had endowed a maintenance fund for poor children at Atina. Nerva's originality consisted in combining the support of children with the financing of farmers and in bringing the scheme under the official control of the State.

It might be added that during the second century the system waxed and multiplied. Private individuals like the Younger Pliny followed the example of the State and endowed such schemes. Soon far more than the five thousand children originally contemplated by Nerva came to be provided for in this way ; and the system, which also spread to the provinces, lasted with interruptions down to the time of Diocletian.

§ 3. CONCILIATION

Nerva, then, by a variety of measures in Rome and Italy, showed his anxiety to avoid the charge of Galbian stinginess. It was fortunate for him that Domitian had not left the fiscus quite so empty as the hostile ancient sources suggest. Whether he was equally solicitous for the provinces there is insufficient evidence to say. The numerous milestones bearing his name do not conclusively prove a provincial road-building programme by him, since many of them belong more rightly to Domitian. All that we can certainly say is that Nerva spent money so freely that at the end of a year he was obliged to appoint an Economy Commission, whose task was to find ways and means for reducing public expenditures.[1]

Open-handed spending was only one aspect of his programme of universal conciliation. He tried to win over everyone of influence and power. To slaves, freedmen and other small fry he could be stern enough, but to men who might have a capacity for mischief he was indulgence itself. It is not surprising that

[1] Or possibly to disentangle *aerarium* and *fiscus* : the Flavians had allowed the two to merge.

his attitude towards the Senate was one of respectful deference :
he was after all the senatorial appointee.   He recalled all exiles
from banishment and allowed them to wreak their vengeance
on some of Domitian's supporters.   To individuals, mostly
senatorials, he restored the property which Domitian had
confiscated.   He issued his coins in the name of the Senate ;
and his land-purchasing and economy commissions consisted of
senators.

This courteous treatment of the Senate seems natural enough.
But Nerva was also indulgent to the infamous *delatores*.   He
either would not, or more probably dared not, take strong
measures against them.   The ancient sources insist that
notorious professional informers were even invited to his table.

One method employed by Nerva to curry popularity was to
canalize public resentment, so far as possible, against the
preceding régime.   The systematic denigration of Domitian
was encouraged, if not inspired, officially.   In general Domitian's
legislation was too sound to be abandoned, and Nerva quietly
retained most of it.   But wherever Domitian's actions could be
abrogated without serious consequence to the State, Nerva
ostentatiously undid them.   His attitude was more than a
little responsible for the uncompromising hostility of the ancient
sources towards Domitian.

Nevertheless the various popularity-hunting measures were
not entirely successful.   According to Dio, although Nerva's
reign lasted only sixteen months, more than one plot was formed
against him.   Only one, however, is explicitly mentioned ; the
conspiracy of C. Calpurnius Crassus, a descendant of the
millionaire triumvir.   This proved abortive ; but it served to
emphasize that the reign needed the enthusiastic support rather
than the sullen acquiescence of the troops.   Towards the end
of 97, indeed, the discontent of the Praetorians came to a head.
Casperius Aelianus, the Prefect who had also served in the
capacity under Domitian, demanded that the murderers of
the last Flavian be surrendered and executed, and Nerva had
no option but to comply.

§ 4.   THE ADOPTION OF TRAJAN

This more than anything else decided him to adopt an
associate and successor who would be able to keep the soldiers
in order.   He had no son of his own, therefore someone else

must be his choice. Like Galba he saw the need of making
early provision for the succession ; unlike Galba, in making his
choice he considered the troops' predilections as well as his own.
In October 97 he passed over his male relatives and selected
M. Ulpius Trajanus, a man who had passed through the
senatorial *cursus honorum*, had distinguished himself as a soldier
under Domitian and had recently been appointed governor of
Upper Germany by Nerva himself. Nerva made Trajan his
full co-regent, and he was not mistaken in thinking that his
appointee could control the troops, for Trajan soon got rid of
the contumacious Praetorian Prefect Casperius.

The adoption of Trajan by Nerva must be considered one
of the most significant events in the history of the Empire.[1]
Most writers see in it the inauguration of a system of succession
that endured for almost a century and provided the Roman
Empire with a series of Emperors under whose beneficent rule
the world prospered as it never had before and seldom has since.
It was only when Marcus Aurelius substituted the dynastic
principle for the adoptive that the government of the Empire
fell once again into weak and evil hands.

Although commonly held, this view is not altogether accurate.
In the second century the system of succession did not differ
radically from that practised by the Julio-Claudians. Under
them, too, the usual thing was for the Emperor to be succeeded
not by a real, but by an adopted son who would be acceptable
to the troops. This system in fact was as old as the Principate
itself. The significant fact about Nerva's choice of Trajan is
not the method employed, but the man adopted. Trajan, so
far from being a Julian, was not even an Italian.

We have already noted that under the Republic the highest
office in the Roman state was reserved for a comparatively few
families which came from the city of Rome itself. It was the
achievement of Augustus to put an end to this unofficial but
very real restriction, so that after him any Italian could aspire
to the consulship. Claudius went a step further when he
proceeded to admit provincials of non-Roman origin.

The same evolution can be seen in the Principate. The
Julio-Claudians, even though most of them chanced to be
born outside of the city, came from old Roman families. The
Flavians on the other hand were an Italian family in the strict

[1] Yet, curiously, it is not reflected in surviving coins of the period.

sense. So now, with the Flavian dynasty extinct, the process is made complete: a man of provincial origin becomes Emperor. Trajan was a Spaniard, the son of a man whom Vespasian had adlected into the senatorial order.

Thus by adopting Trajan Nerva was helping the course of Roman history on its logical and inexorable way. Rome had expanded into the provinces, and the process of assimilation had proceeded far enough to justify the assumption of the imperial purple by a son of the provinces. The provinces were thus beginning to come back to Rome, and the Roman world enters upon its cosmopolitan phase. An inevitable consequence of this was that the sharp distinction between Italy on the one hand and the provinces on the other was bound to disappear. And disappear it ultimately did in the reign of Caracallus at the beginning of the third century.

Actually Nerva's choice of Trajan was a wise one. Trajan was a capable and sober man, and a loyal servant of the Empire, who enjoyed the respect of the troops. Even now, however, the soldiers possibly left something to be desired in the way of whole-heartedness. At any rate, as we shall see, Trajan, like Claudius before him, embarked on a vigorous foreign policy immediately after his accession. His probable motive was to bolster his régime.

For the time being Nerva's consort in the Principate, who does not seem to have had much personal esteem for his adoptive father, did not trouble to come to Rome. He remained on the Rhine; and he was still there when Nerva died only some three months after making the adoption (January, 98). He was buried in Augustus' mausoleum.

Nerva's short reign is of some importance for the history of the Principate. Despite the very analogous situation, he did succeed in preventing a recurrence of a year of anarchy such as 69; and in so doing he won over the Senate, without however granting it any real power, for under him the Senate's time was still mostly taken up with the discussion of trivialities.[1] But by his deferential bearing he managed to win senatorial good-will; and he established a tradition of senatorial co-operation with the Princeps which was to endure, except for a brief interlude under Hadrian, throughout most of the next century.

[1] Garzetti, indeed, suggests that Nerva's famed courtesy to the Senate was merely a mask for thoroughly autocratic behaviour.

CHAPTER II

TRAJAN

§ 1. A WARRIOR EMPEROR

TECHNICALLY Trajan was already Emperor before Nerva's death, since all of the imperial powers and prerogatives had been conferred upon him. He did not leave the Rhine and come to Rome immediately, but contented himself with writing a letter to the Senate promising that he would never execute a senator. Then he proceeded to the Danube. The details are vague, but apparently there were disturbances in Pannonia, where the Suebi had been giving trouble in Nerva's reign, and a threat of disturbances from the Dacian King Decebalus. Trajan spent the winter of 98–99 on the Danube, and did not reach Rome until spring of the latter year. His modest entry into the city on foot is described in terms of enthusiastic exaggeration by Pliny, who witnessed it. Obviously his accession excited the liveliest expectations of the senatorial class at least. Before the reign was out all other classes in the State were also to be completely won over : Trajan re-knit the ties which Domitian had loosened.

At its beginning, however, some sections of the population may have felt reservations. At any rate, for two years after his arrival Trajan felt it necessary to practise universal conciliation, and his wife Plotina and sister Marciana, by their unostentatious and even humble behaviour, ably seconded his efforts.

Undoubtedly during these two years Trajan strengthened his position greatly ; already he was unofficially styled Optimus Princeps.[1] Nevertheless he was not entirely assured, and so decided to embark on a vigorous foreign policy, which ultimately brought the Empire to its widest territorial extent. Dacia was the first victim.

§ 2. THE FIRST DACIAN WAR

Trajan's decision to enlarge the frontiers of the Empire was obviously a momentous one. His motives were probably mixed and quite possibly not those that were outwardly professed. To

[1] The title appears on coins in 105 and on inscriptions in 112 : Dio, however, says that it was not conferred officially until 114.

judge from the ancient evidence, his attack on Dacia was officially represented as an attempt to terminate Domitian's alleged policy of weakness on the Danubian frontier. By going there in 98–99 Trajan had already shown that he was pre-occupied with the problem. It may be, of course, that the Dacians regarded Domitian's policy in a very different light than the Romans and had become arrogant in consequence. In such a case Trajan's decision to humble them is under-standable enough. But on the whole it is more likely that Trajan's real motive was different, since he himself subsequently followed Domitian's example : when he weakened the military establishment on the Danube for his Parthian War, he hired Roxolani to guard the frontier.

Undoubtedly Trajan, one of the very greatest soldier-emperors, found military life and expeditions congenial : he is said to have served ten years as a military tribune. Also it may be that, just as Claudius had thought that after almost half a century of Augustan frontiers the time was ripe for a further advance, so Trajan was of the opinion that the Empire had accumulated sufficient strength to warrant an attempt to expand the boundaries bequeathed by Claudius and the Flavians. He may have thought that the restless tribes outside the Empire would interpret the effort to keep the territories of the Empire static as a sign of weakness. Certainly he was right in regarding the " natural " frontier of the Danube as far from perfect. Rivers, mountains and similar natural frontiers look imposing on paper, and undoubtedly they facilitate the task of internal administration.· Smuggling is suppressed, border tolls collected, raids prevented and order generally maintained more easily behind such boundaries. But such boundaries never have proved an effective barrier to determined enemies : a line that looks good on a map is not necessarily a formidable obstacle. Trajan apparently concluded that it was better to prevent a coalition of Rome's potential enemies beyond the Danube by thrusting a wedge of Roman territory into their midst than to rely on the river to hold them at bay. To this consideration he could add another and a cogent one. Claudius had demon-strated that an initial policy of foreign conquest could strengthen a none too secure régime at its outset. Trajan decided to follow his example.

To find pretexts for a Dacian war was not difficult. Trajan could allege that he was desirous of terminating the Domitianic payments to the Dacians and of preventing Decebalus' preparations for aggression. He could plead further that the wealth of the country justified its conquest. Dacia's gold may not have been known to the Romans as early as 100. But apart from this the Romans must have learned from the Greek merchants and the numerous Roman traders, who had for years been flocking to Drobeta on the Danube, that the land was rich. Incidentally, when the zero hour arrived, the presence of these traders probably produced a convenient clash of interests. In the event the gold, silver and captives Trajan obtained from Dacia provided the imperial treasury with a large net profit.[1]

Preparations for the attack began with Trajan's accession. The nine Danubian legions were reinforced ; [2] and to facilitate military operations Tiberius' old road on the Roman bank of the Danube in the region of the spectacular gorge known as the Iron Gates was rebuilt.

The core of Dacian strength lay in Transylvania, a vast natural fortress cupped in the bend of the Carpathian Mountains. Trajan decided to strike at this with a very large army, perhaps with *auxilia* forming its real core : but ten, or parts of ten, legions [3] also participated, in all about 100,000 men.

In 101 part of this army crossed the Danube at Viminacium and made for the Iron Gate Pass through the mountains on the west of Transylvania.[4] Another force seems simultaneously to have crossed the river at Drobeta and to have headed for one of the Carpathian passes to the southeast of Transylvania, possibly the Vulcan Pass. The first force won a hard-fought victory over the Dacians at Tapae, where Domitian's general Tettius Julianus had defeated them *c.* 89. But enemy resistance had not been broken when winter arrived to postpone the decision.

Trajan wintered on the Roman side of the Danube and had

---

[1] On Trajan's policy in Dacia see E. T. Salmon, *Trans. Amer. Philol. Assoc.*, LXVII (1936), p. 83 ff.

[2] One of the six legions Domitian had left on the Danube, XI Claudia, was transferred permanently to Durostorum. Trajan also borrowed Legion I Minervia from Germany, although whether for his First or Second Dacian War is uncertain.

[3] I Adiutrix, XIII Gemina, XIV Gemina, XV Apollinaris in Pannonia ; II Adiutrix, IV Flavia Firma, VII Claudia in Upper Moesia ; I Italica, V Macedonica in Lower Moesia ; XI Claudia newly transferred to Durostorum.

[4] This is made clear by the one surviving fragment of Trajan's own commentaries.

to fend off a sudden raid by the Roxolani. It was probably in the first instance to commemorate the successful repulse of these Roxolani that the famous 60 foot high circular monument (*Tropaeum Traiani*) was erected at Adamclisi, the probable scene of Oppius Sabinus' defeat *c.* 85. The rude sculptures, with which it was originally encased, now preserved at Bucharest, appear to depict Roxolani rather than Dacians. The *tropaeum* was not completed, however, until 109 when the Dacian Wars were over. The defeats of Sabinus and Fuscus could then appropriately be regarded as avenged and the monument dedicated to Mars Ultor.

In 102 Trajan again crossed the Danube, this time with his forces undivided, apparently at Drobeta. He succeeded in forcing his way into Transylvania through one of the Carpathian passes, either the Vulcan or the Red Tower Pass, and compelled Decebalus and the Dacians to accept a humiliating peace. Roman garrisons were left in Transylvania and the Banat. Dacia, however, was not annexed : at this stage Trajan may have been primarily interested only in scoring a military success as an aid to strengthening his régime. He returned to Rome, celebrated a triumph, and received the title of Dacicus.

§ 3. THE SECOND DACIAN WAR

The Dacians, however, were not tamely prepared to allow a Roman Emperor to seek popularity at their expense. Having secretly rearmed they, early in 105, overwhelmed the Roman garrisons north of the Danube and then proceeded to raid Moesia across the river. Trajan himself at once hurried to the Danubian area and assembled a larger army than ever. After 102 he had enrolled two new legions,[1] had divided Pannonia *c.* 103 into two provinces, an Upper and a Lower, and had increased its garrison to five legions.[2] As a result, in 105 he mustered all or parts of thirteen legions for the renewed assault on Dacia.[3] With this vast army he crossed the Danube

---

[1] II Traiana and XXX Ulpia Victrix, which replaced V Alaudae and XXI Rapax. Both the latter had been wiped out in Domitian's reign.

[2] X Gemina had been brought to Vindobona. This left only four legions in the Germanies, a striking proof of Domitian's pacification of the Rhine.

[3] The ten he used in the First War and, in addition, XXX Ulpia Victrix, and X Gemina and I Minervia, the former transferred and the latter borrowed from Lower Germany : P. Aelius Hadrianus, the future emperor, commanded I Minervia.

at Drobeta early in 106 by means of the famous bridge which the Syrian architect Apollodorus had built: some of its stone pillars are still standing.[1]   After marching to the River Aluta (*Olt*), he proceeded upstream to the Red Tower Pass over the Carpathians.   By this route he forced his way into Transylvania, stormed Decebalus' capital, thoroughly subjugated the country and annexed it to the Empire.

This new province of Dacia extended at first from the River Tisia (*Theiss*) on the west to the Aluta on the east, and as far north as the *colonia* of Porolissum.   Thousands of Dacians were transported to the southern side of the Danube and replaced by settlers mostly drawn from the eastern portions of the Empire. The *colonia* Ulpia Traiana replaced Sarmizegethusa,[2] and a provincial *concilium* was established at Aquae.   Many roads were built and the natural resources of the country, including its gold, extensively exploited.   The province of Dacia, indeed, became an outpost of Latinity on the northern side of the Danube; and to this day the area speaks a Latin language. But it was above all as a military bastion that it was important to the Roman Empire.[3]   It served to split up Rome's trans-Danubian enemies, who were potentially a formidable menace; and it performed this rôle with success for more than a century and a half.   It was not until the reign of Aurelian that the Romans abandoned Dacia.

§ 4.   ANNEXATION OF ARABIA PETRAEA

In 106 or thereabouts Trajan also annexed Arabia Petraea, which lay astride the trade-routes to the east and was the last buffer state remaining between Syria and Parthia proper. Ever since Pompey's day it had been a client kingdom ruled by the King of the Nabataeans; it was inhabited for the most part by Arab nomads, although it contained some wealthy cities, notably Petra.   Trajan decided to follow Augustus'

[1] Its superstructure was of wood.

[2] The site, Ulpia Traiana, is usually stated to have been Decebalus' capital, but this is not confirmed by archaeological investigation.

[3] Its first governor, D. Terentius Scaurianus, probably commanded three legions: XIII Gemina encamped at the *colonia* of Apulum; I Adiutrix; IV Flavia Firma.   The Danube frontier was strengthened further by the five legions in Upper and Lower Moesia and the four legions Trajan left in Upper and Lower Pannonia.

example of ultimately annexing the eastern client kingdoms. When Dabel, the client king of Arabia Petraea, died *c.* 105, A. Cornelius Palma, the governor of Syria, was ordered to occupy his country. Part of it was annexed to Syria, while the more southerly portions, which extended to and included Sinai, became a separate province with its capital at Bostra. It was garrisoned by the Syrian legion VI Ferrata.[1]

§ 5. BUILDING PROGRAMME IN ROME

Trajan now desisted for a space from foreign adventures and devoted his attention to internal administration. Both in Italy and in the provinces he was a tireless worker.

In Rome itself he left striking memorials of his energy. One might mention his Baths and the theatre which he began in the Campus Martius. The most spectacular of all was his Forum, dedicated in 112, which is easily the biggest of all the imperial fora. It was Domitian who had conceived the idea of a chain of such fora when he cleared the area north of the Forum Romanum, in the vicinity of the Argiletum, and built the so-called Forum Transitorium or Pervium, which Nerva coolly claimed as his. For his own Forum Trajan invoked the services of Apollodorus. A large space between the Capitoline and Quirinal was cleared, the col joining the two hills being literally cut away. The Forum was graced by the statue-bedecked Basilica Ulpia, which served as a law-court, and by two libraries containing Latin and Greek volumes respectively. Between them rose Trajan's famous Column surmounted by a statue of the Emperor. It still stands adorned by reliefs, which ascend to the top in a continuous spiral and depict scenes from Trajan's Dacian Wars : its overall height was 128 feet. The Forum was approached from Augustus' Forum by way of a triumphal and richly sculptured arch, and it was surrounded by a double colonnade. This Forum with its variegated marbles, bronze roof-tops, gilded horses and countless statues can perhaps be regarded as a gratification of the Emperor's passion for building. Nevertheless its libraries at least served a useful purpose ; and this is even truer of the shopping centre which flanked its north side.

[1] The new legion II Traiana replaced this latter in Syria.

§ 6. DOMESTIC POLICY

Theoretically the Senate administered Italy, but no Emperor scrupled to interfere, least of all Trajan. He had his agents supervising the finances of Caere and other municipalities in Italy and placed a praetorian legate in charge of the Transpadane region. Inscriptions everywhere reveal his interest in public works. He built harbour installations at Ostia and Centumcellae, the ports for Rome, and at Ancona and Brundisium, the ports on the Adriatic. Highways received particular attention : the Via Traiana from Beneventum to Brundisium, finished in 109, supplemented the less serviceable, more southerly portion of the ancient Via Appia. Some of the bridges he built are still in use to-day. Aqueducts, too, were not neglected. The Aqua Traiana of 109 brought water to Southern Etruria, while the Acqua Paola still supplies modern Rome.

Such amenities, however, were of very little use if the people were not there to use them. In an effort to stimulate the birth-rate Trajan continued and expanded Nerva's scheme of *alimenta*,[1] but these alone were hardly adequate. Therefore Trajan took the additional step of making children eligible for the monthly corn-dole and for the occasional per capita cash distribution. Although himself a native of Spain, he did not want Italy to lose its position of primacy in the Empire through a dwindling of its rising generation. His concern first and foremost for Italy is shown by various measures.

In earlier days when senators were all Romans, or at least Italians, their capital was normally invested in Italian land. By now, however, many senators were non-Italian. It is possible that these new men would have found capital investment in Italy attractive in any case. But Trajan refused to leave the matter to chance : he insisted that they should invest at least a third of their capital in Italian land. One result of this was a re-settlement of some of the derelict portions of the Roman Campagna.

But there were other than centripetal tendencies at work in the Roman Empire. The provinces were indeed coming to Rome in the form of the new nobility ; but it is also true that

[1] Indeed we are chiefly informed about the *alimenta* from Trajanic inscriptions which describe how the system functioned at Veleia in the Po valley and at Beneventum in the south, where the Ligurians known as Baebiani were settled.

Rome and Italy were going to the provinces. Government service alone must have taken many Italians abroad; and opportunities for quick wealth must have taken many more; probably there was considerable emigration. Nerva had tried to discourage it; Trajan may have gone further and flatly prohibited it.[1] Italy no doubt was still very populous, but Trajan was evidently perturbed at the prospect of a possible decline. His notorious reluctance to grant the *ius trium liberorum* to any except bona fide fathers of three proves his anxiety about the birth-rate.

§ 7. THE CURATORES

The departure of municipal aristocrats to the Senatorial Order was a serious loss to local governments. Trajan therefore attempted to rehabilitate municipal life or at any rate to keep it at a high standard. Exactly how far the municipalities in Italy had declined is a moot point. Most of them were undoubtedly still well peopled and flourishing. But Trajan detected the seeds of future decay in the inefficiency and wastefulness of local authorities, especially in the field of finance. To remedy this he appointed officials known as *curatores*, who took local finances out of the hands of the local authorities. Caere in 113 is the first Italian city known to have received a civic commissioner of this type; but there were undoubtedly others. Nor were they confined to Italy. In the senatorial provinces such *curatores* became fairly common. The free cities (*civitates liberae*), which were outside the control of the provincial governor, had in many cases allowed their internal affairs to become chaotic. Trajan did not hesitate to intervene. In 109, for example, he sent a certain Maximus to Achaea with orders to regulate the affairs of such free cities as Athens, Sparta and Delphi.[2] In the senatorial province of Bithynia the situation was even worse, for there not only the free cities but all the communities stood in urgent need of a controlling hand from the central government. Trajan acted boldly. C. 111 the province was tempor-

---

[1] This is not certain; it depends on a disputed interpretation of a passage in the *Historia Augusta*, *Marc. Aur.*, 11, 7.

[2] Maximus may have been technically a *corrector* rather than a *curator*. The competence of the former official does not seem to have been restricted to financial matters or even to one community, as seems to have been the case with the *curator*.

arily transferred from the Senate to the Emperor, who appointed
the Younger Pliny as its governor.   The correspondence between
the Emperor and Pliny has been preserved, and it throws a vivid
light on provincial affairs.   Like Trajan's legislation, it indicates
that the Emperor was a man who sought to combine humanitarianism with discipline and efficiency.   Certainly the central
government in Trajan's day kept a very close eye on every
detail of provincial life.   Although he was primarily concerned
with financial rehabilitation, he was also particularly interested
to see that the ban on illegal clubs and organizations, which
might form a political menace, should be rigidly enforced.
Pliny's attempts to suppress such organizations included a
rather half-hearted attack on Christianity in Bithynia (p. 323).
The central government also concerned itself in every other
conceivable activity.   Public works, education, religion, local
government were all carefully supervised.   Incidentally, Trajan
found in Pliny a conscientious servant to perform this kind of
work.

Needless to say, this painstaking interest in the welfare of
his subjects was very much to Trajan's credit ; and undoubtedly
the appointment of *curatores*, both in Italy and in the provinces,
did much to end abuses and promote efficiency.   Nevertheless
it is questionable whether such paternal care was not a step
in a dangerous direction.[1]   There can be such a thing as too
much efficiency : it can reach the stage where it stifles initiative
and self-reliance.   What begins as an emergency measure, well
tended by an occasional careful appointment, is likely to become
a permanent system supervised by a regular State department
indifferently served by a host of minor and mediocre civil
servants.   Local authorities might get into the habit of relying
on the officials sent out from the central government ; or they
might indignantly resent the interference of these latter and
lose all interest in the affairs of their own community.   Local
patriotism, the driving force of municipal government, would
disappear ; and it should be remembered that the municipalities,
unlike Rome, had an atmosphere of real political life.   Local
elections were genuinely contested, and there was freedom of
speech on topics of local interest.   Once officials of the central
government intervened all this healthy activity might come to
an end.

In Trajan's day this was scarcely the case.   He regarded
the appointment of *curatores* as something quite exceptional,

---

[1] Augustus' local *praefecti iure dicundo* foreshadow Trajan's *curatores*.

and he selected them with care, skill and restraint. But in a later age, under Emperors who were less able or less tactful in their choice, the system expanded apace into a very rank growth. Unimaginative Emperors, seeing no other way to arrest the decline of the municipalities, resorted over-hastily to this solution. Ultimately a veritable army of bureaucrats, the majority of them simply officials who understood nothing but the literal letter of their commission, descended upon the municipalities. The result was that they tended to promote the atrophy which they were supposed to cure. Exactly where the vicious circle began cannot be determined : the decay of municipal institutions necessitated the appointment of *curatores*, and the *curatores*, by ruthlessly imposing themselves on the local communities and depriving the local magistrates of the power to make decisions, fostered a listless disintegration. These evils belonged to a later age than Trajan's ; but it is certainly arguable that he initiated that paternalism on the part of the central government which was to have such dire consequences for the Late Empire. His motives were clearly of the best. He genuinely wished to promote urbanization. He was seeking to be a just ruler and a wise benefactor ; and as far as his own generation was concerned, the solutions he found were admirable enough.

In his day the Empire as a whole was excellently governed. The upper classes supplied him with competent, imperial servants drawn from all over the Empire, including the eastern provinces. His most trusted helper was a Spaniard, the able L. Licinius Sura, whose death *c.* 108 was a very real loss to the Emperor and the Empire.

Besides providing the provinces with roads, bridges,[1] aqueducts and similar material benefits, whose remains can be seen in many parts of the Empire to this day, Trajan also gave them mental ease. The provincials could go about their business with the reassuring knowledge that the central government was taking thought for their physical security, both from within and without the Empire. Within the Empire they were pro-tected against rapacious and malevolent governors. Only four provincial governors, two of them significantly from

---

[1] The most spectacular being the Alcantara bridge built over the Tagus in Spain in 105. To the construction of this bridge the neighbour-ing municipalities also made a contribution. (Dessau, *Inscr. Lat. Sel.*, 287.)

Bithynia, had to be put on trial for maladministration, and these may have been Nerva's appointees, for they were tried in the early part of the reign. The letters of Pliny certainly suggest that Trajan would not tolerate provincial misgovernment.

§ 8.   TRAJAN AND THE FINANCES

There is, however, another side to Trajan's administration. He disbursed large sums, which somehow had to be made good. His extension of the *alimenta* and other measures for the improvement of Italy, his vast building projects, whose dedications were invariably accompanied by the lavish shows and spectacles of which he was very fond,[1] his abolition of *aurum coronarium* and the lucrative treason trials, his waiving of some of the funds previously obtained from the inheritance tax, his enlarged grain dole and cash distributions,[2] the mobilization of his two new legions and of *equites singulares*, all these things had to be paid for by the fiscus.[3] And Nerva's spending for popularity had left the fiscus with no accumulated surplus. It is true that for the most part Trajan postponed his spending orgy until after he had acquired his booty from Dacia, which consisted of large quantities of gold and silver and of numerous captives who could serve as gladiators. Indeed it may be that his Dacian conquests paid for many of the expenditures of his reign. It has frequently been asserted that he resorted to debasement of the currency (of his silver coins, to be specific) in order to get the sums he needed. But the really trustworthy evidence for this would be the coins themselves, and careful examination of Trajanic silver issues does not reveal debasement : if anything, the quality of the silver in Trajan's coins is rather better than that in the coins of his immediate predecessors. We know that Trajan carefully supervised the treasuries of the Roman State : his scrupulous, if in fact fictitious, separation of the *aerarium* from the *fiscus* proves it. Evidently his care was not confined to the organization of the treasuries but extended also to their stock-in-trade, the coins.

[1] In 107, to celebrate his return to Rome, he gave games that lasted a hundred and twenty-three days and used up eleven thousand gladiators (more than Augustus had needed in his whole reign).

[2] Which amounted to six hundred and fifty denarii a head in Rome during the reign.

[3] He imitated Augustus in keeping the fiscus separate from the *aerarium* (reversing Flavian practice).

§ 9. THE PARTHIAN WAR ; REVOLT

Trajan attempted to protect his subjects against external attack by his forward frontier policy. The annexation of Dacia secured the Danube frontier. But the incorporation of Arabia Petraea did not solve the recurring problem of the eastern frontier, which despite Flavian attention remained an Achilles' heel. Recent events in the east were a cause for foreboding. The Alans and other Caucasian tribes, themselves pressed forward by Huns from Central Asia, were threatening Armenia ; and this ripple of population was bound to surge forward against the imperial frontiers. A sage and prudent Emperor like Trajan could not ignore the threat. Unfortunately there was no natural boundary in the east, and no natural inclination towards romanization to make the task of defence any easier. Accordingly Trajan decided on a radical solution of the problem. Instead of attempting to keep a Roman nominee as King of Armenia, either with or without Parthian approval, he decided to annex the country once and for all. But the annexation of Armenia was not likely to be permanent so long as the potentially hostile country to the south of it was independent. An enemy in Mesopotamia would have the advantage of operating on inner lines against the semicircle of Roman lands stretching from Syria by way of Cappadocia to Armenia. In other words, the annexation of Armenia entailed the annexation of Mesopotamia. Trajan did not flinch at the prospect ; on the contrary, it is quite likely that he, as a soldier-emperor, found it congenial.

On strategic grounds one will hardly cavil at his decision. But a general has to do more than consider the appropriate strategy. He must also bear in mind his available resources : men and money enter into the calculation as well as geography. Augustus evidently thought that the Empire did not dispose of sufficient power to make the permanent conquest of Armenia and Mesopotamia feasible. However, since Augustus' day, so Trajan might argue, the Empire's strength had increased sufficiently to justify the venture. He could reasonably argue that it would place no additional strain on the imperial finances, since the contemplated conquests could be made to pay for themselves on the analogy of Dacia. The annexation of Arabia Petraea had probably taught him that considerable sums could be raised from levies exacted upon goods in transit along the

routes to the orient. There were several such routes across
Mesopotamia ; and it is significant that when Trajan reached
Babylon he immediately began to levy tolls on the horses and
camels crossing the Euphrates and Tigris.

But imperial ventures of the type envisaged by Trajan
require a large expenditure of men as well as of money. The
Empire and the new conquests together could possibly have
resisted the financial strain ; the demands on military man-power
were to prove too great. Trajan's cousin and successor Hadrian,
foreseeing this, probably warned him against the adventure ;
but Trajan either overestimated the Empire's man-power
resources or else, which is far more probable, he thought it less
risky in the long run to take a chance and try to achieve his
purpose with the legionary material at his disposal. Doubtless
he counted on internal quarrels in Parthia facilitating his
task. The event proved Trajan wrong. But should he be
severely criticized for attempting to maintain the grandeur
of Rome ?

As a pretext Trajan could have adduced the support which
Parthia invariably gave to the " false Neros " who had
periodically appeared. He preferred, however, to avail himself
of the situation in Armenia. Without consulting Rome,
Chosroes, King of Parthia, had recently appointed Exedares,
the son of his brother and predecessor Pacorus, to the throne of
Armenia.[1] This was a breach of the agreement with Nero.
Trajan already had reason to suspect Parthian designs. For
King Pacorus, whom Chosroes had succeeded c. 110, had been
in communication with Decebalus during the Dacian Wars.
Trajan now regarded the enthronement of Exedares in Armenia
as a *casus belli* and declared war. He himself set sail for Syria
in October of 113. (See maps, pp. 251, 299.)

Chosroes, seeing that Trajan was in earnest, sent envoys
who met him at Athens with the suggestion that Exedares
should be deposed and that Chosroes, with Rome's permission,
should appoint his other nephew, Parthamisiris, in his stead.
Exedares was in fact deposed. But Trajan refused to commit
himself and continued on his way to Syria, arriving at Antioch
in January of 114. There he mobilized the army of Syria
and called upon the client kings of the eastern borderlands
to furnish contingents. Some of them, notably Abgarus

[1] This is how the author interprets the text of Dio LXVIII. 17.

of Osrhoene and Mannus of Arabia Deserta, ignored the request.[1]

In the spring of 114 Trajan moved over the Upper Euphrates by way of Samosata or Melitene and quickly reached Satala in Armenia, where local princes, satraps and chieftains assembled and promised loyalty to him. Even Parthamisiris humbly offered to lay aside his regal pretensions and begged for an audience. Trajan granted it to him at Elegeia, ten miles west of Erzerum. Parthamisiris was forced to do obeisance and lay his crown at Trajan's feet. Trajan did not return it to him, but formally pronounced Armenia a Roman province and temporarily placed it under the control of the governor of neighbouring Cappadocia.[2] He then apparently returned to Antioch for the winter of 114–115.

So far the Emperor had scored an easy victory, largely because Chosroes of Parthia was engrossed by an uprising led by a certain Manisares and probably fostered by Rome. Thus Trajan had not really come into contact with the enemy. He realized clearly, however, that Parthia would not acquiesce in his annexation of Armenia, and therefore he moved quickly with the ultimate intention of incorporating Parthia as well. With his left flank secured by his bloodless conquest of Armenia, a frontal assault on the main adversary seemed safe. Consequently, when he moved over the Euphrates in the spring of 115, he used the important Zeugma crossing. He imitated Agricola's procedure in Britain and left garrisons at strong points along his line of march. At Edessa, in Osrhoene, King Abgarus hastily revised his earlier attitude and was graciously pardoned by Trajan. From here the Roman army marched one hundred and fifty miles to Nisibis, whence Lusius Quietus and his Mauretanian cavalry advanced to seize Singara. The Upper Euphrates area was thus overrun, and the province of (Northern) Mesopotamia acquired.

A centurion named Sentius was now sent to Media Adiabene to demand that its King, Mebarsapes, transfer his allegiance from Parthia to Rome. Mebarsapes replied by imprisoning Sentius, and his defiance was supported by King Mannus of Arabia Deserta. By now Roman reconnaissance units had

[1] Presumably Trajan had also summoned forces from all over the Empire, although the exact strength of his army is unknown. Two of the three Dacian legions, I Adiutrix and IV Flavia Firma, certainly participated.

[2] Cappadocia was apparently no longer administered jointly with Galatia (see above, p. 250).

doubtless reached the Upper Tigris. But the end of the campaigning season had arrived, and the troops were obliged to winter at Nisibis preparing boats and wagons for the next year's campaign. Trajan himself returned to Antioch for the winter (115–116).

The campaign of 116 was preceded by a terrible earthquake at Antioch (December 13, 115), which almost took the Emperor's life and caused widespread death and destruction. From the stricken city Trajan made his way to his army at Nisibis, and the campaign for 116 began. Its main objective was the Parthian capital, Ctesiphon. Before moving against it, however, Trajan turned to Media Adiabene and formally incorporated it as the new province of Assyria, rescuing his centurion Sentius in the process. He was now ready to settle accounts with Parthia. How he reached Ctesiphon is uncertain. Dio's statement that he sailed down the Euphrates as far as Babylon and then proceeded overland to the Tigris is not very credible. But, by whatever route, he did get there. Chosroes had fled from the city, but his treasure fell into Trajan's hands. A fourth province, Parthia, was added to the Empire : the title Parthicus, awarded him in February 116, seemed well earned.

The Emperor, however, did not stop here. After a march to the Persian Gulf he made his way to Babylon in order to winter there. But it was now made clear that he had undertaken a task beyond Roman strength. He had won territories, but not victories ; the Parthians had traded space for time. The garrisons Trajan had left behind at various strong points revealed themselves as inadequate to police the far-flung conquests. Insurrection flared up ; the strong points of Edessa, Nisibis and Seleucia fell to the insurgents ; and Trajan's whole line of communications was disrupted. Lusius Quietus managed to retake Nisibis, while the legionary commanders, Sex. Erucius Clarus and Ti. Julius Alexander, were similarly engaged at Seleucia. But their departure weakened Trajan's army, which Trajan moved on from Babylon to Ctesiphon. Meanwhile, however, the Parthians had gathered a strong force commanded by Chosroes' brother,[1] Sanatruces, and his son Parthamaspates. Trajan was forced to resort to Rome's traditional method for dealing with the Parthians, provocation of internecine strife among them. He was successful, but the price came high. Parthamaspates demanded the Parthian crown as his reward

[1] Or possibly his nephew.

for moving against Sanatruces. Trajan complied, although it meant renouncing his new province of Parthia. He and Parthamaspates then overcame the forces of Sanatruces in a hard-fought battle. Parthamaspates was duly crowned King of Parthia at Ctesiphon. Such a victory for Trajan was a purely nominal one and proved short-lived. Parthamaspates was expelled by Chosroes the moment the Roman forces evacuated Ctesiphon. Trajan's attempt to conquer Lower Mesopotamia had failed.

He still hoped, however, to save something of his original scheme by consolidating his hold on his three other new provinces. But here, too, failure ultimately overtook his efforts. The city of Hatra in Mesopotamia refused to make submission, and late in 116 Trajan tried to reduce it by siege. The rigours of winter arrived to foil his efforts, and finally he had to lead his tired and battered army back to Antioch (early in 117).

Unfortunately the trouble had not confined itself to Mesopotamia. The Jews hated the Romans bitterly ; and their hatred embraced all the Gentiles among whom they were living and not the least the Greeks. Now in 116 the Jews of Judaea made no move ; doubtless they still remembered the terrible lesson of 70. But the Jews of the Dispersion, who were mainly settled in Mesopotamia, Cyprus, Egypt and North Africa, were fanatically bent on revenge. Those in Egypt and North Africa were in revolt already in 115 ; and in 116 those in Mesopotamia joined the mounting insurrection in Trajan's rear. As it spread from country to country the rebellion was marked by ghastly atrocities. A million people are said to have lost their lives. In Cyprus the insurgents gained control and conducted a hideous massacre of the Greeks. The city of Salamis was obliterated and a quarter of a million Gentiles are said to have perished. In Cyrene the blood-letting was on an equally formidable scale. In Egypt the Prefect, M. Rutilius Lupus, was actually besieged in Alexandria. Nor were the risings confined to the Jews. As the ancient source puts it : " The Moors were provocative, the Sarmatians were preparing invasion, the Britons could not be held under the Roman yoke."

Trajan took energetic measures. In Mesopotamia Lusius Quietus, in Africa Marcius Turbo restored some semblance of order ; the former became governor of Judaea, the latter soon went to Dacia. Trajan himself set out for Rome, whence he planned to direct operations against the widespread revolts.

But it was left to his successor to bring the disturbances fully to an end, for Trajan himself never reached Rome.

§ 10. THE "ADOPTION" OF HADRIAN

The sixty-four-year-old Emperor had only got as far as Selinus when he was smitten with a sudden stroke and died within a few days (not later than August 9, 117). Until the time of his stroke Trajan, a man without children, had not formally indicated a successor. His wife Plotina and the Praetorian Prefect Acilius Attianus,[1] who were with him at the end, asserted that on his death-bed he had adopted his second cousin, the forty-one-year-old P. Aelius Hadrianus,[2] who as governor of Syria was at Antioch. A despatch reached Hadrian, informing him of his alleged adoption, on August 9, and the army of the east acclaimed him Emperor two days later : whence Hadrian, on the Vespasianic model, reckoned August 11 his *dies imperii*.

Whether Trajan did in fact adopt Hadrian we shall never certainly know. In any event scarcely any other choice for Emperor was possible. Hadrian was Trajan's nearest male relative. Although of Picentine ancestry,[3] he had been born on January 24, 76 of a senatorial family settled in Spain, Italica in Baetica being reckoned his place of origin.[4] At an early age he had obtained Trajan and another eminent son of Italica, Acilius Attianus, as his guardians ; [5] and he was at once marked out for a public career. His youth was mainly passed in Rome : he received an education there and imbibed a lasting enthusiasm for Greek studies. Thereafter he obtained considerable experience in civil and military matters. He passed through the regular senatorial *cursus honorum*,[6] and saw military service

---

[1] He was a Spaniard from Italica and had succeeded Ti. Claudius Livianus, who was Praetorian Prefect for most of Trajan's reign.

[2] Hadrian's grandmother and Trajan's father were brother and sister.

[3] His name derives from the town of Hadria in Picenum.

[4] He was actually born in Rome. Italica, his official *patria*, later had its status raised from *municipium* to *colonia*.

[5] Hadrian's father died in 85.

[6] Vigintivirate (94) ; Military Tribunate (with Legio II Adiutrix in Pannonia, 95 ; with V Macedonica in Lower Moesia, 96 ; with XXII Primigenia in Upper Germany, 97) ; Quaestorship (101) ; Plebeian Tribunate (105) ; Praetorship (106) ; Consulship (108). He was also *praefectus urbi c.* 91 (for the *Feriae Latinae*).

in Spain (90), Pannonia (95), Moesia (96), Germany (97), and with Trajan in Dacia. He also was with Trajan in the east, although we do not know that he played a prominent military part there. He had been governor of Lower Pannonia and was governor of Syria in 117. Clearly for a man of forty-one such a career was far from ordinary. In addition he had enjoyed some quite exceptional honours. It was he who had conveyed the congratulations of the Danubian legions to Trajan on the latter's adoption by Nerva in 97, and he had been appointed commander of a legion before holding the praetorship and governor of a province containing legionary troops before holding the consulship. To cap all, he was not only Trajan's nearest male relative, but in 100 he had also married the Emperor's nearest female relative, his grandniece Vibia Sabina.

Clearly, whatever Trajan's motive in not formally adopting him (and it cannot have been mere carelessness), no other successor to the soldier-emperor was possible. Any other nominee would surely have found in Hadrian a very real pretender; and almost certainly civil war would have resulted. The story of Trajan's death-bed adoption, marked as it is by some very suspicious circumstances, is not very convincing. The whole episode reads more like a *coup d'état* than a genuine adoption.[1] But it was as well for the Empire that it was officially and generally accepted.

§ 11. OPTIMUS PRINCEPS

The reign of Trajan has always been regarded as one of the very best periods in Roman history, the period when the Empire reached its short-lived apogee. Ancient writers regularly allude to Trajan in terms of the highest praise, if not adulation. A man who evoked such universal admiration must have possessed very considerable virtues; and imperfectly informed though we are about the scope and intention of much that he did, we do know that he was responsible for very real achievements. They are not unfairly set forth in the sculptures on the magnificent arch which was dedicated to him at Beneventum in 114. Here we see Trajan popular with gods and with soldiers, with ordinary civilians and with business

---

[1] Scandal alleged that Plotina forged the adoption because she was in love with Hadrian. She was little, if any, older than the latter.

men ; and allusion is made to his military victories and his care for the children of Italy.

At the same time these ancient encomia cannot be reckoned free from exaggeration. The literary tradition derives mainly from senatorial sources, and Trajan more than any other emperor succeeded in winning the goodwill of the Senate. This is somewhat surprising, for on matters of basic policy he was as ruthlessly autocratic as any of the Flavians. He did not hesitate, for example, to take the province of Achaea away from the Senate and entrust it to his own legate, C. Avidius Nigrinus, and he even continued the Flavian policy of giving increased importance to the Equestrian Order. It is under him that we find the first equestrian financial secretary, L. Vibius Lentulus, in 114 ; and it was he who first appointed equites to certain procuratorial posts, e.g. *procurator aquarum, procurator monetae*. It is worth adding that as a corollary he rigorously controlled his freedmen. It is possible that the Senate of his day, composed as it largely was of provincials like himself,[1] could be more easily won over than the proudly stubborn Senate of Julio-Claudian times, which consisted largely of haughty republican families. But it was above all the Emperor himself, by his own character and personality, who must be given credit for the improvement in relations between Princeps and nobility. In other words, the spirit of his autocracy was different from Domitian's. It was not a case of Trajan contenting himself with less power, but of using it differently.

His popularity, then, must be attributed partly to the revulsion of feeling from the hated Domitian, partly to the conciliatory policy inaugurated by Nerva and consistently followed by himself. But above all his own tactful, genial and winning personality is responsible. The senators were not the only ones who felt its impact. The soldiers worshipped an Emperor who shared their hardships and tore up his own clothing to bind their wounds. The plebs loved an Emperor who provided fine shows and caught their imagination with his victories. Trajan was equally studious of the predilections of the Senate. To individual senators he appeared at once urbane and natural ; he mingled with them on terms of easy social equality. He dined, he hunted and in general he conducted himself with no more ostentation than any private member of the Order. His

---

[1] Trajan himself created many eastern senators ; and in the next reign only some thirty senators bear old Roman names.

modesty, indeed, was remarkable. Thus he, the greatest
of soldier-emperors, was satisfied with thirteen imperial salutations, whereas Augustus had received twenty-one, Claudius
twenty-seven, Vespasian twenty and Domitian twenty-two.

The Senate, as a body, he treated with grave respect. He
always consulted it and sought its advice ; and even though
he allowed it no real power in matters of high importance, he
did give individual senators something more to do than merely
idle their time away in debates on trivial issues. It was under
Trajan, for instance, that the senatorial Prefect of the Grain
Dole emerged again from his obscurity. He was anxious
not to be guilty of faults either of commission or omission that
might offend the Senate. For the last fourteen years of his
reign he avoided the office of consul : in all he was consul only
six times, thus forming a glaring contrast with the Flavians.
When on his campaigns, he punctiliously sent back reports to
the Senate, and he always insisted that no terms which he
struck with the enemy were valid unless and until the Senate
ratified them. A possible explanation of his failure to adopt
Hadrian is that he wanted to avoid the appearance of imposing
his choice upon the Senate.[1]

The result of all this was that the Senate convinced itself that
at long last the Principate and liberty were reconciled. It
seemed to trust the Emperor. Not only did it bestow upon him
the title of Optimus Princeps, but it even deified every member
of his immediate family.

If we have regard only for the basic realities, which were
that the Emperor disposed of the armed force and was prepared
to use it if need be quite autocratically, we might argue that
it was a matter of small importance in the last analysis whether
the Emperor gained senatorial affections or not. That is not
altogether a fair view of the situation. The Senate, representing
as it did the educated upper classes, exerted very wide moral
influence ; and it was not the least of Trajan's services to the
Empire that he produced an atmosphere of cordiality in the
court and in noble circles generally. If it was the Flavians
who won over the provincial armies to the abstract idea of the
Principate, it was Trajan who won over the Senate. In this
the Flavians had conspicuously failed : Domitian, indeed,

[1] It is also possible that the existence of rival court factions, Licinius
Sura supporting Hadrian and A. Cornelius Palma and Avidius Nigrinus
opposing him, made a decision on the matter of adoption difficult.

instead of reconciling the Senate had gone out of his way to alienate it.

Not only was Trajan himself responsible for many measures of good government (and considering the necessities of the time the paternal supervision, which his administration exercised over hard-pressed communities and individuals, was a measure of good government), but he also bequeathed to his successors the tradition of real co-operation between Princeps and Senate. A sullen atmosphere of suspicion, intrigue and conspiracy is not an ideal one for the central government of a great Empire with its pressing daily tasks. Such an atmosphere it was that Trajan succeeded in dispelling. Thanks very largely to him the Emperors of the second century were able to devote their attention to the cares of State with considerably more freedom from worries of a political kind than the Emperors of the first century. It was in an environment not surcharged with menace that they could proceed to the further development of Trajan's humanitarian measures. If some of these measures were developed by less able Emperors to the point where, much later, they became a peril to the State—by the well-known process of *corruptio optimi pessima*—he cannot in all fairness be held solely responsible.

Even his much criticized imperialist adventures in the east should not be impatiently dismissed as the schemes of a military megalomaniac bent on imitating and rivalling Alexander the Great. His expedition against Parthia did end in failure and widespread revolts. But it had succeeded in convincing the outside world that Rome still possessed formidable military might and could not be provoked with impunity. It is doubtful whether the pacific policies of Trajan's own immediate successors would have had more than a remote chance of success, if he had not impressed Parthians and others with a profound respect for Rome's arms.

The ancient picture of Trajan as an emperor of almost super-human excellence cannot be fully endorsed. But that he was one of the very best men ever to wear the imperial purple no one can reasonably dispute. Two and a half centuries later the Senate at a new Emperor's accession could still wish for nothing better than that he should be " more successful than Augustus and more virtuous than Trajan." [1]

----

[1] Eutropius, VIII, 5, 3.

CHAPTER III

HADRIAN

§ 1. THE SUCCESSION OF HADRIAN

PLOTINA, together with Hadrian's mother-in-law, Matidia, and Acilius Attianus, at once hastened to Rome. Hadrian for the time being remained in Syria, but sent a letter to the Senate apologizing for the fact that consultation with regard to his " adoption " had not been possible, and requesting that the Senate vote divine honours to Trajan and confirm his own elevation to the purple, but to confer no unsolicited honours upon him ; and he made the usual promise of a new Emperor, that with him service to the State would always come first and that he would never put a senator to death. This attitude of respect towards the Senate was in the true Augustan tradition and was to be a marked feature of the reign. Nevertheless it hardly altered the facts of the situation. The Senate actually had no option, since the army had already acclaimed Hadrian. The Senate, accordingly, formally recognized him, and granted Trajan the honour of deification, burial within the *pomerium* [1] and a posthumous triumph ; annual Parthian games were even instituted.

Hadrian obviously was bidding for senatorial support. The equivocal nature of his " adoption " and the consequent dubious legitimacy of his succession made him feel insecure. It is significant that he paid the troops a " double donative " and tried to enhance his authority by stressing the fact that by adoption he was the son of one *divus* and the grandson of another, and had secret instructions from Trajan for his projected programme, a programme which he knew would prove unpopular. Other emperors who felt precarious at their accession—Gaius, Claudius, the Nerva-Trajan combination—had sought to strengthen their positions by a policy of expansion. Hadrian, however, was planning just the reverse. Convinced by the widespread disturbances at the end of Trajan's reign that the Empire had reached and perhaps even surpassed the limits of its resources in money and perhaps in men as well, he proposed to terminate Trajan's forward policy abruptly. He was not indeed prepared

[1] His ashes were placed in the pediment of his Column.

to tolerate separatism. Calm was quickly restored in Palestine, Egypt and Cyrenaica. His most trusted general, Q. Marcius Turbo, was immediately sent to quell the disturbances in Mauretania, and the rising in Britain was suppressed without delay. Hadrian himself managed to prevent the Sarmatians and Roxolani from attacking across the Danube.

But he set his face against additions to the Empire. He at once recalled the troops from the Lower Euphrates and thus renounced Trajan's new provinces, leaving the area to client kings. On the continent of Africa the existing frontiers were the furthest limit he would tolerate. In Britain he would countenance no resumption of Agricola's northward advance. In the north the Rhine was to remain the boundary. On the Danube he contemplated an evacuation of Dacia.[1] This, how-ever, would have brought ruin to the numerous settlers beyond the Danube ; and his friends convinced him that public opinion, already none too happy at his policy of apparent weakness on the frontiers, was not prepared to tolerate this extreme step. Dacia thus remained part of the Empire and was soon divided by the trusty Marcius Turbo into an Upper and Lower Province, separated by the River Aluta. Hadrian also retained Trajan's province of Arabia Petraea.

§ 2. THE EXECUTION OF THE FOUR CONSULARS

Even before Hadrian made his intentions with regard to the frontiers unmistakably clear, opposition to his régime was gathering. At the very beginning of the reign Attianus wrote to warn him that Baebius Macer, the City Prefect, M'. Laberius Maximus, Trajan's exiled Dacian commander, and C. Calpurnius Crassus, a former opponent of the Nerva-Trajan régime, were potential trouble-makers. Crassus, indeed, tried to escape from his place of exile and was slain, " without Hadrian's orders," in consequence. No action, however, was taken against the other two. Hadrian preferred a policy of clemency.

This fact, however, did not obviate executions. A plot in which many were implicated is said to have been formed against the new Emperor's life. Its exact details cannot be discovered owing to the discrepancies in the ancient sources. On getting

[1] This at least appears to be the implication of the destruction of the wooden superstructure of Apollodorus' bridge over the Danube at Drobeta, which according to Dio occurred in Hadrian's reign.

news of it Hadrian, who had apparently wintered at Nicomedia (117–118), hastened to Italy, perhaps by way of the Danubian provinces, and reached Rome on 9th July (118). By then, however, his supporters in the Senate had taken matters into their own hands and executed the four ringleaders. All four were ex-consuls and close friends of Trajan : L. Publilius Celsus, A. Cornelius Palma, the conqueror of Arabia Petraea, the Mauretanian Lusius Quietus, and C. Avidius Nigrinus, who almost certainly was the governor of Trajan's province of Dacia at the time and seems to have been the chief figure in the conspiracy. There cannot be much doubt that these men, who had probably opposed Hadrian's adoption during Trajan's lifetime, strongly protested against his policy of retreat on the frontiers, and that it was this that caused their ruin. Hadrian always maintained that their execution had taken place without his knowledge or consent ; this looks like an attempt to push responsibility on to Attianus, who obviously was an alarmist. Senators nevertheless believed that Hadrian had broken his promise not to execute a senator and had himself engineered the murders through Attianus. Nor did these suspicions disappear when Hadrian replaced Attianus with Marcius Turbo in the post of Praetorian Prefect : [1] for it was noted that Hadrian, in his own words, bestowed upon Attianus the highest honour he could : consular insignia and membership in the Senate. It was an honour that befell many another equestrian in Hadrian's reign.

The executions were never forgotten by the Senate, and they saddled Hadrian with a lasting reputation for cruelty. However, whatever the facts, the prompt and vigorous action against the four consulars did silence opposition among the nobility to the frontier policy. But Hadrian thought it prudent to try and increase his popularity by bribing the urban mob with lavish donatives and splendid gladiatorial games and by solemnly promising never to mete out to senators any punishment except such as the senatorial court itself ordered.

§ 3. FRONTIER POLICY

Hadrian's purpose was to return to the Flavian frontiers, strictly delimit them and strengthen them with fortifications.

---

[1] The rumour that he planned to execute Attianus proves how the darkest motives were attributed to the devious Hadrian who never remained anyone's friend for long.

He hoped thus to keep the Empire out of foreign wars. The merits of this policy have been endlessly debated. Peace did reign on the frontiers until the end of his reign, the native kings beyond them, large and small alike, being his "friends." But the obvious and perhaps fatal flaw in the policy was that it made insufficient allowance for the fact that states and empires may expand or contract, but they hardly remain static. Any system of frontier defences, no matter how powerful, will not keep a determined enemy at bay for very long. Hadrian's did so a little longer than might have been expected, because Trajan's military exploits had engendered a certain respect for the Empire's military might in the nations beyond the frontiers. Hadrian had no doubt availed himself of this prestige when in personal interviews he managed to persuade the menacing kings of the Roxolani and the Parthians to keep the peace in 118 and 123 respectively.[1] But nations like these were also ready to exploit to the full the first sign of military deterioration.

Hadrian realized that the only chance of success for his policy lay in keeping the frontier armies and posts at the highest peak of efficiency. But this was no easy task, since troops can only be kept at the razor edge of keenness by being actively employed in operations of war : prolonged garrison duty is a notorious destroyer of morale and discipline. Hadrian sought to overcome this danger by continual tours of inspection through the provinces : half his reign was spent in travelling about the Empire. So far as one man can keep an inactive army at the peak of its efficiency, Hadrian did so by means of constant manœuvres and reviews. No detail was too small to escape his attention ; his energy was unflagging, and he introduced a variety of reforms, all calculated to improve the army. Tactics and training, and even the organization of the legion, were modified.[2] Promotions and furloughs were granted for merit and not by favour. The comforts of the men were increased, those of the officers reduced. The extant fragments of the addresses he delivered to the troops in Africa evince Hadrian's lively interest in all their activities.

[1] The King of the Roxolani was Rasparaganus ; Chosroes was still the Parthian monarch.

[2] He doubled the size of the first cohort in the legion, and also gave enhanced importance to the cavalry. (The details in connexion with the latter are uncertain.) On his virtuosity as a soldier, see *Historia Augusta, Hadrian*, 14, 10 : armorum peritissimus et rei militaris scientissimus.

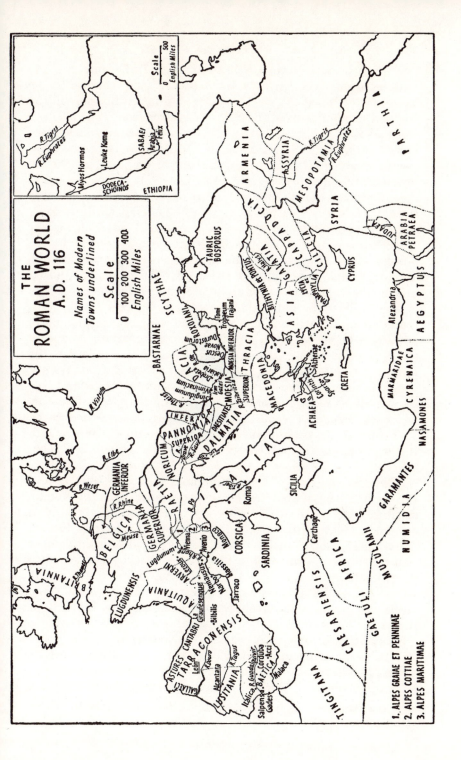

THE
ROMAN WORLD
A.D. 116

Names of Modern
Towns underlined

Scale
0   100 200 300 400
English Miles

Scale
0   500
English Miles

1. ALPES GRAIAE ET PENNINAE
2. ALPES COTTIAE
3. ALPES MARITIMAE

Under him the army was devoted and efficient. As the military centre of gravity was still moving eastwards, he assigned eight legions to the eastern frontier instead of the Flavian six; and he kept them upto full strength. But the other frontiers were not greatly weakened, certain outward appearances notwithstanding. For example, on the Danube Trajan had had twelve legions ; Hadrian reduced them to ten, his two Dacian provinces having only one between them ; but such a reduction in strength was more apparent than real, since Hadrian was using the *auxilia* more extensively. Probably he followed Vespasian's example and made these auxiliary troops serve in areas far from their countries of origin. But he let them serve under native officers who had risen from the ranks, instead of under Roman knights. And he employed them on a large scale. Indeed under him the *auxilia* approximate more and more to the legions. They become almost exclusively infantry troops, receiving virtually the same training and weapons as legionaries ; and they begin to be used as permanent garrison troops in stone frontier forts.[1] As if to emphasize the similarity, the legionaries had their length of service increased from twenty years to the twenty-five served by the auxiliaries, while their personnel was recruited for the most part on the spot. Even the legionary officers, except the very highest ones, ceased to be Italians. Of course provincials had been finding their way into the legions long before Hadrian's day, but he enrolled them eagerly.

The increased use of the *auxilia* and the de-Italianization of the legions contributed to the disappearance of what Roman spirit still remained in the army. When we add that Hadrian organized local militias which had nothing at all really Roman about them, not even their traditions, we can see that under him the Roman army took a long step forward on the road to its ultimate barbarization. Under Hadrian only the Praetorian Guard, which he made a really élite and not just a pampered corps, remained mostly Italian. Once it ceased to be such, as it did before the end of the second century, the complete barbarization of the army was only a matter of time.

Hadrian's army did efficiently guard the frontiers. Nevertheless it was debatable how long this state of affairs would last, once the memory of Trajan's military prowess had become dim

[1] The duties they previously performed were taken over by the so-called *numeri*.

and Hadrian had been succeeded by another Emperor less
energetic, less peripatetic and less able to galvanize a long idle
army into the necessary state of military efficiency. In fact
at the end of his reign the Caucasian tribes attacked Cappadocia,
and the reign of his successor witnessed some serious frontier
troubles.

§ 4. HADRIAN'S TRAVELS

Hadrian's prolonged journeys throughout the provinces were
thus caused in the first place by his desire to keep the army in
a state of skilled readiness. That, however, was not his only
motive. His capacious and versatile mind was interested in
much else besides military matters—in law, order, good government, morals, sport, science, art, literature and the beauties of
nature.[1] His innate curiosity contributed powerfully to his
decision to travel throughout the Empire. His behaviour on his
travels was indeed often that of the ordinary tourist : he gaped
at the tombs of historical figures such as Ajax, Epaminondas,
Alcibiades and Pompey ; he climbed mountain-tops to enjoy
the view at sunrise, and in Egypt he visited all the sights and
monuments.

The itineraries, and even the chronology, of his journeys are
by no means certain. His first prolonged absence from Rome
began late in 120 or early in 121. He travelled to Gaul (Lugdunensis), Upper Germany, Raetia, Noricum, Lower Germany,
Britain and back to Gaul (Narbonensis). Thence he proceeded
to Spain (122–123) and may himself have terminated the war
in Mauretania, the prosecution of which had been interrupted
by Turbo's appointment as Praetorian Prefect. From 123 to
125 he was in the Greek-speaking east : Syria, Cappadocia,
Bithynia, Mysia, the Aegean Islands, Thrace, the Tauric
Bosporus, Pannonia, Macedonia and Greece. Athens was his
headquarters for six months (September 124 to April 125).
He left many memorials of his presence both there and in other
Greek cities, although it is by no means certain from Pausanias'
narrative whether they date from this or subsequent visits.
He arrived back in Rome by way of Sicily late in 125 or early
in 126. Even now, however, his journeys were not over. In
127 he toured Italy and in the next year Africa. It was likewise
in the year 128 that he began another trip through the provinces.
This time he visited Greece, Asia Minor, Syria and Judaea In

[1] Omnium curiositatum explorator.—Tertullian, *Apologia*, 5.

130-1 he was in Egypt. Then he came to Syria again and to
Pontus by an overland route. From there he apparently
returned to Greece in the autumn of 131. But news of the
Jewish revolt took him back to the east, and Rome did not see
him again until late in 132 or early in 133. Thereafter he seems
to have lived chiefly in the capital, where he relieved himself of
the tedium of administrative routine by indulging his passion
for literature and the arts of music, architecture, sculpture and
painting.[1]

§ 5. FIXED FRONTIER DEFENCES

Hadrian's supervision of the military needs of the Empire
has bequeathed a spectacular memorial in the Roman Wall in
Britain. The literary sources tell us little about events in
Britain during the thirty years following Agricola's recall. Yet
incidents must have occurred, since there could hardly have
been peace on the northern frontiers of the province. The
Roman garrisons were too thinly dispersed over a long vulnerable
line stretching from the Tyne to the vicinity of Perth. A
gradual retreat from these advanced positions towards the
present Scottish border was inevitable, and even this new
position was none too secure, for a serious uprising at about the
time of Hadrian's accession wiped out Legion IX Hispana.
Hadrian therefore decided to establish a firm frontier along the
general line of Agricola's Stanegate between the Solway and the
Tyne. Elaborate frontier fortifications were erected, although
their plan was changed more than once before the system was
completed. Perhaps they result from Hadrian's visit to Britain.
They consist of a V-shaped ditch and, immediately south of
it, a monumental structure, Hadrian's Wall. Just south of the
Wall lies the so-called Vallum.[2] The ditch, north of the Wall,
was some twenty-seven feet wide and ten deep. The Wall
itself, built c. 122-128 with a core of lime concrete and a facing
of dressed stone, was seventy-three miles long [3] and about
fifteen feet high on the average. Along it there was a fortlet
with a sally-port at every mile and a signal turret at every five
hundred and forty yards. In addition forts, ultimately sixteen

[1] The ancient authors also say that he spent his time, especially
towards the end of life, in foul immoralities : such scandals can be
ignored.
[2] " Vallum " is a misnomer.   [3] That is, eighty Roman miles.

in number, were built onto the Wall. The Wall was originally intended to be ten feet thick[1] throughout and with its crenellated parapet on the north side and its rampart walk it was clearly a formidable barrier. Legionaries built it, but some fifteen thousand auxiliaries from various parts of the Empire manned it.[2] The Vallum, a flat-bottomed ditch with a mound on either side of it, was built after the Wall, its purpose being to keep civilians away from the military defence zone manned by the soldiers.

Hadrian's wall, which should be sharply distinguished from the wall erected between the Forth and the Clyde under his successor, is the best preserved of all Roman frontier fortifications. Its garrison could issue through its sally-ports to deal with marauders from the north. Moreover it has been aptly described as an " elevated sentry walk " designed to prevent raids, and to assist in holding down the natives to the south by cutting communications between the tribes on either side. It performed a police as well as a military function, and despite the periodic attacks upon it,[3] it enabled Rome to maintain her authority firmly this far north for almost three hundred years.

There is no certain evidence that Hadrian built fixed defences of this sort in the Danubian provinces. Traces of fortifications can still be seen in Dacia, but they may not be due to Hadrian or even to any other Roman. Nor can the earthworks in the Dobrudja be attributed to him.

In Germany and Raetia, however, he did erect fortifications where there were no natural barriers such as rivers. These were palisade fortifications, their main purpose being to mark the civil frontier, to facilitate administration, to hinder smugglers and to provide a boundary line between Roman and barbarian. The most famous of them is a two-hundred-mile section of the so-called German *limes* between the Rhine and the Danube, which ran roughly parallel with the Rhine from the River Vinxt to the crest of the Taunus ridge, where it turned north-east for about fifty miles, then south to the Main. This river formed

[1] Owing to modifications in plan it only reaches such a thickness at its foundation and not always there.

[2] Under Hadrian the legions remained in camps farther south: II Augusta at Caerleon, XX Valeria Victrix at Chester, and VI Victrix Pia Fidelis, which had been brought from Vetera in Lower Germany to replace the lost IX Hispana, at York. XIV Gemina, which had left Britain in order to help suppress Civilis in 70, did not return to the island.

[3] For example, in the reign of Septimius Severus.

the boundary as far as Miltenberg, where the palisade began again and went as far as Lorch. " This continuous palisade consisted of split oak-trunks nine feet high embedded in a ditch four and a half feet deep and fastened together on the inside by cross planking." [1] Apparently neither the continuous earthen bank and ditch nor the strong forts of the German *limes* system are to be attributed to Hadrian.

His hundred-mile-long Raetian frontier palisade was a continuation of the German. It ran from Lorch eastwards through Württemberg and Bavaria to Eining (near Regensburg) on the Danube.

§ 6.   HADRIAN'S INTEREST IN THE PROVINCES

The Emperor's journeys were dictated by an interest in the welfare as well as in the protection of his subjects. No doubt his visits to the various parts of the Empire put the provincials to considerable expense, despite his insistence on an absence of pomp and ceremonial : he himself, so far as possible, travelled bareheaded and on foot. But as his successor was to remark, a Princeps cannot travel without his retinue being burdensome to the provincials. In addition, the many honorific temples,[2] statues, festivals and inscriptions must have cost large sums.

The provincials, however, got much in return, for useful public works were undertaken everywhere.[3] Corinth and Athens both obtained aqueducts, Ephesus and probably Trapezus new harbour installations. New roads and bridges were built in many areas, for example in Spain and the Danubian provinces. Hadrian almost doubled the size of his favourite Athens, by adding to it a quarter appropriately named Hadriano-polis : a still surviving arch separated it from the old city. Nevertheless, Hadrian's lavish temples, buildings, baths and games failed to rescue the cities of Greece from their slow decline : this is expressly recorded of Megara but is true of them all.

In civil matters in the provinces, as in military, no detail was too small to escape his attention. He was just as eager to

---

[1] B. W. Henderson, *Life and Principate of the Emperor Hadrian* (1923), p. 147.

[2] The temple he built at Cyzicus was reckoned one of the " Wonders of the World."   Ultimately the cost for this must have come from the provincials.

[3] " You may see memorials of his journeys in most of the cities of Asia and Europe."—Fronto, *Principia Historiae*, 10.

adjust the domestic troubles of a university in Egypt as to relieve a food shortage in the cities of Asia Minor. He took his duties as codifier of the Draconian, Solonian and other laws at Athens just as seriously as his interviews with the various client kings on the frontiers. He interested himself in the local finances of Ephesus and in the rebuilding of areas devastated by earthquake.

Like practically all the other great statesmen of antiquity, Hadrian was an assiduous founder of cities. During his reign many were established in the Danubian provinces. We might also mention Forum Hadriani in Lower Germany ; Colonia Julia Hadriana Avenio (*Avignon*) in Gaul ; Stratonicea, Hadrianotherae, Hadriani, and more than one Hadrianopolis in Asia Minor ; and above all the famous city in Thrace which is still called Adrianople. Indeed it was under Hadrian that the urbanization of the Empire reached its climax. He was the first emperor to give municipal rights to the civil settlements that had grown up around the great frontier camps ; previous emperors had refused to give such settlements charters of incorporation as *municipia*.

Nevertheless, despite or possibly because of his excessive care for the provincial towns, signs of municipal decay in the provinces manifested themselves in his reign. Like Trajan he found himself obliged to send his own controllers, one of whom was the famed philanthropist Herodes Atticus, to administer financially embarrassed cities. Like Trajan, too, he had to take the province of Bithynia out of the hands of the Senate.[1] Even more significant was his policy in the matter of the Roman citizenship. The full citizenship he never conferred very readily, but he was generous with the grant of Latin status, a new species of which, the Greater Latinity (*Maius Latium*), he seems to have devised. In towns which enjoyed only the ordinary Latin status the local magistrates automatically acquired the Roman citizenship as of yore ; whereas in towns which enjoyed Greater Latinity all the members of the local senate (*decuriones*) obtained it. The object was to make the office of decurion more attractive : Pliny's correspondence with Trajan shows that men were beginning to shun it because of its financial liabilities.[2]

The provincials, grateful for his unceasing labours on their behalf, honoured Hadrian with high-sounding and in some cases extravagant titles. Some of these merely reflect the

[1] The Senate obtained Pamphylia by way of compensation.

[2] Adlection into the Senatorial Order deprived the cities of many wealthy men.

flattery of local officials ; but many of them are quite sincere.
Thus he is called Restorer (e.g. Restitutor Galliae), Benefactor,
Liberator, Panhellenios, Redeemer of the Universe. The east,
as might have been expected, went further than the west and
did not hesitate to style him a god : it even called him Helios,
Zeus, Divine Saviour of the World.

Owing to the political implications of Caesar-worship, every
Roman Emperor had to manifest a certain degree of interest in
religious cults, observances and ritual ; and Hadrian did so,
one ancient source even going so far as to suggest that he played
the rôle of Numa to Trajan's Romulus. He could scarcely discourage worship of himself as divine, although the address which
he wrote to his soul on his death-bed indicates that he was
well aware that he was no god. But his interest in religious
practices was not dictated exclusively by political motives.
Sometimes his motives seem to have been sentimental, as for
example at Athens, where he presided at the Greater Dionysia,
built temples to the Olympian and the Panhellenic Zeus, and
established a Panhellenic Synod and Panhellenic Games. In
other instances his motives seem to have been largely superstitious : [1] he was not only initiated into the mysteries of the
Cabiri at Samothrace and those of Orpheus at Eleusis, but he
even instituted some mysteries of his own at Ephesus and
Smyrna, not to mention the mysteries and oracle in honour of
his Asiatic, Greek-speaking catamite Antinous, whose death in
Egypt in 130 was also celebrated by the foundation of a new
city, Antinoopolis, peopled by Greco-Egyptian veterans.[2] But
nowhere does he seem to have been interested in religion for
spiritual reasons : he simply was not interested in moral or
metaphysical speculation. He was quite nonchalant about
philosophy—his meeting with Epictetus did not evoke his
enthusiasm—and he was equally indifferent about religion.
Certain types of ritual might pique his curiosity, but passionate
religious devotion he could not understand. It is therefore
not surprising that his handling of the Jews—most passionate
of all religionists—was tactless and led to serious trouble.

[1] Cf. his well-known craze for forecasting the future by means of
astrology or numerical calculations.
[2] Hadrian's passion for Antinous is all the stranger in view of his
notorious dislike for freedmen. Traces of the Antinous-cult survived
in Greece for two hundred years.

§ 7. THE JEWISH REVOLT

Hadrian may have shared the usual Gentile prejudice against Judaism to begin with ; if he did, it was exacerbated by the riots which the Jews of the Dispersion had started at the end of Trajan's reign and which those of Judaea, although they remained quiet, would be suspected of instigating. When Hadrian visited Judaea in 130, Jerusalem was still in ruins ; he therefore proposed to rebuild it as a *colonia* called Aelia Capitolina. But conscious of the sentimental appeal which the city could make as the traditional centre of Jewry, he decided to end its Jewish character once and for all : Jews were forbidden to set foot there except on one day a year.[1] It was to be peopled with Greeks or hellenized people, and on the very site of the holy Temple itself the worship of Jupiter and the Emperor was instituted. For the Jews this was a studied insult, and in 132 they rose in revolt. Led by a so-called Prince of Israel, Simon, and an erudite Rabbi, Akiba, they established themselves at the stronghold of Bether and from there conducted guerrilla operations against which Tineius Rufus, the governor of Judaea, and C. Publicius Marcellus, the governor of Syria, made little headway. Hadrian therefore summoned Faustinus Julius Severus from Britain to direct operations and himself crossed over to Antioch to be in close touch with the situation. Severus finally succeeded in stamping out the rebellion in 135.[2] The new Jewless Jerusalem was built and later became a pillar of the Christian Church. Many Jews were sold into slavery abroad, and Judaea was changed into the new consular province of Syria Palaestina with two legions.

Even before 135 the Jews of the Dispersion had outnumbered those in Judaea several times over : some estimates reckon the population of the eastern provinces as twenty per cent Jewish. After 135 the antipathy between these Jews and their Gentile neighbours became ever more marked, especially as Christianity began to spread widely. The anti-Christian reaction of the Jews was to repudiate Greek and employ Aramaic : Hellenistic Jewry gradually disappeared. The anti-Semitism of

---

[1] For Hadrian's general edict forbidding circumcision, see E. M. Smallwood in *Latomus*, XVIII (1959), p. 334 and XIX (1961), p. 93.

[2] The rebellion lasted three and a half years and cost the lives of over half a million people. At least six legions participated : III Cyrenaica, III Gallica, VI Ferrata, X Fretensis, X Gemina, XVI Flavia Firma.

the Gentiles expressed itself in heavy taxation and ultimately, after the christianization of the Empire, in the exclusion of Jews from careers which had been open to them in pagan times, the army for instance.

Christianity, the offshoot of Judaism, did not fare badly under Hadrian. The Christians in Judaea refused to join the rebellion and they certainly were not excluded from Jerusalem. The story of numerous Christian martyrs under Hadrian is late and unreliable; actually he instructed an eastern governor, C. Minicius Fundanus, to punish proved Christians for their membership in an illegal association, but to disregard anonymous accusations and abstain from heresy hunts. In fact Hadrian, little interested as he was in spiritual matters, could hardly have troubled himself with Christianity, and as a result the Church under him enjoyed peace.

§ 8. DOMESTIC POLICY

Hadrian's inept handling of the Jewish situation was exceptional. Usually his personal attention and care were productive of well-being and contentment throughout the provinces.

That is not to suggest that Rome and Italy were overlooked. There too his eagle eye was everywhere, although Trajan's labours for the prosperity and welfare of Italy did not leave a great deal for him to do. Tangible memorials of his interest in the capital still exist. On the Velia he dedicated a temple of his own design to Venus and Rome, probably on April 21, 135 : for political reasons he enthusiastically promoted the worship of Venus, the ancestress of the Romans. In the Campus Martius he set up the famous " Temple of Neptune " or Hadrianeum, with its sculptured representations of the provinces,[1] and the rebuilt Pantheon. On the right bank of the Tiber he commenced a large mausoleum for himself and his heirs ; it was approached by a handsome bridge and is still one of the most outstanding monuments of Rome (Castel Sant' Angelo). He is also said to have erected a colossal temple in honour of Trajan and Plotina when the latter died in 122. Outside the city proper he virtually rebuilt the town of Ostia, and at Tibur he erected a large villa on the banks of the Anio.

Of greater moment for the well-being of the people as a whole, however, was his supervision of the public finances.

[1] Intended, perhaps, to suggest that the distinction between the provinces and Italy was now disappearing.

Trajan had bequeathed an awkward problem of financial rehabilitation, but Hadrian did not shirk it. On the contrary, he paraded his interest in public finances, possibly with the intention of convincing the public that his unpopular frontier policy was enjoined upon him by financial need. Certainly his peace policy must have helped him to preserve financial equilibrium. But he was not concerned to hoard a large surplus : he was shrewd without being stingy. The splendid spectacles he provided, the numerous buildings he erected, both in Italy and the provinces, and his gesture in 118 in making a public bonfire in the Forum of the records of some nine hundred million sesterces' worth of irrecoverable bad debts owed to the fiscus, all prove that he was not niggardly. Nor did he resort, like Gaius or Nero, to confiscation ; he relied rather on care, efficiency and the elimination of unnecessary expenditures. Thus he drastically reduced the money gift which Italy and the provinces made to a new Emperor (*aurum coronarium*), and ordered that there should be a minute examination of public finances every fifteen years to prevent the accumulation of a fresh set of bad debts. The wasteful system of tax-farming, the abolition of which had begun under Augustus and been furthered by the Flavians, almost completely disappeared under Hadrian. The inheritance tax was henceforth collected by twenty *procuratores hereditatum* instead of tax-farmers. He appointed special *advocati fisci* to safeguard the interests of the treasury in law-suits and a procurator to supervise the Crown Lands (*saltus*).[1] These imperial estates thereby obtained efficient management. The peasants (*coloni*) who worked them paid contributions in kind or in forced labour to middlemen (*conductores*), who in turn rented them from Hadrian's new procurator; but Hadrian himself kept a vigilant eye on the middlemen, and by allowing the peasants to appeal directly to himself he prevented them from being severely exploited. Indeed, where the Crown Lands had been allowed to become derelict, Hadrian gave the peasants " squatters' rights " at a very low rental and occasionally at no rental at all.

His financial measures seem to have saved the State from threatened bankruptcy. At any rate his coins show no deterioration of quality.

---

[1] These *saltus* were mostly situated in Africa.—Specimen texts, and commentary, by R. M. Haywood, in Frank, *Economic Survey of Rome*, IV, p. 89 f.

§ 9.   CODIFICATION OF THE LAW

In the field of law as well as of finance he sought to introduce a semblance of order.   In fact, his work on Roman Law is one of the chief glories of his reign.

Roman law proper was statute law, and we have noted that under the Principate the sources of new law were the Emperor (see above, p. 32) and the Senate (by its *senatus consulta*, which, however, required the Emperor's prior approval).   But some confusion existed owing to the survival of the republican practice of permitting urban magistrates to publish an *edictum perpetuum*, that is, a statement of the general programme of legal procedure and interpretation which the magistrate proposed to follow during his tenure of office.   No doubt most of the clauses in such an *edictum perpetuum* were tralatician : in other words, the magistrate took over his predecessor's *edictum*. Nevertheless cases would inevitably occur in which, to suit the particular circumstances, he would have to interpret the existing laws in such a way as to add to or modify them : the magistrate in other words, like an English judge, could virtually make laws (although, unlike an English judge, he was not necessarily bound by the precedent set by a predecessor). Such a system tended to make for some uncertainty and a lack of continuity, and in any event was scarcely likely to recommend itself to an autocratic Emperor.   Therefore Hadrian decided to end this state of affairs by codifying, not the body of statute law, but the accretions to it in the form of the *edictum perpetuum* ; and he planned to give his new code a universal and permanent binding force.   The magistrates henceforth would be obliged to accept it and administer it as it stood without either altering it or adding to it.   Additions to it would, of course, be periodically needed.   But when such cases arose they would be settled by the Emperor's decision, not by some magistrate's interpretation.   In other words, there would be one less way by which the making of new law could escape the Emperor's control.   It is noteworthy that Hadrian actually used his authority as the source of new law to promulgate edicts of a humanitarian character.

For the actual work of codification Hadrian appointed a famous African jurist, Salvius Julianus, grandfather of the future Emperor, Didius Julianus.   He completed his task by 129, and the publication of the code had a great influence on the development of Roman law by giving an impetus to legal studies, which within less than one hundred years produced two of the most illustrious names in Roman jurisprudence, Papinian and Ulpian.

Hadrian was interested in the administration as well as the codification of the law. Indeed it may have been his efforts to administer the law efficiently that convinced him of the need for its codification. Thus he appointed four circuit judges of consular rank (*quattuorviri consulares*), each of whom toured a given district of Italy. This innovation relieved litigants of the expense of bringing appeals to Rome and the courts of the Emperor and City Prefect of much congestion. But, by seeming to reduce Italy to quasi-provincial status, they were unpopular, especially with the Senate ; and this soon led to their suppression.[1] But their revival with some modifications two reigns later proves that they were needed.

To improve the standard of justice in the Emperor's own court Hadrian regularized his own group of assessors. All emperors regularly sought advice from official " friends " in legal as well as administrative matters, so that this was no radical innovation. The group which he used as his judicial *consilium* included the most famous jurists of the day, such as Juventius Celsus, Salvius Julianus and Neratius Priscus. Their task was to advise the Emperor on points of law, and amongst them there were to be found knights as well as numerous senators.[2]

§ 10. THE EQUITES AND THE CIVIL SERVICE

This, however, was only one of the tasks which Hadrian had for members of the Equestrian Order. He was not content to seek efficiency merely in the financial and legal spheres ; he wanted it in the Civil Service as a whole.

Augustus, Claudius and the Flavians between them had done much to create a fairly good administrative machine. But the Imperial Civil Service was never likely to be a really efficient instrument unless it lost its rather anomalous character. It had originated from the household of the Princeps, and even though many of its officers by now were obtained from other sources,

---

[1] See below, p. 316.

[2] But the *consilium* containing knights could not sit in judgment on senators. Herein Hadrian reversed Domitian's procedure, who had also included knights in his (unofficial) *consilium*.

imperial freedmen still held many of its posts. A body of such mixed composition was bound to have its shortcomings. To Hadrian belongs the credit for regularizing it. After him the members of the Imperial Civil Service, though under the Emperor's absolute control, were public servants and not the mere personal agents of the Emperor. The first Princeps had already pointed the way by making extensive use of the knights. Hadrian followed this lead, and made the Equestrian Order the body which was henceforth to supply the Civil Service. The secretaryships and other administrative positions which in the past had all too frequently been held by freedmen were henceforth given to knights,[1] and naturally those which already hitherto had been filled by knights continued to be so held. In addition, knights were appointed to the new posts which came into being owing to Hadrian's efforts to obtain efficient administrative control in all branches of State activity. We must beware, however, of exaggerating bureaucratic developments under Hadrian; his equestrian functionaries numbered no more than 107 according to a recent estimate.

Hadrian thus created a purely civil career for the knights, and he carried this policy to a logical conclusion by no longer requiring of every eques the military services which up until now all members of the Order had been obliged to perform. This incidentally ultimately had an interesting effect on the office of Praetorian Prefect, for he became a legal officer and presided over the Emperor's judicial *consilium*.

This momentous change in the Civil Service, for it was hardly anything less, may have been dictated in part by Hadrian's well-known dislike for the freedman class. But it could also have been due to his desire to make the Civil Service, theoretically at any rate, an instrument of the State and not just a collection of the Emperor's personal agents. Its undoubted effect was to increase the efficiency of public administration and the importance of the Equestrian Order. The equestrian titles *vir egregius* and *vir perfectissimus*, for procurators and prefects respectively, were devised perhaps now, although they only came into official use later, when likewise the highest knight of all, the Praetorian Prefect, was called *vir eminentissimus* : a similar senatorial title, *vir clarissimus*, had been in common use even before A.D. 100.

[1] The freedmen do not disappear entirely : they are found in minor clerical positions after Hadrian. For that matter some of the knights Hadrian used were of freedman origin.

§ 11. HADRIAN AND THE SENATE

The Equestrian Order did not obtain its enhanced importance at the expense of the Senatorial ; the additional functions it assumed had not hitherto been performed by senators. Nevertheless it is only too likely that the Senate resented and was jealous of the increase in equestrian prestige. An aristocracy is bound to lose some of its authority when another aristocracy attains to a position in the State similar to its own. Moreover the new arrangement advertised the monarchical element in the Principate more openly ; for although the Civil Service now became nominally a State organism, the Equestrian Order was in effect brought under the exclusive control of the Princeps.

Consequently the Senate as a whole never really liked Hadrian, even though he did treat it with the greatest courtesy and deference, attending its meetings scrupulously, harshly criticizing earlier Emperors who had detracted from its dignity, and insisting that membership in it was the highest honour a man could obtain. For twenty years he kept his promise not to put a senator to death. He refused to listen to appeals against the judgments of the Senatorial High Court ; and to conciliate the Senatorial Order he avoided the consulship : in all he held it only three times and generally opposed iterated consulships. His attitude to individual senators was genial, and he was on terms of easy friendship with many of them. His relations with the body were such that he could absent himself for prolonged periods from Rome without undue qualms ; for twenty years no conspiracies were formed against him. There was then no open hostility between him and the Senate.[1]

But there was also no genuine affection. The Senate did not fail to note that Trajan had used Hadrian extensively and had been intimately associated with him, yet he had never, unless perhaps on his death-bed, paid him the honour of officially pronouncing him his successor. Indeed such honours as Trajan had bestowed on Hadrian seemed to be at Plotina's instigation : Hadrian himself remarked at the time of her death that he owed the Empire to her. The Senate concluded that Trajan, whose judgment they trusted, had detected serious deficiencies in Hadrian. The Senate also was not particularly pleased by the fact that Hadrian dated his reign, not from the day the Senate recognized him, but from the day the army acclaimed him. And it may have resented the fact that he preferred to

---

[1] Like Trajan, he paraded the ostensible independence of the *aerarium.*

promulgate new laws by issuing *constitutiones principis*, whereas preceding Emperors had usually employed the more indirect and, to the Senate, more flattering method of getting senatorial decrees passed.

On the whole the senators seem to have suspected that Hadrian was being crafty when similar conduct by the equally autocratic Trajan would have seemed merely tactful. His reputation with many senators was most melancholy because of the memory of the four consulars executed in 118. Perhaps they even despised his interest in fine arts and things Greek.[1]

It was at the end of his reign particularly that the relations between him and the Senate became more strained, and he ceased to be the genial, humanist Emperor. This was due, in part at any rate, to an incurable disease which attacked him *c.* 135,[2] and made him very testy and irritable by the pain it caused. The ancient sources even suggest that his physical torments turned him mad and that the Senate suffered in consequence at his hands. At the time of his death a number of senators are said to have been awaiting execution by his orders.

§ 12. THE SEARCH FOR A SUCCESSOR

When illness assailed him Hadrian had to give thought for the succession. He had no children of his own, and even if he had had, he might have preferred to imitate, not Vespasian, but his other predecessors. Adoption had from the outset been the normal method of providing for the succession.

Whether Hadrian planned to adopt his only living male blood relation, his great-nephew, the eighteen-year-old Cn. Pedanius Fuscus Salinator, we cannot say. Fuscus was the grandson of Hadrian's ninety-year-old brother-in-law, L. Julius Ursus Servianus. Forty years earlier Hadrian and Servianus had had a serious quarrel in Upper Germany where Servianus was governor and Hadrian a military tribune in Legion XXII Primigenia. But more recently the two men seem to have been reasonably friendly : at any rate Servianus obtained the

---

[1] Even as a boy Hadrian had been nicknamed " Graeculus," and it may have been in imitation of Greek philosophers that he grew a beard and thereby started the fashion that prevailed at the imperial court throughout the second century.

[2] The symptoms are those of tuberculosis ; towards the end he seems to have been afflicted with dropsy as well.

consulship—his third—in 134. There was apparently a general expectation that Fuscus would be nominated, and in 136 there may have been plotting and intrigue on his behalf. All that can be said for certain is that Hadrian suddenly executed both Fuscus and Servianus. This increased the hatred felt for him by the senators who, remembering the fate of the four consulars, began to fear a reign of terror.

In the summer of 136 Hadrian proceeded to adopt L. Ceionius Commodus Verus, who was henceforth called Aelius Verus. The choice was not popular with the senators, possibly because they felt that Hadrian had passed by men of distinction and ability like A. Platorius Nepos in order to choose one whose chief recommendation seemed to be that he shared the Emperor's taste in literature : there is no evidence that he was a blood relation of Hadrian. Actually Verus might have made a good Emperor. As governor of Pannonia, an office to which Hadrian at once appointed him, he acquitted himself quite well. Hadrian, however, like Augustus, had difficulty in retaining his heirs, for Verus died of tuberculosis on January 1, 138.

Fortunately Hadrian already had his eye on another possibility, and on February 25, 138, he adopted a fifty-one-year-old senator of blameless life, T. Aurelius Fulvus Boionius Arrius Antoninus. Technically Antoninus may have been a near relative of Hadrian : he appears to have been related to Hadrian's " mother," Plotina, the wife of Trajan. Hadrian conferred upon him not only the Imperium Proconsulare and Tribunician Power, but even the *praenomen imperatoris* as well. At the same time, in order to make the succession fully secure for many years, he obliged Antoninus to adopt two sons. The one was Antoninus' nephew, the seventeen-year-old Marcus Annius Verus (or Marcus Aurelius as he came to be known, when he later became Emperor). The other was the seven-year-old Lucius, son of Aelius Verus. The analogy with Augustus' arrangements, when Tiberius was adopted, is obvious and becomes even more striking by reason of the marital relationships which strengthened these ties of adoption : Marcus married Antoninus' daughter Faustina (the Younger), and Lucius ultimately married Annia Lucilla, one of the children of this union.

The choice of Antoninus was wise ; he became one of the best of Emperors. The choice was also popular, for Antoninus was a prominent senator and respected by the Order. Hadrian's selection of Marcus to succeed Antoninus also had much to recommend it : he was a serious youth and his devotion to duty, when he later became Emperor, was remarkable. Similar praise can scarcely be accorded his co-heir Lucius ; and it is curious that Hadrian should have forced upon Antoninus the adoption of this seven-year-old, about whose capacities he obviously could have known but little. No doubt it must be attributed to his affection for Lucius' father, Aelius Verus.

§ 13. THE END OF THE REIGN

Death brought a merciful relief to Hadrian's physical agony. He died " hated by all " at Baiae on July 10, 138, and his ashes were deposited in his new mausoleum. The Senate, despite the urgent pleas of Antoninus and the release of the senators awaiting execution, sought to withhold divine honours from Hadrian. Actually it was only by threatening to refuse to undertake the government on any other condition that Antoninus induced the Senate to change its mind. Even then he was obliged to abolish the unpopular *quattuorviri consulares*. Because Antoninus had thus in true filial fashion obtained the apotheosis of his adoptive father and at the same time saved certain senators from execution he was henceforth officially styled Pius.[1]

Thus passed away one of the most remarkable of the Roman Emperors. In his meticulous attention to constitutional problems, as well as in his enigmatic character, he reminds us of the man whom he publicly proclaimed his model, Augustus. In his care for the Empire as a whole he is reminiscent of Claudius ; in his rigid supervision of the imperial finances he was another Vespasian ; in his interest in literature, fine arts and things Greek generally he resembled Nero ; in keeping a very firm grasp on the helm of the State he was not unlike Trajan. Hadrian thus was a many-sided figure : a statesman and soldier, an administrator and architect, a legalist and littérateur, a traveller and toiler. With equal facility he could solve constitutional problems, supervise military training, play musical instruments, or produce easy if not very remarkable verses. In his own

---

[1] That this was the reason for his receiving the cognomen seems indicated by coins : see P. L. Strack in *Jour. Rom. Stud.*, XXI (1931), p. 145. For other possible explanations of the title see A. Birley, *Marcus Aurelius*, p. 64 f.

person he seems to epitomize that cosmopolitanism which came to be one of the outstanding features of the Empire. The historian Tacitus may choose to limit his mental horizon to Rome and Italy ; the satirist Juvenal may rail at a Rome that has ceased to be Roman : Hadrian is a citizen of the world, equally at home anywhere in the Empire. He saw that all parts of the Empire were inter-dependent, that the welfare of each was necessary to the welfare of all, and that the duty of the Emperor was owed impartially to them all alike. He almost regarded Italy as just a province. He wanted an integrated Empire.

But while there was something most attractive about this, there was also a notable defect. Cosmopolitanism has never really inspired men : it has failed to catch their imagination. So far at least in the world's history, it has not been possible to find a spiritual basis for it ; men are not prepared to pay it a whole-souled devotion. In this it differs from patriotism, which is not just the refuge of a scoundrel but often inspires emotions of the noblest kind and imbues men with a singleness of purpose, which in the past has contributed powerfully to national greatness and human progress. It is herein that cosmopolitanism fails. Hadrian himself exemplifies this. Vast as was the range of his interests, unflagging as was his energy in practically all human activities, he still lacked something. A catholic curiosity about everything does not entirely compensate for the lack of a passionate devotion to one single ideal and cannot in itself provide a man with a scale of values.

Hadrian even exhibited a very opinionated cosmopolitanism and passionately defended it in his cultural pursuits.[1] His villa at Tibur is not the result of adherence to any one architectural principle or theory of beauty ; it is a *mélange* of the sights and monuments he had seen on his travels, all reproduced in miniature : the Lyceum, the Academy, the Stoa Poicile, Canopus, Tempe, etc. Similarly in literature, despite an apparently real interest, his taste and sense of values were quite uncertain. Ennius or Vergil, Cato or Cicero, Caelius Antipater or Sallust, Antimachus or Homer—his preferences seem erratic to us. At the theatre he was quite capable of severely criticizing and simultaneously rewarding an actor, which suggests a curious instability of judgment.

In matters of state such an attitude ultimately was bound to lead to serious results. Hadrian, with his characteristic energy

---

[1] " Semper in omnibus varius."—*Historia Augusta, Hadrian,* **14, 11.**

and versatility, sought to perfect the State machinery everywhere. It would be wrong to say that he was not a man of purpose : he made it his aim to weld the Empire efficiently together within the frontiers upon which he had decided. But efficiency for its own sake is not enough : it must have some ulterior aim, it should serve the spiritual purposes of the State. In the cosmopolitan world of Hadrian it is not easy to discover whether the State really had any high moral purpose at all. Hadrian himself had no spiritual convictions ; he was only remotely interested in such things. The result was that the efficiency he succeeded in introducing into all branches of public life was basically soul-less. It could, and for a while undoubtedly did, contribute to the material well-being of the Empire as a whole : as Gibbon long ago insisted, the succeeding Age of the Antonines from the material point of view was one of the most prosperous in human history.

But departments of state that are coldly efficient become a deadening bureaucracy ; officers like Hadrian's *advocati fisci* were an ominous innovation.

Hadrian's passion for organization meant that he, more than any other of Augustus' successors, introduced changes and reforms into the Principate. They were changes, however, that were to result in the growth of a bureaucratic machine, whose efficient red tape stretched its tentacles into the farthest corners of the Empire, throttled initiative and finally squeezed out its very life's blood.

CHAPTER IV

THE RISE OF CHRISTIANITY

§ 1. THE ROMAN ATTITUDE TOWARDS RELIGION

OF all the institutions which developed in the Roman Empire during the period with which this volume deals, none was to be more permanent or to have a more profound effect upon subsequent history than the Christian Church, whose beginnings coincided almost exactly with those of the Principate.[1] Yet superficially at any rate Christianity did not play a very important rôle in the history of the first century and a half of our era. References to it are sporadic and casual,[2] the most noteworthy being in the reign of Nero when the first recorded persecution of Christians by the Roman government occurred The brutalities perpetrated by Nero have left a widespread misconception of official policy towards Christianity. It is popularly believed that the imperial government with unceasing and uncompromising cruelty ruthlessly persecuted a band of saints and martyrs. This is not the case. Even in the third century A.D., the century of the great persecutions, government action against the Christians was far from being continuous. In our period not only did the central government fail to take steps against the new religion immediately it made its appearance, it also failed to universalize Nero's policy.

In most things the attitude of the Roman government was one of *laissez faire*. It did indeed lay down various regulations which it insisted should be scrupulously observed. Otherwise, however, it interfered as little as possible with the economic activities, the everyday customs and the religious practices of the various nationalities within the Empire. It did not ruthlessly impose the Latin language or the Roman religion. It did indeed foster and from the time of Domitian even demand Caesar-worship ; but this could be described as a political rather than as a religious gesture.

In general, the Roman Empire tried to deal justly by all,

---

[1] Jesus Christ's dates cannot be definitely fixed : He was born between 10 and 4 B.C. ; the crucifixion occurred in either A.D. 29, 30 or 33.

[2] Cassius Dio, in particular, is very reluctant to make any allusion to Christianity.

by citizens and non-citizens alike. The spread of humanitarian ideas is in fact one of the most attractive features of the Principate. The Romans cannot be accused of religious intolerance : on the contrary, throughout their history they showed a tendency to welcome and assimilate foreign gods into the Roman pantheon. This is understandable enough, since for polytheists an extra god or two will make very little difference. Sometimes the newly admitted gods were identified with their Roman counterparts : in the Roman Empire we encounter a multiplicity of local deities, many of them with outlandish names which are completed by the addition of the name of some Roman god such as Jupiter.[1]

Actually Roman tolerance went even further than this. The central government was prepared to tolerate an intolerant and aggressive religion, provided that it remained local and did not constitute a real threat to the Empire as a whole. In Judaea at any rate their general practice was to interfere as little as possible with Jewish customs, and even in the Dispersion the Jews enjoyed certain privileges.

On the other hand, the Roman government always reserved the right to step in and take strong action where any religion seemed to constitute a threat to public order or to public morals. As early as 186 B.C. the Senate had suppressed certain Bacchanalian rituals throughout Italy even though to do so it had been obliged to disregard the treaty rights of Rome's Italian allies.[2] At various times certain foreign cults were excluded from Rome. The cult of Isis, for example, was banned in the first century B.C.; [3] and as we have seen, Domitian expelled foreign religions from the city c. A.D. 90. A religion that was guilty of practices which outraged the Roman moral sense also obtained very short shrift. Thus Druidism with its rite of human sacrifice was relentlessly extirpated.

§ 2. THE BEGINNINGS OF CHRISTIANITY

Christian practices and ritual, of course, were not of the type that the Romans would regard as outrageous. Nor did the Romans at first anticipate that Christianity would constitute a threat to public order. Its founder had, indeed, aroused enough opposition among certain sects in Judaea to lead the

---

[1] Cf. the analogous Christus-Sol : J. Toynbee–J. B. Ward-Perkins, *The Shrine of St. Peter*, pp. 21, 74.

[2] Livy XXXIX, 8–19.   [3] Cass. Dio XL, 47.

Jews to demand and receive the right to execute Him. But the Romans did not regard this as anything out of the ordinary, for Judaea was in a more or less permanent state of turbulence arising out of religious quarrels.

The beginning of the Christian Church is described in the first chapter of *Acts*: "Then returned they unto Jerusalem from the mount called Olivet, which is from Jerusalem a sabbath day's journey. And when they were come in, they went up into an upper room . . . the number of names together were about an hundred and twenty." To the Romans this at first looked like just another Jewish heresy. As such it did not concern them unduly. Knowing none of these things, they regarded the persecution of Christians by Jews in Judaea as regrettable but normal among Jews: the stoning of a Stephen probably made little impression on the cynical Roman, and the attitude of Gallio at Corinth is typical. However, once the religion began to make headway among the Gentiles, the Roman government had to give it closer attention; and the spread of Christianity among the Gentiles, although at first frowned upon by a Judaizing party within the Church itself, was rapid, thanks largely to the missionary zeal of St. Paul. Paul's Epistle to the Romans implies that within a quarter of a century of Christ's crucifixion there was a fairly large Christian community in Rome itself. After the destruction of Jerusalem in A.D. 70 the new religion made even greater headway among the Gentiles, and Jewish Christianity was either absorbed into the Gentile churches or fell away in curious heresies.

§ 3.   THE EARLIEST PERSECUTIONS

The Roman government could now no longer mistake Christianity for a mere Jewish heresy and regard it with a more or less cynical detachment. That, however, is not to say that the government was forthwith obliged to persecute, for it would not feel impelled to step in unless public order or public morals seemed endangered. It might be thought that a religion professing the tenets of Christianity would not endanger either. But unfortunately something that is intrinsically good and valuable in itself may provoke disorder. A golden apple is presumably a precious object; but it can sow dissension even among goddesses. The Christians could be regarded by the authorities as a source of unrest because of their unpopularity

with their pagan neighbours. There can be very little doubt
that for the first 100 years after the crucifixion of Jesus Christians
were generally disliked and even positively hated. For this
there were several reasons. One was economic : the silver-
smiths at Ephesus were not the only suppliers to the pagan
cults, who saw a threat to their profitable livelihood in the
number of conversions to the new creed. Another was prejudice
arising out of ignorance : the Sacrament of the Last Supper
was ignorantly construed as cannibalism. The habit of the
early Christians of addressing one another indiscriminately as
" brother " and " sister " led to the belief that they were guilty
of incest. Their assertion that Christ was " King " fostered
the conviction that they were actively disloyal. But probably
the biggest cause of enmity towards them was their own
attitude. That it tended to be self-righteous we cannot reasonably doubt. The early Christians became a sect apart, who
were convinced of the imminence of the Second Coming. The
Kingdom of Heaven was at hand : St. Paul himself, in his earlier
days at least, obviously expected to witness it. Therefore they
did not hesitate to proclaim the approaching final doom of this
wicked world, a doom from which they, the chosen few, would
be spared. The early Christians literally expected to see the
mighty put down from their seats and the men of low degree
exalted through an act of God. Relying on this conviction,
they consciously or unconsciously assumed an attitude of
arrogance. This was something that their pagan neighbours
would hardly relish. Christian teachings might be a stumbling-
block to the Jews and foolishness to the Greeks : to the pagans
in general they sounded like downright misanthropy.[1] They
naturally reacted to this by conceiving a lively hatred for the
people whom they suspected of hating them. And this hatred
was exacerbated by the false deduction that the Christians
must be antagonistic to the existing social order since they
seemed to advocate celibacy and seemed to split up families by
converting certain of their members. In his famous account of
the Neronian persecution Tacitus makes the revealing remark
that the Christians were punished " because of hatred of the
human race." It is not quite clear whether Tacitus means
the hatred of the Christians *for* the human race or the hatred

[1] Consider the effect on pagan ears of such an assertion of Jesus' as
Luke 12, 49, which Moffatt translates : " I have come to throw fire on
earth ; would it were kindled already."

of the Christians *by* the human race : in effect he means both.

The general ill-will of the surrounding pagans must have led to many an isolated and purely unofficial incident of persecution. The Roman government itself, of course, must have known that popular suspicions of Christian depravity were false. Provincial governors like Pilate, Gallio, Festus and Pliny had investigated the new religion with some care and found no vice in its adherents. The Emperor Trajan thought them such harmless fanatics that, in effect, he ordered Pliny, his governor in Bithynia, to connive at their activities. Hadrian's instructions to Minicius Fundanus, the governor of Asia, were not very dissimilar. Nevertheless, as Tertullian later pointed out, whenever natural disasters occurred such as fire, flood or famine, the pagan public would lay the blame on the Christians ; and, to avoid communal rioting, the central government would respond to the popular feeling and take action against the Christians. In our period persecutions were local and probably not numerous. Yet they did occur : under Trajan, for instance, both Ignatius, the bishop of Antioch, and Symeon, the bishop of Jerusalem, and under Hadrian Telesporus, the bishop of Rome, were martyred.

If the officials decided to humour the popular whim and persecute the Christians, it was easy enough for them to find a pretext. The Christians were technically guilty of forming an association, something which the Principate, sensitive to the political possibilities of clubs and organizations, had frowned upon from its earliest days. We even find Trajan, a practical man and an Emperor reasonably secure of his position, viewing the formation of a fire brigade at Nicomedia with uneasy qualms. Another charge that could be levelled against the Christians, from the time of Domitian on at any rate, was their refusal to participate in the official Caesar-worship. Faithful to their Lord's injunction to render unto Caesar the things that were Caesar's, they were usually willing, and indeed eager, to pray *for* Caesar. But that was not making the political gesture of praying *to* him. There were, then, these two charges that could be brought against Christians, and then they would suffer for His name's sake. There was apparently no universal and comprehensive edict against Christianity in our period, although it certainly seems to have been a *religio illicita* early in the second century.[1]

---

[1] Sherwin-White, *Letters of Pliny*, pp. 778 f.

§ 4. THE SPREAD OF CHRISTIANITY

It is perhaps not irrelevant to enquire how the new religion spread so widely and so rapidly in the face of the initial hostility of a large proportion of the population. A decrease in the intransigence of the Christians themselves was no doubt primarily responsible. In the case of any new gospel later converts seldom display the same violent intolerance as the earliest adherents. This was especially true of the Christians. As prospects for the Second Coming became more and more indefinitely postponed—" until the times of the Gentiles be fulfilled "—they themselves became distinctly more mellow. In the second century their spokesmen, instead of assailing pagan wickedness with fierce invective, had recourse to reasoned apologetic.[1] At the same time, as the Christians and their practices became better known, their way of life and general behaviour won men's respect. Their conduct and bearing impressed men. Instead of being regarded as anthropophagous and incestuous traitors they slowly and gradually came to be known as people who tried to pass all the days of their life in holiness and righteousness, and who tried to guide their feet into the way of peace. Their determination to love their neighbours as themselves little by little led to the disappearance of the story about hatred of the human race. Men began to be disposed in favour of these people whose word was their bond.

Simultaneously another influence was at work. We have already seen that the Roman Empire did not arouse the fiery enthusiasm of its subjects. The average inhabitant of the Empire could pursue his daily life in reasonable security, and he was content to accept the material comforts that the Empire bestowed. But this did not satisfy his spiritual needs. Nor could he make the omission good in the closed field of politics. Only to the favoured few was there an outlet in the big administrative posts. The unprivileged many were forced to find an outlet in the empty formalism of Caesar-worship, in the brutalizing spectacles of the arena, or in the sterile study of philosophy. Philosophical theories, although they appeal strongly to a more or less select group of esoterics, will never catch the imagination of the masses, who need the fervour of a religion. The spread

---

[1] Cf. the Apologies of Aristides and Justin Martyr addressed respectively to Hadrian and Antoninus Pius.

of the mystery religions in the Roman Empire is very significant. Their very multiplicity, however, paradoxically conditioned men's minds to monotheistic ideas, for the average worshipper, at a loss amid the conflicting claims of many religions, solved the problem by simply identifying all the many gods, and such syncretism is a long step forward on the road to monotheism. Even the philosophers with their belief in a single Universal Reason animating the world were moving in the same direction. The various mystery religions, however, tended to degenerate into mere ritual, which could not satisfy men spiritually. Men therefore began to turn to Christianity. In the spiritual desert of materialism, it was a monotheism with a message, and in it men could find a deep reality. Its devotees, at first, had seemed to be possessed merely of an inflexible obstinacy ; but their stead-fastness in the face of persecution and even death ultimately convinced men that they possessed a source of spiritual comfort and strength. Small wonder is it that Christianity gained additional converts, and not merely from the depressed and servile classes. Had Christianity remained a religion of the downtrodden and the slaves it could scarcely have survived : indeed the poor were so busily occupied in scrambling to obtain their daily bread that they had little leisure to reflect on the merits of praying that it be given them. Christianity gradually made its way into the middle and upper classes. Already in the reign of Domitian the evidence indicates that Christians were to be found in the very highest circles.

By the time that the great universal persecutions got under way in the third century, when the government acted on its own initiative rather than under the spur of popular resentment against the Christians, the religion had obtained too firm a hold to be suppressed. Indeed its empire-wide organization was precisely the chief reason why the government moved against it. But by then it was too late : the Christian Church was too well established to be eradicated.

CHAPTER V

LITERATURE AND ART IN THE
EARLY SECOND CENTURY

§ 1. GREEK WRITERS

THE triumph of Christianity, however, and the great spiritual impulse that produced it, really belong to a later age. In the period of Trajan and Hadrian it is in literature and art that we chiefly seek our information on the intellectual life and atmosphere.

One of the most famous names in all literature belongs to this period, that of Plutarch of Chaeronea (*c.* 46–126). In the wide range and catholicity of his interests Plutarch resembled Hadrian himself, for besides his celebrated *Parallel Lives* of notable Greeks and Romans he wrote on numerous other topics. In all these miscellaneous writings Plutarch is first and foremost a moralist. He owes his success largely to his kindly sincerity, a sincerity that appears all the more genuine since his Greek is not imbued with the prevailing rhetoric : he writes in a gossipy style all his own.

A contemporary Greek writer, Dio of Prusa (45–115), despite his appellation of Golden-Mouth (Chrysostom), is not so appealing. His style is much more rhetorical ; it is a good example of the so-called Second Sophistic. However, his speeches are quite serious and, as might be expected from their author's adventurous life, in close touch with practical realities. Like contemporary Latin writing they are satirical in tone, but will strike most readers as dull.

§ 2. YOUNGER PLINY

Latin literature is not radically different from what was produced under the Flavians. The Younger Pliny (*c.* 62–113), for example, although vain of his literary ability, shows no profundity of thought or vigorous originality. His nine books of *Letters* constitute a pleasant commentary on contemporary life and reveal another side to Roman society than that depicted by the satirists. Evidently the life of a Roman gentleman was comfortably bourgeois rather than intellectually stimulating.

Despite its graceful Latinity, Pliny's style is not altogether unaffected by the rhetorical training to which the well-to-do were exposed in their youth. Although not greatly in evidence in the *Letters*, rhetoric infects the *Panegyricus*, a fulsome and tiresome speech thanking Trajan for appointing Pliny to the consulship. Pliny's correspondence with Trajan is also extant ; but although of the greatest historical value, it is scarcely work of marked liter ary merit.

§ 3. TACITUS

In the reigns of Trajan and Hadrian *libertas*,[1] that is the right to venture one's opinions without risking one's neck, was notoriously reconciled with imperial rule. Nevertheless the most substantial achievements of literature, which ought to be an extension of existence as well as a criticism of life, were still in the negative rather than in the positive field. Men of genius contributed satire rather than more constructive types of literature.

Cornelius Tacitus (*c.* 55-120) was not, indeed, avowedly a satirist, but an historian giving an account of the first century A.D.[2] But his approach was that of the satirist ; he gives the impression of being a profoundly disillusioned man. His work abounds in cynical reflections on his own day and on human nature generally. This may be the result of the narrowness of his senatorial viewpoint : usually he deliberately refuses to extend his vision beyond Rome, and life in Rome was not of the type to inspire noble minds. In Tacitus we seek in vain for any appreciation of the world-wide panorama of the Empire or any realization of its growing cosmopolitanism ; his prejudices are those of a republican Roman noble. But this is not to deny the brilliance of his work. He is one of the very greatest of historians, and his style is equally brilliant. His clipped, epigrammatic sentences with their infinite variety and un-translatable nuances show the full possibilities of the rhetoric so fashionable in that age. It is magnificent writing.

---

[1] On *libertas*, see Wirszubski's book cited in the Bibliography.
[2] The *Annales* covered the period from 14 to 68 ; the *Histories* the period from 68 to 96. The *Agricola* and *Germania* are accounts of Britain and the Rhine frontier respectively in the same period.

§ 4. JUVENAL

A contemporary of Tacitus and sharer of many of his prejudices was the avowed satirist D. Junius Juvenalis (55–138), who like Tacitus came from one of the earliest parts of Italy to be romanized.[1] In sixteen hexameter poems Juvenal savagely attacked the follies and foibles of the day. His picture of Rome is identical with Martial's and is presented with the same indecency of language. The literature, the behaviour of women, the ubiquity of Levantines, the gross materialism and the rampant depravity of the capital, all form the butt of Juvenal's verse. And these things are stigmatized in the prevailing rhetorical style. Indeed one is uncertain whether the rhetorician or the moralist should be given pride of place. What are we to say of a writer who for the sake of a climactic effect rebukes Nero's histrionism even more bitterly than his matricide? Concerning the power and vigour of his verse, however, there can be no argument.

§ 5. SUETONIUS ; FLORUS

Juvenal was the last great Latin author. Of his lesser contemporaries, C. Suetonius Tranquillus (c. 75–140) is famous for his *Lives of the Caesars*, which formed part of a larger biographical work. But these enjoy a notoriety disproportionate to their literary merit. Suetonius does indeed write straightforwardly with an almost total lack of rhetoric. But he is read chiefly because he is of great value to the historian as one of our principal surviving sources of information on the first century: Suetonius obviously accomplished genuine research. The *Lives* are vitiated, however, by their indifference to chronology and their predilection for scandal. Suetonius is over-fond of salacious gossip ; indeed his penchant for ferreting out unsavoury tales lost him his post as Hadrian's *ab epistulis Latinis*. Apparently he participated in the campaign of whispers about Sabina, Hadrian's wife.

Annaeus Florus (*fl.* 130) is of much less importance. He was a rhetorician who compiled an epitome of Livy's history and wrote some graceful but slight poems.[2] A civilization that

---

[1] Juvenal apparently came from the Volscian country, Tacitus from the Sabine (or possibly the Cisalpine).

[2] Florus the rhetor, Florus the epitomator, and Florus the poet are probably identical. But, in the view of the present writer, Florus was not the author of the *Pervigilium Veneris*, one of the loveliest poems in Latin.

resorts to résumés and abstracts of earlier works instead of producing original works of its own is definitely beginning to age. Florus' literary activities were a sure sign of the times.

Hadrian, both by example and encouragement, sought to foster literature, but it was in vain. The stream of classical literature had not exactly dried up, but it had become stagnant. Hadrian himself, instead of looking forward, fixed his eyes upon the past. In his aesthetic tastes he was the most archaizing of all the emperors.

§ 6. ART BEFORE THE REIGN OF HADRIAN

The art of the age, no less than the literature, portended a period of intellectual sterility. Some no doubt will argue that Roman art in any event scarcely merits serious consideration, and it is of course true that it was heavily indebted to the Greeks. Nevertheless, it did contribute original features of its own. Italian taste is secularly for the baroque ; the Greek aim was rather to produce ideal types. The adjective " classical " strictly belongs only to Greek art.

The practical nature of the Romans was reflected in their art. Instead of attempting to portray ideal beauty or abstract ideas, it tended to be realistic, representing various phases of everyday life. This led Roman artists to include subjects to which Greek artists were usually indifferent, children for instance. It also explains why so much of Roman art is commemorative, and evolved forms, such as the continuous narrative picture, the better to describe outstanding exploits. Roman sculpture, stucco decoration, metal work, cameos and jewels frequently have this pictorial quality : they depict momentary incidents in a story or career rather than the essential character of the thing represented. Hellenic influence nevertheless is present, and the resulting clash between Roman instinct and Greek education is not always harmonious.

The sculpture of the Augustan Age, as revealed in the reliefs of the Ara Pacis and the numerous portraits of Augustus, exhibited the typical Roman realism. But it was not free from a certain stiffness and awkwardness. The Ara Pacis reliefs, for example, give no illusion of depth.

The same was probably true of Augustan painting to judge from the little of it that survives. The frescoes in the so-called House of Livia on the Palatine, like the paintings of the second and third styles at Pompeii, with all their painstaking detail, formal carefulness and sobriety of subject-matter, are essentially two-dimensional.

Under the Julio-Claudians, however, there was a gradual improvement in technical skill. Already in Augustus' day an unknown painter created the illusion of a real garden on a wall of the imperial villa at Prima Porta, while portrait sculptors began to produce excellent pieces. Their representations of the members of the imperial family were no doubt rather stylized and flattering ; as the French critic wittily puts it : " There is art and there is official art." [1] But the less sycophantic portraits of private individuals, women with their varying coiffures as well as men, are very human. And the sculptors were equally good with animals, as the numerous equestrian statues or the wolfs' heads from the ships at Nemi testify.

By the time of Nero and the Flavians the artists had to some extent succeeded in reconciling Greek classicism with Roman realism. Flavian sculpture is Roman in that it represents individuals rather than ideal types ; yet it is not lacking in Greek refinement, and it is most skilfully modelled.

Painting, too, displays technical excellence : foreshortening is a common feature in the frescoes of the fourth style at Pompeii. In fact, by Nero's day artists were sure enough of their technique to be able to give rein to their Italian instinct for the baroque without restraint.

Consequently the art of the second half of the first century contains a suggestion of fantasy. One only has to recall the obliquely held standards floating in a sea of space in the Arch of Titus reliefs, or the swarms of maenads, satyrs and the like that feature many of the Pompeian wall-paintings of this era. Even so simple a device as the acanthus scroll or hanging festoon, which is an original Roman contribution to both sculpture and painting, tends to become fanciful : other things than ox-heads appear between the garlands. The very word " grotesque " derives, significantly enough, from the *grotte* of Nero's Golden House with their somewhat eccentric frescoes.

§ 7.   ART AND ARCHITECTURE UNDER HADRIAN

Reaction against this tendency began under Domitian.[2] The Trajanic paintings on the so-called Bridge of Caligula on

---

[1] The caricature of Claudius as Jupiter is the exception that proves the rule ; it is the sculptural counterpart to Seneca's *Apocolocyntosis*.

[2] Domitianic reliefs recently found in the Cancelleria are classical in style.

the Palatine are marked by reserve and painstaking care for detail. The Trajanic reliefs on the elaborate Arch at Beneventum and on the Arch of Constantine, the figures on Trajan's Column, and the rather more lively scenes on the anaglypha of the Forum indicate a tendency to return to severer, classical standards.

Under Hadrian the reaction became complete: the neo-classical Antinous-type dominated sculpture. So true is this that sculpture in the round for a while replaces the historical reliefs so beloved by the Romans. It is no doubt true that this was not just " sterile classicism." [1] The artists were putting into practice the lessons learned in the preceding century, and they delighted in exhibiting their mastery over difficulties. Sculptors, for instance, did not hesitate to work in hard and intractable materials such as diorite and porphyry.

Architecture tells the same story, and perhaps even more emphatically, since it was something in which the Romans excelled. In architecture their original contributions are notable: one thinks of the Italic temple, whether of the three-cella or circular type; of the high podium with its flight of steps; of the triumphal arch; of the column with spiral reliefs; and above all of the skilful use of the vault.[2] A practical people with a gift for organization might have been expected to produce the wonders of Trajan's Forum with its adjoining shopping-centre.

The material prosperity of the second century provided the wherewithal for extensive building enterprises; and great monuments resulted. It was in Hadrian's reign that the Pantheon, in all the perfection of its present beauty, was built.

Yet new architectural principles were not evolved. It was rather a case of exploiting earlier conceptions to the full. Hadrian's mausoleum is merely an enlarged version of the traditional Italic circular drum with conical tumulus. The device of a mighty hall spanned by a cross-vault enabled engineers to erect public structures of impressive proportions; yet it had been developed in the time of Nero and had been skilfully employed for Domitian's mighty palace on the Palatine and Trajan's vast Baths.

The unquestioned skill with which the second-century artists

---

[1] See above, p. 317.

[2] Nevertheless their debt to Greece, even in architecture, was large : e.g. the pediments and columns of Roman temples are Greek in type.

and architects made use of the principles evolved in an earlier age produced works of variety and complexity ; it is not for nothing that " The Grandeur that was Rome " has become one of our favourite clichés.   Nevertheless the fact remains that no new intellectual contributions were being made, and when all the possibilities of the old ones had been exhausted decadence was bound to ensue.   Already in the second century sculpture, for instance, tended to become stereotyped.   For all of the attention to individual portraiture, the influence of Hadrian can be seen in the bearded busts of the succeeding emperors. Creative art like creative literature was ceasing to be produced.

Incidentally it is of interest to note that the constitutional evolution of the Empire is reflected in its art.   In the reliefs of the Ara Pacis the Emperor is truly a Princeps, merely the first among various Roman nobles and senators.   In later monuments the personality of the Emperor comes to dominate everything.

APPENDIX I

THE OFFICIAL NAMES AND THE DATES OF THE EMPERORS

IN the following list the name by which the Emperor is usually known is printed in capitals.

27 B.C.–A.D. 14	Imperator Caesar AUGUSTUS
14–37	TIBERIUS Julius Caesar Augustus
37–41	GAIUS Caesar Augustus Germanicus
41–54	Tiberius CLAUDIUS Caesar Augustus Germanicus
54–68	Imperator [1] NERO Claudius Caesar Augustus Germanicus
	Servius GALBA Imperator Caesar Augustus
69	Imperator Marcus OTHO Caesar Augustus
69	Aulus VITELLIUS Imperator Germanicus Augustus [2]
69–79	Imperator Caesar VESPASIANus Augustus
79–81	Imperator TITUS Caesar Vespasianus Augustus
81–96	Imperator Caesar DOMITIANus Augustus Germanicus
96–98	Imperator NERVA Caesar Augustus Germanicus
98–117	Imperator Caesar [3] Nerva TRAIANus Optimus Augustus Germanicus Dacicus
117–138	Imperator Caesar Traianus HADRIANus Augustus [4]

[1] Augustus' *praenomen imperatoris* was revived by Nero, who, however, did not use it invariably. His ephemeral successors in 69 did not always place it first in their list of names. From the reign of Vespasian, however, it invariably stands first.

[2] Vitellius refused to assume the name of Caesar. Tacitus (*Hist.*, iii. 58) says that he was willing to take it during the last days of his reign, but there is no evidence that he actually did so.

[3] Hitherto the practice of the Emperors with regard to the position of the name of Caesar varied. From the reign of Trajan it invariably stands second.

[4] The name Augustus usually heads the list of the Emperor's *cognomina.*

APPENDIX II

THE SOURCES

OUR knowledge of the consecutive history of the Early Empire is derived chiefly from the works of Tacitus, Suetonius and Cassius Dio. The value and importance of these authors vary in accordance with their native ability, their historical methods, or the extent to which their works have survived.

Pride of place must be given to TACITUS, who between A.D. 85 and 125 produced works covering the reigns of all the Emperors from Tiberius to Domitian inclusive ; in addition, his *Germania* and *Agricola* are valuable accounts of certain frontier districts. Fierce debate has failed to determine exactly what sources he used. The view that his normal practice was to depend almost exclusively on one main source and only occasionally glance at others does not recommend itself to the present writer. There is no need to disbelieve Tacitus' own statement that he consulted the official archives. Besides these he must have used the works of various historians of the first century A.D. whose names have survived without their works. He actually cites Cluvius Rufus, a senatorial who wrote on the period from Augustus to the death of Nero ; Fabius Rusticus, a friend of Seneca who described the same period ; and the Elder Pliny, an equestrian who wrote an account of the German wars and also continued the annalistic account of the early Principate left by Aufidius Bassus (another non-senatorial, whose work had broken off abruptly, possibly at A.D. 47). Presumably Tacitus also used the historical writings of M. Servilius Nonianus, a senatorial, and the Elder Seneca, an equestrian, neither of whom, however, went beyond the death of Gaius or possibly even of Tiberius ; and it is improbable that he overlooked the memoirs of Emperors, Empresses and generals, or pamphlets by Stoics, nostalgic republicans and the like. Besides the matter of his sources, there is also the question of his outlook and methods. Tacitus himself was a practical man of affairs, a celebrated advocate and the holder in succession of the various offices in the senatorial career. He was personally and intimately acquainted with the imperial system that he was describing, and presumably he served it loyally in the various official positions which he held. That is not to say, however, that he was enamoured of it. He himself criticizes earlier historians whose habit it was to describe an Emperor's reign under the influence of fear while he lived and under the influence of recent hatreds when he was dead, and he tells us that he himself consciously sought to avoid this practice. Nevertheless his picture of the Principate is not altogether free from prejudice. He was convinced that absolute power has a demoralizing effect, and the longer he lived under the Principate, the more he was impressed at the way that autocracy inevitably leads to degeneration. Moreover, although himself probably of provincial birth, he evinces comparatively little interest in the provinces. His prose style varies. The *Dialogus de Oratoribus*, now usually agreed to be by him, is relatively Ciceronian ; his latest, the *Annals*, best exhibits his famed variety and epigrammatic terseness. A similar development can be seen in his view of the Principate. In his earlier works he notes how the all-pervading influence of the Princeps had brought about a decline in oratory ; in his latest he has formed the conclusion that the Principate has demoralized everything. The high and sensitive idealism of his youth has turned into disillusionment ; he remains a moralist, but a cynically pessimistic one. Nor is this all. His view is that these evils could have been avoided under a senatorial régime. His outlook is not only anti-imperial, but positively pro-senatorial. This is not due, as is sometimes rashly asserted, to his dependence on senatorial sources : he consulted equestrian and imperial writers as well as senatorial. It is due partly to his exposure to the customary rhetorical education with its academic evocation of an idealized Republic, and above all to his membership of the Senate, which despite its continuous recruitment from non-senatorial families remained stubbornly conservative. His senatorial outlook is clearly shown by his choice of subject. Rome itself, the seat of the Senate, occupies his canvas very largely to the exclusion of everything else. It is not that he is uninformed about life in the Empire : his *Agricola* and *Germania* prove the opposite. But he is engrossed with the capital since it is there, and not in the provinces, that the degeneration inherent in the Principate is most manifest. Tacitus' painstaking care and anxious avoidance of *ira et studium* prevented him from stating facts that were false : his accuracy on questions of fact is generally conceded. But obviously a man with his outlook must be reckoned a hostile witness against any Emperor. His manner of presenting facts and his interpretation of them convey an impression of the Empire that cannot be accepted uncritically ; one must always be on one's guard against allowing his innuendoes to pass for statements of fact. But despite his shortcomings Tacitus is easily the best authority we have for our period. Unfortunately the extant portions of his work only cover the reign of Tiberius (except the years 29 to 32), the last half of the reign of Claudius (47–54), the reign of Nero (down to 66), and the events of 68–70 : they also include a good deal of scattered information about the Flavians.

SUETONIUS helps to fill the gaps in Tacitus' account, since his *Lives of the Caesars* (Augustus to Domitian inclusive) have survived. Suetonius was a man of very wide interests, who had exceptional facilities for obtaining information : he was for a time Hadrian's archivist (*ab epistulis*). Similar posts (*a studiis, a bibliothecis*), probably under Trajan, had also provided research opportunities. Such a writer inevitably presents much evidence of great value. Furthermore, as he was a member of the Equestrian Order, which was usually loyal to the Principate, he was free from Tacitus' senatorial prejudices, except insofar as he reproduces those of his sources. (Presumably he knew the same sources as Tacitus, although apparently the ones he chose to rely on were different, except for the year 69.) Suetonius' performance unfortunately was not commensurate with his opportunities. He sought above all to entertain. This caused him to include too much that is pruriently scandalous or superstitiously miraculous. Moreover he lacks a strong critical faculty : he actually calls Claudius' conquest of Britain " a campaign of little importance." He is much too prone to indulge in rash generalizations and is guilty of inaccuracies which a more critical writer would have avoided. As a result his *Lives* are very uneven in merit : even those of them which can be reckoned really good are not all equally so. His account of the Flavians, for example, is unduly compressed. His historical methods are sometimes sound, but usually faulty. Generally he is content to give an account of the Emperor's boyhood, then catalogue all of his good deeds and conclude with an account, frequently salacious, of his bad actions. In other words his biographies lack a firm chronological framework.

For the latter we have to turn to CASSIUS DIO, a third-century Greek-speaking senator of provincial origin, who wrote an annalistic history of Rome from 753 B.C. to A.D. 229 in eighty books. Besides repairing Suetonius' chronological deficiencies (not always accurately), Dio also provides us with an account of the period after Domitian's death, beyond which neither Tacitus nor Suetonius had ventured. This is of particular importance for the reigns of Nerva and Trajan ; since the *Historia Augusta*, a collection of imperial biographies, duller than and inferior to those of Suetonius, purporting to be written by six authors possibly in the late fourth century, only begins with Hadrian (for whom indeed the lives of *Hadrian* and *Aelius Verus* are of prime importance). Unfortunately Dio's work has not survived entire. It is reasonably complete down to A.D. 54 ; thereafter we are dependent on epitomes of him compiled by Xiphilinus in the eleventh century and Zonaras in the twelfth (and, for the period from Trajan on, Zonaras is only epitomizing Xiphilinus). Dio was a very serious writer : he studied for ten years and wrote for twelve. Presumably he read the same sources as Tacitus and Suetonius, although almost certainly he did not prefer the same ones. Tacitus and Suetonius themselves must also have been familiar to him since he claims to have perused everything of importance that had been written on Roman history. As Dio was a provincial, he was free from the prejudices of the capital, and to judge from his admiration of the imperial autocrats of his own day he also entertained no anti-imperial bias.   Hence he often proves a useful corrective to Tacitus, in his accounts of Tiberius and Claudius, for example. His ability, however, was by no means equal to his industry.   He is not lacking in the critical faculty, but his judgment is at times unsound.   Like Suetonius he generalizes over-hastily.   Nor is he free from factual inaccuracies.   He sometimes seems to forget that the constitutional practices of his own time might have developed much later than the early days of the Principate.   Nevertheless, as he alone provides us with a continuous narrative of Augustus' reign and, in a fairly bulky epitomized form, of the period from 70 to 138, it is obvious that he is an indispensable source.

Besides these main sources, various other writers supply incidental information amounting in all to a substantial quantity. STRABO, an accurate and disinterested recorder, gives us a valuable geographical description of the Roman world, non-Italian as well as Italian, in Augustus' day. VELLEIUS PATERCULUS hurriedly produced a two-book compendium of Roman history in A.D. 30, the latter portions of which provide us with the "official" view of the reigns of Augustus and Tiberius : it is significant that Velleius, the time-serving careerist, feels it incumbent on him to flatter Tiberius and even Sejanus without stint. PHILO supplies valuable if rhetorical information on the Jewish community in Alexandria during the reigns of Gaius and Claudius.   An even more important source for anything relating to the Jews down to A.D. 70 is JOSEPHUS.   He has, however, to be used with care as his chronology is faulty, and any references to his own exploits and behaviour are suspect. PLUTARCH has bequeathed Lives of Galba and Otho, but they add little to what we learn from other authors. Various scraps of information can also be gleaned from the epitomators (FLORUS in the reign of Hadrian ; EUTROPIUS and AURELIUS VICTOR in the fourth century ; OROSIUS in the fifth) ; from the technical writers (VITRUVIUS, who was personally acquainted with Augustus' building programme ; FRONTINUS, who supervised Rome's water supply in Flavian times ; PAUSANIAS, who had inspected Hadrian's improvements in Athens ; the fourth-century writer VEGETIUS, who gives an interesting if not always accurate account of the imperial army) ; and from the Byzantine scholars (JOHN MALALAS, the sixth-century writer on eastern affairs ; the "SUDA," a tenth-century lexicon). It goes without saying that the various literary figures, who have been discussed in the text (above, pp. 114, 263 f., 326 f.), are also valuable in that they give us some idea of the intellectual, moral and material life and atmosphere of their times.

To supplement the literary sources there are the epigraphic, papyrological, numismatic and archaeological finds. These are obviously of the greatest possible value ; and it is extremely fortunate that, precisely when the literary sources become increasingly jejune (that is, after A.D. 70), this non-literary material becomes more plentiful. But even for the earlier period we are heavily indebted to it ; in quite recent years, for instance, epigraphy has thrown considerable light on the reigns of Augustus and Claudius. It is, of course, obvious that inscriptions and coins by themselves cannot provide a connected account of the history of the period, least of all of the internal history ; and the archaeological monuments, e.g. those at Adamclisi, sometimes cannot be certainly interpreted at all. It is equally obvious that official documents cannot invariably be accepted at their face value : the *Res Gestae* of Augustus, for instance, is chiefly intended to justify the ways of the Princeps to men. Even so, the non-literary material is indispensable. The inscriptions shed accurate light on life in the provinces, on imperial administration, on chronology, on army matters (including troop movements and wars), on prosopography. Coins likewise illuminate the chronology and, in addition, indicate the policies and personal appearance of the various Emperors and the emotional movements throughout the Empire : they even tell us something of states outside the Empire such as Parthia. It is no exaggeration to say that our knowledge of the Principate has been revolutionized by intensive study of these non-literary sources.

APPENDIX III

A NOTE ON THE IMPERIUM CONSULARE

THE view adopted in the text is that the real basis of Augustus' power was the so-called Imperium Proconsulare, which was given to him for periods of ten years, being invariably renewed at the end of each decennium. (On two consecutive occasions, in 18 and 13 B.C., Augustus is described as receiving it for only five years, but the ten years, that were thus made up, were manifestly regarded as constituting a single ten-year period : Dio LIV, 12, 5).

Dio (LIII, 14, 7 ; 15, 4 ; 32, 5) makes it clear that, from the middle of 23 B.C. onwards, Augustus was never without the Imperium Proconsulare, not even inside the *pomerium*, and it was by virtue of it that he administered the imperial provinces ; moreover, still according to Dio, the Senate voted that in every province Augustus' authority should be superior to that of the governor (by which Dio must mean that Augustus could wield his Imperium Proconsulare in the senatorial as well as in the imperial provinces). In other words, from 23 B.C. on, Augustus enjoyed what modern scholars have agreed to call *imperium maius*, a concept of the *imperium* that had developed in the closing years of the Republic (see V. Ehrenberg in *Amer. Journ. Philology*, LXXIV, 1953, pp. 113-36). This should not be taken to mean that the Princeps continuously and actively interfered in the administration of the senatorial provinces. On the contrary, we must assume that normally not Augustus but the proconsuls of those provinces were responsible for everything that took place in them : otherwise surely there would have been virtually no real difference between a senatorial and an imperial province. Augustus' *imperium*, therefore, was normally dormant so far as senatorial provinces were concerned, but he could nevertheless intervene in them if for any reason his duties should demand that he do so ; and in the event that he was obliged thus to intervene, no clash of authority could ensue since his *imperium* was not just equal, but was specifically recognized as superior, to theirs. Thus Augustus would escape the embarrassment to which Pompey had been subject when, under the Gabinian Law, he had been invested with an *imperium* equal to that of any provincial governor for fifty miles inland from the sea (Volume V, p. 154) : such an *imperium* had not positively obliged the governors to co-operate with Pompey, much less to obey him. No senatorial proconsul would be able to be recalcitrant when faced with the superior *imperium* of Augustus ; the latter could legally expect, and even demand, obedience. That Dio is right in saying that Augustus possessed an *imperium maius* from mid-23 B.C. onwards is the conventional view, even though admittedly the expression *imperium proconsulare* does not occur in republican Latin. And, in fact, the epigraphic evidence puts the matter beyond reasonable doubt : inscriptions from Achaea and Cyrene reveal that Augustus' *imperium* was valid in both these senatorial provinces (see W. Vollgraff in *Mnemosyne*, XLVII, 1919, p. 263 f. ; F. de Visscher, *Les édits d'Auguste découverts à Cyrène*, p. 46 f.).

The real problem is the nature of his *imperium* before he resigned the consulship in the middle of 23 B.C. Many scholars argue that in those years he could not have possessed proconsular *imperium* at all, since it would have been anomalous, if not indeed constitutionally absurd, for one who was consul to be also simultaneously proconsul (cf. now the remarks of P. A. Brunt and J. M. Moore, *Res Gestae Divi Augusti*, Appendix, pp. 82–84). Therefore they conclude that in those years the basis of his authority was his consular *imperium*, in the provinces no less than in Italy, since a consul (according to Cicero, *Ad. Att.*, VIII. 15, 3) had the right to " approach " any province. Attractive though the argument is, the present writer does not find it cogent. Dio (LIII, 13, 1) says that when Augustus' huge *provincia* (the Spains, the Gauls, Syria, Egypt) was assigned to him by the Senate in 27 B.C., his *imperium* in it was to last for ten years. Dio (LIII, 11) also makes it clear that at that time there was no general expectation that Augustus would be continuously consul for those ten years. This surely implies that the *imperium* then conferred on Augustus was envisaged as potentially proconsular. Indeed, apart altogether from the length of its tenure, Augustus' *imperium* would almost certainly have been regarded as proconsular in any case because of the areas in which it was going to be exercised. For it had been standard republican practice since Sulla's day for an *imperium* that was tenable in a *provincia* overseas to be proconsular (see H. Last in *Camb. Anc. Hist.*, IX, p. 294), the consular *imperium* being normally restricted to Italy (as was also the case from 27 B.C. on, according to Dio LIII, 13, 6). Hence, in the text, the view set forth is that Augustus' Imperium Proconsulare dates from 27 B.C. Between that year and 23 B.C. Augustus did indeed exercise consular *imperium*, but only in Italy ; the moment that he left Italy for his *provincia* his *imperium* became (automatically) proconsular.

Good evidence for this is supplied by the cases of Narbonensis and Baetica. In the division of provinces between Senate and Princeps in 27 B.C. these were certainly intended for the former. Yet they were not actually assigned to the Senate until some years later : in the years immediately after 27 B.C. both were imperial (Dio LIV, 4 ; R. Syme, *The Roman Revolution*, pp. 326, 395). The reason for this, in the present writer's view, is that at the time of the division of the provinces in 27 B.C. Augustus knew that within a few months he would certainly be visiting Narbonensis and possibly Baetica as well (since his projected itinerary included the Iberian peninsula) and therefore he had to be sure that his *imperium* was legally valid in both places. Evidently Augustus feared that it might not be legally valid if it was not specifically so defined, since a consul normally wielded his *imperium* only in Italy and a proconsul his only in his own *provincia*. The fact that Augustus' *provincia* in 27 B.C. included Narbonensis and Baetica, even though only temporarily, is most significant, since it implies that if they had been senatorial provinces he would legally have had no *locus standi* in them.

One must, therefore, assume that between 27 and 23 B.C. Augustus did not wield *imperium* in any province, either senatorial or imperial, as a consul; one must assume further that he did wield it in the imperial provinces as a proconsul; and one must assume still further that he did not wield it at all in the senatorial provinces. Until his *imperium* was made *maius* the senatorial proconsuls in their *provinciae* were juridically the equal of the Princeps in his, and it was only in 23 B.C., as Dio says, that Augustus obtained an *imperium* that was *maius*. From then on he had the legal right to wield it everywhere.

APPENDIX I

GENEALOGICAL TREE OF THE JULIO-CLAUDIAN EMPERORS

THIS stemma does not profess to be complete; it merely seeks to indicate the relationships of the first five Emperors.

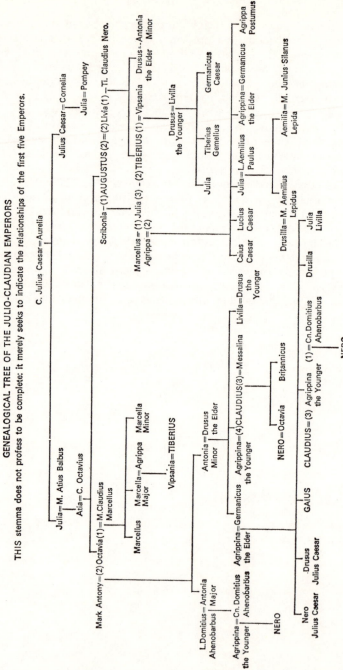

SELECT BIBLIOGRAPHY

(It would be obviously impossible in a one-volume history of the Early Empire to give more than a brief selection from the great mass of material. The following bibliography for the most part contains items that have appeared within the last fifteen years. As they are usually well documented, they will serve as a guide to additional literature and in particular to articles in the learned journals, which are not here listed but which are carefully recorded in *L'Année Philologique* every year.)

1. GENERAL HISTORIES, WORKS OF REFERENCE, &c.

Barrow, R. H.	*The Romans.*	Harmondsworth, 1949.
Cagnat, R.	*Inscriptiones Graccae ad Res Romanas pertinentes.*	1901–
Cary, M.	*Geographic Background of Greek and Roman History.*	Oxford, 1949.
	History of Rome.	London, 1935.
Charlesworth, M. P.	*The Roman Empire.*	Oxford, 1951.
Cook, S. A., Adcock, F. E., Charlesworth, M. P. (edd.)	*Cambridge Ancient History,* Vol. X (1934); Vol. XI (1936).	
Daremberg, C., Saglio, E. (edd.)	*Dictionnaire des antiquités grecques et romaines.*	Paris, 1877–1919.
Dessau, H.	*Inscriptiones Latinae Selectae.*	Berlin, 1892–1916.
	Geschichte der römischen Kaiserzeit.	Berlin, 1924–1930.
De Ruggiero, E.	*Dizionario epigrafico.*	Rome, 1895–
Dittenberger, W.	*Sylloge Inscriptionum Graecarum* (3rd ed.).	Hildesheim, 1960.
Klebs, E., Dessau, H., von Rohden, P.	*Prosopographia Imperii Romani* 1898: since 1933 a new edition by E. Groag and A. Stein has been appearing.	Berlin, 1897–.
Kornemann, E.	*Römische Geschichte: II, Die Kaiserzeit.*	Stuttgart, 1954.
Macurdy, G. H.	*Vassal Queens and Some Contemporary Women in the Roman Empire.*	Baltimore, 1937.
Marquardt, J.	*Römische Staatsverwaltung* (2nd ed.).	Leipzig, 1881–1885.
Mattingly, H., Sydenham, E. A.	*The Roman Imperial Coinage,* Vol. I (1948) and II (1926).	London.

Mommsen, T.	*Römisches Staatsrecht*, Vol. I (3rd ed.); Vol. II (3rd ed.); Vol. III.	Basel, 1952.
Passerini, A.	*Linee di Storia Romana nell' Età Imperiale.*	Milan, 1949.
Pauly, A. F., Wissowa, G., Kroll, W. (edd.)	*Realencyclopädie der classischen Altertumswissenschaft.*	Stuttgart, 1894–
Platner, S. B., Ashby, T.	*Topographical Dictionary of Rome.*	Oxford, 1929.
Sandys, J. E.	*Companion to Latin Studies* (4th ed.).	Cambridge, 1929.
Starr, C. G.	*Civilization and the Caesars.*	Cornell, 1954.
Wagenvoort, H.	*Roman Dynamism.*	Oxford, 1947.
Westbury-Jones, J.	*Roman and Christian Imperialism.*	London, 1939.

2. MONOGRAPHS, SPECIAL STUDIES, &c.

Abel, F. M.	*Histoire de la Palestine.*	Paris, 1952.
Abbott, F. F., Johnson, A. C.	*Municipal Administration in the Roman Empire.*	Princeton, 1926.
Baillie Reynolds, P. K.	*The Vigiles of Imperial Rome.*	London, 1927.
Balsdon, J. P. V. D.	*The Emperor Gaius.*	Oxford, 1934.
Barini, C.	*Triumphalia.*	Turin, 1952.
Barrow, R. H.	*Slavery in the Roman Empire.*	London, 1928.
Béranger, J.	*Recherches sur l'aspect idéologique du principat.*	Basel, 1953.
Berchem, D. van	*Les distributions de blé et d'argent.*	Geneva, 1939.
Berlinger, L.	*Beiträge zur inoffiziellen Titulatur der römischen Kaiser.*	Breslau, 1935.
Birley, E.	*Congress of Roman Frontier Studies.*	Durham, 1952.
	Roman Britain and the Roman Army.	Kendal, 1953.
Burn, A. R.	*Agricola and Roman Britain.*	London, 1954.
Carcopino, J.	*Daily Life in Ancient Rome.*	Yale, 1940.
Charlesworth, M. P.	*Trade Routes and Commerce of the Roman Empire.*	New edition, 1963.
	Five Men: Character Studies from the Roman Empire.	Harvard, 1936.
	Documents Illustrating the Reigns of Claudius and Nero.	Cambridge, 1951.
Cheesman, G. L.	*The Auxilia of the Roman Imperial Army.*	Oxford, 1914.
Christescu, V.	*Istoria militară a Daciei romane.*	Bucharest, 1937.
Ciaceri, E.	*Tiberio.*	Rome, 1944.

Coleman-Norton, P. R. (ed.) — *Studies in Roman Economic and Social History in Honour of A. C. Johnson.* — Princeton, 1952.

Collingwood, R. G., Myres, J. N. L. — *Roman Britain and the English Settlements.* — Oxford, 1937.

Crook, J. A. — *Consilium Principis.* — Cambridge, 1955.

Curtius, L. — *Die Wandmalerei Pompeijs.* — Leipzig, 1929.

Davies, O. — *Roman Mines in Europe.* — Oxford, 1935.

Debevoise, N. C. — *Political History of Parthia.* — Chicago, 1938.

Degrassi, A. — *I Fasti Consulari dell'Impero Romano.* — Rome, 1952.

De Robertis, F. M. — *Il Diritto Associativo Romano.* — Bari, 1938.

Duff, A. M. — *Freedmen in the Early Roman Empire.* — Oxford, 1928.

Durry, M. — *Les cohortes prétoriennes.* — Paris, 1938.

Ehrenberg, V., Jones, A. H. M. — *Documents Illustrating the Reigns of Augustus and Tiberius.* — Oxford, 1955.

Forni, G. — *Il Reclutamento delle Legioni da Augusto a Diocleziano.* — Milan-Rome, 1953.

Fortina, M. — *L'Imperatore Tito.* — Turin, 1955.

Frank, T. (ed.) — *Economic Survey of Ancient Rome.* — Baltimore, 1934–40.

Fuchs, H. — *Der geistige Widerstand gegen Rom.* — Berlin, 1938.

Gagé, J. — *Recherches sur les jeux séculaires.* — Paris, 1934.
Res Gestae Divi Augusti. — Paris, 1950.

Garzetti, A. — *Nerva.* — Rome, 1950.

Graf, H. R. — *Kaiser Vespasianus.* — Stuttgart, 1937.

Grant, M. — *From " Imperium " to " Auctoritas."* — Cambridge, 1946.
Aspects of the Principate of Tiberius. — New York, 1950.
Roman Imperial Money. — London, 1954.

Gwynn, A. — *Roman Education from Cicero to Quintilian.* — Oxford, 1926.

Hammond, M. — *The Augustan Principate in Theory and Practice.* — Harvard, 1933.

Henderson, B. W. — *Life and Principate of the Emperor Nero.* — London, 1903.
Civil War and Rebellion in the Roman Empire, A.D. 68–70. — London, 1908.
Life and Principate of the Emperor Hadrian. — London, 1923.
Five Roman Emperors, A.D. 69–117. — Cambridge, 1927.

Holmberg, E. J. — *Zur Geschichte des cursus publicus.* — Uppsala, 1933.

Homo, L. — *Vespasien, l'empereur du bon sens.* — Paris, 1949.

346   THE ROMAN WORLD : 30 B.C. TO A.D. 138

Johnson, A. C.	*Egypt and the Roman Empire.*	Ann Arbor, 1951.
Jones, A. H. M.	*The Cities of the Eastern Roman Provinces.*	Oxford, 1937.
	The Herods of Judaea.	Oxford, 1938.
Klingner, F.	*Die Geschichte Kaiser Othos bei Tacitus.*	Leipzig, 1940.
Klose, J.	*Roms Klientel-Randstaaten am Rhein und an der Donau.*	Breslau, 1934.
de Laet, S. J.	*Portorium.*	Bruges, 1949.
Lambrechts, P.	*La composition du Sénat romain.*	Antwerp, 1936.
Lepper, F. A.	*Trajan's Parthian War.*	Oxford, 1948.
Levi, M. A.	*Il Tempo di Augusto.*	Florence, 1950.
	Nerone e i Suoi Tempi.	Milan, 1949.
Loane, H. H.	*Industry and Commerce of the City of Rome, 50 B.C.–A.D. 200.*	Baltimore, 1938.
Magdelain, A.	*Auctoritas Principis.*	Paris, 1947.
Magie, D.	*Roman Rule in Asia Minor.*	Princeton, 1950.
Magi, F.	*I Rilievi Flavi del Palazzo della Cancelleria.*	Rome, 1946.
Marañon, G.	*Tiberius : a Study in Resentment.*	London, 1956.
Mattingly, H.	*The Imperial Civil Service of Rome.*	Cambridge, 1910.
	The Man in the Roman Street.	New York, 1947.
Maxey, M.	*The Occupations of the Lower Classes in Roman Society.*	Chicago, 1938.
Momigliano, A.	*Claudius : the Emperor and his Achievement.*	New edition, 1963.
d'Orgeval, B.	*L'Empereur Hadrien.*	Paris, 1950.
Paribeni, R.	*Optimus Princeps.*	Messina, 1927.
Parker, H. M. D.	*The Roman Legions.*	Cambridge, 1958.
Passerini, A.	*Le Coorti Pretorie.*	Rome, 1939.
Patsch, C.	*Der Kampf um den Donauraum.*	Vienna, 1937.
Pflaum, H. G.	*Les procurateurs équestres sous le haut empire romain.*	Paris, 1950.
Pippidi, D. M.	*Autour de Tibère.*	Bucharest, 1944.
Premerstein, A. von	*Vom Werden und Wesen des Prinzipats.*	Munich, 1937.
Reinhold, M.	*Marcus Agrippa.*	Geneva, N.Y., 1933.
Rice-Holmes, T. E.	*The Architect of the Roman Empire.*	Oxford, 1928, 1931.
Richmond, I. A.	*Roman Britain.*	Harmondsworth, 1955.

Rogers, R. S.	*Some Imperial Virtues of Tiberius and Drusus Julius Caesar.*	Baltimore, 1943.
	Criminal Trials and Criminal Legislation under Tiberius.	Middletown, 1935.
	Studies in the Reign of Tiberius.	Baltimore, 1943.
Rostovtzeff, M. I.	*Social and Economic History of the Roman Empire.*	Oxford, 1957.
Schmitthenner, W.	*Oktavian und das Testament Caesars.*	Munich, 1953.
Schulz, F.	*Principles of Roman Law.*	Oxford, 1936.
	History of Roman Legal Science.	Oxford, 1946.
Scott, K.	*The Imperial Cult under the Flavians.*	Stuttgart, 1936.
Scramuzza, V. M.	*The Emperor Claudius.*	Harvard, 1940.
Sherwin-White, A. N.	*The Roman Citizenship.*	Oxford, 1939.
Shipley, F. W.	*Agrippa's Building Activities in Rome.*	St. Louis, 1933.
Smith, C. E.	*Tiberius and the Roman Empire.*	Baton Rouge, 1942.
Starr, C. G.	*The Roman Imperial Navy.*	Cambridge, 1960.
Stauffer, E.	*Christ and the Caesars.*	London, 1955.
Stein, A.	*Der römische Ritterstand.*	Munich, 1927.
Stevenson, G. H.	*Roman Provincial Administration.*	Oxford, 1939.
Strong, E.	*Art in Ancient Rome.*	London, 1930.
Sutherland, C. H. V.	*The Romans in Spain, 217 B.C.– A.D. 117.*	London, 1939.
	Coinage in Roman Imperial Policy, 31 B.C.–A.D. 68.	London, 1951.
Syme, R.	*The Roman Revolution.*	Oxford, 1952.
Tanzer, H. H.	*The Common People of Pompeii.*	Baltimore, 1939.
Taylor, L. R.	*The Divinity of the Roman Emperor.*	Middletown, 1931.
Tibiletti, G.	*Principe e Magistrati Repubblicani.*	Rome, 1953.
Toynbee, J. M. C.	*The Hadrianic School.*	Cambridge, 1934.
de Visscher, F.	*Les édits d'Auguste découverts à Cyrène.*	Louvain, 1940.
Vittinghoff, F.	*Römische Kolonisation und Bürgerrechtspolitik.*	Mainz, 1952.
Volkmann, H.	*Zur Rechtssprechung im Principat des Augustus.*	Munich, 1935.
Walker, B.	*The Annals of Tacitus.*	Manchester, 1952.

Wallace, H. le R.	*Taxation in Egypt from Augustus to Diocletian.*	Princeton, 1938.
Warmington, E. H.	*The Commerce between the Roman Empire and India.*	Cambridge, 1928.
Westermann, W. L.	*The Slave Systems of Greek and Roman Antiquity.*	Philadelphia, 1955.
Wirszubski, C.	*Libertas as a Political Idea at Rome.*	Cambridge, 1950.
Wiseman, F. J.	*Roman Spain.*	London, 1956.
Zancan, P.	*La Crisi del Principato nell'anno 69 D.C.*	Padua and Milan, 1939.

The important work that has appeared on the Early Empire during the past half-century is briefly discussed by C. G. Starr in *Journal of Roman Studies*, Vol. L, 1960, pp. 149–160. The following recent works are of great interest and value.

Adcock, F. E.	*Roman Political Ideas and Practice.*	Ann Arbor, 1959.
Birley, E.	*Research on Hadrian's Wall.*	Kendal, 1961.
Blake, Marion E.	*Roman Construction in Italy,* Vol. II.	Washington, 1959.
Bowersock, G. W.	*Augustus and the Greek World.*	Oxford, 1965.
Cerfaux, L., Tondrian, J.	*Le Culte des souverains dans la civilization gréco-romaine.*	Tournai, 1957.
Charles-Picard, G.	*Auguste et Nerone, le secret de l'Empire.*	Paris, 1962. California
Deininger, J.	*Die Provinziallandtage der römischen Kaiserzeit*	Munich and Berlin, 1965.
Esser, A.	*Cäsar und die julisch-claudischen Kaiser im biologischärtzlichen Blickfeld.*	Janus Books, 1958.
Garzetti, A.	*L'Impero da Tiberio agli Antonini.*	Bologna, 1960.
Gordon, A. E. and J. S.	*Album of Dated Latin Inscriptions.*	University of Press, 1958.
Grant, M.	*Roman History from Coins.*	Cambridge, 1958.
Grenade, A.	*Essai sur les origines du principat.*	Paris, 1961.
Hadas, M.	*A History of Rome.*	London, 1958.
Hammond, M.	*The Antonine Monarchy.*	Rome, 1959.
Harmand, L.	*L'Occident romain.*	Paris, 1960.
Kahrstedt, U.	*Kulturgeschichte der römischen Kaiserzeit.*	Bern, 1958.

Kelly, J. M.	*Princeps Iudex.*	Weimar, 1957.
Latte, K.	*Römische Religionsgeschichte.*	Munich, 1960.
Levick, B.	*Roman Colonies in Southern Asia Minor.*	Oxford, 1967.
Lugli, G.	*La tecnica edilizia romana.*	Rome, 1957.
Mattingly, H.	*Roman Imperial Civilization.*	London, 1957.
McCrum, M., Woodhead, A. G.	*Select Documents of the Flavian Emperors.*	Cambridge, 1961.
Millar, F.	*A Study of Cassius Dio.*	Oxford, 1964.
Oliva, P.	*Pannonia and the Onset of Crisis in the Roman Empire.*	Prague, 1962.
Palm, J.	*Rom, Römertum und Imperium.*	Lund, 1959.
Pareti, L.	*Storia di Roma,* Vol. IV (1955), Vol. V (1960).	Turin.
Pareti, L., Brezzi, P.	*History of Mankind II : The Ancient World.*	New York, 1965.
Questa, C.	*Studi sulle fonti degli Annales di Tacito.*	Rome, 1960.
Romanelli, P.	*Storia delle province romane dell' Africa.*	Rome, 1959.
Schmitz, H.	*Colonia Claudia Ara Agrippinensium.*	Cologne, 1956.
Smallwood, E. M.	*Documents of Gaius, Claudius and Nero.*	Cambridge, 1967.
Smallwood, E. M.	*Documents of Nerva, Trajan and Hadrian.*	Cambridge, 1966.
Smith, R. E.	*Service in the Post-Marian Roman Army.*	Manchester, 1958.
Strong, D. E.	*Roman Imperial Sculpture.*	London, 1961.
Syme, R.	*Tacitus.*	Oxford, 1958,
Timpe, D.	*Untersuchungen zur Kontinuität des frühen Prinzipats.*	Wiesbaden, 1962.
Vitucci, G.	*Ricerche sulla praefectura urbi in età imperiale.*	Rome, 1956.
Welch, G. P.	*Britannia : the Roman Conquest and Occupation of Britain.*	Middletown, Conn., 1963.
White, K. D.	*Historical Roman Coins,* 44 B.C.– A.D. 55.	Grahamstown (S. Africa), 1958.

INDEX

Augustus, 123–8 132–4, 138, 142, 143, 147, 149, 155, 158, 164–8, 172, 175, 211, 214–17, 219, 229, 237, 252, 272, 273, 278, 285, 295, 309, 311, 315, 316, 329, 337–40 ; appellate jurisdiction of, 4, 22 ; building programme of, 29, 30 ; efforts to find a successor, 14, 16, 17, 33–8 ; indifferent health of, 14, Part One *passim*, 1–122 ; significance of the name, 9, 10 ; its adoption by later emperors, 32 ; travels in the provinces, 12, 34 ; A. and Caesar-worship, 28–9 ; and the army, 95–101 ; and the censorship, 7, 21 ; and the citizenship, 47, 85, 86 ; and the consulship, 13, 45–8 ; and the finances, 31, 32 ; and the Imperium proconsulare, 8–10, 33–8 ; A's provincial arrangements, 74–9, 102–13
Aurelian, 278
Aurelius, *see under* Antoninus Pius
Aurelius, Marcus, 52, 213, 216, 272, 311, 315, 316
Aurelius Victor, 337
Aurum Coronarium, 91, 284, 309
Auxilia, Auxiliaries : 86, 96, 97, 112, 130, 160, 203, 212, 239, 276, 300, 303
Avenio (= Avignon), 305
Aventine Hill, 143
Avidius Nigrinus, 293, 297

Babylon, 286, 288
Baebius Macer, 296
Baetica, *see under* Spain
Baiae, 150, 316
Balbus, Cornelius, commander against the Garamantes, 106
Barea Soranus, 186
Basila, Helvius, 270
Basilica Ulpia, 279
Bassus, Annius, 207
Bassus, Aufidius, historian, 334
Bassus, Seleius, poet, 219
Bastarnae, 247
Batanaea, 252
Batavi, 99, 151, 205, 238–40
Bath (= Aquae Sulis), 162
Baths : of Agrippa, 30 ; of Nero, 180 ; of Titus, 223 ; of Trajan, 279, 331
Bato, chief of the Breuci, 110
Bato, chief of the Daesitiates, 110
Bavaria, 304
Bedriacum, 202–5, 208 ; first battle of, 204 ; second battle of, 208
Belgica, *see under* Gaul
Beneventum, 280, 291, 331
Berenice, 222
Berytus, 3
Bether, 307
Birth-rate, 25, 84, 260, 270, 280, 281
Bithynia, 77, 281–2, 284, 301, 305, 323
Black Forest, 241

Black Sea, 105, 162, 192, 250
Blaesus, Junius, 127, 130, 154
Boadicea, *see* Boudicca
Bocchus, 106
Bohemia, 110, 111
Boionius, *see under* Antoninus Pius
Bonna (= Bonn), 232, 239, 240, 245
Bosporan Kingdom (= Tauric Bosporus), 105, 301
Bostra, 279
Boudicca, 92, 191, 192, 210, 245
Breuci, 110
Breviarium Imperii, 92
Brigantes, 245
Brigetio, 249
Britain, 78, 83, 148, 163, 165, 171, 191, 197, 201–5, 207, 210, 211, 216, 222, 232, 234, 238, 240, 242, 247, 255, 256, 261, 287, 289, 296, 301, 307, 327, 336 ; annexed by Claudius, 159–62 ; Augustus' policy towards, 112 ; frontier fortifications, 302, 303 ; Gaius' abortive expedition to, 152 ; under the Flavians, 245, 246
Britannicus, son of Claudius and Messalina, 171–3, 175, 176
Brixellum, 204, 205
Bructeri, 241
Brundisium, 280
Brutus, Julius Caesar's murderer, 184, 340
Burebista, 247
Burrus, *see under* Afranius Burrus
Byzantium, 218

Caecina Alienus, 188, 201–9, 221
Caecina, Aulus, commander in Lower Germany, 127
Caecina Paetus, 158, 220
Caecina Severus, legate of Moesia, 110
Caelian Hill, 182, 219
Caelius Antipater, 317
Caenis, 216, 231
Caepio, Fannius, 13
Caere, 281
Caerleon (= Isca Silurum), 245, 303
Caesar as a title, 32, 196, 199, 200, 201, 205, 225, 333
Caesar, Gaius, grandson of Augustus, 33–7, 136, 340
Caesar, Julius, 3, 6, 8, 11, 29, 30, 47, 51, 53, 75, 84, 85, 99, 102, 117, 121, 148, 149, 157, 164, 165, 171, 215, 247, 264, 340
Caesar, Lucius, grandson of Augustus, 33–7, 340
Caesarea, 196
Caesariensis, *see under* Mauretania
Caesar-worship, 28, 29, 60, 66, 67, 82, 124, 149, 162, 214, 230, 241, 306, 307, 319, 323, 324 ; deification of dead emperor, 38, 143, 149, 174, 221, 224 295

INDEX

357

Flavians, 79, 101, 207–52, 260, 268, 269, 272–3, 293, 300, 309, 311, 335, 336

Flavianus, Tampius, 206

Flavius Clemens, 235, 236

Flavius Sabinus, brother of Vespasian, 210

Flavius Sabinus, cousin of Domitian, 231

Flavius Vespasianus, *see under* Vespasian

Fleet, *see under* Navy

Florus, Annaeus, 328, 337

Florus, Julius, 131

Fonteius Agrippa, 247

Fonteius Capito, 200

Forth River, 246, 303

Forum : Augustus, 30, 36, 279 ; the Forum Romanum, 6, 30, 201, 279, 309, 331 ; Nerva's (*forum transitorium* or *pervium*), 279 ; Trajan's, 257, 279, 331 ; Vespasian's, 219

Forum Hadriani, 305

Fosse Way, 160, 162, 245

Freedmen, 19, 25, 54, 56, 64–70, 85, 88, 170, 175, 183, 187, 189, 200, 234, 270, 292 ; disabilities of, 65 ; in the Civil Service, 54, 56, 312 ; Claudius and the freedmen, 69, 159, 165, 167 ; in the fire brigade, 19, 66 ; freedmen and Caesar-worship, 66 ; freedmen prefects, 54, 56, 68, 178 ; freedmen procurators, 54, 56 ; Hadrian's policy, 306, 312 ; *liberti Caesaris*, 68, 69, 228

Frisii, 128, 163

Frontiers and Frontier Policy, 78, 79, 128–30, 237–52, 275–9, 285–90, 296–304

Frontinus, Julius, 232, 234, 245, 267, 337

Fronto, Pactumeius, 215

Frumentationes, 59, 280

Fucinus Lake, 169

Fuscus, Cornelius, 207, 248, 277

Fuscus Salinator, Pedanius, 314, 315

Gades, 214, 254

Gaetulians, 106

Gaetulicus, Lentulus, 131, 151

Gaius (= Caligula), 5, 33, 63, 74, 136, 141, 144, 146, 157, 158, 163, 165, 166, 168, 171, 172, 177, 179, 183, 185, 186, 189, 195, 198, 199, 215, 217, 224, 230, 295, 309 ; reign of, 147–56

Gaius Caesar, grandson of Augustus, 33, 35–7, 136, 340

Galatia, 79, 105, 193, 250

Galba, 198–200, 210, 213, 217, 218, 238, 268, 269, 272 ; early career, 151, 168, 188, 189

Galerius, Gaius, 136

Galilee, 195, 196

Gallaeci, 107

Gallia, *see under* Gaul

Gallicus, Rutilius, 241

Gallio, 321, 323

Gallus, Aelius, 105

Gallus, Annius, 203, 204, 240

Gallus, Asinius, 159

Gallus, Cestius, 196

Gallus, Cornelius, 13, 50, 106

Gallus, Rubrius, 247

Games, 3, 59, 143, 148, 152, 158, 179, 222, 223, 229, 230, 284, 292, 297 ; Panhellenic, 306 *See, too, under Ludi*

Garamantes, 106

Gaul, 12, 34, 68, 74, 78, 82, 83, 107, 108, 109, 130, 148, 151, 153, 159, 163, 164, 180, 202, 212, 213, 238, 240, 242, 255, 257, 301, 305 ; disunity in, 131, 188, 201, 239 ; Aquitania, 79, 108 ; Belgica, 79, 108, 112, 131 ; Cisalpine Gaul, 97 ; Gallia Comata, 164 ; industrial development, 256 ; Lugdunensis, 79, 108, 131, 301 ; Narbonensis, 77, 78, 84, 108, 143, 164, 203, 301 ; nationalist aspirations of, 188, 240 ; Transalpine Gaul, 164, 208

Germanicus, nephew of Tiberius, 37, 38, 110, 111, 124, 125, 134, 138, 139, 141, 146, 147, 150, 154, 171, 172 ; adopted by Tiberius, 37 ; death, 137 ; journey to the east, 129, 135, 136 ; quells riot on the Rhine, 127 ; trans-Rhenane expeditions, 128, 129

Germanicus, son of Drusus and Livilla, 138, 139

Germanicus, title taken by Domitian, 244, 249

Germans, 73, 151, 160, 213, 238–40, 242, 246 ; fissiparous tendencies of, 109, 111, 128

Germany, 111–13, 163, 205–6, 209–13, 222, 237, 240, 244, 247, 248, 276, 277, 291 ; divided into two military districts, 112 ; Lower Germany, 79, 112, 113, 127, 131, 186, 200–3, 232, 233, 240–2, 245, 277, 301, 303, 305 ; organized as two provinces, 112 ; Upper Germany, 79, 112, 113, 127, 131, 186, 199, 200–3, 232, 233, 240–2, 245, 272, 290, 301, 314

Gessius Florus, 196

Getae, 109, 247

Golden House of Nero, 182, 219, 330

Gracchi, 259

Graeculus, nickname for Hadrian, 314

Graufesenque, La, 256

Greece, 82, 116, 182, 186–90, 301, 302, 306